SAP S/4HANA® Management Accounting Certification Guide

SAP⁷ PRESS

SAP PRESS is a joint initiative of SAP and Rheinwerk Publishing. The know-how offered by SAP specialists combined with the expertise of Rheinwerk Publishing offers the reader expert books in the field. SAP PRESS features first-hand information and expert advice, and provides useful skills for professional decision-making.

SAP PRESS offers a variety of books on technical and business-related topics for the SAP user. For further information, please visit our website: *www.sap-press.com*.

Theresa Marquis, Marjorie Wright

SAP S/4HANA® Management Accounting Certification Guide

Application Associate Exam

Rheinwerk

Publishing

Editor Megan Fuerst
Acquisitions Editor Emily Nicholls
Copyeditor Yvette Chin
Cover Design Graham Geary
Photo Credit Shutterstock.com/1164813766/© INGARA
Layout Design Vera Brauner
Production Hannah Lane
Typesetting SatzPro, Krefeld (Germany)
Printed and bound in the United States of America, on paper from sustainable sources

ISBN 978-1-4932-1842-4
© 2019 by Rheinwerk Publishing, Inc., Boston (MA)
1st edition 2019

Library of Congress Cataloging-in-Publication Data
LCCN: 2019017644

Contents at a Glance

Dear Reader,

Some events are more difficult to prepare for than others.

Take pet ownership. A few years ago, my family decided to adopt a dog—a ten-year-old, overweight beagle with a loud bark named Oliver—from our local animal shelter. First came the weeks of study: how to introduce an adult dog to a new home; how to spot and correct negative learned behaviors; how to identify breed-specific health issues, and so on. We quickly learned that there's no limit to the time you can spend on internet searches, but there is a limit to just how ready you can possibly be for a new furry family member.

Other milestones are easier to prepare for. Take certification exams! For your SAP S/4HANA Management Accounting certification, there's no need to wade through pages of Google search results. Lucky for you, this book contains all of the guidance, tips, and practice questions you need to be confident about your CO knowledge and skills on exam day. (Although, unfortunately, test preparation won't result in a new puppy.)

What did you think about *SAP S/4HANA Management Accounting Certification Guide*? Your comments and suggestions are the most useful tools to help us make our books the best they can be. Please feel free to contact me and share any praise or criticism you may have.

Thank you for purchasing a book from SAP PRESS!

Megan Fuerst
Editor, SAP PRESS

meganf@rheinwerk-publishing.com
www.sap-press.com
Rheinwerk Publishing · Boston, MA

Contents

3   Cost Center Accounting

4   Internal Orders

7   Profitability Analysis

8   Profit Center Accounting

9   Reporting

Preface

The SAP PRESS Certification Series is designed to provide anyone preparing to take an SAP certification exam with all of the review, insight, and practice you'll need to pass the exam. The series is written in practical, easy-to-follow language that provides targeted content focused on what you need to know to successfully take the exam.

Target Audience

This book is specifically written for those preparing for the SAP Certified Application Associate—SAP S/4HANA for Management Accounting Associates C_TS4CO_ 1809 exam, so if you've purchased this book, you're obviously interested in successfully passing the certification exam. We'll focus on core SAP S/4HANA management accounting skills: overhead management accounting (controlling, CO), product cost planning, cost object controlling, profitability analysis, and more.

Using this book, you'll gain a thorough understanding of the exam structure and what to expect in taking it. You'll receive a refresher on key concepts covered on the exam and will be able to test your skills via sample practice questions and answers. The book is closely aligned with the course syllabus and the exam structure, so all of the information provided is relevant and applicable to what you need to know to prepare. We'll explain SAP products and features using practical examples and straightforward language, so you can prepare for the exam and improve skills for your day-to-day work. Each book in the series has been structured and designed to highlight what you really need to know.

Structure of This Book

Each chapter begins with a clear list of the learning objectives, such as:

Techniques You'll Master

- How to prepare for the exam
- Understanding the general exam structure
- Practice questions and preparation

From there, you'll dive into the chapter and get right into the test objective coverage.

Throughout the book, we've also provided several elements that will help you access useful information:

- Tips call out useful information about related ideas and provide practical suggestions for how to use a particular function.
- Notes provide relevant asides or other resources to explore that will help you with the topic under discussion.
- Warnings draw your attention to points that often cause confusion or are ignored.

The following boxes are examples of these elements:

Note

This certification guide covers all topics you need to successfully pass the exam and provides sample questions similar to those found on the actual exam.

Tip

This book contains screenshots and diagrams to help your understanding of the many information modeling concepts we'll cover throughout the guide.

Warning!

This book is meant to review and supplement the knowledge gained from standard SAP Education training.

Each chapter that covers an exam topic is organized in a similar fashion, so you can become familiar with the structure and easily find the information you need. A typical chapter will be organized with the following structure:

- **Introductory bullets**
  The beginning of each chapter discusses the techniques you must master to be considered proficient in the topic for the certification examination.

- **Topic introduction**
  This section provides you with a general idea of the topic at hand to frame future sections and includes objectives for the exam topic covered.

- **Real-world scenario**
  This part describes a scenario to provide you with a real-life case where these skills would be beneficial to you or your company.

- **Objectives**
  This section provides you with the information necessary to successfully passing this portion of the test.

- **Key concept refresher**
  This section outlines the major concepts of the chapter. We'll identify the tasks you'll need to understand or perform properly to answer the questions on the certification examination.

- **Important terminology**
  Just prior to the practice examination questions, we'll review important terminology including definitions of various terms covered in the chapter.

- **Practice questions**
  The chapter will then provide a series of practice questions related to the topic of the chapter. The questions are structured in a similar way to the actual questions on the certification examination.

- **Practice question answers and explanations**
  Following the practice exercises are the solutions to the practice questions. As part of the answer, we'll discuss why answer options are correct or incorrect.

- **Takeaway**
  This section provides takeaways or reviews areas you should now understand.

- **Summary**
  Finally, we conclude with a summary of the chapter.

Now that you have an idea of how the book is structured, the following list will dive into the individual topics covered in each chapter:

- **Chapter 1: SAP HANA, SAP S/4HANA, and SAP Fiori**
  The focus of this chapter is to explain the architecture of SAP HANA, the scope and deployment options of SAP S/4HANA, and the basic functions of the SAP Fiori user interface (UI).

- **Chapter 2: Organizational Assignments and Process Integration**
  The focus of this chapter is to explain organizational assignments and the way

CO business processes integrate with others in SAP S/4HANA. We'll review key concepts related to CO and integration.

- **Chapter 3: Cost Center Accounting**
  The focus of this chapter is to explain the key cost center accounting concepts for master data, primary and adjustment postings, and period-end close.

- **Chapter 4: Internal Orders**
  The focus of this chapter is to prepare test takers for coverage of internal orders in the exam. It reviews the key internal order concepts for master data, integrated transactions, period-end close, and planning and budgeting.

- **Chapter 5: Product Cost Planning**
  The focus of this chapter is to explain the key concepts around product cost planning methods and basics, discusses variations of cost estimates and the costing run process, and identify other additional functions.

- **Chapter 6: Cost Object Controlling**
  The focus of this chapter is to understand functionalities for valuation by period and by order. We'll also walk you through some key sales order-related scenarios.

- **Chapter 7: Profitability Analysis**
  The focus of this chapter is to explain the organizational structures, master data, and actual data flow of CO-PA, in addition to key reporting concepts.

- **Chapter 8: Profit Center Accounting**
  This chapter prepares test-takers for coverage of profit center accounting in the exam. We'll review the key profit center accounting concepts for master data; integration with financial accounting (FI), materials management (MM), and sales and distribution (SD); and period-end close.

- **Chapter 9: Reporting**
  This chapter provides an overview of the reporting tools used for CO, including SAP S/4HANA-specific tools and standard SAP reporting tools like the Report Painter and drilldown reports.

Practice Questions

Let's go over some background information about the test questions before you encounter the first few in the chapters. Just like the exam, each question has a basic structure:

- **Actual question**

  Read the question carefully and be sure to consider all the words used in the question because they can impact the answer.

- **Question hint**

  Although not a formal term, we provide hints that tell you how many answers are correct. If only one is correct, normally, the question will tell you to choose "the correct answer." If more than one is correct, like the actual certification examination, the question will indicate the correct number of answers.

- **Answers**

  The answers to select from depend on the question type. The following question types are featured in this book:

  - Multiple response: More than one correct answer is possible.

  - Multiple choice: Only a single answer is correct.

  - True/false: Only a single answer is correct. These types of questions are not used in the exam but are used in the book to test your understanding.

Summary

With this certification guide, you'll learn how to approach the content and key concepts highlighted for each exam topic. In addition, you'll have opportunities to practice with sample test questions in each chapter. After answering the practice questions, you can review explanations for each answer where we'll dissect each question by explaining why answers are correct or incorrect. The practice questions will provide insight into the types of questions you can expect on the exam, what the questions look like, and how the answers relate to the question. Understanding the composition of the questions and seeing how the questions and answers work together is just as important as understanding the content itself. This book gives you the tools and understanding you need to be successful. Armed with these skills, you'll be well on your way to becoming an SAP Certified Application Associate in SAP S/4HANA for Management Accounting.

Introduction: The Path to Certification

Techniques You'll Master

- Understand the relevant certification offerings for management accounting (CO) in SAP S/4HANA

- Find the courses required for the certification

- Learn techniques for taking the certification exams

- Identify further relevant SAP Education offerings in SAP S/4HANA

- Explore additional resources for financials in SAP S/4HANA

- Expand your knowledge and keep your skills up to date

This chapter paints the big picture of the SAP S/4HANA Management Accounting Application Associate exam and certification. It teaches you about the different levels and offerings for SAP S/4HANA financial certifications, identifies resources for study, and provides certification-test-taking advice.

With SAP S/4HANA, SAP has introduced a new breed of enterprise resource planning solutions to keep businesses ahead of the technological wave and to support customers in becoming truly digital businesses. SAP S/4HANA is the most important product in the SAP portfolio and CO is still at the very core of the processes and functionalities supported. As more customers adopt SAP S/4HANA, the number of projects worldwide also increases greatly, leading to a need for more implementation and support consultants who understand the core financial functions.

In this chapter, we'll establish that the SAP S/4HANA Management Accounting Application Associate certification is the right certification for you. We'll also go over the details of the certification and the SAP Education materials that are essential to achieve the certification. We'll discuss the ways you can access the SAP Education materials and then we'll go over some tips to prepare for and succeed in passing the certification examination. Finally, we'll look at some additional resources you might find useful when preparing for the exam and as you continue your journey with SAP S/4HANA.

Who This Book Is For

There is hardly any SAP project worldwide that doesn't require project members familiar with CO processes and configuration. This was true for SAP ERP and is true for SAP S/4HANA. This makes CO consultants with good skills and solid experience a valuable and sought-after resource for both SAP partner firms and SAP customers.

This book covers a broad and deep scope of core CO configuration and business processes in the SAP S/4HANA system. As such, this book is an excellent starting point for those of you who are just getting introduced to CO. For example, you might be a new hire at an SAP implementation partner, an IT support consultant whose company is upgrading to SAP S/4HANA, or a graduate looking to kick-start a career in SAP.

The book is also a great way for more experienced consultants to get back to the basics. Often, as you gain more experience, you become specialized in a specific part of the SAP financials world. This book will help you look again at the complete picture of CO and at the same time get upskilled to the specifics of SAP S/4HANA.

Those working as business users with CO in SAP also often want to expand beyond that role to get a deeper and broader understanding of the implementation or to support consultant roles.

Developers wanting to specialize in financials or to gain a good understanding of the common business processes that are configured with SAP S/4HANA can also find value in this book, even just as a reference if they aren't interested in the certification aspect.

The book is designed around the latest 1809 version of the SAP S/4HANA system and certification; however, because it covers core processes that are by now quite mature, the knowledge found here should support future versions of the product as well.

Certifications for SAP Financials in SAP S/4HANA

We'll first review the portfolio of certifications from SAP that might be of interest to you. Then, we'll go into the details of the C_TS4CO_1809 certification.

Useful SAP S/4HANA Certifications Overview

SAP offers an expanding portfolio of certifications for SAP S/4HANA, many of which might be interesting for the CO consultant. The following is a list of potentially relevant certifications that might interest you (the first three are relevant in a broader scope):

- **C_TS410_1610: SAP Certified Application Associate—Integrated Business Processes in SAP S/4HANA**
  This certification indicates that you have a solid understanding of the integrated processes in SAP S/4HANA, including the SAP Fiori user experience (UX), financial and management accounting, human capital management (SAP ERP Human Capital Management and SAP SuccessFactors), procure-to-pay, plan-to-produce, warehouse management in SAP, order to cash, project system, and SAP Enterprise Asset Management (SAP EAM).

Although a business processes course, this is immensely useful for any consultant's understanding of the nearly end-to-end scope of the SAP S/4HANA solution offering.

- **C_ACTIVATE05: SAP Certified Associate—SAP Activate Project Manager**
  SAP Activate is the implementation methodology replacing ASAP. All projects related to SAP S/4HANA will be based on some form of the SAP Activate methodology. Even if you're not a project manager or don't aspire to become one, understanding how a project works, what accelerators are offered, and what implementation options are available is of great use for a consultant.

- **C_S4IMP_1610: SAP Certified Associate—SAP S/4HANA Implementation Scenarios for Architects**
  This is a certification that is probably best suited to the admin/Basis consultant; however, the underlying courses (S4H01 and S4H100) are great resources for understanding the SAP S/4HANA adoption scenarios for new implementations and system conversions alike.

- **C_TS4CO_1809: SAP Certified Application Associate—Management Accounting with SAP S/4HANA**
  The certification for which this book is created and the best starting point for any new CO consultant.

- **C_TS4FI_1809: SAP Certified Application Associate—SAP S/4HANA for Financial Accounting Associates (SAP S/4HANA 1809)**
  This is the equivalent certification to the one this book covers, only for the consultants more focused on financial accounting (FI). This is a very useful certification also for CO consultants who want to play more generalist roles in projects. Because FI and CO are becoming increasingly integrated, this is a logical next learning step for the CO consultant.

- **P_S4FIN_1809: SAP Certified Application Professional—Financials in SAP S/4HANA for SAP ERP Finance Experts**
  This certification is the level-up certification from the application associate certifications in FI and CO. It's for the experienced professional who has a good knowledge level in both FI and CO and has upskilled to SAP S/4HANA. It's the only professional certification available for FI with SAP S/4HANA.

- **C_S4CFI: SAP Certified Application Associate—SAP S/4HANA Cloud—Finance Implementation**
  This certification is crucial for consultants wanting to participate in SAP S/4HANA Cloud implementations as finance experts. The content prerequisites

cover both project setup and implementation topics (SAP Activate and the fit-to-standard workshop), as well as the broadest scope of finance knowledge of any SAP certification. You'll be required to understand a fairly detailed level of financial accounting, management accounting, financial operations, treasury management, group reporting, innovation applications that use the cloud platform, and more. Because the certification is updated every three months, you'll also have to complete a "stay-current" assessment for every new product release to maintain your certification status. Therefore, you'll need to maintain a learning hub subscription.

All mentioned certifications and most certifications on offer for SAP Education have the same format:

- *Length of exam:* Up to three hours.
- *Exam questions:* Eighty questions, either multiple choice or multiple selection.
- *Exam location:* Can be taken either at a certification center or online through the SAP Certification Hub.

The SAP Certification Hub is a subscription-based cloud offering. You subscribe annually and can make six certification attempts in this period. This means that if you always pass on the first try, you could potentially get six different certifications. For each individual certification, you get up to three tries, meaning you can fail to pass no more than two times for each subscription. You can try the previous version of the certification (if it is still available) or wait for the release of the next version (usually released in the first quarter of the new year).

> **Note**
> You can find more information at *https://training.sap.com/shop/course/cer006.*

Depending on your location, you can also visit a certified certification partner and take the certification in a moderated classroom. For more information, visit *https://training.sap.com,* or call your local training contact (the number is provided at the training shop site).

You can find up-to-date learning offerings by area on the SAP Training Web shop at *https://training.sap.com/learning.* Here the education content is categorized into **Learning Journeys** (Figure 1), which are interactive maps that guide you through the complex and sometimes confusing SAP Education offerings.

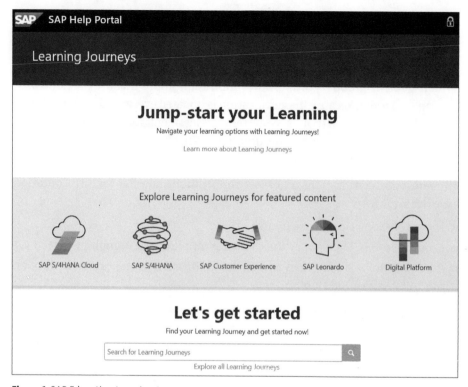

Figure 1 SAP Education Learning Journeys

The C_TS4CO_1809 Certification

The certification covered in this book is to SAP S/4HANA what the C_TFIN22: SAP Certified Application Associate – Management Accounting with SAP ERP was for SAP ERP. In other words, this certification is the common starting point for many SAP CO professionals. Both the new certification and the underlying course materials are based on those of SAP ERP, so if you're familiar with or certified in the SAP ERP certification, you should have no problem identifying the delta and passing the certification exam for SAP S/4HANA.

The C_TS4CO certification will likely, but not necessarily, continue to have an annual release cycle for the perceivable future to match the annual release cycle of the SAP S/4HANA system. However, as mentioned, because core Customizing and functionality are covered, the certification won't be obsolete the day after you take it. The same goes for the validity of this book as a reference and for future releases of the certification.

Certification Exam Format

As you can see in Figure 2, which is a screenshot from the SAP Training Web shop, the certification exam is an associate-level exam, meaning it's assumed the exam taker has at least one year of hands-on experience in a role relevant to CO with SAP S/4HANA (or SAP ERP) and has excellent knowledge of the prerequisite education courses.

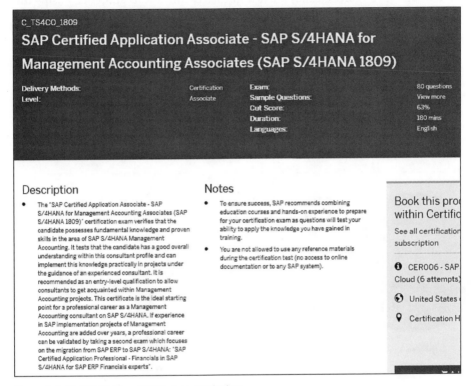

Figure 2 C_TS4CO_1809 on SAP Training Web Shop

The certification exam consists of 80 questions of the following types:

- Multiple choice, for which you must select one correct answer out of the four available options
- Multiple select (type 1), for which you must select the two correct answers out of the four available options
- Multiple select (type 2), for which you must select the three correct answers out of the five available options

There are no other question types than these. Note that you must get all answers correct for each question for the question to be considered correctly answered.

To pass the 1809 certification, you must answer 63% of the questions correctly. This means you must answer 51 out of 80 questions completely correctly. The percentage for the pass rate might be changed in future versions of the exam as it depends on the rated difficulty of the question items in the certification. As mentioned earlier, you can take the certification at a certification center or by using the cloud offering at your own home. For current information on both options, you can check the SAP Education web shop at *https://training.sap.com/shop/certification* or call your local SAP Education office.

After passing the certification exam, you get a printed certificate, and you can access the Credential Manager from the SAP Education web shop to manage your certifications (*https://training.sap.com/shop/content/Credential-Manager*). In addition, you'll receive a digital badge (Figure 3), which you can display on your profile in social media platforms and in emails.

Figure 3 SAP Global Certification Digital Badges

Scope of the Certification Exam

The book is modeled closely to the topic areas of the certification (Figure 4). The book covers the same exact areas and scope as the exam itself and the academy courses on which the certification is based.

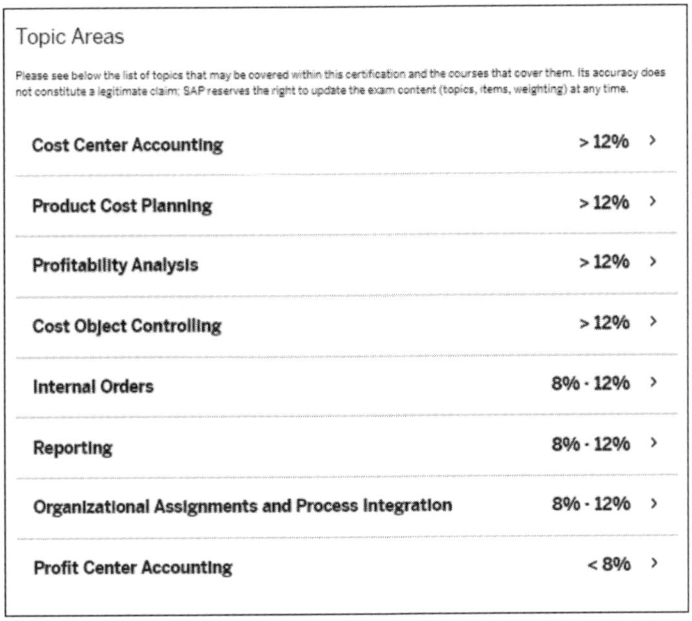

Topic Areas

Please see below the list of topics that may be covered within this certification and the courses that cover them. Its accuracy does not constitute a legitimate claim; SAP reserves the right to update the exam content (topics, items, weighting) at any time.

Topic	Weighting	
Cost Center Accounting	> 12%	>
Product Cost Planning	> 12%	>
Profitability Analysis	> 12%	>
Cost Object Controlling	> 12%	>
Internal Orders	8% - 12%	>
Reporting	8% - 12%	>
Organizational Assignments and Process Integration	8% - 12%	>
Profit Center Accounting	< 8%	>

Figure 4 Certification Topic Areas

The approximate weighting and approximate number of questions you can expect per area are detailed in Table 1.

Topic	Percentage (%)	Approximate Number of Questions	Book Chapter
SAP HANA and SAP S/4HANA	–	–	1
Organizational assignments and process integration	8 – 12	6	2
Cost center accounting	>12	12	3
Internal orders	8 – 12	12	4
Product cost planning	>12	13	5
Cost object controlling	>12	13	6

Table 1 Topic Weighting

Topic	Percentage (%)	Approximate Number of Questions	Book Chapter
Profitability analysis	>12	12	7
Profit center accounting	<8	6	8
Reporting	8 – 12	6	9

Table 1 Topic Weighting (Cont.)

SAP Education Courses

You can select from quite a few different course options to gain the knowledge required for the certification exam:

- **Individual courses:**
    - S4F12: Cost Center and Internal Order Accounting in SAP S/4HANA (five days)
    - S4F23: Product Cost Planning in SAP S/4HANA (five days)
    - S4F25: Cost Object Controlling in SAP S/4HANA (five days)
    - S4F29: Profitability Analysis in SAP S/4HANA (four days)
    - S4F28: Profit Center Accounting in SAP S/4 HANA (two days)
- **Academy courses:**
    - TS4FO3: Management Accounting in SAP S/4HANA – Academy I
    - TS4FO4: Management Accounting in SAP S/4HANA – Academy II
- **E-Academy course:**
    - TS4F4e: SAP E-Academy – Management Accounting in SAP S/4HANA

Note

The individual courses are also available as e-learnings; just add an "e" to the end of the course names.

If you're new to the subject of CO with SAP, it's a good idea to also check out the prerequisite course, S4F20, Business Processes in Management Accounting in SAP S/4HANA (five days), which is also available as e-learning S4F20e. For all these courses, the latest materials as of the date of publishing for this book are in collection 11 and refer to SAP S/4HANA 1809. The likely next version of the materials will refer to SAP S/4HANA 1909, which is due to be released in September 2019. However, these won't be available until the tail end of 2019 at the earliest, and the certification for SAP S/4HANA 1909 is likely to be made available in 2020.

> **Tip**
>
> *Collections* are semiarbitrary course version numberings that generally map a course to a specific product release. For SAP S/4HANA, you can assume that the higher the collection number, the newer the course, and the courses with the same collection number all refer to the same system version.

Always go for the newest collection of materials available. You can find the newest materials referenced in the relevant learning journey (Figure 5). The scope of the content for these courses isn't due to change dramatically, but each version of the course gets a little better, as is true for the product as well. SAP S/4HANA is maturing very quickly, and the small adjustments and enhancements made in mature modules go along nicely with rapid changes and improvements that occur in parallel.

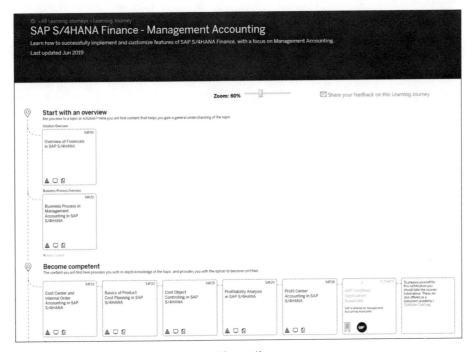

Figure 5 SAP S/4HANA Finance: Management Accounting

To keep up to date with what learning materials are available for CO in SAP S/4HANA, you should check the relevant learning journey (Figure 5). Here you can see the offerings categorized in sections. You can see the academy track, which also leads to the certification in the **Become competent** section. The learning journey is interactive, so clicking on the course links will take you to the latest version of each course. If you have an active (paid) SAP Learning Hub subscription, you can get directly routed to the course material (select **E-book** or **E-learning**). An assessment is also available for each course, and the assessment groups all assessment questions available in the course content into a single test that can be used to gauge your understanding of each topic. Finally, there is a link for SAP Live Access, which provides a PDF of all the relevant exercises and details for booking a live-access training system to practice on.

Ways to Learn

You can choose to learn and consume the standard SAP Education courses in a variety of ways:

- *Classroom training* is the most obvious way to learn, especially when you're new to the subject. The inherit and undeniable advantages are an environment that offers immediate live feedback from an expert trainer, networking with trainees with whom you've shared goals, minimal "real-work" interruptions during the day, and a system at your disposal to perform all exercises during the training. At an SAP training center for the scope of the CO academy (or individual courses), you'll receive four printed versions of the relevant books (one for each course or week of the academy), which average more than 400 pages each.

- *Remote classroom* training is a kind of Internet-based training that utilizes a conferencing application. It approximates the classroom experience, so you still have a live trainer to ask questions, system access to perform exercises and learners with whom you may interact. However, the experience isn't quite the same as in a classroom.

- *eAcademy training* through SAP Education is a third option for consuming the materials. With this option, you receive the following:
  - Online learning content in an e-learning format consisting of presentation slides with audio commentary, recorded system demonstrations, and practice simulations
  - SAP's training system for hands-on experience with live training systems to reinforce your learning and test scenarios on your own
  - Student manuals in electronic form (without the audio simulations)
  - Help desk support, with a guarantee that all queries are answered within 24 hours on Monday through Friday

- Technical support for the system via online web conferencing and scheduled expert instructor sessions, as well as the Ask the Expert feature

■ *SAP Learning Hub* (*https://training.sap.com/shop/learninghub*) is the newest in the line of offerings from SAP. This is a cloud-based offering with an annual subscription. SAP Learning Hub consists of three major offerings bundled in one:

- Access to learning content in the SAP Education catalog. This includes all SAP S/4HANA content on the day the content is released (and before any classroom events have taken place). Figure 6 shows an example search for the content available for CO in SAP S/4HANA. Course content is delivered either in e-book format, which is like a PDF version, or as an e-learning, which includes multimedia elements and recorded demo/practice simulations.

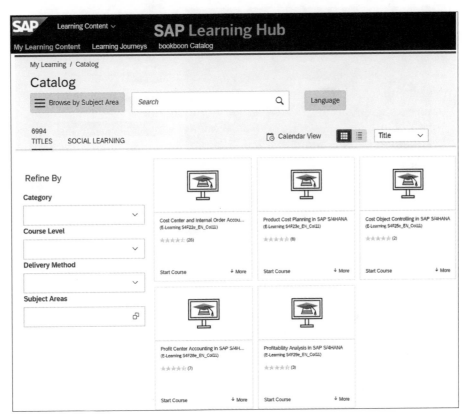

Figure 6 Course Content on SAP Learning Hub

- Access to the SAP Learning Rooms that are available for many SAP lines of business, including CO (Figure 7). A learning room is a virtual forum where

SAP Learning Hub subscribers can interact, ask questions, make proposals, discuss business cases, find materials and links, join webinars, and get informed about the newest developments in individual areas. Each learning room has a lead trainer assigned to create original content, facilitate discussions, answer questions, and generally overlook things and make sure all is running smoothly for participants.

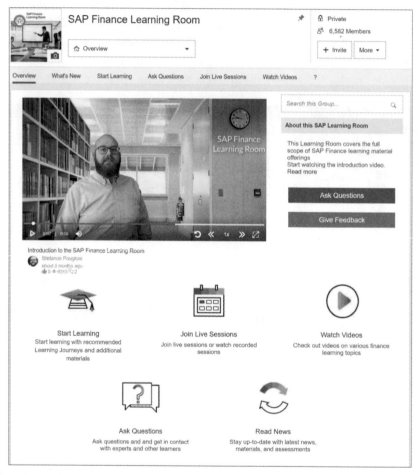

Figure 7 SAP Finance Learning Room

- SAP Live Access allows you to deploy training systems configured specifically to support the courses on the SAP Learning Hub. To gain access, you need an SAP Learning Hub subscription, but you also need to purchase a separate contingent/voucher that gives you 20 hours of system access. You can suspend and resume your system activities as needed. You can also change to a different course and order a new system within the allotted time. All current and future financial courses for SAP S/4HANA are planned and designed to support SAP Live Access. In Figure 8, you can see the SAP Live Access portal and some of the SAP S/4HANA courses available to order.

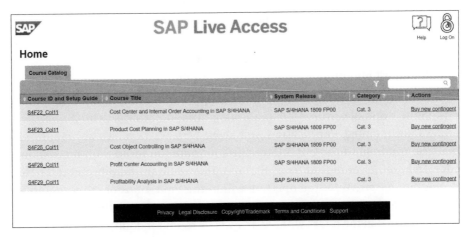

Figure 8 SAP Live Access Catalog

As a complete offering, the SAP Learning Hub is a good way to gain the knowledge required to pass the certification. In addition, however, it's the offering with the most overall value because you get access to much more learning content, including the latest releases from SAP Education.

Tips for Taking the Certification Exam

Let's now go over a few tips that will help better prepare you for the exam. Studying the education materials is truly the key to passing the certification, but we'll also analyze the question types you'll answer, and finally list a few tips and tricks for before and during the exam.

Realign Your Perspective

The main objective of this book is to help you pass the certification exam for C_TS4CO_1809: SAP Certified Application Associate—SAP S/4HANA for Management Accounting Associates (SAP S/4HANA 1809). This isn't the same as preparing you for real-life consulting projects. Although the requirements for the exam and real-life consulting overlap to a great extent, and SAP releases materials with content and exercises that are relevant for consultants, remember that this certification (and any application consultant-level certification) tests knowledge of the specific materials it's based on. In other words, though your own experience will contribute a lot to your success in the certification exam and experience is arguably the single most important indicator of ability (at least until a certain experience level is reached) in the real world, this isn't true for the certification. For the certification, knowledge and an understanding of the material and scope of the courses is most important.

For a consultant, life is full of choices, options, multiple paths, balance, and trade-offs. In the world of certification, the truth is absolute; it's clear-cut, it's detailed, and it's documented. Certification isn't about best practices; it's about the only practice. You might hear that SAP certifications are too focused on book knowledge and are disconnected from real life. This criticism may be accurate to a degree, but we strive for the opposite within the limitations of creating a 100% foolproof certification exam for which all questions can be answered through what is learned in the books without any wiggle room for doubt.

A recent graduate who has the test-taking methodology all figured out and the process of sitting down to take an exam fresh in his memory will have an equal but different advantage from that of the seasoned professional who is tested and uses his knowledge each day to solve problems for customers.

What we're trying to say here is that yes, you need to study the education materials. The exam isn't an exercise in memorization, but it's built around the book content.

What to Expect When Taking the Exam

As mentioned, the exam is based on multiple choice and multiple selection questions. All questions must have answers found directly or easily deduced from the course book content.

In this section, we'll look at an example from each category based on questions found in the sample questions PDF from the certification exam page, as shown in Figure 9.

> A profit center standard hierarchy contains all profit centers that are assigned to which organizational unit?
>
> ○ Client
> ○ Plant
> ○ Controlling area
> ○ Operating concern

Figure 9 Multiple Choice Example

The multiple-choice question type is the most straightforward and is usually a very specific question with a single very specific answer. In the example question in Figure 9, you're asked where in the system the profit center standard hierarchy is assigned. To answer this, you must know the configurations made for a controlling area, which is the correct answer.

Figure 10 shows a sample multiple selection question in which you must select two options as correct out of the four. Again, this is a simple question with simple answer options because it's testing knowledge of system functions, not of English. SAP avoids adding unneeded scenario information to a question; most of the time, every element of a question is important, so read the question carefully, and read the question twice to make sure you have it. There's time, so don't rush it.

> You need to assign a company code to a controlling area.
> Which settings must be identical for both organizational objects?
> Note: There are 2 correct answers to this question.
>
> ☐ Operational chart of accounts
> ☐ Currency
> ☐ Operational posting periods
> ☐ Fiscal year variant

Figure 10 Multiple Selection: Two Correct Out of Four

> **Note**
> Another thing to keep in mind is that the test questions aren't written to trick you. You can take the question at face value. There may be important details, but they aren't designed to trip you up; instead, they are there to check that you comprehend a subject rather than just have it memorized.

In the multiple selection question, you need to select both correct answer options to have the answer marked correct. SAP doesn't give points for half a correct answer because it doesn't deduct points for a wrong answer. The simple sample question here is correct when you select both the operational chart of accounts and fiscal year variant answer options.

One level up the difficulty ladder is the multiple choice question with three correct options out of five, as shown in Figure 11. One additional answer option adds one further parameter to consider and ultimately a greater chance of getting it wrong. In addition, it usually takes a bit longer just to read through it all and take it in. The question here is where results analysis is available in SAP S/4HANA. When you're sure of an answer, then it's correct; don't overthink it. Marking down the ones you're sure of leaves you with a simpler question. You know one answer is correct, so you now have a two out of four question instead of a two out of five question. If you know two answers for sure, then you're left with a one out of three question. It seems obvious, but eliminating options is the best way to get them out of mind and out of sight. Concentrate on the real dilemma; don't keep going over the ones you know. The same goes for wrong answer options. Writing convincing wrong answers is challenging, so take advantage of this: when something looks out of place, know that it probably is. Eliminating one answer from the possible correct options leaves you with three correct out of four, which is much easier. If the direct knowledge approach doesn't work, go ahead with the process of elimination. Knowing what is incorrect is as important as knowing what is correct for the certification.

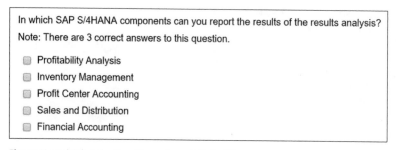

> In which SAP S/4HANA components can you report the results of the results analysis?
> Note: There are 3 correct answers to this question.
>
> ☐ Profitability Analysis
> ☐ Inventory Management
> ☐ Profit Center Accounting
> ☐ Sales and Distribution
> ☐ Financial Accounting

Figure 11 Multiple Selection: Three Correct Out of Five

You'll have three hours to go through all exam questions. This gives you a little over two minutes per question. Questions are designed to be readable in 30 seconds on average, so that should leave you plenty of time to go through the full exam. Stay relaxed and don't worry about the time; concentrate on the question at hand, and if you're unsure of the answer, move on. The system keeps track of questions that haven't been answered. Before submitting the exam as final, always answer all questions to the best of your ability. There is no penalty for wrong answers, so submitting no answer is a wasted chance at an educated guess.

SAP allows you to retake a certification exam up to three times. Both the order of the questions and the order of the answers in a question are randomized. In other words, you won't get new questions if you retake the same exam, but the questions will be mixed.

Tips and Tricks

The following are some useful tips to use when preparing for the exam:

- Bulleted lists in materials are a great resource for creating questions, especially multiple selection questions, so always keep your eyes open for them.
- Use the assessment questions in the materials and in this book to gauge your understanding of a topic. If you don't understand something, reread the relevant section, check the correct answer details, and, if needed, ask a question in an online forum or community.
- There's a lot of content to cover, so give yourself the time required to study all of it. You won't be able to review all of it the night before the exam, so it's better to invest in a good night's sleep rather than another review cycle.
- Get to the exam center or be ready for the cloud examination early. Remove as many additional stress factors as possible; being late shouldn't be something you should have to worry about.
- Avoid or at least don't put too much stock into answering "certification" questions outside official SAP resources. These are usually badly written, and many times answered incorrectly. The education courses (and this book) give you plenty to work with.

Here are some tips for during the exam:

- Answer all questions, and bookmark the questions you're unsure of to revisit them. This allows you to focus on specific ones instead of wasting time on selections you made confidently.
- Experience has shown that your initial selection is usually better than a revised one. Be cautious of going back over questions and answers too many times.
- Don't worry too much about time. In most cases, you'll be able to go over the questions two or three times if you want to.
- You don't have to get it all correct. Don't stress out because you hit two or three questions in a row of which you're unsure. Try to rationalize and keep your cool.
- Read the question a couple times, and confirm you understand the question by restating it in your own words. Then move to the answer options and read

through all of them thoroughly. Even if it's multiple choice and you identify the right answer, always read all answer options.

- Eliminate the answer options that don't make sense or are obviously wrong. Usually one of the wrong answers sticks out as incorrect, and the fewer options you have, the better the chance of selecting the right one.

- In some cases, there might be answer options that are paired. This means that if one answer is correct, then the other must be wrong. Because both can't be correct, you must select one of the two in any case.

- Questions might look similar or might cover the same topic. Although SAP avoids having too many questions that overlap, it does happen. Watch out for the differentiators in the question and answer options, and treat them as new questions.

Additional Learning Resources

Undoubtedly, gaining the knowledge to pass the certification exam is important; a certification is valuable in the job marketplace, and it does verify at least a certain level of knowledge. However, in the IT field especially, innovation never stands still; plus, the sheer scope of the SAP product offerings, even just for CO, is truly awe-inspiring.

Not strictly for preparation of a certification, but in the general scope of learning more about different areas and keeping your knowledge up to date, the following subsections provide a few useful resources for you to consider.

Stay-Current Materials

These materials are created and provided by SAP Education in direct cooperation with the development departments that build the solutions. Stay-current materials are released and made available on the SAP Learning Hub (requires a valid license) for every major product release on the day the product is released to customers. For the on-premise edition of SAP S/4HANA, a new set of learning programs is created at least annually (Figure 12 shows the learning programs made available for SAP S/4HANA 1809) and updated as needed to include features released with every new feature and service packs throughout the year.

SAP S/4HANA 1809 - Stay Current
Learning Programs
CUSTOMERS/PARTNERS

Dear all,

today, SAP announced the general availability of SAP S/4HANA 1809, the latest release of SAP S/4HANA. The following stay current learning programs are available now to make sure you keep their knowledge up-to-date for the innovations shipped with this new release.

Overview & Cross Topics	Finance
Scope, Innovation and Technical Highlights	Accounting
Embedded Analytics Innovations Overview	Group Reporting
Master Data Governance	Treasury Management
	International Trade

Industries	LoB Solutions
Oil & Gas	Sourcing and Procurement
Consumer and Mortgage Loans	Manufacturing
Fashion and Vertical Business	Supply Chain
Retail for Merchandise Management	Transportation Management
Commercial Project Management	Sales
Commodity Procurement and Commodity Sales	Asset Management
Commodity Risk Management	Portfolio and Project Management
Utilities	R&D/Engineering
Insurance	Environment, Health & Safety

Figure 12 Stay Current for SAP S/4HANA 1809

With stay-current programs, you get access to live and recorded webinars, information for useful links, and presentations of what is new, how new features work, and how to implement the new features in the system. The content is delta in nature by default, so it's ideal to continue to stay current on new functionality after you gain a baseline knowledge from SAP's full-scale education courses. The education courses will take a subset of what's new to filter back into the core learning curriculum, and sometimes features or functions are large and important enough to warrant a completely new course.

SAP Best Practices Explorer

The SAP S/4HANA system deployment and the SAP Activate methodology is closely integrated with the SAP Best Practices. A new system will generally use a best practices package as the baseline on which a customer will build its own processes (or in some cases, the customer will change its processes to match the best practices). Through the SAP Best Practices Explorer (*https://rapid.sap.com/bp*, shown in Figure 13), you can access detailed definitions of the best practices solution scopes, test scripts detailing the steps to perform various business processes, and business process diagrams that graphically depict processes steps.

Figure 13 SAP Best Practices Explorer for SAP S/4HANA

SAP Help Portal

The SAP Help Portal (*https://help.sap.com*; Figure 14) is an additional go-to place for finding detailed information on SAP products.

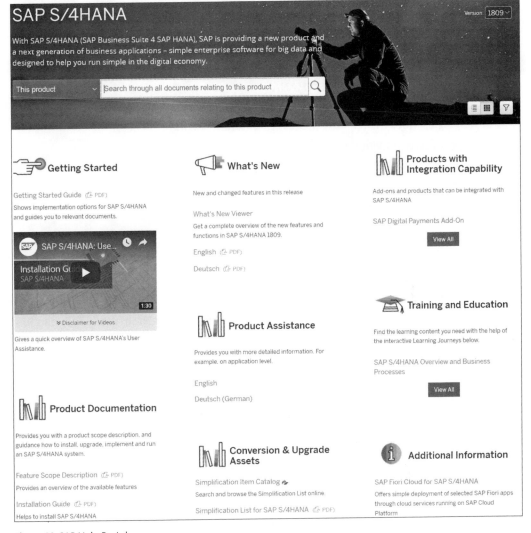

Figure 14 SAP Help Portal

Especially for admin information, it offers a wealth of details. With every release of SAP S/4HANA, you can expect the following documents to be made available:

- **What's new viewer**
  Offers a complete overview of the new features and functions in every new release of SAP S/4HANA
- **Feature scope description**
  Provides an overview of the available features
- **Installation guide**
  Helps you install SAP S/4HANA
- **Upgrade guide**
  Describes the upgrade process to different software versions
- **Conversion guide**
  Supports the conversion from SAP ERP to SAP S/4HANA
- **UI technology guide**
  Gives information on the UI implementation
- **Security guide**
  Enables the implementation of a secure system landscape
- **Operations guide**
  Helps you operate your system
- **Simplification list**
  Describes features that aren't in scope for SAP S/4HANA in comparison to SAP ERP and provides alternatives

SAP Product Assistance

The SAP Help Portal has a link to **Product Assistance** (lower middle of the screen in Figure 14). This is what was formally known as the SAP Library, and it has information for each application and many processes in SAP S/4HANA, including configuration steps. Figure 15 shows a page with details on **Controlling (CO)**; on the left, you can see the tree menu with details for each area of the same.

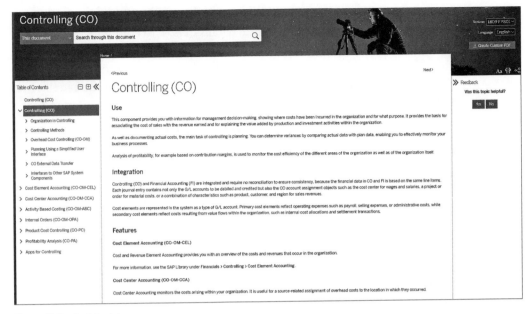

Figure 15 Product Assistance

SAP User Enablement Videos

The user enablement videos created by SAP for SAP Enable Now showcase basic best practices tasks performed in an actual system environment. These can be a great way for people without access to an SAP S/4HANA system to understand how the business processes are executed within the system using the SAP Fiori interface. You can access them for various SAP applications, including SAP S/4HANA, via the blog post at *http://s-prs.co/485600*.

Tip
The demos are always kept up to date with the newest product release, and new simulations are often added as well.

SAP Fiori Apps Reference Library

The SAP Fiori apps reference library is an extremely important resource for you to keep an eye on (*http://s-prs.co/485601*). Here you'll see every app made available for SAP Fiori. You can quickly find newly released apps and apps that have changed. For native SAP Fiori apps, you can find a short description of their functionality; for all apps, you get analytical details of how to configure them in your system. In Figure 16, you can see an example for the Monitor Payments app, in which the application details can be viewed for the different product releases (SAP S/4HANA, SAP S/4HANA Cloud, SAP ERP, etc.). In the search box, you can filter via many different parameters, such as line of business, product, release, and so on.

Figure 16 SAP Fiori Apps Reference Library

SAP Community

The SAP Community is another great way to gain valuable knowledge and get assistance from other expert community members (*http://s-prs.co/485602*; Figure 17). There are many blog posts available containing useful how-to guides and plenty of questions already answered.

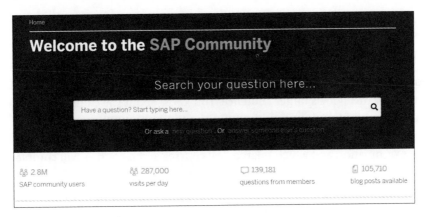

Figure 17 SAP Community

openSAP

openSAP is SAP's free massive open online course (MOOC) enterprise offering (Figure 18).

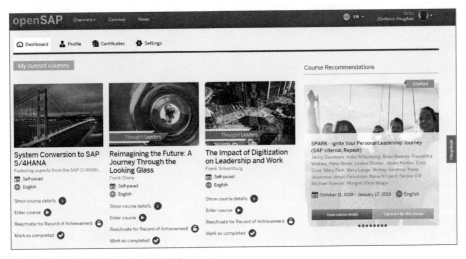

Figure 18 openSAP Enterprise MOOC Courses

It has a wealth of ongoing and previously run courses for several topics focusing on true innovation, such as machine learning, big data, Internet of Things, and more. There isn't a lot of content for CO specifically, and the detail level the courses go into usually isn't very deep, but this makes it a fantastic resource to keep up with all the latest innovations and trends without requiring prior knowledge of the topics.

Summary

You should now understand the various SAP S/4HANA certification options that are relevant for this book's target audience. You know about the exam structure, topic weighting, and required pass score for the C_TS4CO_1809 exam. You now know which SAP Education training courses you can review or attend for your certification examination and which related SAP courses and resources will complement and further enhance your knowledge and skills.

In the next chapter, we'll dive right in to the exam topics, starting with an introduction to and overview of SAP HANA and SAP S/4HANA.

Chapter 1

SAP HANA, SAP S/4HANA, and SAP Fiori

Techniques You'll Master

- Explain the SAP strategy for digital transformation
- Describe the SAP framework for the digital enterprise
- Understand the role of the SAP Cloud Platform and SAP Leonardo
- Review basic SAP HANA technology
- Describe the scope of financials for SAP S/4HANA
- Choose the relevant deployment option for SAP S/4HANA
- Explain the SAP Fiori design pillars
- Use the SAP Fiori launchpad
- Describe the basic SAP Fiori application types

In this chapter, we'll explore the architecture of SAP HANA, describe the scope and deployment options of SAP S/4HANA, and discuss the basic functions of the SAP Fiori user interface (UI).

Real-World Scenario

As a consultant, you need to understand the underlying architecture that the SAP S/4HANA system is built on. SAP HANA is at the core of the SAP strategy, and you need to feel comfortable explaining this technology to your customers in simple terms. SAP HANA is a faster database, but there's more information you should be able to pass on without scaring nontechnical people off. SAP HANA is often perceived as expensive, so understanding technologies such as compression and columnar store on a high level can help you build a case to alter this perception for your potential customers.

The SAP S/4HANA system is a separate product line from the old SAP ERP system. SAP ERP is no longer the default go-to enterprise resource planning (ERP) platform for SAP. This was a huge change and a business decision with quite a large risk for SAP. It has proven to be successful, and more and more customers are persuaded by the true benefits of the new system. But what's special about it? How difficult is it to adopt? How can customers move to SAP S/4HANA, and do they risk losing the (potentially) millions they have invested in the "old" software? You need to be able to explain the reasons for this move by SAP and what it means for new and existing SAP customers.

Finally, SAP Fiori is the default graphical user interface (GUI) for end users in SAP S/4HANA, so you need to be able to use it with confidence, explain its components, and describe the benefits it brings. You should also have knowledge of how the tile groups, tile catalogues, roles, and users cooperate to form what the user sees on his own SAP Fiori launchpad.

Objectives of This Portion of the Test

The management accounting (CO) certification exam does not test your general knowledge of SAP HANA, SAP S/4HANA deployment options, and SAP Fiori applications. However, as more CO transactions and reports move to SAP Fiori, as a CO consultant, you will need a good understanding of the following topics:

- SAP HANA in-memory architecture
- SAP S/4HANA products, and architecture for financials
- Deployment options for SAP S/4HANA
- SAP Fiori launchpad features
- SAP Fiori application types

Key Concepts Refresher

Digital transformation is motivating innovation in business, and in this section we'll describe SAP's intelligent enterprise vision and strategy, as well as show how SAP HANA and SAP S/4HANA are at the core of this strategy. We'll go over the basic SAP HANA architecture and look at the technology that enables SAP HANA to be the innovation platform of the future for SAP.

In addition, we'll discuss the SAP S/4HANA solution, deployment options, and system landscape. Finally, we'll look at the SAP Fiori user experience (UX) and analyze basic generic functions, application types, and administration tools.

Digital Transformation

Because the technological world is expanding with unprecedented speed, it's imperative for businesses to not only catch up with these advances but also use them to their competitive advantage. Computers and software are traditionally considered supportive to business, and digital transformation brings the digital world to the forefront of innovation and makes it a key business driver on its own. Digital transformation in business implies the adoption and use of technologies such as big data, the Internet of Things (IoT), mobile, artificial intelligence (AI), and social media to drive business innovation and growth.

Intelligent Enterprise Framework

The effect of digital transformation can be felt across business functions such as marketing, operations, human resources, administration, and so on. It forces organizations and people to rethink and optimize how they execute business processes and how they can benefit from adopting automation in their day-to-day activities. SAP is investing heavily to support all facets of the digital enterprise and has adopted a strategic framework to help businesses run while utilizing the cutting edge of enterprise technology.

The SAP strategy for supporting the intelligent enterprise is focused on three key product offerings:

- **Intelligent suite**
  The intelligent suite includes all the SAP applications that support the end-to-end business processes of the enterprise (Figure 1.1).

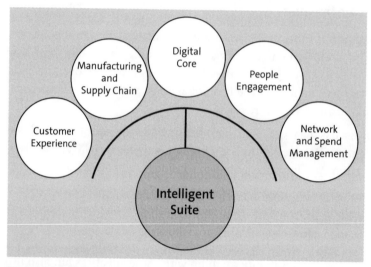

Figure 1.1 Intelligent Suite

- **Digital platform**
  The digital platform refers to SAP Cloud Platform, an open business platform for building and delivering business applications. The strategy put forward by SAP is to shift development focus from the core solutions into the SAP Cloud Platform to ensure the greatest flexibility both for SAP and third-party developers while maintaining a lean and stable core.

- **Intelligent technologies**
  The third and final component revolves around the SAP Leonardo offering. SAP Leonardo is a technology framework that combines multiple modern technological tools that can be used to improve applications by providing automation, detection, and prevention capabilities, among others. Some of the key words for SAP Leonardo technologies include artificial intelligence and machine learning, blockchain, data intelligence, big data, IoT, and analytics.

Traditional business applications and ERP software packages aren't designed to fully support businesses throughout this digital transformation journey. SAP saw this growing gap as an opportunity more than 10 years ago and created SAP HANA to be the core building block of business software that not only supports but drives digital transformation. Today, SAP HANA is at the core of virtually all SAP product development. But what is SAP HANA, and why is it so important?

SAP HANA Architecture

In its simplest form, SAP HANA is a database management system. It performs all the expected database functions of storing and retrieving data for applications that sit on top of it, but SAP HANA is unique in how it performs these tasks. In addition, SAP HANA has embedded advanced analytics capabilities such as predictive analytics and text analysis, mining, and search. SAP HANA also offers application development services supporting a variety of programming languages. Finally, SAP HANA offers a slew of data access, administration, and security support services. Clearly, SAP HANA is much more than "just" a really fast database.

Interesting as all the features are, we'll concentrate on the database architecture. We won't get too technical, and we'll keep things in scope both for the certification and the CO associate role. The SAP HANA database has three standout features that work together and make it unique:

- **In-memory database**
  Using RAM to store all data has only even been imagined as a possibility in the past decade or so. Memory is faster than disk storage—in fact, much faster. In best-case-scenario sequential reads, the best solid-state disks today can read data at about 3 GB/s. Modern, fast memory reads, writes, and copies at rates around 60 GB/s. That's a factor of 20 against best-case-scenario disk drive speed. Of course, this method is more expensive, but these costs usually aren't prohibitive for enterprises. In addition, the data storage capacities supported aren't as large, but modern servers can support tens of terabytes of capacity. The memory size limitations aren't critical in any but the most extreme cases due to the other features of SAP HANA, described in the next list items.

- **Aggressive compression**
  All major databases support compression, but what you save in space, you lose in speed. SAP HANA uses smart techniques to make compression a viable option while sacrificing little speed. You can expect data in an SAP HANA database to be compressed by a factor of 10 on average, meaning neither acquisition

cost nor storage capacity is a huge factor. One of the ways SAP HANA avoids losing speed is by inserting only new data rather than editing existing entries; decompressing and recompressing for changing entries is a costly proposition. By only adding entries and appending the old ones, SAP HANA doesn't go through the compress/decompress cycle. With versioning, the system knows always to read the latest entry for a given data set. This brings us to another major technical difference that allows larger compression, discussed in the next list item.

- **Columnar data storage**
  SAP HANA uses the columnar data store type for two major reasons:
  - Much better compression
  - Faster data retrieval for queries (when only a subset of the full table data set is required)

  Column storage also works great for data aggregation (SAP HANA is used for ad hoc aggregation a lot) and parallel processing. Column storage is more commonly found in online analytical processing (OLAP) applications (e.g., business warehouse systems), rather than online transaction processing (OLTP) systems (which a typical ERP system might be considered), for which row storage is considered faster. Although SAP HANA supports both types of tables (developers can decide what works for their use case), the columnar store is where SAP HANA shines.

Technology Enablers for Success with SAP HANA

Most databases are designed to work optimally with the technology available at the time of their design. The de facto approach before SAP HANA was for applications to minimize disk access requirements and perform calculations in the code. However, as technology continues to progress, this design is no longer the only way to go. The following are the main technology drivers and trends that led SAP to invest in SAP HANA:

- **Large-volume, extremely high-bandwidth, affordable memory**
  Memory has always been much faster, but 20 years ago, it was inconceivable to be able to purchase and take advantage of the volumes that we can today.
- **New-generation microprocessors with multiple cores and larger optimized caches**
  CPUs can now access data at much higher rates than in the past.

- **Expandable modular data centers**
  Modular data centers now can be expanded by adding servers for more memory and processing power to scale to any new sizing requirements.

- **Cloud computing applications**
  These apps are used more and more by customers as an alternative to investing in on-premise software, even for critical backend components. Customers save on IT costs, and their solution is always up to date. The subscription model makes the cost of ownership more transparent and increases flexibility because the buy-in is smaller.

SAP S/4HANA

SAP S/4HANA is the current ERP solution from SAP. As the name implies, it's optimized for SAP HANA. In fact, unlike all previous ERP solutions from SAP, it will only work on SAP HANA. SAP S/4HANA comprises the SAP S/4HANA Enterprise Management digital core, the component closest in scope to the SAP ERP solution, and various line of business (LoB) solutions, which are generally cloud solutions that are SAP products gained through mergers and acquisitions and that have been and are being optimized to work together as a seamless, integrated solution (Figure 1.2).

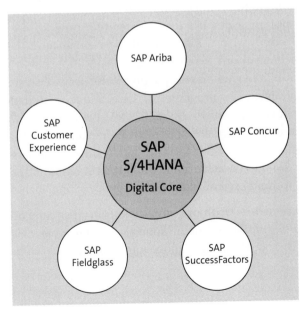

Figure 1.2 SAP S/4HANA: Digital Core

The following are the main LoB solutions you should be aware of:

- SAP C/4HANA, the customer experience and engagement suite
- SAP SuccessFactors and SAP Fieldglass for human resource management
- SAP Concur for travel management
- SAP Ariba for sourcing and procurement

Now let's explore the digital core, in which you'll find the financial components this exam is about. SAP S/4HANA is a new breed of ERP system written specifically with two major goals in mind:

- **Writing code to take advantage of SAP HANA**
  SAP removes architectural redundancies to simplify and speed up the system. New code was developed for the core system architecture that did away with the aggregation tables the old system relied on. The system doesn't use separate totals tables to store values; instead, totals are calculated on the fly from the line items. The system also did away with the index tables used for reporting because SAP HANA is fast enough to work on the line item level. Indices increase code complexity and have been removed. These are ambitious simplification steps that seem incompatible with the second goal.

- **Safeguarding existing customer investments**
  Writing a completely new logic for the SAP S/4HANA system was and is ambitious, but doing so while maintaining compatibility with custom code written for the previous SAP ERP system seems like it would require some form of witchcraft. However, this is exactly what SAP programmers have managed. The exact description of the mechanism isn't in scope for this certification, but in a nutshell, SAP HANA compatibility views make it possible to replicate obsolete tables on the fly. In this way, an existing program that, for example, reads data from an index table (that was removed in SAP S/4HANA) can continue to retrieve the data because the system creates an on-the-fly replication of the original table. Another manifestation of this goal is the option SAP offers to customers to transform their SAP ERP systems into SAP S/4HANA systems and continue business as usual without extensive downtimes.

Figure 1.3 shows how data is accessed for traditional applications that use compatibility views and aggregates, along with the simplification achieved from reading directly from line item tables with SAP HANA-optimized apps.

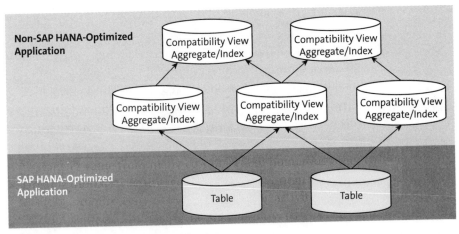

Figure 1.3 SAP HANA Application Simplification

> **Note**
> For a little history, the first component of the SAP ERP to be "simplified" through module unification and removal of aggregates was Finance with the introduction of the universal ledger in the SAP Simple Finance 1503 add-on (internally at SAP, this release was referred to as SFIN2.0). The financials-only version of SAP S/4HANA was originally sold as a separate product in parallel to the complete SAP S/4HANA suite, but they have now been consolidated into a single, complete product.

SAP S/4HANA Deployment Options

There are currently four deployment options for SAP S/4HANA that customers can choose from, as detailed in Table 1.1.

	SAP S/4HANA Cloud, Multitenant Edition	SAP S/4HANA Cloud, Single Tenant Edition	SAP S/4HANA, Private Option Managed by SAP	SAP S/4HANA On-Premise
Functional Scope	Core ERP and select LoB processes	Full functional SAP S/4HANA scope	Full functional SAP S/4HANA scope	Full functional S/4HANA scope
Innovation Cycle	Quarterly	Two per year	Annual	Annual

Table 1.1 SAP S/4HANA Deployment Options

	SAP S/4HANA Cloud, Multitenant Edition	SAP S/4HANA Cloud, Single Tenant Edition	SAP S/4HANA, Private Option Managed by SAP	SAP S/4HANA On-Premise
Licensing	Subscription	Subscription	Mixed	Perpetual
Infrastructure	Shared public cloud	Dedicated system in cloud	Customer system in SAP HANA Enterprise Cloud	Customer infrastructure

Table 1.1 SAP S/4HANA Deployment Options (Cont.)

For simplicity, and from a functional consultant perspective, you can simplify this to two editions: SAP S/4HANA Cloud (the first column, multitenant edition), for the scope and customizing possibilities are limited; and SAP S/4HANA (the other three columns), which provides the full scope of functionality and configuration flexibility.

> **Tip**
>
> SAP naming conventions mandate that when referring to the on-premise editions, the product is SAP S/4HANA. The cloud edition is referred to as SAP S/4HANA Cloud.

> **Warning!**
>
> The certification and this book focus only on SAP S/4HANA (the on-premise version).

SAP S/4HANA Adoption

Customers have three major options to start using SAP S/4HANA: a new implementation, system conversion, or landscape transformation. Let's drill down into these adoption options:

- **New implementation**
  In this case, customers can move from their legacy system (SAP ERP or a non-SAP system) and implement SAP S/4HANA from scratch. This scenario is also known as a *greenfield approach*. Customers with older, highly customized ERP solutions might prefer this option to clean up their systems and start over. This option is available for all editions of SAP S/4HANA.

- **System conversion**

  This is for customers who want to convert their existing SAP ERP system into an SAP S/4HANA system. The benefit is that customers can move to SAP S/4HANA without a reimplementation and with no major disruption to existing business processes. Once the conversion is completed, customers can gradually update their processes to adapt to SAP S/4HANA and SAP Fiori. This option is available for on-premise and private cloud customers of SAP S/4HANA.

Tip

The specific tasks required of a CO consultant during a system conversion project are a part of the SAP Certified Application Professional—Financials in SAP S/4HANA certification curriculum. However, this is out of scope for the application associate certification.

- **Landscape transformation**

  This adoption method is for customers who want to consolidate their landscapes or to selectively bring data into an SAP S/4HANA system.

  For example, through Central Finance, customers can take advantage of the features and advantages of the Universal Journal and reporting using the SAP S/4HANA system. In this case, the source systems remain intact and business transactions are still performed in the source systems. Landscape transformation scenarios work on premise and may selectively work with the cloud deployment as well.

The SAP S/4HANA System Landscape

System landscapes can vary greatly depending on the customer requirements and legacy ERP systems in use. A new installation for SAP S/4HANA would typically require two basic productive systems: the SAP S/4HANA backend server and an SAP Gateway server. The SAP S/4HANA backend is, of course, a required component because without it, there is no ERP system. The SAP Gateway server is where the connections and settings to SAP Fiori are established. You can access both with the traditional SAP GUI. Figure 1.4 shows the **SAP Logon** window with the two system setup we use in SAP Education courses for most SAP S/4HANA Finance courses: **T41** is the backend server, and **T4N** is the gateway server.

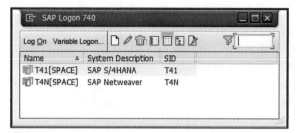

Figure 1.4 SAP Logon Screen with SAP S/4HANA Backend and SAP Gateway Server

Note
SAP Fiori is in theory an optional component of SAP S/4HANA; however, you aren't taking full advantage of SAP S/4HANA without it and as the product matures and is enhanced, you are utilizing fewer and fewer of the new developments for it.

The SAP Fiori User Interface

SAP Fiori is the common design paradigm for SAP. The SAP Fiori design language affects the look and feel of all things SAP, not only the interface of the new SAP S/4HANA system. SAP recognized that everyday apps are becoming simpler to use and more flexible. Business software needs to keep up with this development or else the disconnect between "work software" and "daily apps" will cause issues in user acceptance, satisfaction, and productivity.

To create apps in SAP Fiori, you use the SAPUI5 framework. This framework is in turn based on the open source OpenUI5 framework, with the addition of a few extra SAP-specific tools. SAPUI5 is an open-source framework; that is, anyone can use it and implement improvements. The main development tools to work with SAPUI5 include HTML5, CCS3, jQuery, and JavaScript. Basing the entire development platform on open standards with general and broad acceptance ensures that a lot of people will be familiar with the tools needed to develop SAP Fiori apps and that the apps have great compatibility with multiple device platforms.

SAP Fiori User Experience Paradigm

The SAP Fiori design and user experience paradigm is built on five principles:

- **Role-based**
  Applications should be focused on providing the functionality required for a

specific task. Complex screens with infinite selection options and one app for doing everything isn't the aim.

- **Responsive**
Apps should be usable on multiple devices and be able to adjust their interface to fit the device size, input methods, and so on.

- **Simple**
Apps should not need a manual or special training to be used. The apps should be designed for a single user and use case and require no more than three screens end to end.

- **Coherent**
The design has to be coherent between apps, and users should feel instant familiarity when accessing new apps. Also, apps should be designed with technical coherence as well, meaning they can be ported to other systems and speak the same language.

- **Instant value**
Apps need to be useful immediately, meaning they need to be easy to install, configure, and deploy in your IT landscape. On the user side, the purpose of the apps should be clear, and users should have no problem learning how to use them. Ideally, users who have seen a couple of SAP Fiori apps in action should be able to move on to other apps without needing help or training.

SAP Fiori for SAP S/4HANA

SAP Fiori for SAP S/4HANA refers more specifically to the apps available for the system. The SAP development teams are constantly developing new native applications for SAP Fiori to replace the traditional and usually "busier" SAP GUI apps that SAP S/4HANA inherited. Native applications can also make use of all the exciting new technology available with SAP S/4HANA, such as conversational UI, machine learning, immersive experiences, and the like. SAP S/4HANA Finance has a good head start, and quite a few native applications are already available.

In addition to the native SAP Fiori apps, you can also launch SAP GUI apps from the SAP Fiori launchpad. These apps will be launched in the web browser with an SAP Fiori "look" design theme called Belize (see Figure 1.5). The scope of the SAP ERP apps is huge, and not immediately having to replace everything at once gives SAP some breathing room to create useful and simpler native applications without sacrificing scope coverage. Customers can always develop their own apps as well, and easily adding SAP GUI apps to SAP Fiori allows any legacy custom ABAP apps to work through SAP Fiori.

You can see an example of the SAP Fiori-look classic applications in Figure 1.5. The basic design elements for these apps include:

- A text-based toolbar instead of icons
- All labels right-aligned
- New design icons with common design language
- Condensed table rows
- The SAP Fiori header **Back** button replacing the in-app navigation controls
- Redesigned tab strips (the active tab highlighting)
- Processing and closing actions moved to the footer of the screen

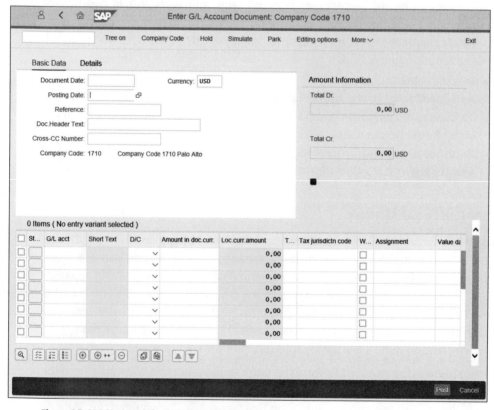

Figure 1.5 SAP Fiori Look for HTML SAP GUI App

Tip

SAP GUI apps are referred to by SAP in the new system as *SAP S/4HANA classic applications*.

SAP Fiori apps fit into one of three categories:

- **Transactional apps**
  Apps used to perform operations such as master record creation and maintenance or posting transactions. For example, the Clear Incoming Payments app,
  shown in Figure 1.6.

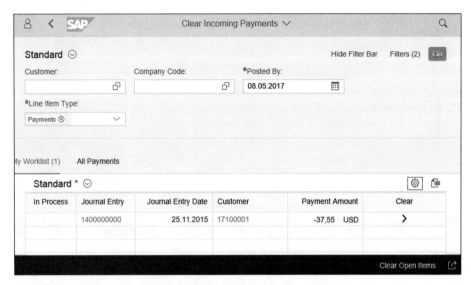

Figure 1.6 Transactional Application Example: Clear Incoming Payments

- **Analytical apps**
  These are detailed reports used to drill down to finer details or "zoom out" to
  the organization level you need. One of these, **Overdue Payables**, is shown in
  Figure 1.7.

- **Factsheet apps**
  Quick overviews of a specific object, with the basic details and even some key
  performance indicators (KPIs) in one screen. You can often navigate directly via
  links from one factsheet to another for related objects. Figure 1.8 shows an
  example of this, the Supplier Invoice Search app.

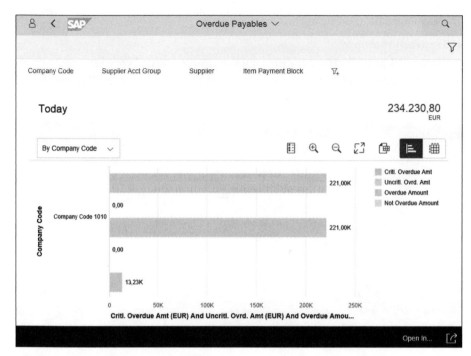

Figure 1.7 Analytical App Example: Overdue Payables

Figure 1.8 Factsheet App Example: Supplier Invoice Search

The SAP Fiori Launchpad

The SAP Fiori launchpad is the user access point to the system (as shown in Figure 1.9). It's a customizable web-based interface from which all the apps a user has assigned can be launched. The apps don't need to be from one specific system; the tiles can launch apps and links for any system that's connected and compatible.

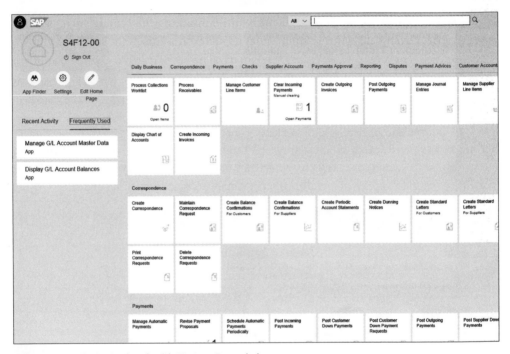

Figure 1.9 SAP Fiori Launchpad, with Me Area Expanded

Let's explore the important characteristics and functionalities of the SAP Fiori launchpad:

- You access it from a web browser with a fixed URL. The URL can be shared with anyone on the network. If they have a username and password and are authorized, they will be able to log on without further installations of local software (see top of Figure 1.10).

- Apps are displayed as tiles (or, rarely, as text links). The tiles can be static, meaning they have a fixed icon, or active. Active tiles show some important information directly without needing to be clicked on. Active tiles update displayed information at customizable periodic intervals and can be helpful to provide a quick status overview for topics of interest, such as open payments, number of open workflow messages, and more. You can see the active tile for the Cumulative Totals app in Figure 1.10.

Figure 1.10 Browser View of SAP Fiori

- Advanced search functionality isn't limited to applications; there is a dropdown list to search for many characteristics. The system will display information for the searched-for object directly in a factsheet, as shown in Figure 1.11.

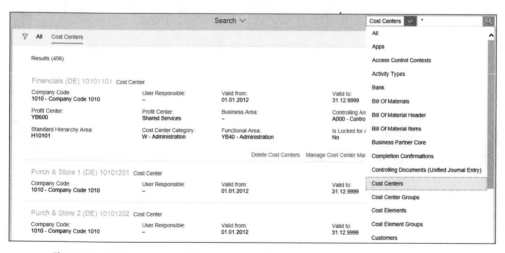

Figure 1.11 SAP Fiori Launchpad: Search for Cost Centers

- An end user can customize the apps and app groups displayed in his SAP Fiori launchpad. Selecting the **Edit Home Page** option (shown previously in the **Me** area in Figure 1.9) will allow a user to reposition apps, remove apps, add apps (that the user has access to), move groups, add groups, rename groups, and remove groups completely. A user can at any time reset groups back to their default.

> **Warning!**
> The scope of apps each user can open, the initial grouping of apps, and the apps included in these standard groups are all controlled by an administrator.

Within most native SAP Fiori apps, and especially for reports, a user has the option to save the current view (with whatever inputs have been made) as a new tile. Clicking on the tile directly from the SAP Fiori home page will execute the app with the settings defined when the tile was created. This is useful, for example, in KPI reports when you want to have easy access to information for a specific combination of characteristic values.

Customers can use their own themes to fully customize the look of the SAP Fiori launchpad. The colors, background, logos, fonts, and so on can all be changed from the SAP-standard-delivered theme. You can design multiple themes, and users can select from among them. All such customizing is done with the UI theme designer, as shown in Figure 1.12.

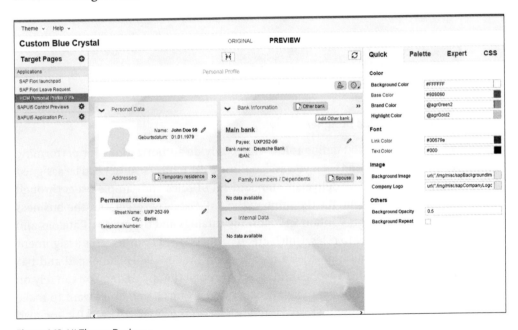

Figure 1.12 UI Theme Designer

The user can select the **Settings** option in the **Me** area to display information for his or her user account, as shown in Figure 1.13. This is also where users select the theme and default language and region settings. Under **User Profiling**, the user can enable customized search (which tracks the user's activity to tailor search results) and, if enabled, clear the search cache. Finally, the user can set default values proposed by apps for many system attributes, such as company code, plant, planner profile, and so on.

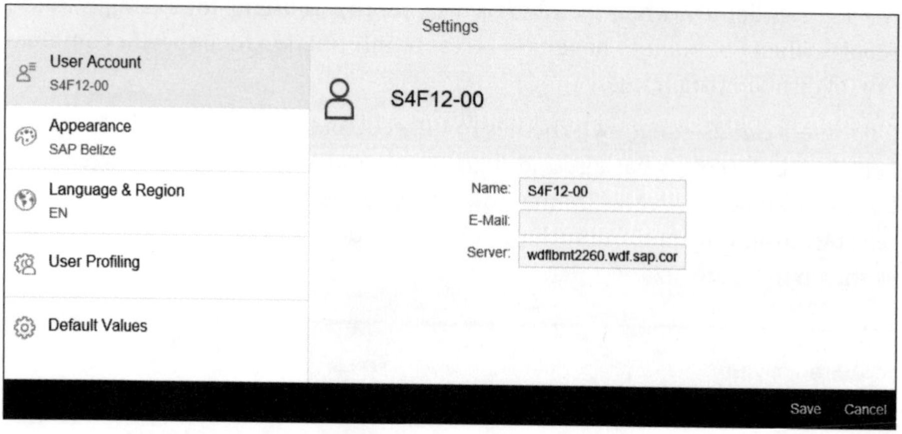

Figure 1.13 SAP Fiori Launchpad User Settings

SAP Fiori Launchpad Designer

In SAP S/4HANA, you define roles, which provide authorizations for performing various functions, and then you assign these roles to users. A user can be assigned to multiple roles. SAP delivers a standard set of roles and sample users through best practices content. It's the same in the SAP Gateway server, but the business roles you assign here contain SAP Fiori tile catalogs and tile groups. Catalogs and groups are assigned to roles, which are in turn assigned to users. This assignment defines which application tiles a user sees on the SAP Fiori launchpad and has authorization to add to groups and launch through the app finder. You can rely on the many SAP-delivered standard catalogs and groups if you don't want to make changes, or you can use them as a reference for your own. With the SAP launchpad designer, you create the catalogs and the groups for your SAP Fiori launchpad, as shown in Figure 1.14.

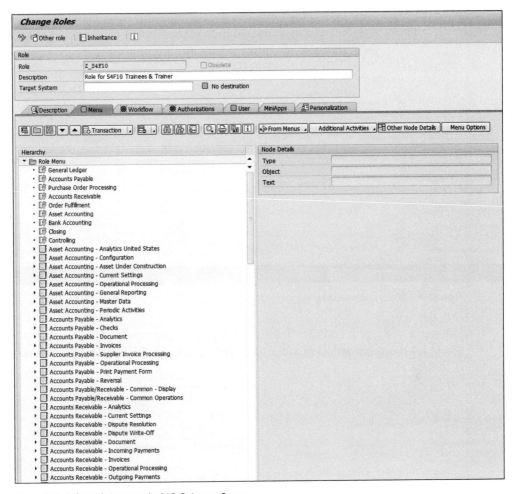

Figure 1.14 Role Maintenance in SAP Gateway Server

SAP Fiori catalogs hold configuration information for apps. Here you maintain names, subtitles, icons, and other options for the more technical settings for your tiles (these are useful to understand, but completely out of scope for this book). After you've created a catalog, you assign it to a role (and the role to a user). The application tiles inside the catalog define the applications a user has access to. If a tile is included in an SAP Fiori tile group to which a user is assigned, but the tile isn't in any of the catalogs assigned, the user won't be able to see the tile. You'll need to assign the catalog to the user that the tile is in. You can create as many catalogs as required to meet the needs of end-user roles (see Figure 1.15).

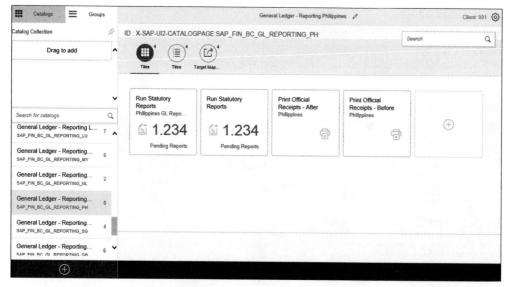

Figure 1.15 SAP Fiori Launchpad Designer: Catalogs

The name of a group and the tiles included in that group are assigned in the SAP Fiori tile group configuration in the SAP Fiori launchpad designer (see Figure 1.16).

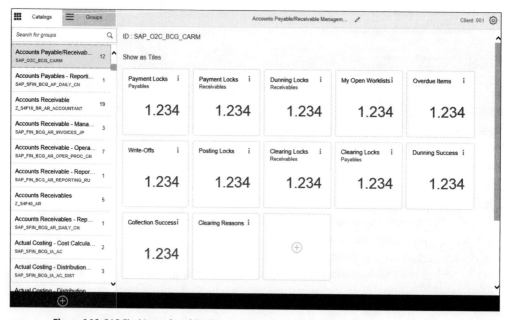

Figure 1.16 SAP Fiori Launchpad Designer: Groups

You can add tiles to the group from many different catalogs, but the user must be assigned to all the relevant catalogs to see and use the tiles. You can select whether the end user will be allowed to change a tile group on their own launchpad or not. Finally, you select whether apps will be displayed as tiles or as links.

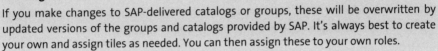

> **Warning!**
> If you make changes to SAP-delivered catalogs or groups, these will be overwritten by updated versions of the groups and catalogs provided by SAP. It's always best to create your own and assign tiles as needed. You can then assign these to your own roles.

Important Terminology

In this chapter, the following terminology was used:

- **Columnar store**
  Data is stored in columns instead of in the more traditional rows; this allows speedier read performance and greater compression capabilities. The downside is suboptimal transactional processing.

- **In-memory technology**
  Data storage in RAM instead of in disks to capitalize on lower latency and read/write times. The technology still makes use of disks for historic data and backup purposes.

- **SAP Cloud Platform**
  The SAP Cloud Platform is a development and deployment platform that aids the creation of intelligent, integrated, and mobile-ready applications to support business operations.

- **SAP Fiori**
  A new common design paradigm for all SAP applications. The design goal is to make business apps intuitive to use and available on all platforms and devices. SAP Fiori is based on the following design principles: role-based, responsive, simple, coherent, and instant value.

- **SAP Fiori for SAP S/4HANA**
  A group of applications that are designed for SAP S/4HANA. There are three basic app types: transactional, analytical, and factsheets.

- **SAP Fiori launchpad**
  The end-user interface "cockpit" for SAP Fiori that is accessed through any modern web browser without extra software requirements. It displays several

applications in flat, rectangular forms called *tiles*. The applications available depend on the user's role and authorizations. The SAP Fiori launchpad offers many Customizing options for the end user, such as theme selection, custom grouping, and displayed application selection.

- **SAP Fiori launchpad designer**
  Administrator interface to customize the catalogs and groups available in the system. You define the configuration for SAP Fiori tiles in the **Catalog** section and for the tiles included in groups in the **Group** section.

- **SAP Gateway server**
  The server used to connect SAP Fiori to one or more SAP S/4HANA, SAP ERP, SAP Business Warehouse (SAP BW), and other such backend systems. SAP Fiori application configuration is performed here, as well as SAP Fiori user maintenance.

- **SAP Leonardo**
  SAP Leonardo is a collection of intelligent technologies that can be utilized in conjunction with the SAP Cloud Platform to develop next-generation applications. Relevant technologies include machine learning, IoT, analytics, blockchain, data intelligence, and big data.

- **SAP S/4HANA**
  The new ERP system from SAP that leverages SAP HANA to simplify the code and data structures. It's designed to be the digital core for all business applications of the customer and to allow businesses to go digital. It's offered on premise with a traditional ownership model and in the cloud with a subscription model.

Practice Questions

These practice questions will help you evaluate your understanding of the topics covered in this chapter. Although none of these questions will be found on the exam itself, and this topic will not be specifically tested on the exam, they will allow you to review your knowledge of the subject. Select the correct answers, and then check the completeness of your answers in the next section. Remember that on the exam, you must select all correct answers and only correct answers to receive credit for the question.

1. Which SAP technological products provide the platform required for SAP to support the digital transformation of an organization? (There are two correct answers.)

☐ **A.** SAP HANA

☐ **B.** SAP Leonardo

☐ **C.** SAP Fiori

☐ **D.** SAP Cloud Platform

2. Which component of the framework for the intelligent enterprise includes SAP Leonardo?

☐ **A.** Intelligent suite

☐ **B.** Digital platform

☐ **C.** Intelligent technologies

☐ **D.** Machine learning

3. You want to develop a substantial enhancement for the purchase-to-pay process in your SAP S/4HANA system. Where does SAP recommend you perform this enhancement?

☐ **A.** SAP Leonardo

☐ **B.** SAP Fiori

☐ **C.** SAP Cloud Platform

☐ **D.** SAP S/4HANA core

4. True or False: SAP S/4HANA (on premise) can be deployed on cloud infrastructure.

☐ **A.** True

☐ **B.** False

5. The SAP HANA database relies on which of the following technologies for storing data? (There are three correct answers.)

☐ **A.** In-memory

☐ **B.** Aggregation

☐ **C.** Indexing

☐   **D.** Columnar store

☐   **E.** Compression

6.   Data in the SAP HANA database is stored in which two ways? (There are two correct answers.)

☐   **A.** Random

☐   **B.** Vector

☐   **C.** Column

☐   **D.** Row

7.   True or False: In an environment of systems using SAP HANA, you can perform both OLAP and OLTP processing without duplication of the data for the SAP BW and SAP ERP systems.

☐   **A.** True

☐   **B.** False

8.   SAP HANA makes extensive use of which high-speed hardware technology to offer more speed?

☐   **A.** Read-only memory

☐   **B.** Solid-state drives (SSDs)

☐   **C.** Graphics processing units (GPUs)

☐   **D.** Multicore CPUs

9.   True or False: SAP S/4HANA replaces SAP ERP, and development and support are shifted completely to it.

☐   **A.** True

☐   **B.** False

10.   Which of the following product lines does the SAP S/4HANA system rely on for procurement functions?

☐   **A.** SAP Concur

☐   **B.** SAP Ariba

☐   **C.** SAP SuccessFactors

☐   **D.** SAP C/4HANA

11. What technology did SAP leverage to eliminate aggregate tables from the SAP S/4HANA system while maintaining compatibility with many legacy programs?

☐   **A.** Columnar store

☐   **B.** Compatibility views

☐   **C.** Data aging

☐   **D.** Indices

12. True or False: Choosing between SAP S/4HANA and SAP S/4HANA Cloud, multitenant edition is also a matter of required scope.

☐   **A.** True

☐   **B.** False

13. True or False: The only version of the public cloud edition of SAP S/4HANA Cloud a customer can be on is the latest released version.

☐   **A.** True

☐   **B.** False

14. A user wants to add an application to his or her SAP Fiori home page but can't find it in the app finder. What does the admin have to do?

☐   **A.** Assign the corresponding SAP Fiori tile group to the user.

☐   **B.** Assign the corresponding SAP Fiori tile catalog to the user.

☐   **C.** Add the tile to a tile group already assigned to the user.

☐   **D.** Add the corresponding tile catalog to the tile group.

15. Where can an SAP Fiori end user change the theme of his or her SAP Fiori launchpad?

☐   **A.** In the Me area of the SAP Fiori launchpad

☐   **B.** In the Tile Catalog area of the SAP Fiori launchpad designer

☐   **C.** In the Tile Group area of the SAP Fiori launchpad designer

☐   **D.** In the UI theme designer

16. True or False: Anyone with an appropriate user name and password can log on to the SAP Fiori launchpad through a web browser.

☐   **A.** True
☐   **B.** False

17. What kind of customizations can users make to their SAP Fiori launchpads? (There are two correct answers.)

☐   **A.** Change the name of tile groups.
☐   **B.** Create their own tile groups.
☐   **C.** Change the names of tiles.
☐   **D.** Change the icons on tiles.

18. Which of the following are SAP Fiori design principles? (There are two correct answers.)

☐   **A.** Role-based
☐   **B.** Routine
☐   **C.** Rational
☐   **D.** Responsive

19. You use the search in your SAP Fiori launchpad to loop up information for a cost center. What kind of app is used for the information shown in the search results?

☐   **A.** Transactional
☐   **B.** Factsheet
☐   **C.** Analytical
☐   **D.** List

Practice Question Answers and Explanations

1. Correct answers: **A, D**
    SAP HANA is SAP's default platform to support the digital transformation for businesses. In addition, the SAP Cloud platform provides the infrastructure and tools for developing next-generation applications.

2. Correct answer: **C**

   SAP Leonardo is a collection of technology innovations, so intelligent technologies is the correct answer here. Artificial intelligence, mostly currently through machine learning, is only one of these technologies supported by SAP Leonardo.

3. Correct answer: **C**

   Traditionally, such enhancements are made directly in the core SAP ERP component. This will indeed still work today in your SAP S/4HANA system; however, SAP wants to shift such development to the SAP Cloud Platform. This is part of a strategy to keep the core running lean and as close to standard as possible. The other answers are wrong because SAP Leonardo is a technology framework, which you can use when you develop apps but not to directly build apps on; and SAP Fiori represents the UI level, so you would incorporate SAP Fiori as the default user interface of your enhancement, but it is not where the enhancement is developed.

4. Correct answer: **A**

   True. There is no limitation on the location of the hardware that the on-premise version of SAP S/4HANA is deployed on. A customer can choose (compatible) third-party cloud vendors other than SAP. If a customer chooses to go with SAP as the cloud infrastructure vendor for an "on-premise" SAP S/4HANA deployment, the product is called SAP S/4HANA Cloud, private option; with other vendor infrastructure, it's just SAP S/4HANA.

5. Correct answers: **A, D, E**

   In-memory is the most obvious answer here; columnar store is the preferred SAP HANA data storage technique; and through compression, SAP HANA manages to cut down on the infrastructure costs and support larger customers. On the other hand, aggregates are supported but should be avoided as the idea is to have all the data at the highest granularity to provide flexible reporting. The same is true for the indices because with SAP HANA, they offer little speed improvement and sacrifice too much in the way of flexibility because they must be predefined and adding reporting characteristics is difficult.

6. Correct answers: **C, D**

   Column store is the preferred method for SAP HANA as discussed because it's better for reading data. Row storage is preferred by classic databases and is supported fully by SAP HANA.

7. Correct answer: **A**

   True. SAP HANA was designed to fulfill the goal of combining optimal OLTP and OLAP processing in one database. This simplifies the process of answering questions such as "How did I come up with this number?" and saves on IT resources by requiring fewer systems to support.

8. Correct answer: **D**

   With many streams of data to process and large requirements for communication between memory and the CPU cache, you can use a lot of CPU cores at the same time. Even though GPUs might seem the most out of place here, they offer tremendous calculation power and are developing faster than CPUs. Although many companies are considering using some of their special characteristics in the business application world, and we might be hearing of more of these exploits in the future, for now, they aren't used by SAP HANA. SSDs offer a big boost to traditional databases, and because SAP HANA uses disk drives for many non-speed-critical processes (e.g., backup and aged data), they can be used with SAP HANA. Unfortunately, they don't offer much in the way of improved speed due to the architecture. Read-only memory is irrelevant.

9. Correct answer: **B**

   False. SAP S/4HANA is the successor to SAP ERP, but it doesn't replace it. There is still a huge customer base that relies on SAP ERP, and SAP has promised support until 2025 (at the time of publication) for these customers.

10. Correct answer: **C**

    SAP Ariba is the product that supports the SAP S/4HANA digital core with procurement. SAP Success Factors is for human resources, SAP Concur is for travel management, and SAP C/4HANA supports everything around the customer experience.

11. Correct answer: **B**

    Compatibility views can be materialized on demand for data in line item tables of the SAP HANA database to support programs that read old aggregate and index tables that are no longer in the system.

12. Correct answer: **B**

    False. The product scopes still vary with SAP S/4HANA being the more complete solution currently. The SAP S/4HANA Cloud solution is a better fit for new subsidiaries of large enterprises or companies interested in a lean digital core solution that is always up to date with the latest features and functions and that can live with the (decreasing) limitations of the multitenant cloud solution.

13. Correct answer: **A**

    True. Quarterly updates in the realm of the multitenant public cloud solution are always required. A customer can't choose to skip a product release cycle because the system is upgraded for all at the same time. All other editions, including SAP S/4HANA Cloud, single-tenant edition give customers more flexibility when selecting their upgrade path and frequency.

14. Correct answer: **B**

    The SAP Fiori tile catalog defines which tiles a user is authorized to use. If the user isn't assigned to the right catalog, he or she won't see the application tile even if it's part of a group he or she is also assigned to.

15. Correct answer: **A**

    An end user will only typically have access to the SAP Fiori launchpad; other SAP Fiori tools are for admins. The Me area is where users control all changeable settings for their SAP Fiori launchpads, including theme selection.

16. Correct answer: **A**

    True. No special software needs to be installed; all modern, up-to-date web browsers with HTML5 support will work. In our training system, we recommend using the Google Chrome browser because it seems currently to offer a better speed/compatibility mix.

17. Correct answers: **A, B**

    Changing the name and look of tiles can only be done in the catalog view of the SAP Fiori launchpad designer. End users can only access the SAP Fiori launchpad where they can manage their tile groups.

18. Correct answers: **A, D**

    SAP Fiori principles mandate that applications should be role-based, catering to specific tasks performed by specific users. SAP Fiori apps should also be responsive, adjusting their interface to work optimally for different devices.

19. Correct answer: **B**

    The result will be displayed with a factsheet app, which will provide key facts for the object you searched for. You will have the option to navigate to a transactional app, such as Manage Cost Centers, or an analytical app, such as a cost center report. The List answer option is not an official app type in the SAP Fiori design language.

Takeaway

You now have a good overview and understanding of the SAP HANA database. You understand the benefits of the SAP HANA architecture and the technologies that it uses to improve on traditional disk-based databases. You also got an introduction to the SAP intelligent enterprise strategy and new product portfolio that supports it, namely the SAP Cloud Platform and SAP Leonardo (together with SAP HANA, SAP S/4HANA, and the other cloud LoB solutions).

In addition, you got a thorough introduction to SAP S/4HANA, the successor to SAP ERP and the core software required for SAP's vision of the digital business revolution. You understand the deployment options available and should be able to determine which option best fits a customer's needs.

Finally, you gained insight into the SAP Fiori design paradigm and what it means specifically for SAP S/4HANA. You learned about the basic SAP Fiori tools and how the tile catalogs and groups control the apps a user sees and can use.

Summary

You've gained a high-level understanding of SAP HANA, SAP S/4HANA, and SAP Fiori. You can now explain the basic concepts and benefits of these to customers and can propose deployment options. You can also help users with basic SAP Fiori operations.

This chapter is the only one not directly related to CO in SAP S/4HANA. However, the knowledge here is very important for both new and experienced consultants with no prior experience with SAP S/4HANA.

In the next chapter, we'll cover organizational assignments and the way CO business processes integrate in SAP S/4HANA.

Chapter 2

Organizational Assignments and Process Integration

Techniques You'll Master

- Distinguish between external statutory accounting and internal management accounting (CO)
- Manage organizational units in CO
- Configure the operating concern
- Configure the controlling area
- Configure CO versions
- Understand the concept of cost objects
- Identify integration points between CO and other SAP business processes

Creating the organizational structure is the initial step in defining overhead cost controlling, otherwise known as CO. In this chapter, we'll focus on the functions available for CO in SAP S/4HANA Finance for defining organizational units and maintaining the configuration required to activate CO.

Real-World Scenario

Your task, as a CO consultant, is to capture your customers' internal cost reporting requirements and recommend the appropriate CO configuration to meet these needs and optimize their systems. Before making recommendations about CO organizational units, you'll need to become familiar with the components of CO so you can design the organizational units appropriately.

Financial accounting (FI) is the primary integration with CO. When you define the CO organizational structure, it will link directly to FI organizational structures. The interaction between FI and CO will depend on the controlling area definition. Transactions cannot directly cross controlling areas, meaning FI company codes in different controlling areas cannot transfer costing data directly. Additionally, FI data and CO update the same major table for reporting in SAP S/4HANA. This integration requires you to have a broad understanding of FI processes that will trigger CO postings as well as of CO postings that don't impact FI reporting.

In addition, CO is closely integrated with other lines of business (LoBs). The organizational structure in the other LoBs will link to the controlling area through the FI organizational structure. Configuration in these LoB areas will impact your configuration and could adversely affect the CO area. As a CO consultant, the broader your understanding of standard SAP processes, the more successfully you'll define CO structures. The total areas you need to consider depend on the SAP components you're implementing for your customers. Likely, consultants in other LoBs will not be aware of how they adversely affect your work. Thus, you'll need to translate your requirements and record interactions, so that configuration settings do not conflict.

Objectives of This Portion of the Test

This portion of the certification exam will test your understanding of CO organizational units, as well as the available options for connecting to other organizational units. We'll also introduce you to the concept of the cost object. Specific types of cost objects will be used throughout this book.

The certification exam expects you to have a good understanding of the following topics:

- Define controlling areas and activate the CO components
- Define operating concerns for profitability analysis (CO-PA)
- Define CO versions
- Configure the assignment of interrelated organizational structures

> **Note**
> The organizational structure and process integration topic makes up 8% – 12% of the total exam.

Key Concepts Refresher

Every SAP system has two main areas: the application area and the configuration or implementation guide (IMG). In this chapter, we'll discuss the enterprise structure of an SAP system, which is defined in the IMG. We'll show you how to define organizational units relevant to CO and describe how other business processes interact with CO. Defining organizational structures is the first step you'll perform in configuration. You also will learn how the features of CO are impacted by the organizational structure. We'll discuss how the organizational structures are built through assignments. In addition, we'll illustrate how organizational assignments interact with each other to provide business process integrations.

Let's start with an introduction to configuration tasks. At a high level, most configuration falls into three main steps: First, you'll define a structure, which means giving components in your structure names. Then, the structure needs to be maintained with the required technical settings. Finally, any interrelationships with other structures need to be assigned. These assignments will support integration across the system. You'll see this theme recur throughout the book.

Positioning Management Accounting

To begin any discussion of overhead controlling, you must first understand its position in relation to FI, which is legally required for any ongoing business venture. FI provides a standardized reporting structure and maintains the details needed to meet statutory requirements. FI is designed to adhere to standard accounting practices and legally mandated details. The general ledger (G/L), which is fully integrated with all other operational functions, records all value-related details to meet these reporting requirements.

A fundamental challenge exists with FI: While FI can meet all external reporting requirements, it lacks the detail required to meet internal business reporting needs. Often, financial information is recorded at a higher level of detail. CO contains the functions necessary to report enhanced detail for internal operations. While building from key information in legal reporting, CO includes functions to provide additional flexibility for internal reporting.

Note that not all postings for financial reporting will flow over to CO. Instead, CO monitors and tracks operational functions. In other words, CO tracks designated expense and revenue postings from FI, as well as cost and revenue details from other LoBs. CO excludes all financial postings to the balance sheet. In addition, CO can make postings that have no direct financial impact and includes an extensive set of tools to provide period-end allocations.

Organizational Units for Controlling

A critical first step to implementing an SAP system is to design its organizational structure. This design will translate a real-life company or business model into the SAP organization's structure. This structure will significantly impact how an SAP system operates.

Each level of the organizational hierarchy identifies individual units related to the business. The controlling area level could have one or many individual controlling area units, depending on business needs. The levels of the organizational hierarchy may have direct or indirect links to units at other levels of the hierarchy. You can also create specific guidelines on how organizational units at each level are associated to the next level. The organizational-level connections provide the basis for SAP business process integration while providing the foundation for the reporting and analysis of business functions.

Let's walk through the specific organizational levels you'll work with in CO.

Client

The client is the top organizational level of any SAP system. The client is a complete set of self-contained master data, applications, and tables. A client will contain a set of ABAP programs, master data tables, transactional tables, configuration tables, and the Data Dictionary. In the SAP table structure, some tables will be identified as client specific, meaning unique to this client, while other tables will be designated as cross-client, meaning common to several client structures.

Warning!

Making changes to cross-client tables carries a certain amount of risk and should be done with great caution. Since a client represents a business group, and the data in each client is designed to be kept separate from other clients, changing a cross-client table could have adverse effects on other clients. Each time you access a cross-client table, the system will issue a warning.

The client overview and client detail screens, shown in Figure 2.1 and Figure 2.2, respectively, display the information defining each client.

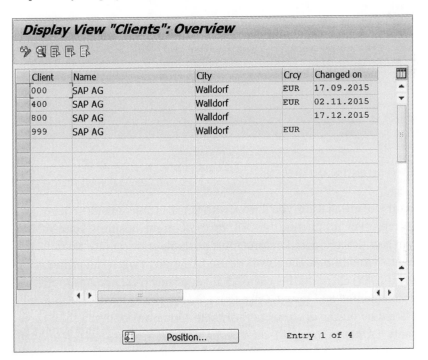

Display View "Clients": Overview

Client	Name	City	Crcy	Changed on
000	SAP AG	Walldorf	EUR	17.09.2015
400	SAP AG	Walldorf	EUR	02.11.2015
800	SAP AG	Walldorf		17.12.2015
999	SAP AG	Walldorf	EUR	

Position...   Entry 1 of 4

Figure 2.1 Client Overview (Transaction SCC4)

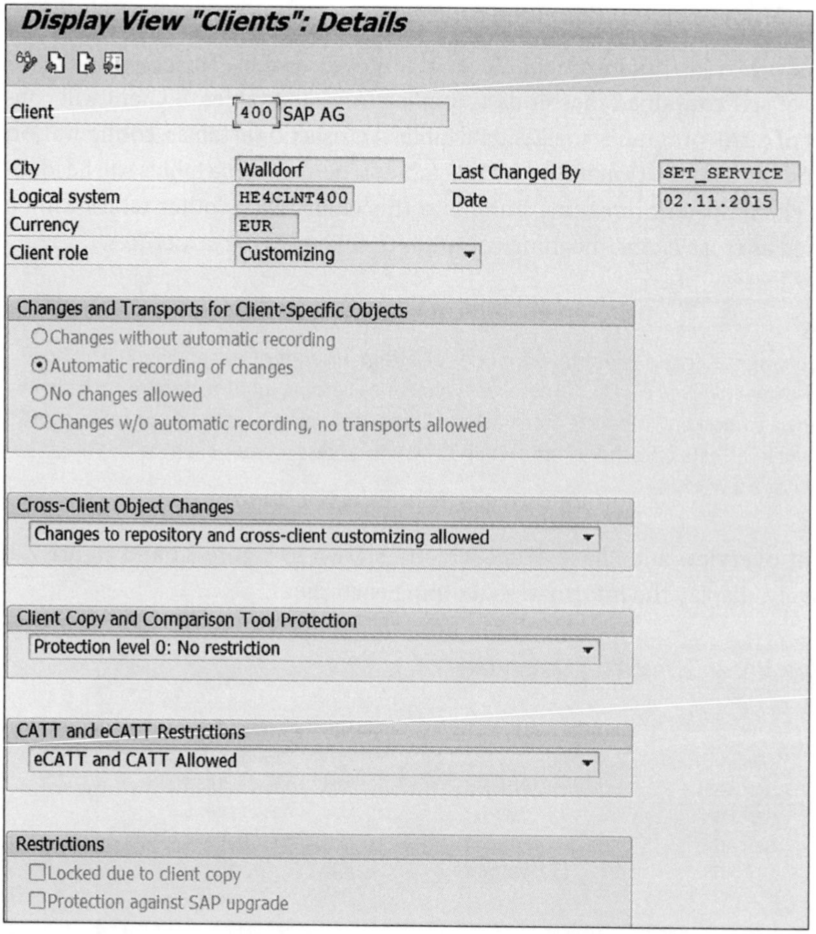

Display View "Clients": Details

Client	400 SAP AG

City	Walldorf	Last Changed By	SET_SERVICE
Logical system	HE4CLNT400	Date	02.11.2015
Currency	EUR		
Client role	Customizing ▼		

Changes and Transports for Client-Specific Objects

○ Changes without automatic recording
◉ Automatic recording of changes
○ No changes allowed
○ Changes w/o automatic recording, no transports allowed

Cross-Client Object Changes

Changes to repository and cross-client customizing allowed   ▼

Client Copy and Comparison Tool Protection

Protection level 0: No restriction   ▼

CATT and eCATT Restrictions

eCATT and CATT Allowed   ▼

Restrictions

☐ Locked due to client copy
☐ Protection against SAP upgrade

Figure 2.2 Client Details (Transaction SCC4)

In a standard SAP installation, you'll work with at least three separate clients. One client will represent production (PROD), or the current business concern. The PROD client is critical to operations and must be stable and accurate. To fulfill this requirement, two additional clients will be used. One client will be identified as the development (DEV) client. In this client, changes or technical updates to the system are implemented and tested. Once these changes have been validated, they are transferred by means of a transport or table copy from DEV to a third client, called quality (QUAL). In the QUAL client, your business analysts can test and validate these changes. If any issues or concerns arise, additional changes are made in the DEV client and transported again to the QUAL client.

Once the relevant business unit signs off on a change, the change is transported to PROD. This process reduces risks by avoiding reckless changes to the PROD client. While each client may have a complete set of data and tables, DEV and QUAL may not exactly match the PROD system. These other clients may only contain a subset of the PROD client. Unless a backup for the PROD client, not all clients need to have all the production master data. A DEV client, for example, may have test data created for the express purpose of testing system changes. Trying to keep data synchronized across all clients can be quite cumbersome, but can be facilitated by a system installation architecture like the one shown in Figure 2.3.

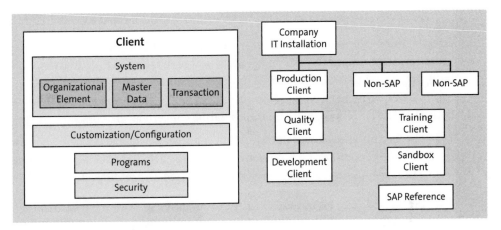

Figure 2.3 Client Architecture

The SAP system landscape may also contain other clients. Usually, the first client set up for a new installation is called a "sandbox." After the system goes live, you can keep this sandbox client so that you can perform "what-if" testing of a new functionality without impacting your live production landscape.

Perhaps you can set up a client designated for training. This client can be built with current master data that matches the training materials. This training client could allow your users to opportunity to gain hands-on experience without risk to your PROD client.

With the completion of the initial system setup, many companies will make a system copy and freeze this first copy as an SAP reference. This client can serve as a permanent replica of the initial system, which allows development teams to compare current changes against the initial system. In large, complex businesses, you might find multiple production clients utilized by different divisions. These clients could represent how your IT infrastructure has developed over time, perhaps through the acquisition of new business units.

Your complete IT landscape may also contain non-SAP environments. These third-party systems may also be connected to, and interact with, the SAP system frequently. These systems are connected through a remote function call (RFC) connection. A few common systems are the corporate email servers, tax calculation systems, or transportation planning systems.

Operating Concern

An operating concern is the first level of the CO organizational structure, residing directly below the client. An operating concern represents a view of external market segments for the enterprise and is necessary to activate CO-PA. Later, in Chapter 8, you'll find that CO-PA has two options: account-based CO-PA and costing-based CO-PA. Whether you use account-based CO-PA or costing-based CO-PA or both, these activities take place on the operating concern level.

To begin the configuration of the operating concern, you'll give it a name and an ID. The identification for each operating concern is a 4-character, alphanumeric code. The naming conventions for the operating concern are shown in Figure 2.4.

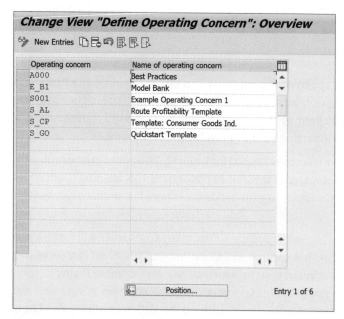

Figure 2.4 Define Operating Concern

Once you've created the operating concern code, you can maintain its initial settings, as shown in Figure 2.5. In this step, you'll determine whether account-based CO-PA, costing-based CO-PA, or both are activated. You'll need to define the currency to be used in the operating concern as well as the fiscal year variant. Each SAP transaction is recorded with a period designation. These periods are defined in the fiscal year variant. This fiscal year variant must match the assigned controlling areas. To maintain data consistency, the periods must be equivalent between the operating concern and controlling area, even though the currency may be different. If costing-based CO-PA is activated, you can assign a second currency.

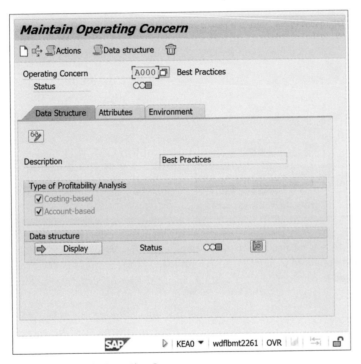

Figure 2.5 Maintain Operating Concern

After the operating concern has been activated, you can assign the relevant controlling areas, which we'll discuss in the next section. Assignments between controlling areas and operating concern can have a 1:1 relationship or an *n*:1 relationship. Figure 2.6 shows the assignment process.

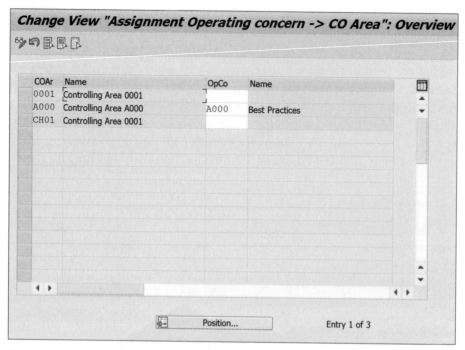

Figure 2.6 Assign Operating Concern to Controlling Area

Note

In an SAP S/4HANA system, you can still activate costing-based CO-PA. However, account-based CO-PA has been enhanced in SAP S/4HANA with many of the features of costing-based CO-PA. You'll need to consider whether costing-based CO-PA is needed.

Controlling Area

Internal business transactions are captured in the controlling area, which is the key organizational unit in CO. Internal allocation transactions are captured on cost objects. The level of detail provided by CO components allow specific cost monitoring and process flows. Primary costs are revenue and expense accounts that are transferred from external accounting. Overhead costs can be captured and then further allocated with secondary costs. You can allocate costs only within a controlling area. Cost objects refer to only one controlling area.

Define Controlling Area

To initiate the controlling area, you'll need to name it and assign a code. The naming convention for the controlling area is similar to the operating concern, a 4-character alphanumeric code, as shown in Figure 2.7. Even though the controlling area is a separate organizational element, you'll see that controlling areas are closely tied to FI settings. Once the name is active, basic settings for the controlling area will need to be defined.

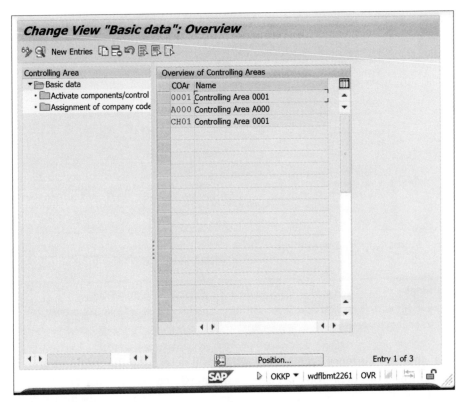

Figure 2.7 Define Controlling Area

Basic Settings

The initial configuration settings, shown in Figure 2.8, include currency details. The first setting, the **CoCd>CO Area** dropdown list, affects currency, and your choice depends on whether you'll later assign one company code or many company codes to your controlling area. Even though you may only have one company code right now, choosing the **Cross-company-code cost accounting** option would allow more company codes to be added in the future.

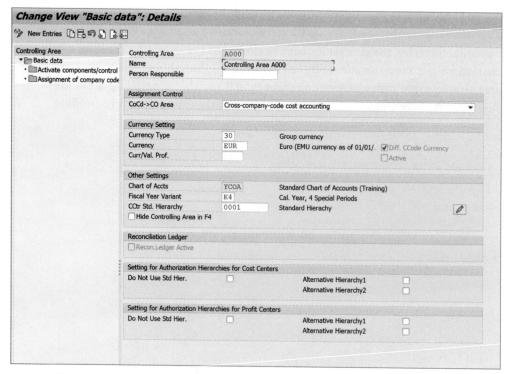

Figure 2.8 Basic Controlling Area Settings

 Warning!
Be cautious with these settings. Some settings, especially those related to currency, cannot be changed later.

Next, choose a **Currency Type** setting, which will determine the default currency for the controlling area. You can choose a unique CO currency or use one of the FI currencies. The usual choice is **30 Group currency**, which is a currency in FI. Selecting the **Diff. CCode Currency** setting will activate a second CO currency, thus allowing local company code currency evaluations.

Once the currency has been determined, the operating chart of accounts (**Chart of Accts**) is identified.

A **Fiscal Year Variant** must be defined for controlling area postings. The fiscal year variant will automatically generate posting periods in all CO transactions. An additional setting is the **CCtr Std. Hierarchy** field. Cost centers must be assigned to a standard hierarchy. The standard hierarchy is a mandatory field, and only one standard hierarchy can be defined per controlling area (see Chapter 3 for a detailed discussion of cost centers). The controlling area settings, as well as the standard hierarchy, are shown in Figure 2.8.

Activate Components Settings

This configuration phase will manage overhead controlling options that are available in the controlling area. In this step, you'll need to have an in-depth conversation with your customer to determine their requirements. You'll activate components in the controlling area, as shown in Figure 2.9, but these components will require additional configuration to complete their functionality. Except for **Projects**, these components will be discussed in further chapters.

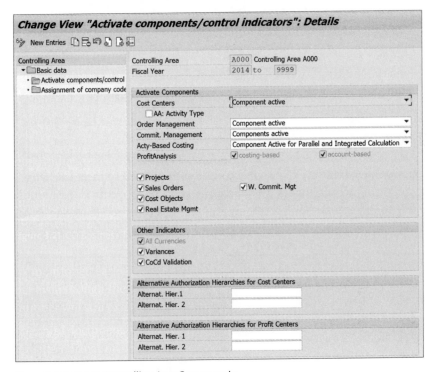

Figure 2.9 Activate Controlling Area Components

> **Note**
> Project systems (PS) is out of scope for this book. Projects are covered in a separate certification (C_TPLM22).

Assign Company Codes

Once you've created a controlling area, you'll need to assign all the relevant company codes, as shown in Figure 2.10. Company codes and controlling areas may have a 1:1 relationship or an *n*:1 relationship. To make an *n*:1 assignment, all company codes must use the same operating chart of accounts and have the same fiscal year variant with the same special periods. In a 1:1 assignment, you must also have only one company code currency.

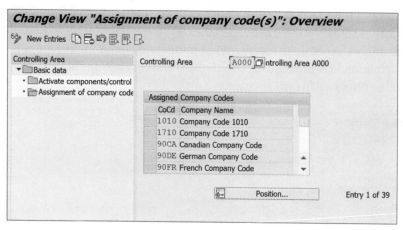

Figure 2.10 Assign Company Codes to Controlling Area

In FI, you may have multiple charts of accounts each defined to meet specialized financial reporting requirements. The operating chart of accounts is the foundation for day-to-day transaction processing and acts as a common language across many business processes.

> **Note**
>
> In SAP S/4HANA, all CO cost elements are now G/L accounts and controlled through the G/L closing variant. However, this feature introduced a constraint on the CO closing process. To supplement the controlling area, close at special periods commonality was added for SAP S/4HANA.

You can assign more than one company code to a controlling area, which enables CO across company codes. While you can define as many controlling areas as necessary, many organizations have chosen to use only one controlling area. Since the controlling area manages internal costing, it also manages how logistics transactions are processed. The link between CO and logistics will be discussed in further detail in subsequent chapters.

Controlling Version

A key function of CO is its ability to record different versions of your data for comparative analysis. With the introduction of versions, you can differentiate between plan and actual data. The term "actual" refers to the value of a business transaction that has occurred during the reporting period. The term "plan" refers an estimate of future transactional values by period. Many individuals in the business community refer to the plan as the annual budget. (SAP reserves the term "budget" to represent funding for a project.)

> **Tip**
>
> Versions are a valuable element in CO. In a controlling area, you can define many different versions. Actual data can only exist in one version. Version 0 is always assigned as actual. Plan data can exist in many different versions. Defining separate plan versions allows you to record data with different assumptions in different versions, which enables you to compare the results of different assumptions.

Versions are first defined with an ID and name, as shown in Figure 2.11. You must also specify which data can be recorded in the version by selecting the relevant checkboxes.

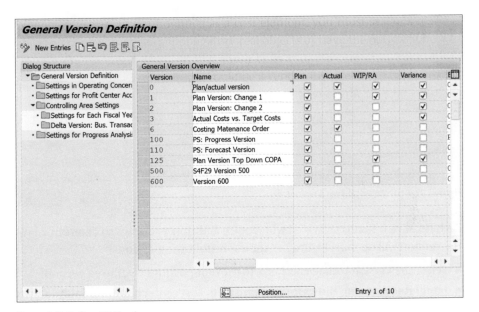

Figure 2.11 Define CO Versions

Once the version is defined, you'll need to activate it for each fiscal year, as shown in Figure 2.12. Fiscal years can be activated in advance. Plan or actual data cannot be recorded in the controlling area until versions have been activated.

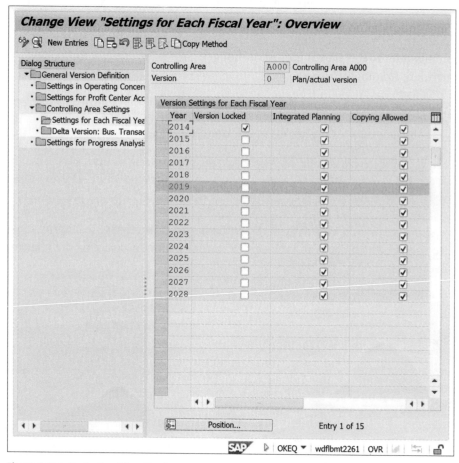

Figure 2.12 Activate Fiscal Year Versions

Each fiscal year that is activated will require additional settings to determine how the version will operate. Figure 2.13 shows the following options:

- Select the **Version Locked** checkbox to prevent postings to unused versions.
- **Integrated planning** allows for the transfer of cost center planning data to different CO components.

- Select the **Copying Allowed** checkbox to permit plan data or actual data to be copied to a different version. SAP records data in multiple currencies; currency translation dictates what rate will be used to translate between currencies for reporting.
- The **Orders/projects** options control whether internal order/work breakdown structure (WBS) element planning in a version is integrated with cost center or business process planning.
- The **Profitability Analysis** section sets the version capable of transfer to CO-PA.

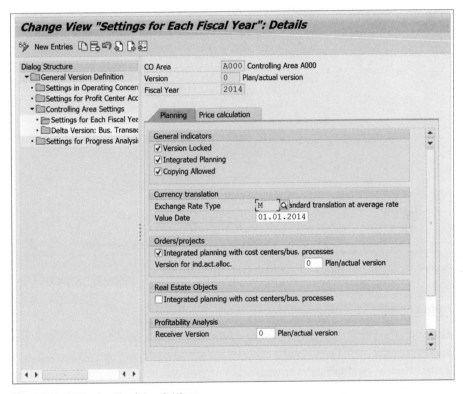

Figure 2.13 CO Version Fiscal Year Settings

The settings under the **Price calculation** tab determine how the system automatically calculates prices and where the results will be stored, as shown in Figure 2.14. Price calculation will be described in more detail in Chapter 5.

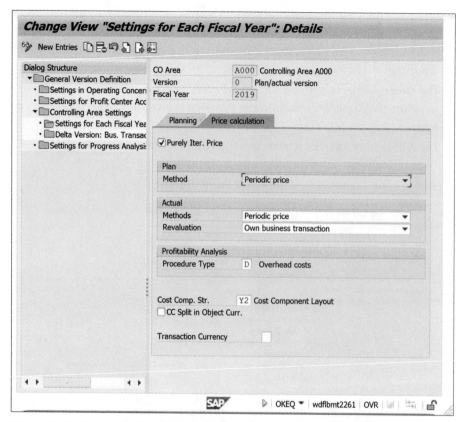

Figure 2.14 CO Version Fiscal Year Price Settings

Profit Center

Although the profit center is a master data element, this object can act like other organizational structures. Profit centers are maintained in the application area (rather than in configuration as with other organizational units). Profit centers are defined at the controlling area level, which allows profit centers to provide operational reporting across all company codes assigned to the controlling area. Profit centers allow for a flexible internal organizational design separate from the rigid company code structure of legal entities. A profit center could represent a geographic region, a division, or a combination of these levels. Profit centers will be discussed in further detail in Chapter 8.

> **Note**
> Profit centers allow you to determine profit and loss (P&L), as well as capital balance sheet reporting, by internally defined areas of responsibility. One significant difference between profit centers and other CO elements is the existence of the balance sheet at the profit center level.

Components of Management Accounting

The components of CO are not explicitly part of overhead cost controlling's organizational structure, but a basic understanding of these components is needed to gain a foundation in CO. Each component of CO provides specific details for process analysis. The appropriate components are activated in the controlling area configuration and will be based on the business process requirements identified during the SAP project implementation. The following components will be discussed throughout this book:

- **Cost and revenue element accounting**
  Cost element accounting classifies costs and revenue by account number. This component provides details to reconcile FI and CO and includes account-level value postings at a cost object level. Two types of cost elements exist:
  - Primary cost elements
  - Secondary cost element
- **Overhead cost accounting**
  Cost centers, internal orders, and business processes provide generic overhead cost tracking. Cost centers and business processes can enable broad cost analysis by department or process. Internal orders provide more encapsulated cost tracking. Overhead cost accounting typically tracks costs that cannot be directly assigned to products or services. During period-end processing, these costs can be assigned to products and services through CO allocation tools. Overhead cost controlling tools include the following:
  - Cost center accounting
  - Internal orders
  - Activity-based costing
- **Product cost controlling**
  Product cost controlling provides cost planning details for products and services. This component accesses data from other SAP components. Product information can be used for tracking and analyzing operations. Cost object

controlling uses production cost objects to monitor and track operations. The features of product cost controlling are:

- Product cost planning
- Cost object controlling
- Material ledger/actual costing

- **Profitability and sales accounting**
  Profitability and sales accounting enable an enterprise-level view of operations and profitability and can be used to determine actual business P&L. CO-PA delivers an external market view of product profitability. Profit centers provide an internal view of a company's financial fitness by individual profit centers or by groups of profit centers. Two components exist in profitability and sales accounting:

  - Profitability analysis (CO-PA)
  - Profit center accounting (PCA)

Cost Objects

Any discussion about CO must include a basic understanding of cost objects. CO is predominantly organized by account number, which must always contain a cost object. A cost object is a cost collector. Think of a cost object of as a bucket or container for a specific type of cost or revenue. Each cost object has specific features and functions. Many cost objects are associated directly to other LoBs. Therefore, many cost objects are only valid if specific business process have been activated.

Possible cost objects, by area, include the following:

- **Overhead management (CO-OM)**
  - Cost centers
  - Internal orders
- **Activity-based costing**
  - Business processes
- **Product cost controlling**
  - Production planning (PP)
    - Production orders
    - Process orders
    - Product cost collector
  - Project system (PS)
    - Work breakdown structure (WBS)
    - Network
    - Activities

- – Enterprise asset management
  - • Plant maintenance (PM) order
  - • Customer service order
- ■ **Profitability and sales accounting**
  - – Profitability analysis (CO-PA)
    - • Profitability segment
- – Sales and distribution (SD)
  - • Sales order item (SDI)

- – Profit center accounting (PCA)
  - • Profit centers

Integration with Other Processes

An SAP system has additional organizational structures for other business processes. The CO organizational structure links either directly or indirectly to other organizational structures to form the foundation for process integration throughout the SAP system. Figure 2.15 shows how organizational units can be connected, which we'll discuss further in the following sections.

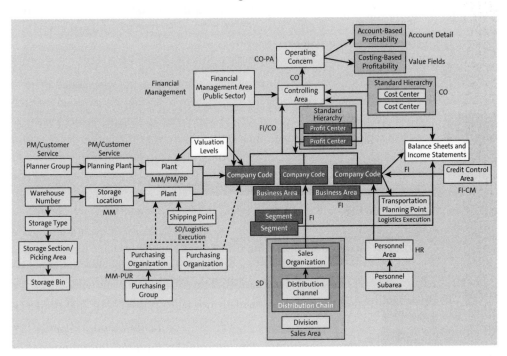

Figure 2.15 SAP Organizational Structure

Finance

FI records value transactions to determine the legal monetary position of your company. FI is based on legal requirements, as defined by accepted accounting standards or local statutory obligations. Data in FI is defined in two views: the balance sheet and the income statement. The balance sheet represents the current overall health and stability of the company and includes assets, liabilities, and equity. The income statement is a view of all activity that has occurred during the period and includes the revenue received during the period and expenses paid out during the period.

Key organizational units in FI include the following:

- **Company codes**
  A company code represents an independent accounting unit, also referred to as a legal entity. Company codes track all value postings across an SAP system. Financial statements and P&L statements are prepared at the company code level to meet legal reporting requirements. Company codes are the central organizational units of external accounting structures that follow legal guidelines and accepted accounting principles.

- **Segments**
  A segment is a subarea of a company. Originally, segments were added to meet accounting principles requiring a dimension of reporting for external market-level financial statements. A segment can represent an area of business or a geographical region. In most cases, the segment is derived through a profit center assignment. The profit center is highly integrated with other business processes and provides a basis for deriving segments. You'll see the profit center and segment in action in Chapter 8.

- **Functional areas**
  A functional area provides the basis for cost of sales accounting and groups expenses by business functions. Functional areas are assigned to master data to link the functional area to business transactions, thus allowing reporting by account number and business function. Financial reports can then categorize expenses into groups, such as sales, administration, production, marketing, and so on.

- **Business areas**
  A business area is an external accounting unit that corresponds to a specific area of responsibility in a company. Value transactions in FI are assigned to a

business area. Business areas can be used to create complete financial statements for internal purposes. Business areas are similar to profit centers; however, profit centers provide additional levels of flexibility.

Logistics

Logistics includes all the functions to manage product and service activities that have occurred over a period. Logistics manages the procurement of goods and services, at specific quantity and value levels. Logistics includes supply chain planning processes, production planning (PP), and resource management. Logistics also includes materials management (MM) with quantity tracking, position reporting, movement tracking, and inventory management. The sales and distribution (SD) function monitors the sale and shipment of products and services. Additionally, this component plans and monitors transportation functions. Key organizational units include the following:

- **Purchasing organizations**

  A purchasing organization negotiates the terms and conditions for procuring goods and services. Purchasing organizations must be directly or indirectly linked to company codes. This organizational unit supports the management of accounts payable transactions in the procure-to-pay (P2P) process. At the transactional level, the procurement of non-stock materials or services will require purchase order items to link cost objects to track the expense transaction. Purchases of stock items will be managed in FI through the balance sheet. These transactions will receive their account assignment through automatic account determination. Automatic account determination is a technical feature used throughout many SAP processes to assist with correct account assignment.

- **Plants**

  A plant is a level of logistics used to segregate, plan, and manage materials. Plants are linked to company codes in configuration. This link supports the valuation of goods and services in FI. Within CO, product cost controlling is recorded at the plant/material level. Cost object controlling is also managed at the plant/material level.

- **Sales organizations**

  A sales organization is responsible for negotiating the terms of a sale and for managing the distribution of goods. The sales organization is connected to company codes in configuration. Sales organizations support FI accounts receivable (AR) processes. SDIs within a sales order can act as cost objects to capture the cost and revenue of make-to-order (MTO) products and services.

Human Capital Management

In human capital management (HCM), the personnel area supports personnel administration. Each personnel area is connected to a company code. The personnel area supports value transactions for payroll and personnel management. Within HCM, each person is assigned to a cost center or inherits the assignment through the HCM organizational structure. This component supports the capture and reporting of personnel expenses.

Important Terminology

In this chapter, the following key terminology was used:

- **Actual**
  An actual value represents the value of transactions that have occurred for a business during the reporting period.
- **Client**
  A client is the top organizational level of an SAP enterprise structure and contains a complete set of programs, configuration, master data, and transactions.
- **Company code**
  A company code is the key structure for legal and statutory reporting. A company code represents a legal entity and enables complete financial statements for external reporting.
- **Controlling area**
  A controlling area is the key organizational structure for CO. This object monitors cost and revenue to enable internal operational reporting.
- **Cost and revenue element accounting**
  Cost and revenue element accounts provide overhead detail by account number. These accounts provide details for reconciling FI and CO.
- **Cost object**
  Cost objects are cost collecting structures used in CO. These objects identify the owner of costs and revenues and provide detail for operational reporting.
- **Fiscal year variant**
  The fiscal year variant identifies the basis of the financial calendar for an organization. A fiscal year variant contains the number of posting periods and the number of special periods and defines the calendar period for the beginning of a fiscal year and the number of calendar days in a period. The fiscal year variant must be consistent across all company codes in a controlling area.

- **Operating chart of accounts**
  A chart of accounts is defined in FI and consists of a list of all account numbers required for posting details in FI. The operating chart of accounts is a list of account numbers used for daily operations postings. All company codes within a controlling area must use this common chart of accounts.

- **Operating concern**
  An operating concern is the top level of the organizational structure for CO. This optional structure is only required when CO-PA is part of the organization design.

- **Organizational structure**
  Creating an organizational structure is a key activity in implementing an SAP system. This structure helps translate a company's operational structure into an SAP enterprise structure. An organizational structure also provides linkages between different organizational elements, which provide the integration between SAP business processes.

- **Overhead cost controlling**
  Overhead cost controlling provides internal operational reporting for a company. This capability has multiple components to meet the reporting needs of your organization, providing more flexibility and more detailed reporting than FI. This component is built on cost and revenue postings in FI but also provides additional tools for posting, allocating, and monitoring internal operations.

- **Plan**
  A plan is an estimate of future expenses and revenue by period and can represent monetary values or quantities.

- **Product cost controlling**
  Product cost controlling is a component of CO and includes product cost planning, product cost controlling, and the material ledger/actual costing. This component is used to plan and valuate products and services as well as monitor production costs.

- **Profitability and sales accounting**
  Profitability and sales accounting are a component of CO to monitor profit and the cost of sales.

- **Profit center**
  A profit center is an optional structure that provides a complete set of financial statements by internal areas of responsibility. The structure of profit centers is defined to meet the reporting needs of each individual company.

- **Versions**

  Versions are used in CO to group data. Only one version of actual data exists, but planning can have many versions. These groupings can be used for comparing different views of operational detail.

 Practice Questions

These practice questions will help you evaluate your understanding of the topics covered in this chapter. The questions shown are similar in nature to those found on the certification examination. Although none of these questions will be found on the exam itself, they will allow you to review your knowledge of the subject. Select the correct answers and then check the completeness of your answers in the "Practice Question Answers and Explanations" section. Remember, on the exam, you must select all and only the correct answers to receive credit for the question.

1.   True or False: Company codes are required for internal CO.

☐   **A.** True

☐   **B.** False

2.   Which of the following components can be activated in the controlling area? (There are two correct answers.)

☐   **A.** Commitments

☐   **B.** Cost centers

☐   **C.** Profit centers

☐   **D.** Production orders

☐   **E.** Currency

3.   True or False: The client is the top organizational structure for external financial reporting.

☐   **A.** True

☐   **B.** False

4. In an SAP S/4HANA system, which settings must be consistent to connect company codes to a controlling area in an *n*:1 environment? (There are three correct answers.)

    ☐ **A.** Company code currency
    ☐ **B.** Fiscal year
    ☐ **C.** Fiscal year special periods
    ☐ **D.** Operating chart of accounts

5. True or False: A standard SAP S/4HANA client will have two main clients: production and testing.

    ☐ **A.** True
    ☐ **B.** False

6. The top level of CO is which the following?

    ☐ **A.** Company code
    ☐ **B.** Controlling area
    ☐ **C.** Operating concern

7. When defining a controlling area, you must choose which of the following? (There are three correct answers.)

    ☐ **A.** Standard cost center hierarchy
    ☐ **B.** Controlling area currency
    ☐ **C.** Cross-company code setting
    ☐ **D.** Standard profit center hierarchy

8. True or False: The operating concern is the top of the overhead controlling structure and requires the activation of costing-based and account-based CO-PA.

    ☐ **A.** True
    ☐ **B.** False

9. Which of the following organizational structures are directly connected to the controlling area?

☐ **A.** Plant

☐ **B.** Business area

☐ **C.** Purchasing organization

☐ **D.** Company code

10. The first step in activating the SAP system is to define what?

☐ **A.** Master data

☐ **B.** Organizational units

☐ **C.** Transactional data

☐ **D.** ABAP programs

11. Which key features are activated in an operating concern? (There are two correct answers.)

☐ **A.** Costing-based CO-PA

☐ **B.** Operating concern currency

☐ **C.** Controlling areas

☐ **D.** Company code

12. Which SAP technical feature allows technical settings to be shifted from one client to another?

☐ **A.** Organizational structure

☐ **B.** Configuration

☐ **C.** Transport

13. Which enterprise structure is used to manage profit by external market?

☐ **A.** Profitability analysis (CO-PA)

☐ **B.** Profit center

☐ **C.** Company code

☐ **D.** Segment

14. Which of the following describes the purpose of CO?

☐   **A.** Operational expense and profit reporting

☐   **B.** External statutory reporting

☐   **C.** Capital detail analysis

15. True or False: Profit centers are optional organizational structures to provide a flexible reporting tool for income statements and balance sheets.

☐   **A.** True

☐   **B.** False

16. True or False: Only one version for actual can be activated for a controlling area.

☐   **A.** True

☐   **B.** False

17. The controlling area version controls which of the following? (There are three correct answers.)

☐   **A.** Ability to post actual data

☐   **B.** Ability to plan across cost centers

☐   **C.** Ability to send plan data to other processes

☐   **D.** Ability to calculate price

☐   **E.** Ability to plan the balance sheet

18. True or False: It is possible to activate both account-based CO-PA and costing-based CO-PA in SAP S/4HANA.

☐   **A.** True

☐   **B.** False

19. True or False: SAP S/4HANA offers the ability to change all configuration settings in the future to meet changing business requirements.

☐   **A.** True

☐   **B.** False

20. True or False: It is possible to connect non-SAP systems to an SAP S/4HANA client.

☐   **A.** True
☐   **B.** False

Practice Question Answers and Explanations

1. Correct answer: **A**

   True. Finance is the foundation of value reporting in SAP and, for legal reasons, company codes are required for all organizations. Not all transactions from finance will have an impact in CO, but for many transactions, a financial posting provides the basis for reporting about internal operations.

2. Correct answers: **A, B**

   Currency is required to define a controlling area but is not a component. Profit centers and production orders are not specifically activated at the controlling area; these elements are master data elements, defined after the controlling area is active.

3. Correct answer: **B**

   False. The client is the top enterprise structure for the entire SAP system. The key organizational element for external financial reporting is the company code.

4. Correct answers: **B, C, D**

   In an n:1 environment, you can designate that company code currency is tracked in a transaction, but this setup is not mandatory. If you choose to track company code currency, different company codes can have different currencies. The mandatory settings for n:1 are an operating chart of accounts, a fiscal year variant, and special periods.

5. Correct answer: **B**

   False. An SAP infrastructure can have any number of clients depending on your business requirements. Production is the most critical client since this client holds all of your organization's operations. The SAP infrastructure is built to update and safeguard this environment.

6. Correct answer: **C**

   The operating concern is the top level in CO and is also an optional structure that is only activated if your company chooses to use CO-PA. A controlling area is a mandatory structure for CO.

7. Correct answers: **A, B, C**

   The standard cost center hierarchy is a required setting for cost center accounting. The name of the hierarchy is set in the controlling area. The profit center hierarchy is not set in the controlling area. The controlling area currency must be identified. You can use a currency defined in FI or use a unique controlling area currency. Even though you could choose a unique currency for CO, in most cases, this approach is not recommended, since FI would not be able to see that currency. The cross-company code settings identify whether the company code to controlling area is 1:1 or n:1. Consider always setting n:1, even where the current environment is 1:1, to allow for future flexibility to add additional company codes later if required.

8. Correct answer: **A**

   True. The operating concern is the top of the overhead controlling structure. The operating concern is the first level below a client in the system structure. Controlling areas reside below operating concerns. A controlling area can be activated without the operating concern; an operating concern is only required if you are activating CO-PA.

9. Correct answer: **D**

   Company codes are directly assigned to controlling area. Plants are connected to the company code. A business area is a financial structure and is not directly associated to the organizational structure that they are otherwise connected to through postings. Purchasing organizations can be directly assigned to a specific plant, directly assigned to all the plants under a company code, or not assigned until the transaction is completed.

10. Correct answer: **B**

    An organizational structure is the first activation once the system is set up. ABAP programs are part of the initial system installation and may be added at any time. Master data and transactions are added once all relevant configurations are complete.

11. Correct answers: **A, B**

    To activate the operating concern, you'll choose the options for costing-based CO-PA or account-based CO-PA. You'll also choose the operating concern currency. You don't set the controlling areas during activation. You'll assign controlling areas after you've activated the operating concern.

12. Correct answer: **C**

    Transports are used to move technical systems settings from one client to another. Organizational structures are the settings in configuration where you'll define how your company will operate within the SAP modules. Configuration consists of maintaining technical table settings that will control how the system will operate.

13. Correct answer: **A**

    CO-PA provides profit information and cost of sales information for external markets. Company codes are defined for external reporting but do not provide market analysis. Segments are available to report external market information for financial reporting but not for reporting profitability. Profit centers are intended for profit analysis but not for analysis by market.

14. Correct answer: **A**

    CO is structured to provide operational detail reporting for expenses and profit. Company code reporting is structured to meet legal or statutory reporting. Company codes also provide capital reporting detail.

15. Correct answer: **A**

    True. Profit centers are flexible reporting tools for income statements and balance sheets. The structure is defined according to your company's requirements and provides an alternative to company codes, which are strictly based on legal requirements.

16. Correct answer: **B**

    False. Controlling areas can have many versions of plan, but only one version of actual. Versions can also be used for specialized purposes. Think of a version as a bucket where SAP can store a set of data for a specific purpose.

17. Correct answers: **A, C, D**

    The version controls whether actual and plan data can be posted. The version does not control planning across cost centers but does control the ability to copy plan data. Versions control whether data can be integrated with other components. If price calculations are needed, then the version must contain settings specifying how the price should be calculated.

18. Correct answer: **A**

    True. In SAP S/4HANA, you can activate account-based CO-PA, costing-based CO-PA, or both. SAP recommends that account-based CO-PA always be activated. Serious discussions should take place to determine whether costing-based CO-PA is still needed, since costing-based CO-PA is not part of the Universal Journal.

19. Correct answer: **B**

    False. While many configuration settings can be changed, other settings are set only one time and cannot be changed later. Many settings also have restrictions on how and when they can be changed.

20. Correct answer: **A**

    True. In many SAP installations, you can use an RFC connection to link non-SAP systems to an SAP system. This link could be required for many different business purposes.

Takeaway

In this chapter, you gained a foundational understanding of the purpose of CO. You saw how the organizational structure for CO is related to financial reporting. You were introduced to the key features of CO, including its organizational units and components. In subsequent chapters, you'll see how these components operate.

Like FI, CO is fully integrated with other business processes. As you'll see throughout this book, CO is also dependent on master data from many other LoBs. Finance does not dictate how CO operates but does influence it. Therefore, a fundamental understanding of FI is needed to design controlling areas appropriately. In future chapters, you'll gain, along with an understanding of finance, a respectable understanding of other business processes as needed.

Summary

In this chapter, the foundation for CO was laid. Now, you should be able to articulate the features of CO and advise clients about possible uses for the organizational structure, which serves as the foundation for integration with other business process.

The principles of how CO operates will be illustrated in future chapters. Each CO component will be defined in detail. You'll see the structure of master data and learn the rules for transactional posting, which will give you the skills to recommend a comprehensive and effective CO structure for your customers.

The succeeding units in this book will begin with the master data structure for each area and begin to build event-based postings and continue on through period-end closing. The first area we'll introduce is cost center accounting, which covers key functions for managing general overhead costs.

Chapter 3
Cost Center Accounting

Techniques You'll Master

- Design the best structure for a standard hierarchy
- Create primary and secondary costs
- Create activity types and statistical key figures
- Update master data in collective processing
- Define event-based postings
- Describe the configuration options that facilitate postings
- Correct original postings
- Execute a direct accounting allocation
- Explain accrual calculations
- Create and execute period-end allocations
- Understand the period lock option

In this chapter, we'll focus on cost centers and cost management. Cost center accounting is a core component of management accounting (CO). This component is activated before any other CO components are activated. Cost centers monitor internal business activities and provide transparency for cost analysis, ultimately providing your business insights into the sources of costs.

Real-World Scenario

As a CO consultant, at this point, you've completed designing the organizational structure for your customer. Now is the time to begin the groundwork for CO. You'll need to impress upon your customers the need to design the system to meet internal reporting requirements as well as statutory requirements, which can be a difficult concept to convey. You'll need to work with the financial accounting (FI) team to complete master data tasks, since all CO accounts are maintained in the FI chart of accounts.

As you begin defining the cost center structure, you'll need to determine all your customer's needs. The management team will need to determine the base structure of the cost center hierarchy, but likely, you'll also work with individual departments to define specific cost center structures within this hierarchy.

CO is highly integrated with all the business processes. Thus, you must facilitate testing with your user community to ensure that the master data is complete and correct. This testing will also require interaction with many other lines of business (LoBs).

Objectives of This Portion of the Test

This portion of the certification exam will test your knowledge of overhead cost master data and cost center accounting business processes. The exam will assess your ability to design master data to meet internal business requirements for cost center accounting and create all the relevant master data records. You will also be evaluated on your knowledge of SAP business transactions and integration points with other SAP processes.

The certification exam expects you to have a good understanding of the following topics:

- Define and create cost centers
- Create cost center hierarchies
- Define alternate cost center groups
- Determine the usage of activity types
- Assign cost center attributes
- Design and define cost center allocations
- Configure settings to support cost center accounting
- Configure period-end closing for cost center accounting

> **Note**
> The cost center accounting topic makes up 12% of the total exam.

Key Concepts Refresher

Cost center accounting is the foundation of CO. Cost centers take costs incurred throughout the period and then allocates these values to associated subareas that incurred these costs. We'll begin with a discussion of cost center accounting master data. Then, throughout this chapter, we'll begin to build the architecture of cost objects, a fundamental concept that will be discussed frequently throughout this book.

> **Note**
> In a strict sense, cost centers are cost collectors. You'll find some people look at them as master data objects, reserving the term "cost object" for other cost collectors, which we'll discuss later in this book. We'll use the term "cost object" to include cost centers.

Often, when you're defining an SAP system, you can look at the process as a series of steps or a set of guidelines. The first step is designing and defining the organizational structure, performed in configuration, as we discussed in Chapter 2. The next step is to define the master data. This chapter begins with that step. We'll define cost centers, activity types, statistical key figures, and cost elements.

Then, we can move to the third step of performing transactions. In cost center accounting, transactions are primary postings, adjustment postings, and period-end postings. Finally, we can perform the final step of reporting and analysis.

Master Data

Cost center accounting master data is structured to facilitate cost collecting and allocations within CO. While company codes in FI and CO both use the same operating chart of accounts, not all accounts are relevant for statutory accounting, and not all accounts are relevant for management reporting. We'll see this distinction throughout our discussion of specific master data elements in the following sections.

Cost Element

Cost elements are accounts used to monitor internal business operations. CO by its nature only tracks current operations or period expenses and revenues. A cost element has no balance sheet items. Cost elements are profit and loss (P&L) accounts in the operating chart of accounts. Additionally, you can exclude P&L accounts that are defined as nonoperational. These specific P&L accounts are reported in FI but excluded from CO.

SAP S/4HANA has brought general ledger (G/L) accounts for FI and cost elements for CO together into one master data object. All cost elements are defined in the FI master data, which has been expanded to include cost element attributes for CO. The common master data structure supports the transactional data stored at a line item level in the Universal Journal, or table ACDOCA. You'll need consider adjusting traditional FI master data fields to accommodate the blending of FI and CO master data.

Once the controlling area has been activated (see Chapter 2), cost elements can be defined. In the controlling area settings, you identified an operating chart of accounts, which tracks daily operational activity. FI can have many different charts of accounts to meet statutory reporting. However, since CO is for internal reporting, you don't need to adhere to those requirements. All cost elements used in CO are contained in the definition of the chart of accounts. The design of the chart of accounts should include account number ranges for all the types of postings found in both FI and CO.

Tip

In many cases, we recommend against logical number ranges due to constraints on flexibility. While defining logical number ranges allow users to distinguish between account types, logical number ranges could deplete the numbers available within a range. For charts of accounts, logical number ranges are beneficial to users and can support reporting. In SAP S/4HANA, all cost elements are G/L accounts. Not all account numbers are relevant for FI reporting. Conversely, not all G/L accounts are relevant to CO reporting.

Cost elements are divided into two types: primary cost elements, which are period expenses and revenues, and secondary cost elements. We'll begin our discussion with primary cost elements, which have a 1:1 relationship with finance income and expenses.

A mandatory master data setting after **Account Number** and **Description** is the **Account Type**, as shown in Figure 3.1.

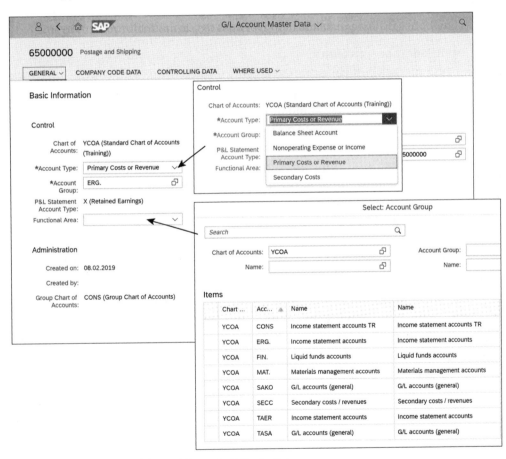

Figure 3.1 Account Types and Account Groups in FI Master Data

This field has been recently added to SAP S/4HANA. The account type categorizes accounts as balance sheet, non-operating expense or income, primary cost or revenue, or secondary cost element. One differentiator for G/L account numbers should be account type. When a new G/L account is created, the account type is selected. You should be certain about the assignment of account type, since this selection can't be changed later.

> **Note**
>
> The balance sheet and non-operating expense or income account types are relevant for FI; primary cost or revenue account types are relevant for both FI and CO. Secondary cost elements are only relevant for CO.

Let's take a closer look at the four mandatory account types, shown in Figure 3.1:

- **Balance sheet accounts**
  CO does not post balance sheet accounts. You can indicate that certain balance sheet items should be posted statistically to a cost object.

- **Non-operating expense and income accounts**
  SAP gives you the ability to post accounts from an income statement only to FI. These accounts will never have a cost object reference. Note that most environments have a few non-operating accounts. An example where this type of account could be relevant is a special FI posting to the income statement only for closing adjustments.

- **Primary cost and revenue elements**
  Primary cost elements are income statement accounts, expenses, and revenues recorded in both FI and CO. Non-operating accounts plus the primary cost elements represent all the accounts in an FI income statement or P&L statement.

Another mandatory field in the account setup is **Account Group**, shown earlier in Figure 3.1. This field has always been required for FI. This field allows you to restrict the number range of accounts and the default settings for the account. You should consider creating an additional account group for cost elements.

The controlling area settings contain a mandatory field for cost elements. FI accounts exist in the chart, and some fields are specific to individual company codes. Cost elements are defined at the chart of accounts level and contain CO-level settings. Cost elements require a **Cost Element Category**, as shown in Figure 3.2. This category is defined by SAP; it determines the types of CO postings that are possible.

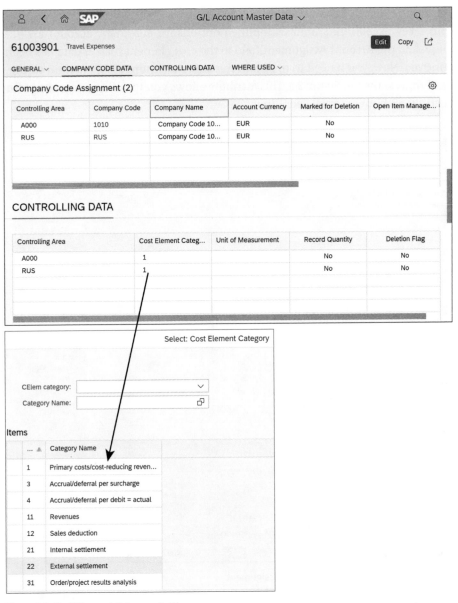

Figure 3.2 Cost Element Category Setting

Warning!
You should be certain about how the cost element is going to be used, since it can't be changed later.

Most cost element fields available in SAP ERP 6.0 are available in SAP S/4HANA, with a key exception. SAP has simplified options for automatic account assignment, and the **Account Assignment** field in the cost element master data has been removed. Now, you'll need to maintain the **Default account assignment** in configuration, as shown in Figure 3.3. This attribute allows you to define a cost object for postings without external user input.

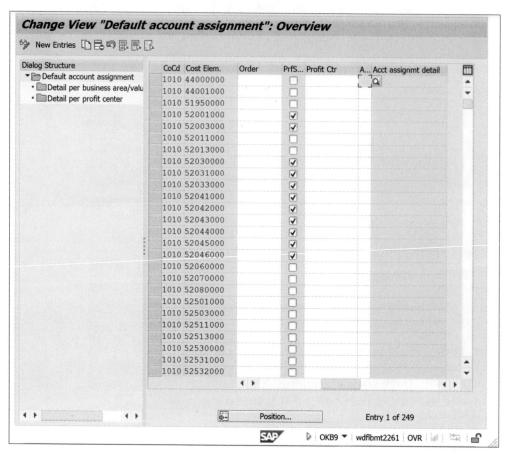

Figure 3.3 Table OKB9 Default Account Assignment

SAP also has a unique setting for two types of balance sheet accounts. Material stock accounts and asset valuation accounts can be posted with statistical values to cost objects. This indicator is the shown in the controlling area settings in Figure 3.4. The first step to activating this option is to create FI account master data with account type balance sheet. The automatic account determination must be configured in material valuation or in asset management. Once that step is complete, the **Apply Statistically** setting will be available in the account master data.

	G/L Account Master Data ⌄				Q

16000000 Land & Ld Improvemts   Edit   Copy

GENERAL ⌄   COMPANY CODE DATA   CONTROLLING DATA   WHERE USED ⌄

Company Code Assignment (72)

Controlling Area	Company Code	Company Name	Account Currency	Marked for Deletion	Open Item Manage...
A000	1010	Company Code 10...	EUR	No	
A000	1710	Company Code 17...	USD	No	
A000	90CA	Canadian Compan...	CAD	No	
A000	90DE	German Company...	EUR	No	
A000	90FR	French Company ...	EUR	No	

CONTROLLING DATA

Controlling Area	Apply Statistically	Change History
A000	Yes	
RUS	Yes	

Figure 3.4 Apply Statistically for Balance Sheet Accounts

Tip
This statistical option is used frequently by organizations that use project systems (PS). This option allows you to track stock or assets acquired for a specific project. This option is only available for these two specific situations.

Secondary cost elements are reserved by CO for allocations and management accounting adjustments. Secondary cost elements, non-operating costs, and balance sheet accounts become reconciling items between FI and CO. In the past, many individuals were frustrated with SAP because FI and CO didn't match, which required considerable effort during period end to reconcile the two areas. Also, during the month, the two areas were not synchronized, which hindered interim reporting. However, SAP S/4HANA provides real-time reconciliation between FI and CO, which has greatly simplified the reconciliation process.

Most settings for primary and secondary cost elements are similar. Secondary cost elements have a unique account type, as shown in Figure 3.1. Secondary cost elements must also have a cost element category. These categories are mandated by SAP and separate from the primary cost element categories. The secondary cost element categories shown in Figure 3.5 determine what type of allocation is being performed.

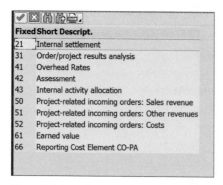

Fixed	Short Descript.
21	Internal settlement
31	Order/project results analysis
41	Overhead Rates
42	Assessment
43	Internal activity allocation
50	Project-related incoming orders: Sales revenue
51	Project-related incoming orders: Other revenues
52	Project-related incoming orders: Costs
61	Earned value
66	Reporting Cost Element CO-PA

Figure 3.5 Secondary Cost Element Category

An additional setting required for account master data is a field status group, as shown in Figure 3.6.

Field status variant: 0010

FStGroup	Text
YB45	Goods/invoice received clearing accounts
YB59	Inventory accounting material stock acct
YB25	Inventory adjustment accounts
YB62	Investment support accounts
YB49	Manufacturing costs accounts
YB06	Material accounts
YB03	Material consumption accounts
YB14	MM adjustment accounts
YBXX	non-operative expense or income
YB64	Other cost accounts (obligatory text)
YB19	Other receivables/payables
YB40	Personnel clearing accounts
YB23	Plant maintenance accounts
YB65	Provisions (transac.type obligatory)
YB12	Receivables/payables clearing
YB71	Reconcil.accts (KIDNO/foreign payment)
YB67	Reconciliation accounts
YB68	Reconciliatn accts (payables - Austria)
YB29	Revenue accounts
YB36	Revenue accts (with cost center)
YB18	Scrapping (MM)
SECC	Secondary GL
YB41	Tax office clearing accounts

Figure 3.6 Field Status Group

This setting controls what fields are required as the master data is used for postings. A separate field status group is advisable for secondary cost elements. Secondary cost elements are not used in financial postings, which could cause issues using field status groups used by FI. You should consider working with the FI team to define a unique field status group for secondary cost elements.

Standard Hierarchy

One of the most beneficial features of CO is the use of hierarchies and groups. Master data groups simplify reporting options, provide collective processing, and summarize data into levels. In Chapter 2, we configured a controlling area. In those settings, a standard hierarchy name was defined for cost centers. This hierarchy now needs to be built, as shown in Figure 3.7.

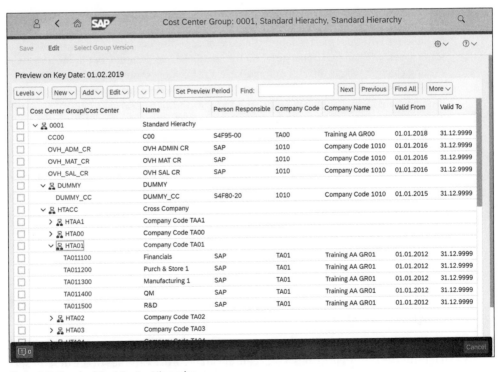

Figure 3.7 Standard Cost Center Hierarchy

The standard hierarchy is a special type of master data group, with only one standard hierarchy allowed per controlling area. All cost centers defined in the controlling area must be assigned to a node in this hierarchy. CO also offers the ability to define as many alternate hierarchies as needed. Cost center assignment in the alternate groups is optional.

Cost Center

Cost centers represent a department or area of responsibility in a business unit. Except in rare occasions, cost centers only collect period costs and not revenues. Cost centers incur costs from other business processes and record many operational expenses, unless expenses are posted directly to other cost objects. Expenses such as payroll, benefits, depreciation, and corporate allocations are posted at the cost center level. The cost center then performs services or provides labor for other cost objects and allocates overhead at period end.

Warning!

Be judicious with your master data settings because settings cannot be changed later. In some cases, you can make changes if no transactions have occurred, but in most cases, making changes will be difficult or impossible. Cost centers should be considered a permanent cost object. These objects can only be deleted if no transactions have occurred, or if no postings, actual or plan, have occurred at the start of a fiscal year. Other elements like assets, internal orders, and activity types cannot be assigned to the cost center. An alternative is blocking the cost center from future postings.

You'll need to define unique alphanumeric IDs for each cost center. In the **General Data** section in the cost center settings, the required fields include:

- Short/Long Description
- Valid From/Valid To
- Person Responsible
- Cost Center Category

User Responsible is optional and represents a user's SAP ID. The **Department** field is also optional and freely definable.

The cost center category is defined by you and defaults settings in the **Control** box that limit the type of postings a cost center can record. Examples of the default settings: actual primary costs, actual secondary costs, plan primary costs, plan secondary costs, and revenue. The configuration setting for cost center category is shown in Figure 3.8.

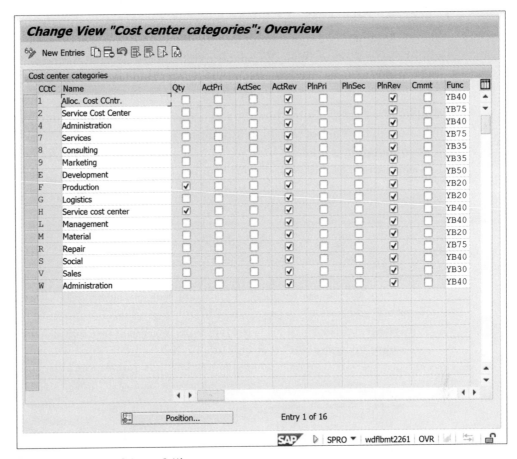

Figure 3.8 Cost Center Category Settings

Note that cost center exists at the controlling area level. Cost centers have the following organizational assignments beyond the controlling area, as found in the **Organizational Units** section shown in Figure 3.9:

- **Hierarchy Area** is the assignment to the standard cost center hierarchy.
- **Company Code** is a mandatory setting.
- **Business Area** is an optional setting depending on the activation of this feature in FI. The same is true of **Functional Area**.
- **Currency** normally defaults from the company code currency defined in FI but also depends on the controlling area settings for currency.

- **Profit Center** is optional; however, it is beneficial if profit center accounting is active. If a profit center is not set, information must be derived by other means in transactions. Profit centers will be discussed throughout the subsequent chapters; however, Chapter 8 focuses specifically on profit centers and the derivation process.

The final set of indicators control how the cost center receives postings. Note that the indicators in the **Control** section lock out the ability to post certain kinds of data. These indicators can default from the cost center category, but then further changes can be made later to the individual cost center.

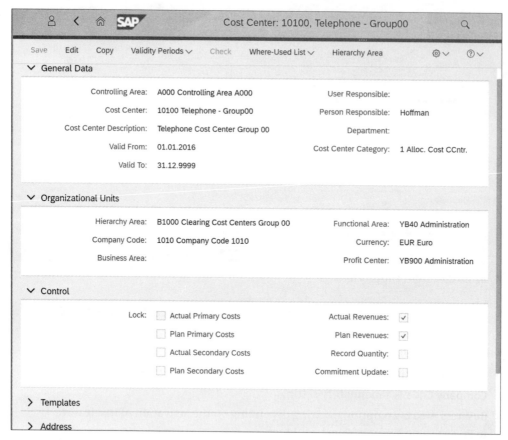

Figure 3.9 Cost Center Master Data

Activity Type

Activity types represent the output or services provided by a cost center. Activity types allow cost centers to allocate costs where they were incurred. Activity types are quantity based and commonly represent internal labor allocations. The value of the activity is recorded with a secondary cost element.

An activity type is CO-level data and uses an alphanumeric name, as shown in Figure 3.10.

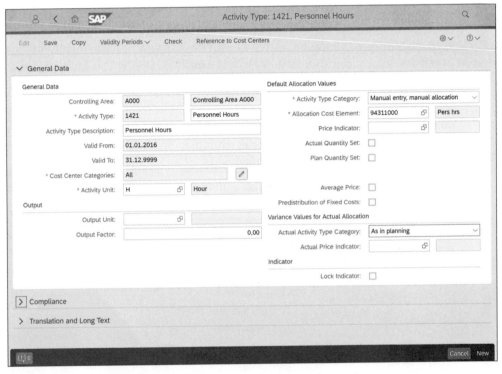

Figure 3.10 Activity Type Master Data

The **Cost Center Categories**, **Activity Unit**, **Activity Type Category**, and **Allocation Cost Element** fields are mandatory. The cost center category will restrict which cost centers can use the activity type. The activity type category is defined by SAP and identifies what type of allocations and price determinations are possible. Examples of activity type categories include the following:

- **Manual entry, manual allocation**: Planned quantities are determined externally and manually entered. Allocation of quantities to other objects is done using internal activity allocation.

- **Indirect determination, indirect allocation**: This process is used when the quantity is difficult to determine. A rule or tracing factor is defined for the system to calculate the planned quantity, and the system uses a rule to automatically allocate the quantity to receivers.

- **Manual entry, indirect allocation**: Planned activity quantities are determined externally and entered. Quantity allocation to receivers is difficult to determine, so a tracing factor is defined, and the system allocates the quantity.

- **Manual entry, no allocation**: Activity quantities can be entered manually, but it's not possible to allocate a quantity to receivers.

Activity types require a planned rate to enable value postings; without a price, an activity type is simply a master data element. As you record an activity, such as quantity consumption, the system will use the price to value the activity, which allows your users to focus on quantities without concern for value.

Each price is assigned to a combination of activity type and cost center. The **Price Unit** represents the quantity of activity relative to the price. The **Cost Element** defaults from the activity type master data. Plan price is shown in Figure 3.11.

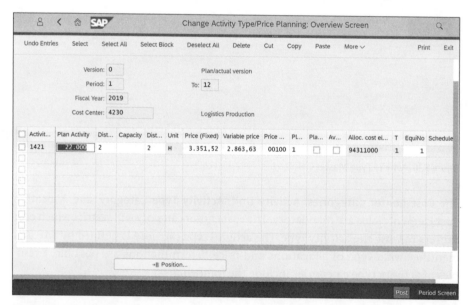

Figure 3.11 Activity Type Plan Price

> **Tip**
>
> Notice that, throughout SAP, prices do not automatically represent a quantity of one unit. Prices should always include the price unit.

You'll need to determine which costs to include in an allocation price. Subsequently, prices can be determined manually or automatically by the system and entered into the **Price Planning** field. Prices determined by the system will require extensive cost center planning to facilitate the price calculation.

Statistical Key Figure

A statistical key figure represents a quantity that can be used as a basis for allocation and provides a flexible base for allocation calculations. The settings for a statistical key figure are rather basic. You'll need to identify an ID, a name, and a unit of measure, and then choose whether the statistical key figure will be fixed or total. Fixed means that the value is stable over time with few changes, the number of trucks, for example. Total represent a value that you expect to change each period, miles driven by a truck, for example. Statistical key figure settings are shown in Figure 3.12.

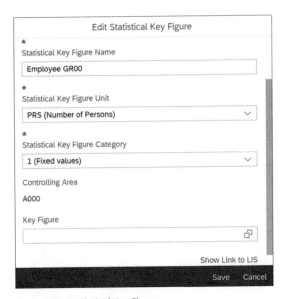

Figure 3.12 Statistical Key Figure

The value of the statistical key figure can be entered manually or can be linked to the Logistics Information System (LIS). When the statistical key figure is linked to an LIS structure, the quantities are updated automatically through the LIS quantity. The alternative is to enter quantities manually during the period-end close process.

Collective Processing

Throughout CO, you'll find the ability to update single objects or to update information collectively. Collectively is vastly preferred because you can easily and efficiently process a vast quantity of information with minimal effort. Singular processing is reserved for resolving errors or providing a detailed review. Let's explore some key master data options for collective processing:

- **Time-based data**
  Master data in cost center accounting, with the exclusion of statistical key figures, can be managed as time-based data with a unique validity period. Changing records with a validity period creates a new master record. Time-based data can be beneficial for segregating reporting by changes in master or by responsibility/ownership. You can specify the periodicity for a field in cost center master data, as shown in Figure 3.13. If you choose not to set a validity period, the record changes are only visible in change documents and not available for reporting.

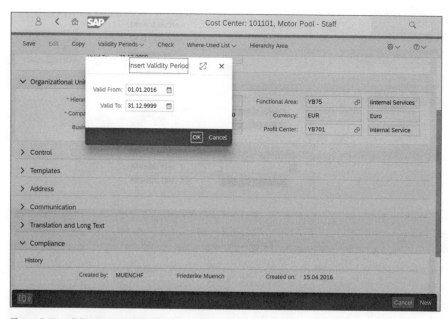

Figure 3.13 Validity Period Setting

You can specify fields as time-based in Customizing, as shown in Figure 3.14. Certain fields are defined by SAP as time-dependent with a mandatory periodicity. For other data fields, you can define the periodicity. A few fields will not be time dependent. Fields like **Hierarchy Area** assignment will take effect immediately.

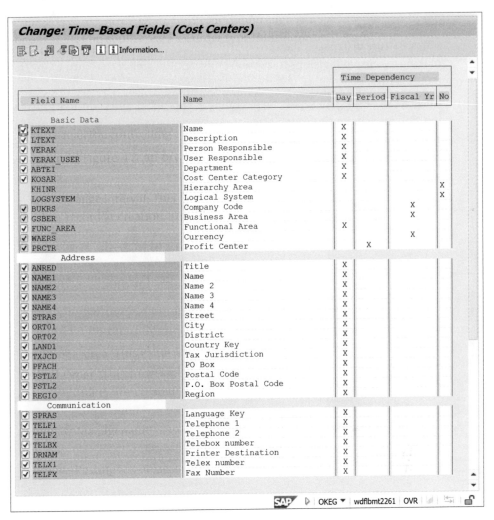

Change: Time-Based Fields (Cost Centers)

Information...

Field Name	Name	Day	Period	Fiscal Yr	No
Basic Data					
KTEXT	Name	X			
LTEXT	Description	X			
VERAK	Person Responsible	X			
VERAK_USER	User Responsible	X			
ABTEI	Department	X			
KOSAR	Cost Center Category	X			
KHINR	Hierarchy Area				X
LOGSYSTEM	Logical System				X
BUKRS	Company Code			X	
GSBER	Business Area			X	
FUNC_AREA	Functional Area	X			
WAERS	Currency			X	
PRCTR	Profit Center		X		
Address					
ANRED	Title	X			
NAME1	Name	X			
NAME2	Name 2	X			
NAME3	Name 3	X			
NAME4	Name 4	X			
STRAS	Street	X			
ORT01	City	X			
ORT02	District	X			
LAND1	Country Key	X			
TXJCD	Tax Jurisdiction	X			
PFACH	PO Box	X			
PSTLZ	Postal Code	X			
PSTL2	P.O. Box Postal Code	X			
REGIO	Region	X			
Communication					
SPRAS	Language Key	X			
TELF1	Telephone 1	X			
TELF2	Telephone 2	X			
TELBX	Telebox number	X			
DRNAM	Printer Destination	X			
TELX1	Telex number	X			
TELFX	Fax Number	X			

SAP ▷ OKEG ▼ wdflbmt2261 OVR

Figure 3.14 Time-Based Master Data

- **Master data groups**
  Earlier in this section, we discussed the standard cost center hierarchy as a special type of master data group. However, you can add additional master data

groups. Membership in these groups is optional. You can also create cost element, activity type, and statistical key figure groups. This feature adds extensive capabilities to CO. Master data groups can be 99 levels deep and as broad as you need. Data elements can belong to separate groups simultaneously.

Master data groups are not time dependent. To see before and after views of data, SAP provides the feature of groups with suffixes. A suffix is a copy of a master data group. Since this copy has a separate name, you can freeze the current structure of a master data group. This feature can be quite helpful if you are making extensive revisions to a group and want the ability to return to the initial structure.

Groups can be used for reporting parameters, allocation, and collective processing. You must grasp the capabilities of master data groups to be an effective CO consultant. The process for creating master data groups is consistent across cost center master data elements. Examples of additional cost center groups are shown in Figure 3.15.

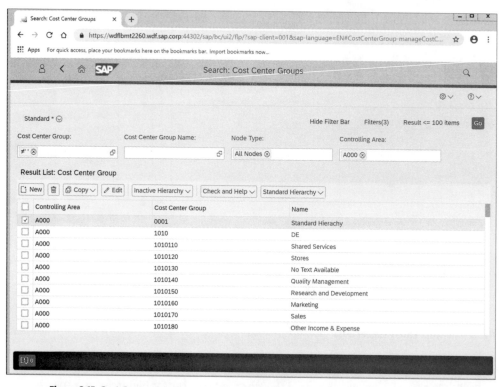

Figure 3.15 Cost Center Groups

- **Selection variant**

  SAP offers several options for managing master data collectively. You must specify to SAP a technique to choose the relevant items. To change a collection of data simultaneously, you'll need to provide settings to determine the appropriate elements by creating a selection variant. The term "variant" will be seen repeatedly throughout this book. In general, a variant is a grouping of pertinent details. A selection variant is a cluster of settings that choose the data elements you wish to manage, as shown in Figure 3.16.

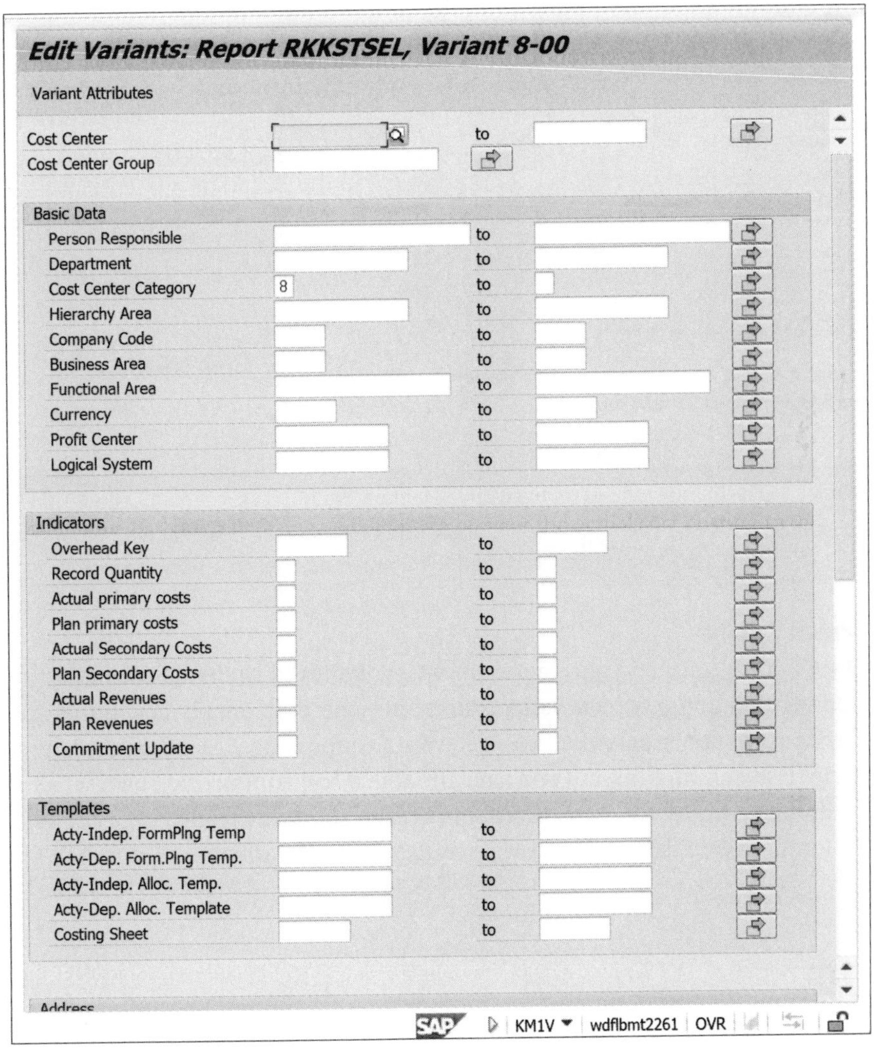

Figure 3.16 Selection Variant Settings

Once you select a field, you can further enhance its selection criteria with various options, as shown in Figure 3.17. An example would be to automatically select the current date and not manually specify the date in the variant.

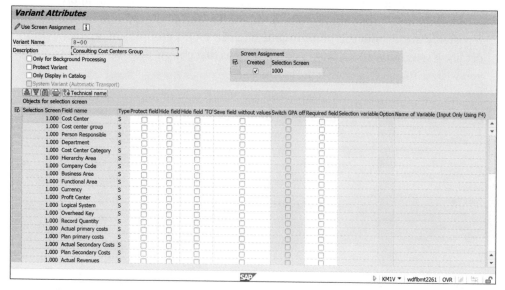

Figure 3.17 Enhanced Variant Settings

> **Note**
>
> You can use a selection variant to automatically add members to a master data group as they are created, which eliminates the need to manually add new members to a group.

- **Screen variant**

  Once you've selected your data elements, you'll need to define the details to update. Building a screen variant simplifies the data details and limits the screen contents to only the fields relevant for updating. SAP offers some predefined screen variants, but you have the ability to customize you own screens, as shown in Figure 3.18. Screen variants are specific to the relevant master data. Different master data elements will require different variants.

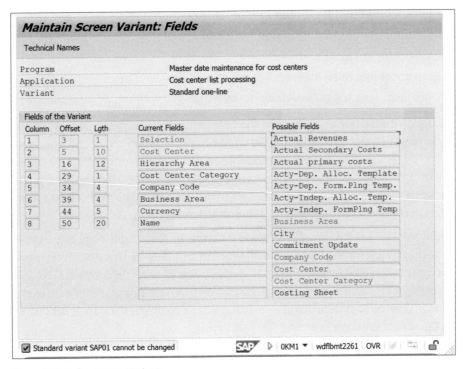

Figure 3.18 Define Screen Variant

Primary Postings

Now that the master data has been created, you can begin posting transactions. The postings for CO fall into a few key categories:

- Real postings from other applications
- Real postings from inside CO
- Statistical postings

The foundation of all CO postings is the assignment of a real cost object and a cost element. Once all the requisite information has been provided, a transaction is completed, and a document will be created.

In the simplest terms, a document is a record of a transaction in the SAP database. Many times, you'll hear about the SAP document principle, which contains the following rules:

- Each relevant module receives a unique document.
- Each document must contain a posting period.
- Each document must balance.
- Each document must have a header and line items.
- Documents can trigger workflows (optional).

The following sections will describe the foundation of documents. Distinct differences exist between CO documents in an SAP ERP 6.0 system and documents in an SAP S/4HANA system. Users may be confused by Universal Journal data displayed as a traditional CO document format, since all of the FI and CO data is displayed in the same line item. While it's not necessary to display FI data and CO data separately, it is beneficial to see the CO data independently from FI.

In the SAP ERP 6.0 environment, data for CO is recorded in tables separate from FI data, thus necessitating separate documents. In an SAP S/4HANA system, only one document is created for the Universal Journal (table ACDOCA). The SAP S/4HANA system still creates a view of the data as a traditional CO document to facilitate analysis for CO without extraneous FI information. Let's go through the steps for setting up document creation in an SAP S/4HANA system.

CO Documents Type

At this point, you can begin posting values to the controlling area. Prior to SAP S/4HANA, CO postings simply needed a number range to create documents but didn't require a specific document type. SAP S/4HANA more closely links FI and CO postings. In SAP S/4HANA, postings for CO will be stored in the Universal Journal, or table ACDOCA, along with FI postings, which means that all CO postings now require an explicit document type.

Postings that are initiated in FI will generate FI document types. With the release of SAP S/4HANA, postings initiated internally in CO require an FI document type specifically for CO. This feature is activated by the new G/L function for real-time replication between FI and CO. After FI creates a CO document type, CO process transactions must be assigned to link the functions, as shown in Figure 3.19. For more granularity in reporting, additional documents types could be used.

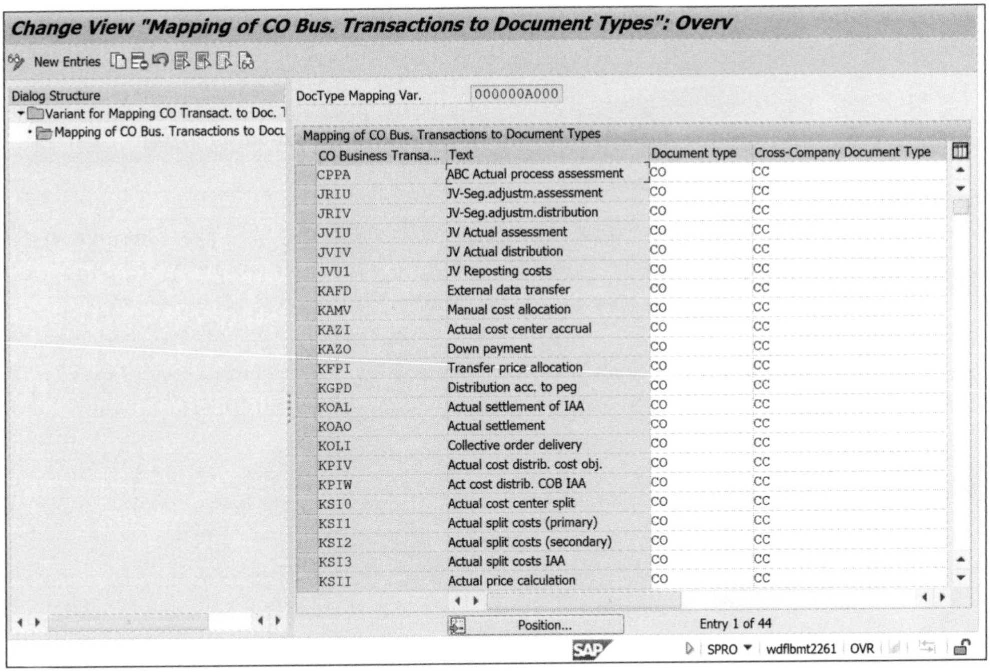

Change View "Mapping of CO Bus. Transactions to Document Types": Overv

New Entries

Dialog Structure	DocType Mapping Var.	000000A000		
▼ ☐ Variant for Mapping CO Transact. to Doc. 1				
• ☐ Mapping of CO Bus. Transactions to Docu	**Mapping of CO Bus. Transactions to Document Types**			

CO Business Transa...	Text	Document type	Cross-Company Document Type
CPPA	ABC Actual process assessment	CO	CC
JRIU	JV-Seg.adjustm.assessment	CO	CC
JRIV	JV-Seg.adjustm.distribution	CO	CC
JVIU	JV Actual assessment	CO	CC
JVIV	JV Actual distribution	CO	CC
JVU1	JV Reposting costs	CO	CC
KAFD	External data transfer	CO	CC
KAMV	Manual cost allocation	CO	CC
KAZI	Actual cost center accrual	CO	CC
KAZO	Down payment	CO	CC
KFPI	Transfer price allocation	CO	CC
KGPD	Distribution acc. to peg	CO	CC
KOAL	Actual settlement of IAA	CO	CC
KOAO	Actual settlement	CO	CC
KOLI	Collective order delivery	CO	CC
KPIV	Actual cost distrib. cost obj.	CO	CC
KPIW	Act cost distrib. COB IAA	CO	CC
KSI0	Actual cost center split	CO	CC
KSI1	Actual split costs (primary)	CO	CC
KSI2	Actual split costs (secondary)	CO	CC
KSI3	Actual split costs IAA	CO	CC
KSII	Actual price calculation	CO	CC

Position...   Entry 1 of 44

SAP   ▷ | SPRO ▼ | wdflbmt2261 | OVR

Figure 3.19 CO Business Process Document Assignment

CO Number Ranges

To start the document process, number ranges for documents must be defined. Number ranges fall into two types: internal and external. For internal number ranges, you'll designate the range, and SAP will assign the next available number. This option is used for documents created automatically by the SAP system. External number ranges are for documents created external to the SAP system. SAP simply ensures that each number is unique.

CO documents can receive numbers from three separate functions: First, FI-CO postings to a primary account will generate an FI document number, since the information is relevant to both FI and CO. This number range is dictated from the FI document configuration. You can reference the CO information through this document view. This posting will also generate a traditional CO document number, triggered from the CO number ranges, as shown in Figure 3.20. This document number provides a uniquely CO view of the information, facilitating reporting at the CO level.

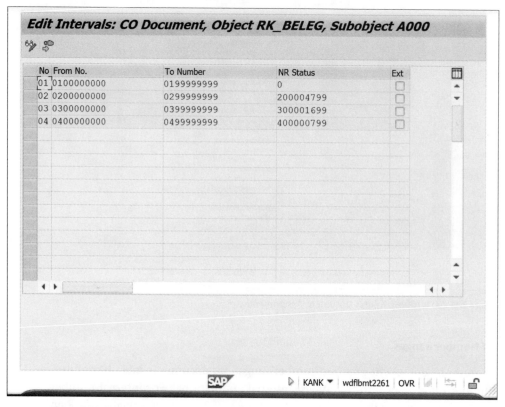

Figure 3.20 CO Number Ranges

Secondary cost element postings, or CO-only postings, still require an FI document type to post data in the Universal Journal. The configuration of the CO document type is required since the all postings to the Universal Journal must maintain an FI document number. The CO document type will still generate the reference CO document number. The CO type configured in FI is assigned to a business transaction, as shown in Figure 3.21. A business transaction represents SAP technical functions, such as settlement, assessment, planning, and so on.

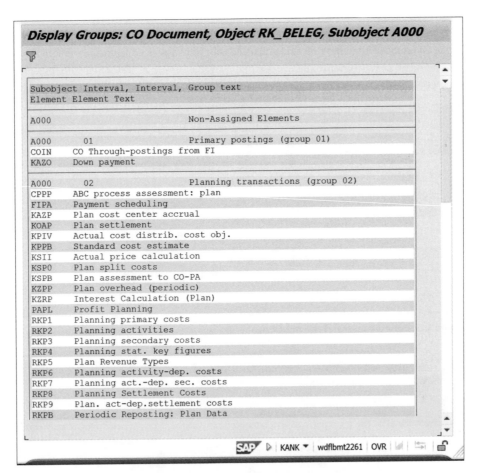

Figure 3.21 CO Business Transaction Assignment

As mentioned earlier, an internal CO posting will generate an FI document number even though the posting is not relevant to FI, and the CO reference document number will still exist in the posting, as shown in Figure 3.22.

The third document number that is possible is initiated by SAP. Some postings are outside normal business processes and may require the creation of a CO document, for example, a material movement that is performed without reference to any other object. Alternatively, a CO document is not needed, but an additional document is required. When an FI posting is created, an internal document is generated, starting with the letter "A." You cannot manipulate this number range. The system-assigned document number is shown in Figure 3.23.

ACDOCA: Display of Entries Found

Search in Table	ACDOCA		Universal Journal Entry Line Items
Number of hits	108		
Runtime	0	Maximum no. of hits	500

Posting Date	Ld	CoCode	Year	DocumentNo	LnItm	GLFY	Account	Ref. doc.	Cost Center	Profit Ctr	Func. Are	BusA	CO Area	Segment	Sender cost ctr	DocNoL	R	TTy	TrTy	BTra
19.01.2018	0L	1010	2018	2300000125	00000	2018	29500100	1015		INTENG			A000	1000_D		0		RMRU	RKL
19.01.2018	0L	1010	2018	2300000125	00000	2018	29500100	1015		T-FLS00			A000	1000_A		0		RMRU	RKL
19.01.2018	2L	1010	2018	2300000125	00000	2018	29500100	1015		INTENG			A000	1000_D		0		RMRU	RKL
19.01.2018	2L	1010	2018	2300000125	00000	2018	29500100	1015		T-FLS00			A000	1000_A		0		RMRU	RKL
12.01.2018	0L	1010	2018	2300000121	00000	2018	29500100	200003804		T-PCB98			A000	1000_B		0		RKU3	RKU3
12.01.2018	0L	1010	2018	2300000121	00000	2018	29500100	200003804		YB600			A000	1000_C		0		RKU3	RKU3
12.01.2018	2L	1010	2018	2300000121	00000	2018	29500100	200003804		T-PCB98			A000	1000_B		0		RKU3	RKU3
12.01.2018	2L	1010	2018	2300000121	00000	2018	29500100	200003804		YB600			A000	1000_C		0		RKU3	RKU3
02.01.2018	0L	1010	2018	2300000120	00000	2018	29500100	300001400		T-PCB98			A000	1000_B		0		RKL	RKL
02.01.2018	0L	1010	2018	2300000120	00000	2018	29500100	300001400		YB600			A000	1000_C		0		RKL	RKL
02.01.2018	2L	1010	2018	2300000120	00000	2018	29500100	300001400		T-PCB98			A000	1000_B		0		RKL	RKL
02.01.2018	2L	1010	2018	2300000120	00000	2018	29500100	300001400		YB600			A000	1000_C		0		RKL	RKL
12.01.2018	0L	1010	2018	2300000121	00000	2018	54300000	200003804	4300	YB600	YB20		A000	1000_C	4230	0		RKU3	RKU3
12.01.2018	0L	1010	2018	2300000121	00000	2018	54300000	200003804	4230	T-PCB98	YB20		A000	1000_B	4300	0		RKU3	RKU3
12.01.2018	0L	1010	2018	2300000121	00000	2018	54300000	200003804	4230	T-PCB98	YB20		A000	1000_B	4230	0		RKU3	RKU3
12.01.2018	0L	1010	2018	2300000121	00000	2018	54300000	200003804	4230	T-PCB98	YB20		A000	1000_B	4230	0		RKU3	RKU3
12.01.2018	2L	1010	2018	2300000121	00000	2018	54300000	200003804	4300	YB600	YB20		A000	1000_C	4230	0		RKU3	RKU3
12.01.2018	2L	1010	2018	2300000121	00000	2018	54300000	200003804	4230	T-PCB98	YB20		A000	1000_B	4300	0		RKU3	RKU3
12.01.2018	2L	1010	2018	2300000121	00000	2018	54300000	200003804	4230	T-PCB98	YB20		A000	1000_B	4230	0		RKU3	RKU3
02.01.2018	0L	1010	2018	2300000120	00000	2018	90639300	300001400	4300	YB600	YB99		A000	1000_C	4230	0		RKL	RKL
02.01.2018	0L	1010	2018	2300000120	00000	2018	90639300	300001400	4230	T-PCB98	YB99		A000	1000_B	4300	0		RKL	RKL
02.01.2018	2L	1010	2018	2300000120	00000	2018	90639300	300001400	4300	YB600	YB99		A000	1000_C	4230	0		RKL	RKL

SAP   ▷ | SE16N ▼ | wdflbmt2261 | OVR

Figure 3.22 Universal Journal (Table ACDOCA)

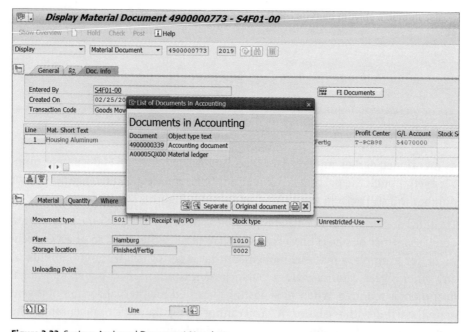

Figure 3.23 System Assigned Document Numbers

Real versus Statistical Postings

In CO, postings are classified as either real or statistical. Before explaining the process of creating posting, let's explore the difference through their different setup rules:

- Each CO posting must have a cost element.
- If you post to cost element, you must have one real or true cost object, also called the account assignment object.
- Cost centers, business processes, and profitability segments are always designated as real cost objects.
- Profit centers are always defined as statistical cost objects. If profit center accounting is activated in CO, at least one statistical posting will always exist.
- Real objects carry real postings, and statistical objects carry statistical postings.
- Postings can include one real cost object and additional statistical cost objects.

> **Note**
> There's one exception: When we post to a cost center and another real object, the cost center gets a statistical posting but remains a real cost object.

When you use an account defined as a cost element, you must assign a real cost object. Cost objects are either obligatory real objects or have the option of becoming statistical at creation. The account assignment state is determined at the time a posting is executed. An example could be a vendor invoice for an expense item where the account is a primary cost element, which requires the assignment of the cost object. The vendor invoice is defined as the *prima nota*, or source transaction, for a CO posting to the Universal Journal. This concept is not new but has become more prevalent in SAP S/4HANA.

The source of immense confusion within CO is the difference between real and statistical postings. Statistical postings are for information only; they allow the reporting of additional details but do not duplicate initial postings. Statistical postings add dimensions to extend and enhance analysis functions.

Keep in mind some key points to differentiate between real versus statistical objects:

- Real objects can be settled.
- Real objects can send or receive allocations.
- Real objects can stand alone in postings.

- Statistical postings only occur at the time of the prima nota.
- Statistical postings cannot stand alone; they must always be accompanied by a real posting.

Postings from Other Applications

Postings from other business areas that impact primary cost or revenue require the assignment of a cost object. The assignment can originate in master data, be derived automatically, or be entered at the time of document creation. The most obvious postings are FI transactions for primary cost elements. In the initial FI line item, a cost object will need to be populated, which can be done manually by a user or through automatic account assignment.

In other business processes, the creation of the CO document may not occur until later in the business process. An example is a purchase order (PO) used to procure consumption items, which requires the assignment of a cost object in the PO line item. The assignment can happen manually as the PO is created, or automatic account assignment will determine the cost object at the time of PO creation.

Persons defined in the human capital management (HCM) area must receive the assignment of a cost center. This is done through an organizational assignment or the master data settings in the personnel record. The execution of a payroll run will post directly to the assigned cost center.

A similar process happens with assets. The asset master record must be assigned to a cost center. At the execution of the depreciation run, the system will post depreciation expenses to the assigned cost center. A sales order recording cost of goods sold (COGS) or billing revenue will derive a profitability segment in CO-PA. You'll see many of these operations throughout subsequent chapters.

Postings within Management Accounting

Once values have been recorded in the controlling area, these values can be further distributed between cost objects. As shown in Figure 3.24, CO internal postings always include a sender and a receiver. A few key elements have been added in the CO data for SAP S/4HANA. CO manual postings now contain a document type, a ledger group, and a valuation date. Normally, these fields are associated with FI, but to combine FI and CO data in the Universal Journal, you now can use these fields for CO postings. Document types will default from the configuration settings unless otherwise dictated. The ledger group will default to the leading ledger unless another ledger is designated.

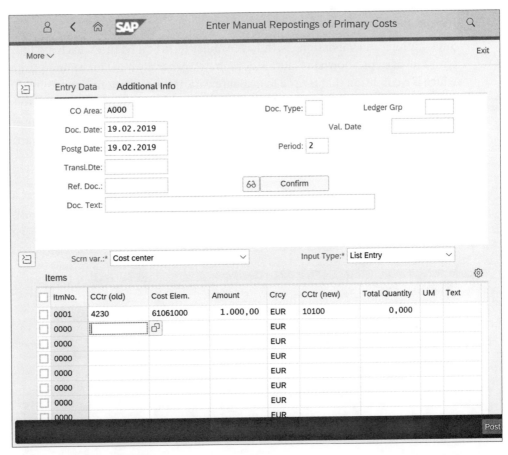

Figure 3.24 Manual CO Posting

Account Assignment Options

CO has options to assist the assignment of cost objects. These options can be used to validate user entries or to post account assignments automatically. Automatic account assignment in table OKB9, shown in Figure 3.3, gives you the ability to associate a cost object directly with a cost element. However, you cannot use logic to derive different cost objects. Once an object is derived, you can still change it within the document.

Substitutions and validations can define rules to determine account assignment logic. Substitutions will automatically enter a cost object, even to the extent of overwriting existing data. Validations do not change data; they just validate that the current data meets existing rules.

Substitutions and validations both have similar technical features. Each are built with a set of steps, shown in Figure 3.25. Each step generally includes a prerequisite, which is a condition that is used to evaluate data. If the condition is met, then the step will be executed. If the condition is not met, then the condition will be disregarded. With a validation, if the prerequisite is met, then the system will issue an acceptance. If the condition is not met, then the system will issue a selected warning or error message.

Warning!

These rules are beneficial but should be used judiciously, or they could become difficult to manage.

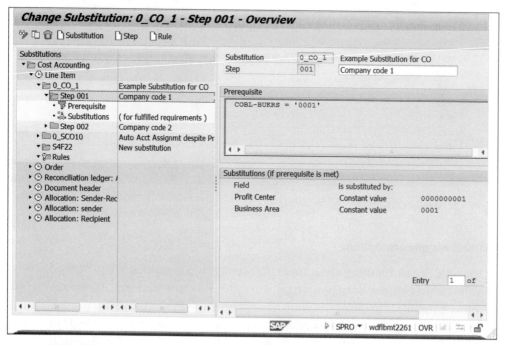

Figure 3.25 Substitution

Adjustment Postings

On occasion, you may find that a posting has cause an error in the CO data, but the FI-relevant information is correct. You'll need to make a correction to the existing data. Several options exist for accomplishing this correction, but some carry risk or have restrictions. You'll need to analyze how the error occurred and determine the best option to correct the data. Analyzing the source of the error could be beneficial and may indicate a technical issue with the system or an issue in a business process.

To correct a CO posting, the following options are available:

- **Reverse original FI document**
  - Pros: Keeps FI and CO in sync. Downstream reporting remains consistent.
  - Cons: Reversing an FI posting can only be carried out in open periods and is not always possible. It also has significant implications on external reporting process governance.

- **Repost line items**
  - Pros: Corrects CO data with a separate document but is linked directly to the FI document. Reversing the FI document will notify the user of subsequent postings. Validates to original values. Allows value to move across cost objects.
  - Cons: Document corrections are 1:1 and the process becomes cumbersome with numerous document corrections. No indication in the original FI document that a subsequent posting exists.

- **Manually repost line items**
  - Pros: Allows changes to total values when significant numbers of documents require changes.
  - Cons: No link to original document. No validation of amounts.

- **Leave original posting and correct in the subsequent period**
  - Pros: Simple option that will avoid impact to FI.
  - Cons: Option is realistic only for immaterial postings. Causes reporting issues in CO if amount is material.

- **Make an FI adjustment posting to trigger an accompanying CO posting**
  - Pros: Keeps FI and CO in sync.
  - Cons: Does not link or impact the original posting. May also raise issues with FI governance.

> **Tip**
>
> If the period is still open and the documents are limited, reverse and repost is the best option and will keep FI and CO synchronized.
>
> In cases where the period is closed, reposting or leaving the posting for future correction is more appropriate. These options generate a link between FI and CO.
>
> Manually reposting line items is the least desirable method due to the lack of integration. However, when numerous documents are involved, manual reposting may be the only option.

Cost Center Reporting

In Chapter 1, you learned about SAP HANA and SAP Fiori apps. Although these should be the preferred options for reporting in SAP S/4HANA, you can still use traditional reporting tools from previous SAP versions. SAP has provided technical functions to accommodate this option. In many cases, you might want to use traditional tools to ease users into the new SAP S/4HANA environment. Businesses may also choose this route to capitalize on their current customized reports. Core data services (CDS) views provide reporting from and replicate data from tables that no longer exist in SAP S/4HANA. These views will be discussed further in Chapter 9.

In this section, we'll discuss two common reporting options used for cost center reporting: list view reports and Report Painter reports. These two tools are traditional reporting functions that use CDS views to replicate data from table ACDOCA. The reports work in the same manner in SAP S/4HANA as they did in previous SAP systems.

List View Reports

One of the most common tools employed for reporting is a list view report. Newer versions of list reports are called ABAP list viewer (ALV) reports. The ALV reports contain enhancements to make the list reports more functional. The basic purpose of a list view report is to provide a list of desired information, such as a list of documents, a list of master data, or a list of details.

A list report has many similarities to a simple Excel spreadsheet. The data is presented in columns and rows, as shown in Figure 3.26. In list reports, you can add or remove fields and columns; change the arrangement of columns; and sort, filter, and total lists. In most list reports, you can also export the list to Excel. After you've formatted a list to the desired view, you can save it for future reference, making it easy to re-create the desired list views.

Cost Center	Acty Type	Cost ctr short text	Act. type short text	COCr	Total Price	Price (Varia...	Price (Fixed)	Prl
10101301	1	Manufacturing 1 (DE)	Machine hours 1	EUR	30,00	10,00	20,00	1
	11	Manufacturing 1 (DE)	Personnel Hours	EUR	35,00	35,00	0,00	1
	2	Manufacturing 1 (DE)	Machine hours 2	EUR	0,00	0,00	0,00	1
	3	Manufacturing 1 (DE)	Setup Production	EUR	30,00	30,00	0,00	1
	4	Manufacturing 1 (DE)	Personel Hours	EUR	0,00	0,00	0,00	1
10101321	101	Services/Consltg(DE)	Service Standard	EUR	0,00	0,00	0,00	1
	102	Services/Consltg(DE)	Service Specialist	EUR	0,00	0,00	0,00	1

Figure 3.26 List Report

Report Painter Reports

Another traditional reporting tool is the Report Painter. Report Painter is the most often used reporting tool in SAP (refer to Chapter 9 for an overview).

The most common standard report used for cost centers is Cost Centers: Actual/ Plan/Variance (Transaction S_ALR_87013611). Report Painter reports are structured with a navigation pane on the left and data display on the right, as shown in Figure 3.27. The information presented on the right is summarized data for the accounts or calculations defined in the report.

Following are the available functions of Report Painter reports:

- Format view with sorts, filters, and summarization
- Export data to Microsoft Excel spreadsheet
- Define threshold values
- Mail reports
- Expand or collapse rows
- Alter number format

- Convert to alternative language
- Produce graphs
- Change view to Excel in place (SAP screen becomes Excel)

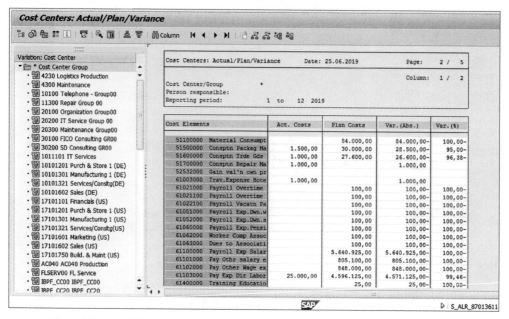

Figure 3.27 Actual/Plan/Variance Report

Report Painter provides three technical functions. The obvious function is reporting, but it also provides two additional functions. In cost center, internal order planning, and CO-PA planning, it controls the screen layout for data entry. Like the reporting area, SAP provides standard planning layouts, allowing businesses to create their own layouts. Report Painter also provides drilldown report forms. Drilldown reports can use the format capabilities of Report Painter to structure a drilldown report. The rows and columns are built in to Report Painter, and then the drilldown report selects the data.

One of the best features of Report Painter reports is the use of a graphical report structure—basically a row and column format—to visualize the report structure without executing a program, as shown in Figure 3.28. You just double-click the areas of the report and choose the data to include.

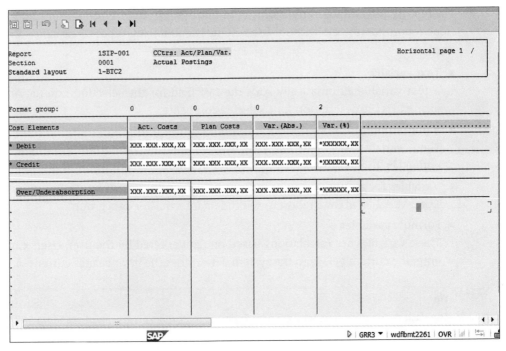

Figure 3.28 Report Painter Screen

Report Painter reports have three basic components that make up the structure of the reports and determine the data and format of the reports:

- **General data selection**
  Criteria specify information to retrieve from the database.

- **Rows**
  Rows contain characteristics or formulas. A characteristic is a data element, such as an account number or activity type.

- **Columns**
  Columns are key figures or formulas. A key figure is a combination of characteristics and a value, such as actual dollars or activity quantities.

To enhance your reports, you can divide the information into sections. You can also add calculated key figures. Calculated key figures are unique sections with formulas using data from sections within the report.

You can use Report Painter to capitalize on master data groups as well. In situations where master data doesn't exist, you can create custom groups called sets.

The reports also employ variables, which allow the system to automatically determine report parameters without user input. The following types of variables are used:

- **Text variable**
  A text variable automatically adds the test field for the selection criteria. An example is the description for a selected cost center.

- **Value variable**
  These variables (e.g., current year, current quarter, or current period) are entered by users or are determined by the system.

- **Variables for groups**
  These variables allow a report to select data for a master data group.

- **Formula variables**
  These variables are calculations based on data entered by the user. Users can enter the current year, and the system determines the prior year as current - 1.

Tip

The easiest approach to creating a new Report Painter report is to copy a standard SAP report. SAP reports can't be altered, but after you save the reports under a different name, you can alter the report.

Period-End Close

At period end, numerous costs and quantities are allocated between cost objects. SAP S/4HANA offers several options for allocating costs. Understanding how an allocation works technically doesn't explain when the different tools are appropriate. Asking a few simple questions can help resolve this problem:

- **Who will be affected?**
  Distribution and periodic repostings are done with primary cost elements and could cross company codes. Assessment and indirect activity allocation post with secondary cost elements, affecting only CO. Accrual allocation with settlement of the internal order can duplicate the accrual in FI. Order settlement can post costs back to FI.

- **What will be sent?**
  Distribution and periodic repostings send primary costs in a 1:1 relationship and are visible to the receiving object. Assessment summarizes primary and

secondary costs into a secondary cost element, making tracking back to the original account from the sender impossible.

- **What is the sender allocating: dollar values or quantities?**
  Indirect activity allocations allocate quantities, while assessments, distribution, periodic reposting, and accruals send dollar values.

- **How am I sending: as a percentage, in amounts, or in portions?**
  Costing sheets accrue based on percentage. Cycle segment allocation allows you to send all three. Cycle segment methods offer a rule-based allocation method to transfer value from many cost objects to numerous other cost objects. The rules can be fixed percentages, fixed amounts, or in variable portions like a statistical key figure.

- **Who is sending?**
  Periodic reposting can send costs from many different types of cost objects. Assessment, distribution, and indirect activity allocations are limited to cost centers and business processes.

- **When am I sending, periodically or object by object?**
  Cycle segment allocations are executed during the period-end close process, allocating costs to and from numerous objects. One rule is followed for many objects. Settlement is executed for individual objects at month end, each with their own allocation rule.

In the next sections, we'll explore allocation methods in more detail. We'll begin the discussion with the accrual calculation, which is probably the least used process but offers the benefit of automating month-end accruals in both FI and CO.

Accrual Calculation

In FI, numerous accruals must be posted at period end. Accruals can be accomplished with different methods. CO has a tool for achieving an accrual calculation using CO data. The accrual can be used as an allocation method solely within CO or can also be used to transfer the posting to FI.

Though SAP offers two methods for calculating an accrual, the most commonly used method is the percentage method. The accrual calculation is defined in Customizing using an overhead calculation, as shown in Figure 3.29, which holds the logic for the calculation.

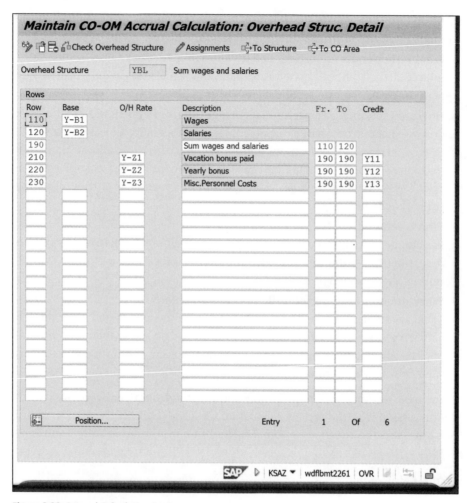

Figure 3.29 Accrual Calculation Logic

The structure defines three items:

- A base value (costs that have been incurred) as a basis for the calculation
- A percentage of overhead to apply
- An order to receive the credit

This allocation structure used for accrual is, in essence, a costing sheet. Costing sheets are a percentage-based allocation method transferring values from a sender to a receiver. Think of a costing sheet as a simple spreadsheet with three components: a base (or information available in the receiver), an overhead (or amount applied to the receiver), and a credit (or sending cost object). The costing sheet is available throughout CO and will be discussed further in Chapter 5.

The accrual calculation uses specific cost elements with the cost element category of accrual and uses an internal order that is defined as an accrual order (see Chapter 4 for more information on internal orders). Upon execution of the accrual calculation, the designated order receives a credit, and the appropriate cost centers are debited, as shown in Figure 3.30.

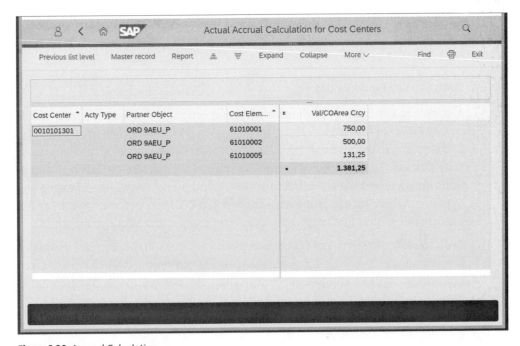

Figure 3.30 Accrual Calculation

You can set up this calculation based on actual data without the additional steps of planning cost ahead of time, which is required in the second method, the target = actual method.

The target = actual method requires plan quantities and values to calculate a target value. The simplest definition of target is *planned price × actual quantity*. To calculate the target, all the planning data for the sending cost object must be entered prior to the start of the period so that the system can calculate a comparison value between the planned value and the actual value.

> **Note**
> Since target = actual requires plan values and quantities to be entered ahead of time, many companies do not use this method since many businesses do not plan at all or plan quantities outside of SAP.

A complementary process can be used to transfer the accrual to finance by settling the accrual order to an FI G/L account. The benefit of the accrual process is that you can use the rich transaction data in CO to automatically calculate accrual versus the traditional method of running a repost and manually calculating the accrual, prior to making a manual posting.

Statistical Key Figure Values

A statistical key figure represents any type of quantity you wish to track, as discussed earlier in the "Master Data" section—POs processed, office square footage, IT tickets processed, and so forth. These quantities can be captured and entered as statistical key figures. These quantities can also be used as tracing factors in allocations or in key performance indicator (KPI) calculations. They offer a flexible and dynamic method for allocating costs throughout CO. Since most statistical key figures are based on actual usage, they offer a more equitable allocation method.

Even though statistical key figure quantities may need to be entered manually, they eliminate the need for complicated calculations required when using a fixed percentage or fixed amount allocation. Once the percentage or fixed amounts have been calculated, these values must still be entered into the allocation tools. Many businesses still use the percentage or amount values since they replicate traditional allocation methods.

Cycle Segment Methods

Periodic reposting, distribution, assessment, and indirect activity allocations use a procedure called the cycle segment method. A cycle is a sequence of steps called segments. Each step contains a group of objects, such as a sender, a group of costs or quantities to allocate, a tracing factor, and a group of receiving objects. Each cycle can contain as many segments as needed. The system executes the complete cycle.

> **Tip**
> If an issue arises with any step, no segments post. If you define 20 steps and the system encounters a problem with step 6, nothing posts for any of the 20 steps. The cycle must be executed multiple times to resolve all issues before any postings occur. For this reason, we recommend keeping the number of steps to a manageable total.

An overview of a cycle segment allocation is shown in Figure 3.31.

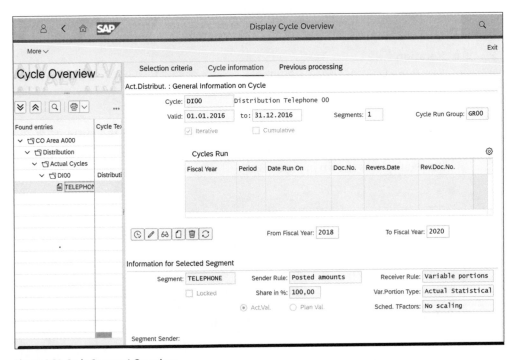

Figure 3.31 Cycle Segment Overview

These allocation methods have similar structures, making it easy for you to develop the skills you'll need to create allocations. In these allocations, using master data groups can be quite helpful. By using the grouping techniques learned in the "Master Data" section of this chapter, you can control updates to allocation segments through master data group updates. Controlling the group members allow allocations to be updated without editing individual segments directly.

Segments need to have rules defined. The first rule you must define is for the senders. Are you sending everything or just partial values? You'll then need to define a rule governing how to apply values to the receiver, called a tracing factor. You can define fixed amounts, fixed percentages, fixed portions, or variable portions. The least understood options are the fixed portions and variable portions options: Fixed portions are ratios you define manually. Variable portions are statistical key figures. With a statistical key figure, SAP automatically calculates the ratios.

SAP will then total all the portions and calculate the allocation amount. The quantity of all designated key figures is totaled, and again the system calculates the correct portions. Statistical key figures allow you to use current quantities to automatically adjust allocation amounts.

Two settings at the cycle level need to be reviewed:

- **Iteration**
  Iteration cycles the calculation to balance to 0, which allows you to ensure the sender balances to 0.

- **Cumulative**
  Cumulative accumulates values from period 1 and applies the current tracing factor to the total, then subtracts values already allocated in previous periods (for example, as shown in Figure 3.32).

	Sender	Receiver	Receiver			
Segment 1	A	B	C			
	AMT 1	Statistical Key Figure	Statistical Key Figure			

Period	Amount	B – Statistical Key Figure	C – Statistical Key Figure	B – Non-Cummulative	C – Non-Cummulative	B – Cummulative	C – Cummulative
1	10,000	50.00	75.00	4,000	6,000	4,000	6,000
2	20,000	50.00	75.00	8,000	12,000	8,000	12,000
3	20,000	250.00	80.00	15,152	4,848	18,172	1,828
4	40,000	100.00	160.00	15,385	24,615	18,042	21,958
5	30,000	60.00	100.00	11,120	18,750	12,986	17,014
6		And so on…					
	120,000			53,786	66,214	61,200	58,800

Figure 3.32 Cumulative Cycle

You should only use this option if the relationships between senders and receivers are stable. Totals for all periods must remain constant, and only the allocation in the current period is adjusted.

The following are the most commonly used cycle segment methods:

- **Periodic reposting**

  The periodic reposting method sends only primary costs elements in a 1:1 relationship from the sender to the receiver. This process is not often used because the sender won't be able to see the results of the allocation. This method does, however, have the benefit of many types of objects being able to act as senders.

- **Distribution**

  Distribution allocates primary cost elements in a 1:1 relationship from cost centers or business processes to other senders. Each account from the sender is visible to the receiver. The original amounts and the allocated amounts are visible to the sender.

- **Assessment**

  Assessment summarizes both primary and secondary costs, then allocates a secondary cost element, cost element category 42, from the sending cost center to a receiver. The original costs and the allocation are visible to the sender, but only the summarized cost element is visible to the receiver.

  The basic assessment definition can have only one secondary assessment cost element in the segment data. As a result, the receiving object sees all the allocation values in one large total amount versus a 1:1 value transfer in distribution. An alternative is to build an allocation structure to group costs into smaller buckets, allowing the receiver to see more detail. These groups can then be assigned to different allocation cost elements. This method does not give a 1:1 cost element assignment but does provide some additional granularity for reporting.

Out of this list, periodic repostings are used the least, since these postings are recorded at the totals level, which prevents the sender from viewing the original amount.

Think of an allocation structure, as shown in Figure 3.33, as a mapping table. The first step is to define group names. The next step is to define source cost elements to use in these groups. These cost elements are posted to the sender. The last step is to assign each group to an assessment cost element that is visible to the receiver. After the allocation structure is complete, the structure ID is entered into the **Allocation Structure** field of the segment in place of the allocation cost element.

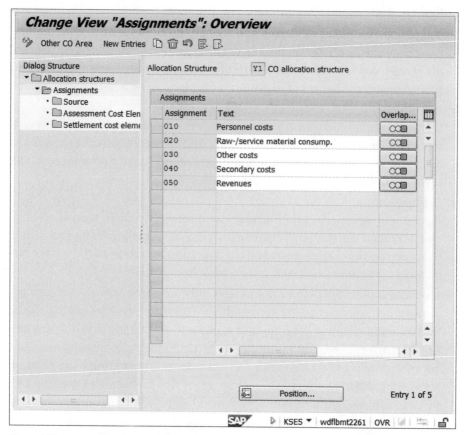

Figure 3.33 Assessment Allocation Structure

In CO, you can track and allocation activity quantities as well as monetary values. Activity quantities are recorded using an activity type. At period end, you may need to realign quantities across cost objects. Two methods exist for making the activity calculation: direct and indirect. The direct option requires knowledge of the quantities on which to base the allocation. The alternative is to use a key to inversely calculate the allocation. Indirect activity allocations transfer activity quantities from a cost center to receivers. The value of the allocation is derived from the activity price. The activity quantity is transferred from a cost center to other receivers. The value is posted using the secondary cost element from the activity type. The quantity allocated and the secondary cost value are visible both to the sender and the receiver. The costs included in the activity price are not readily visible to the sender or receiver.

Tip

Many companies will face an situation where allocations in prior periods were incorrect. One option is to reverse and post a correction in the original period, but doing so presents the complication of adjusting closed periods. Since allocations are CO-based postings and not FI relevant, this adjustment should not be an issue. Even so, for audit reasons, many organizations don't want to touch previous periods.

An alternative is to perform a reverse and rebook. With this technique, the values for segments in previous periods are reversed in the current period. As a result, corrections are visible in the current period postings, without altering closed period data. This approach doesn't impact the values posted in the current period; it simply reverses prior periods and makes these corrections visible in the current period.

The segment's details can now be corrected, and the values are posted in the current period. Prior periods are not impacted, but the total effect is visible, and year-to-date totals are corrected. This correction technique is available for assessments and distribution.

Period Lock

The final step in period-end closing is to lock the period from further postings. The traditional period lock for CO, Transaction OKP1, locks individual business transactions, shown in Figure 3.34, which allows for control by individual CO business functions.

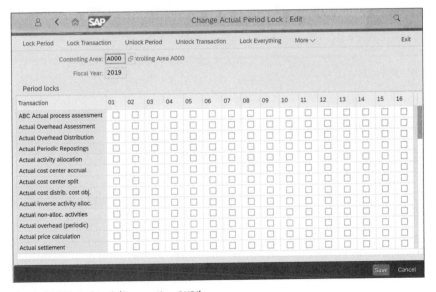

Figure 3.34 Period Lock (Transaction OKP1)

SAP S/4HANA adds an additional layer to the closing process for CO. Since all cost elements are now G/L accounts, the traditional FI lock process also locks CO transactions, as shown in Figure 3.35. SAP has provided a third set of periods in Transaction OB52 to provide additional options for the CO close. You can use both methods in combination or rely only on the FI lock process.

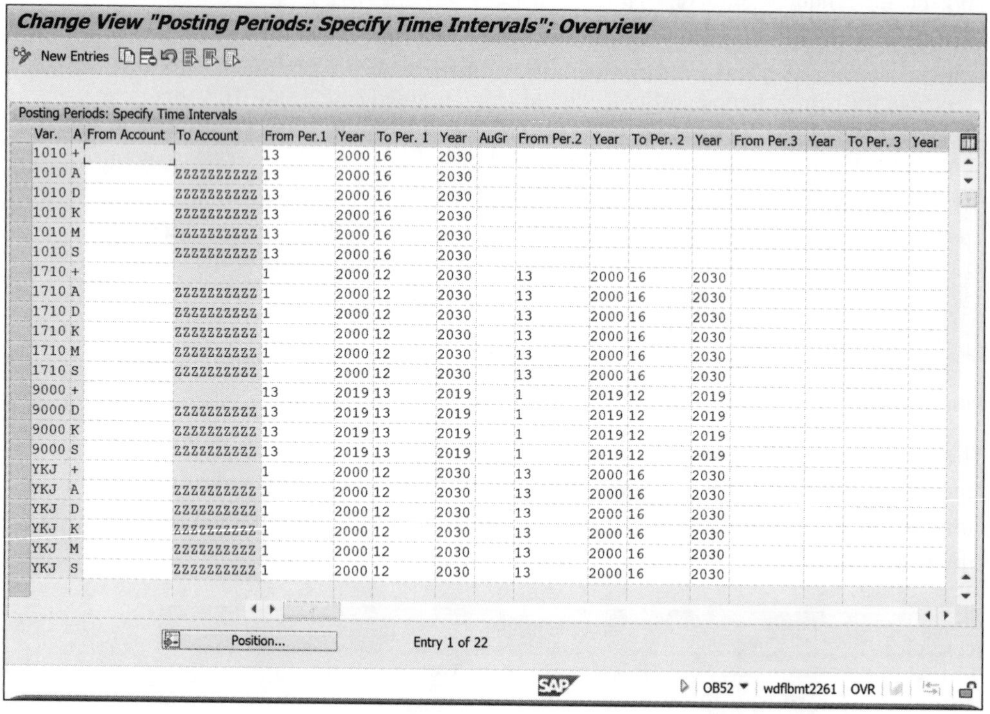

Change View "Posting Periods: Specify Time Intervals": Overview

New Entries

Posting Periods: Specify Time Intervals

Var.	A	From Account	To Account	From Per.1	Year	To Per. 1	Year	AuGr	From Per.2	Year	To Per. 2	Year	From Per.3	Year	To Per. 3	Year
1010	+			13	2000	16	2030									
1010	A		ZZZZZZZZZZ	13	2000	16	2030									
1010	D		ZZZZZZZZZZ	13	2000	16	2030									
1010	K		ZZZZZZZZZZ	13	2000	16	2030									
1010	M		ZZZZZZZZZZ	13	2000	16	2030									
1010	S		ZZZZZZZZZZ	13	2000	16	2030									
1710	+			1	2000	12	2030		13	2000	16	2030				
1710	A		ZZZZZZZZZZ	1	2000	12	2030		13	2000	16	2030				
1710	D		ZZZZZZZZZZ	1	2000	12	2030		13	2000	16	2030				
1710	K		ZZZZZZZZZZ	1	2000	12	2030		13	2000	16	2030				
1710	M		ZZZZZZZZZZ	1	2000	12	2030		13	2000	16	2030				
1710	S		ZZZZZZZZZZ	1	2000	12	2030		13	2000	16	2030				
9000	+			13	2019	13	2019		1	2019	12	2019				
9000	D		ZZZZZZZZZZ	13	2019	13	2019		1	2019	12	2019				
9000	K		ZZZZZZZZZZ	13	2019	13	2019		1	2019	12	2019				
9000	S		ZZZZZZZZZZ	13	2019	13	2019		1	2019	12	2019				
YKJ	+			1	2000	12	2030		13	2000	16	2030				
YKJ	A		ZZZZZZZZZZ	1	2000	12	2030		13	2000	16	2030				
YKJ	D		ZZZZZZZZZZ	1	2000	12	2030		13	2000	16	2030				
YKJ	K		ZZZZZZZZZZ	1	2000	12	2030		13	2000	16	2030				
YKJ	M		ZZZZZZZZZZ	1	2000	12	2030		13	2000	16	2030				
YKJ	S		ZZZZZZZZZZ	1	2000	12	2030		13	2000	16	2030				

Position...   Entry 1 of 22

SAP   ▷ OB52 ▼ wdflbmt2261 OVR

Figure 3.35 FI Period Lock (Transaction OB52)

Important Terminology

In this chapter, the following terminology was used:

- **ABAP list viewer (ALV)**
  A set of ABAP function modules that enhance the readability and functionality of reports.

- **Account assignment object**
  An account assignment object refers to an object to which you post quantities and values in CO. Account assignment objects are required for each CO posting.

- **Accrual**
  The accrual method distributes costs and revenue to the correct period. The process in CO uses a specific type of internal order to post the calculated value during the accrual run.

- **Activity allocation**
  Activity type quantities can be transferred from a cost center to other cost objects using either a manual transaction or an indirect allocation.

- **Activity price**
  Activity allocations require that each activity type has a price. When quantities are transferred, the rate is used to calculate the transaction value.

- **Activity type**
  An activity type is a cost center master data element that represents labor or services provided by a cost center to other objects.

- **Assessment**
  An assessment is an internal cost allocation from a sender cost center to receiver CO objects using a secondary assessment cost element.

- **Cost center**
  A cost center is an organizational unit within CO that represents a responsibility area, an allocation area, or a physical location where costs are incurred.

- **Cost center category**
  A cost center category is an attribute that determines how a cost center will be used.

- **Cost element category**
  A cost element category classifies cost elements by identifying their usage and origin.

- **Cost object**
  Cost objects are internal units collecting the results of costs or revenue from value-add processes. Objects can represent independent units or a group of related objects. These entities can also link to specific business functions.

- **Cycle segment method**
  This method is an allocation process using a rule-based procedure to select senders and distribute costs or quantities to designated receivers.

- **Direct activity allocation**
  This process manually allocates activity quantities from a cost center to other cost objects.

- **Distribution**
  A distribution is an allocation transaction that allocates primary costs. The original cost element is retained in the receiver cost center.
- **Graphical structure**
  Technical structure that organizes data into columns and rows.
- **Periodic reposting**
  This allocation method is based on defined rules to allocate primary costs from a sender to other receivers. The sender does not require a cost center.
- **Prima nota**
  A prima nota is an original document that contains the incoming data for a transaction that leads to a journal entry. This document serves as the anchor for reversing all related documents in a process.
- **Primary cost element**
  A primary cost element is a cost that originates outside CO representing a G/L that is recorded on the income statement.
- **Real cost object**
  A cost object is said to be real when it can carry individual postings without the support of other cost objects.
- **Repost**
  This kind of posting corrects primary costs from the original receiving object under the original cost element.
- **Screen variant**
  A screen variant is a selection of entry fields that are displayed for processing CO data.
- **Secondary cost element**
  A secondary cost element is an account used within CO for allocating costs between cost objects.
- **Selection variant**
  A selection variant is a tool for selecting CO master data using one or more criteria. The selections are entered once and saved in the variant for future use.
- **Set**
  Customized data groups created for use in reports; similar to master data groups.
- **Standard hierarchy**
  A standard hierarchy is a tree-like structure used for organizing CO objects. Business processes, profit centers, and cost centers each belong to a standard hierarchy with all the object contained in a controlling area.

- **Statistical cost object**
  A statistical cost object is used for information purposes only. These objects do not settle or receive allocations. A statistical cost object must always be posted with an additional entity that carries the actual value.

- **Statistical key figure**
  A statistical key figure is a numerical quantity that you can use as a tracing factor in allocations.

- **Text variable**
  The associated text for selection criteria entered in a report.

- **Tracing factor**
  A tracing factor is a rule created to define the basis of transferring values from the sender to the receiver.

Practice Questions

These practice questions will help you evaluate your understanding of the topics covered in this chapter. The questions shown are similar in nature to those found on the certification examination. Although none of these questions will be found on the exam itself, they will allow you to review your knowledge of the subject. Select the correct answers and then check the completeness of your answers in the "Practice Question Answers and Explanations" section. Remember that on the exam you must select all correct answers and only correct answers to receive credit for the question.

1. Which activity type category requires that you enter the price and quantity allocated with activity allocation?

    ☐   **A.** Manual, manual
    ☐   **B.** Manual, indirect
    ☐   **C.** Indirect, indirect

2. Which master data in functions of CO can be grouped? (There are three correct answers.)

    ☐   **A.** Cost elements
    ☐   **B.** Controlling area
    ☐   **C.** Internal orders
    ☐   **D.** Statistical key figures

3. True or False: Cost element master data requires a cost element category.

☐   **A.** True

☐   **B.** False

4. In G/L account master data, each account must contain which of the following?

☐   **A.** Account type

☐   **B.** Cost element category

☐   **C.** Cost object assignment

5. True or False: SAP has mandatory standard hierarchies.

☐   **A.** True

☐   **B.** False

6. Which SAP S/4HANA function provides methods to automatically assign accounts to cost object? (There are two correct answers.)

☐   **A.** Automatic assignment to table OKB9

☐   **B.** Cost object master data

☐   **C.** Substitution

☐   **D.** Field status

☐   **E.** Validation

7. Where are the day-to-day accounts we use for cost centers activated?

☐   **A.** G/L chart

☐   **B.** Local chart

☐   **C.** Operating chart

8. What function does the cost center category provide?

☐   **A.** Available cost elements

☐   **B.** Available profit centers

☐   **C.** Default setting for the cost center

9. CO allocations may need corrections. What is the effect of reverse and rebook?

☐ **A.** Reverse allocations for several months and rebook in the original periods

☐ **B.** Reverse current period and rebook to previous periods

☐ **C.** Reverse value of previous periods and repost the correction in the current period

10. True or False: Cost centers can allocate to many different objects.

☐ **A.** True

☐ **B.** False

11. True or False: An attribute of cost centers is their ability to perform period-end settlement.

☐ **A.** True

☐ **B.** False

12. Where do non-operating expense accounts post?

☐ **A.** Financial accounting (FI)

☐ **B.** Controlling (CO)

☐ **C.** Cost center

☐ **D.** Profit center

13. When comparing manual reposting of costs and repost line items, which is true?

☐ **A.** Manual reposting will link to the original document.

☐ **B.** Repost line items will validate against the FI line item.

☐ **C.** Repost line items will update the original FI posting.

☐ **D.** Manual reposting will create an FI and CO document.

14. What is the feature that distinguishes between fixed and variable cost?

☐ **A.** Variable cost element

☐ **B.** Secondary cost element

☐ **C.** Activity quantity

15. Which allocations use the cycle segment method? (There are two correct answers.)

☐ **A.** Costing sheet

☐ **B.** Periodic reposting

☐ **C.** Assessment

☐ **D.** Direct activity allocation

16. How can you configure cycles for period-end allocation? (There are two correct answers.)

☐ **A.** Create cycles that iterate with each other

☐ **B.** Use different allocation rules within one segment

☐ **C.** Assign several segments to a cycle

☐ **D.** Define allocation for the same cost center in multiple segments

17. What can you specify when you create an activity type? (There are three correct answers.)

☐ **A.** The primary costs G/L account for internal activity allocation

☐ **B.** The valid receiving cost center types

☐ **C.** The valid sending cost center types

☐ **D.** The secondary costs G/L account for internal activity allocation

☐ **E.** The activity type category for allocation

18. What is the highest overhead cost reporting level in CO?

☐ **A.** Company code

☐ **B.** Cost center hierarchy

☐ **C.** Controlling area

☐ **D.** Operating concern

19. When do you select the percentage method for accrual calculation? (There are two correct answers.)

☐ **A.** When you accrue activity-independent costs and an appropriate cost element is NOT available

☐   **B.** When you accrue activity-dependent costs and an appropriate cost element for defining overhead rates is available

☐   **C.** When you accrue activity-independent costs and an appropriate cost element for defining overhead rates is available

☐   **D.** When you accrue activity-dependent costs and an appropriate cost element is NOT available

20.   True or False: You would like to conceal the original cost element in an allocation. You should choose a distribution.

☐   **A.** True

☐   **B.** False

21.   When is the standard hierarchy of the cost center identified?

☐   **A.** When the controlling area is assigned to the operating concern

☐   **B.** When the controlling area is defined

☐   **C.** When the first cost center for a controlling area is created

☐   **D.** When the first company code is assigned to the controlling area

22.   When would you define assessment cycles for the period-end closing in overhead cost accounting? (There are two correct answers.)

☐   **A.** Transfer a primary cost element to the sender

☐   **B.** Transfer primary costs element from an order to a receiver

☐   **C.** Transfer a secondary cost element to the receiver

☐   **D.** Transfer primary and secondary to a secondary cost

23.   Which object can you assign to the cycle segment? (There are three correct answers.)

☐   **A.** Non-operating expense accounts

☐   **B.** Activity prices

☐   **C.** Balance sheet accounts

☐   **D.** Secondary cost accounts

☐   **E.** Statistical key figures

24. Which activities can you perform while you create cost center hierarchies? (There are two correct answers.)

☐ **A.** Append nodes and cost centers to a node of the standard hierarchy

☐ **B.** Assign a standard hierarchy to several controlling areas

☐ **C.** Create a cost center without specifying a standard hierarchy

☐ **D.** Reassign a cost center to another node of the standard hierarchy

25. Which characteristic controls the eligible cost element categories for G/L accounts in SAP S/4HANA?

☐ **A.** Field status group

☐ **B.** Account currency

☐ **C.** Account group

☐ **D.** Account type

26. Which configuration is possible when you assign multiple company codes to a controlling area in SAP S/4HANA?

☐ **A.** The company code currency may differ from the controlling area currency.

☐ **B.** The company code fiscal year variant may differ from the controlling area fiscal year variant in the number of special periods.

☐ **C.** The company code operational chart of accounts may differ from the controlling area operational chart of accounts.

☐ **D.** The company code fiscal year variant may differ from the controlling area fiscal year variant in the number of periods and number of special periods.

27. Which CO currencies can you use for evaluation when you use cross-company code cost accounting? (There are three correct answers.)

☐ **A.** Controlling area currency

☐ **B.** Company code currency

☐ **C.** Object currency

☐ **D.** Transaction currency

☐ **E.** Reference currency

Practice Question Answers and Explanations

1. Correct answer: **A**

   This question is referring to how an activity price is calculated and the quantity allocated. The activity price is calculated manually, and the allocation quantity is entered manually. Indirect means the calculation is carried out by the system.

2. Correct answers: **A, B, C**

   The master data components for cost center accounting can be grouped. Internal orders can also be grouped. Controlling areas cannot be grouped. All master data elements can be grouped, but controlling areas cannot be grouped.

3. Correct answer: **A**

   True. Cost elements are now formed in FI master data, but the cost element category is still required. These categories are the same as those used prior to SAP S/4HANA.

4. Correct answer: **A**

   The account type is a new master data field in SAP S/4HANA that is required for all accounts. The cost element category is required only if cost elements are created. The category is not required for FI balance accounts or income statement accounts. A cost object is not required until postings occur.

5. Correct answer: **A**

   True. Cost centers, profit centers, and business processes require assignments to a standard hierarchy. Other hierarchies can be built for cost center master data elements but are not required.

6. Correct answers: **A, C**

   In SAP S/4HANA, you can still use automatic account assignment with table OKB9. You can use a substitution to automatically set the cost object, but using master data is no longer an option. Validations just verify account assignments; they don't set account assignments.

7. Correct answer: **C**

   The accounts that are used in CO are part of the accounts called the operating chart of accounts. Other accounts may not be a part of daily operations, and these accounts would not be relevant to CO. FI may use other account charts for statutory reporting.

8. Correct answer: **C**

    The cost center category, a required setting, is a method of setting default parameters for a cost center. This category also assigns a key that can be used to include or exclude cost centers from activity type assignments.

9. Correct answer: **C**

    You have the option of reversing allocations in previous periods. A credit posting would be entered and new debit posting created, which would require opening prior periods. Even though allocations are CO relevant, many organizations don't want to allow adjustments after period-end close.

10. Correct answer: **A**

    True. Cost centers can allocate to all types of cost objects. The options available depend on the allocation method. Allocations can send value and quantities to other object types.

11. Correct answer: **B**

    False. Settlement is not possible for a cost center. Orders and projects can settle. Period-end settlement is a process that transfers a current period value to other objects or a G/L account. The detail is still visible, but the overall value of the object is 0.

12. Correct answer: A

    Non-operating costs are only available to FI. These income statement accounts are available for FI reporting when you don't want to include a cost object. The accounts become reconciling items between FI and CO.

13. Correct answer: **B**

    Manual reposting does not link to the original document, but reposting line items does. Reposted line items may link to the FI document and validate against it, but the values won't change. Manual repostings only create CO postings.

14. Correct answer: **C**

    SAP refers to activity-dependent cost as values that vary with changes in activity quantity. No settings distinguish between fixed costs and variable costs. When you post costs without reference to a quantity, these costs are always fixed.

15. Correct answers: **B, C**

    Periodic reposting, distributions, assessments, and indirect activity allocation all use the cycle segment methods. A cycle contains a set of allocation steps, called segments. Activity allocation directly assigns a quantity from a cost center to another cost object.

16. Correct answers: **C, D**

    Cycles cannot iterate with each other; only segments within a cycle can. Each segment only has one tracing factor. Different segments can have different allocation rules but still be assigned to the same cycle. Each segment has an independent set of senders and receivers. You can reuse cost objects and cost elements.

17. Correct answers: **C, D, E**

    Activity types only use secondary cost elements and are an internal allocation. Receivers are not limited to cost centers. The receiver is identified in the allocation process. The cost element category represents possible cost centers. The activity type category identifies how the allocation is executed and how the prices are calculated.

18. Correct answer: **C**

    The controlling area is the top level for overhead reporting. Company code is relevant to FI reporting. Cost center hierarchy is a master data grouping, not an organizational level. Operating concern is the top organizational element of CO, but the cost object is CO-PA.

19. Correct answers: **B, C**

    You would select the percentage method when you accrue activity-dependent costs and when you accrue activity-independent costs and if an appropriate cost element for defining overhead rates is available. Activity-dependent costs are used for the target = actual, since this process is based on quantity.

20. Correct answer: **B**

    False. Distribution is 1:1 primary, which means that the receiver will see everything the sender has as values. The correct option is assessment. Assessments group primary and secondary costs together. The receivers will only see the secondary cost element used for the assessment.

21. Correct answer: **B**

    You'll specify the standard hierarchy for cost centers when you define the controlling area is created. This setting is mandatory and identifies the hierarchy name required for all cost centers created in the controlling area.

22. Correct answers: **C, D**

    You can use an assessment to send primary and secondary costs to a secondary cost element in the receiver. The receiver only sees a secondary cost. Distributions and periodic repostings send only primary cost elements.

23. Correct answers: **B, D, E**

    Non-operating expense accounts are P&L accounts in FI only, so they cannot be allocated in CO. Indirect activity allocations can send activity quantities and prices. Balance sheets are not relevant to CO. Secondary cost elements can be allocated in an assessment. Statistical key figures can be used as a tracing factor.

24. Correct answers: **A, D**

    You can assign a cost center to a standard hierarchy node, but you cannot create new nodes. You can only have a cost center in one controlling area at a time. You cannot create a cost center without specifying a standard hierarchy.

25. Correct answer: **D**

    The new field account type controls what kind of account is being defined. Field status groups control how fields are treated on screen. Account currency doesn't affect CO. Account groups dictate number ranges and default settings.

26. Correct answer: **A**

    Both options (1:1 or *n*:1 company code to controlling area) have the same chart of accounts and fiscal year variant. The only separate posting between the two options is the company code currency, which may be different from the controlling area currency in the *n*:1 option.

27. Correct answers: **A, B, D**

    When assigning a company code-specific controlling area, if the controlling area and company code are in a 1:1 relationship, the currency must be the same. Normally, the object currency is the company code currency.

Takeaway

Cost center accounting, as the foundation for CO, provides tools for performing allocations to other objects at period end, with options to support different business requirements. Cost centers receive most of the primary cost postings from finance and in several cases, the cost center is the mandatory direct receivers of the expense, like asset depreciation. Cost centers should be considered as a permanent cost object. As a result, they are the central reporting structure for CO. Even though you can delete cost objects, a more desirable approach is to lock cost objects to support historical reporting.

Cost centers must be organized into a standard hierarchy. The grouping process is a key feature throughout CO. All cost center master data elements can be grouped. Most CO objects can be grouped, but in many cases, groups are optional. Groups can benefit reporting, change management, and allocations.

A variety of allocation options provide methods for cost centers to transfer cost to alternate cost objects that receive the benefit of the primary expenses. The choice of allocation method is up to you depending on the type of value to allocate (quantities or dollars) and the impact on the receivers.

Summary

The previous chapter laid the foundation of building the organizational structure to support CO. This chapter added to that structure by adding cost centers and cost element master data. Cost centers are the first cost objects that a business unit defines and, in some cases, represent the least expansive use of cost objects. Cost centers provide a general overview of cost usage. The downside of cost center reporting is the volume of data. Trying to find specific data transactions can be difficult and cumbersome.

The next chapter introduces the concept of internal orders, which are designed to capture a specific type of overhead costs. You'll also see many of the concepts discussed in this chapter applied to additional functions in the following chapters.

Chapter 4
Internal Orders

Techniques You'll Master

- Understand the four categories of internal orders
- Create and maintain internal orders
- Understand the requirements for commitment management
- Distinguish between planning and budgeting of internal orders
- Use an overhead costing sheet to debit an internal order
- Understand periodic settlement options

In this chapter, we'll review the design and purpose of internal orders, one of three cost objects in overhead management (CO-OM).

Real-World Scenario

As a controlling (CO) consultant, you'll need an understanding of the benefits of using internal orders as temporary cost objects. SAP's intention with internal orders was to provide a convenient cost collector for short-term events or projects. If your company is sponsoring a company picnic, for example, how could you effectively collect those various expenses and divide up the cost based on attendance? Creating a cost center for an event like this would be impractical. An internal order is an ideal way to post all costs against a single cost object and, through periodic settlement, pass on each receiver's share of the event.

As a CO consultant, you'll need to explain the options available for the configuration of the internal order type, which controls all order parameters, from the order number to the period-end settlement process. You may also need knowledge of how to use overhead costing sheets, which are commonly used with internal orders.

For period-end processing, passing order costs to other cost objects is typically confusing to end users. Having a firm foundation in the configuration of a settlement profile will give you the tools necessary for explaining this process and completing your system design.

Objectives of This Portion of the Test

The objective of this portion of the certification exam will test your understanding of customizing the core objects required for internal order accounting as well as test your understanding of its main business processes.

The certification exam expects you to have a good understanding of the following topics:

- Configure internal order types
- Configure order-related profiles
- Period-end closing activities

- Planning and budgeting
- Commitments
- Daily business operations in internal order accounting

> **Note**
> The internal order accounting topic makes up 8% – 12% of the total exam.

Key Concepts Refresher

In this chapter, we'll discuss the role of an internal order as a master record and order types, as well as describe the configuration that controls the internal order itself. We'll discuss how postings are made to an internal order, the process of internal orders in period-end close, and the optional planning and budgeting features.

Master Data

An *internal order* is a cost object in CO. Often, you may hear this object referred to as a "temporary cost object." The idea is to use these fairly simple cost objects for short-term events (like that company picnic) or even for small projects. Internal orders are not complicated and have far fewer dimensions than project systems (PS).

As the short-term event is taking place, costs are accumulated against the internal order master data in real time as the financial postings occur. At the end of the accounting period, or sometimes the end of the event, the internal order goes through a periodic process called *settlement*. During settlement, the costs collected on the order are assigned to a specific receiver object; settlement is a form of cost, or overhead, allocation.

Four categories of internal orders exist, defined by their usage:

- Overhead orders: These orders are used to collect costs, with settlement to other cost objects.
- Investment orders: These orders are used to collect costs, with settlement to fixed assets. This category may be integrated with investment management (IM) and plant maintenance (PM).
- Accrual orders: These orders are used in a unique design as an offsetting cost object for calculated, or accrued, values in CO.

- Orders with revenue: These orders can be integrated with sales and distribution (SD), or used only in CO, to collect cost and revenue, with settlement to any receiver.

To use internal orders, order management must be activated at the controlling area level, as shown in Figure 4.1.

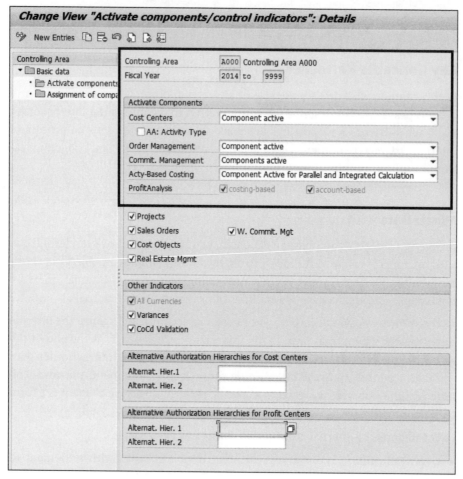

Figure 4.1 Activate Order Management for a Controlling Area

Let's walk through the configuration settings and create an internal order master record.

Internal Order Type

An internal order master record is created by first selecting an appropriate *order type*. All the control functions of the order type are then transferred to the internal order being created.

Order types are created and maintained in Customizing. Each order type represents certain control parameters that should align to a specific business process. For example, you could create an order type that allows settlement only to a fixed asset (this order type could then support assets under construction), or you could create an order type that allows settlement only to a cost center (this order type could then support overhead cost allocations).

An internal order type is created at the SAP client level (see Chapter 2), which means that all the controlling areas of a client can use the same order types.

As shown in Figure 4.2, an order type contains the following important control functions:

- **Number range interval**: This controls the number assigned to the internal order master record at creation. This range can be an internal or an external number range.
- **Settlement prof.**: This controls settlement routine of the internal order.
- **Planning Profile**: This controls how overall values are planned on the internal order.
- **Budget Profile**: This controls order spending by using the availability control feature.
- **Functional area**: This value will default to all orders created from the order type.
- **Model Order**: This function can be used to provide default field values when internal orders are created, for example, a default controlling area, company code, or profit center.
- **Commit. Management**: If selected, this order will be updated with commitments.
- **Revenue Postings**: If selected, orders can collect revenue via the cost element category of a transaction.
- **Integrated Planning**: If selected, orders will participate in integrated planning.
- **Status Profile**: This function controls the lifecycle of the internal order by determining which business transactions can be executed at which phase of the order. A user status profile can be assigned in this field if more control than standard SAP field status is required.

- **Release Immediately**: If selected, orders created will be set to the status REL (released) upon saving the new master record.
- **Order Layout**: This function can be used to control the presentation of the internal order master record, for example, by positioning groups of fields on the various tabs of the order.
- **Field selection**: This function can be used to set the status of the fields of the order master record.

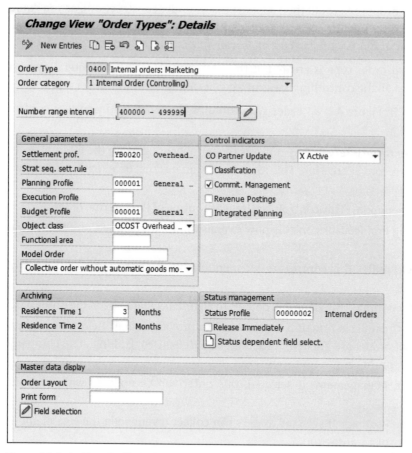

Figure 4.2 Order Type Configuration

Tip
Field status is used to identify fields that are to be hidden, displayed, required, or optional (HDRO), which determines priority in cases of conflict.

Status Management

The various profiles mentioned earlier are created independently of the order type and can be assigned to many order types. We'll review various profiles in later sections of this chapter, but for now, let's briefly explore the status profile. Other profiles have a specific use in certain business processes, but the status profile is important for the entire order lifecycle.

Let's first look at status management purely from a database management point of view. Eventually, master data objects and line item details in our system must be aged or archived simply to manage memory and storage resources. In plain words, you could define an order lifecycle in the following way:

1. Create the master data.

2. Accumulate business transactions.

3. Mark the master data for aging.

4. Mark the line item details for archiving.

In any ERP system, flags on objects and line items direct the system on how to manage that data.

> **Tip**
> What would "order lifecycle" mean within the daily business? Let's look at an example of creating an internal order to capture expenses related to creating a new marketing brochure. This event has a beginning, a middle, and an end. When the order is created at the beginning, perhaps a good idea would be to prevent the actual cost posting to the order until a supervisor has approved the event. Then, once the brochures are complete and all costs are accumulated, preventing any other costs from posting to the order would be paramount. A user status profile can be created to manage these business transactions.

All settings for the status profile are maintained in the Customizing menu.

First, let's discuss the indicators of SAP's standard example of order status, referred to as *system status*:

- **REL** (released): If this status is set, all business transactions can post against the internal order.

> **Warning!**
> If **REL** is not set, then no business transactions can be posted.

- **TECO** (technically complete): If this status is set, limited business transactions can post against the internal order, but no changes can be made to the planned order values.

- **CLSD** (closed): If this status is set, only a few activities are allowed, and no financial postings are allowed. Closed orders can be marked for deletion.

For many companies, these three system status indicators are enough. To activate system status, simply leave the status profile field blank in the order type. Figure 4.3 shows us an example of leaving the status profile field blank ❶ on an order type. To have the order status always set to **REL** upon creation of an order, you must also select the **Release Immediately** checkbox ❷.

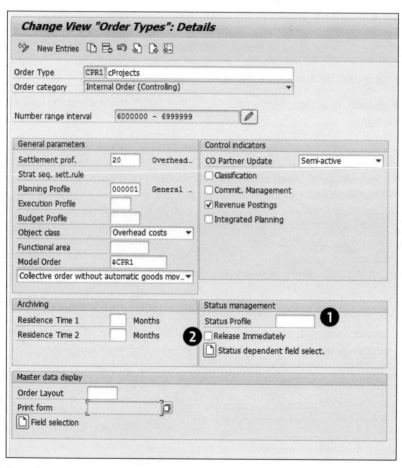

Figure 4.3 Order Type, Status Management Group without Status Profile

If more control is needed over the order lifecycle, then an optional *user status profile* can be created and assigned to the order type, as shown in Figure 4.4.

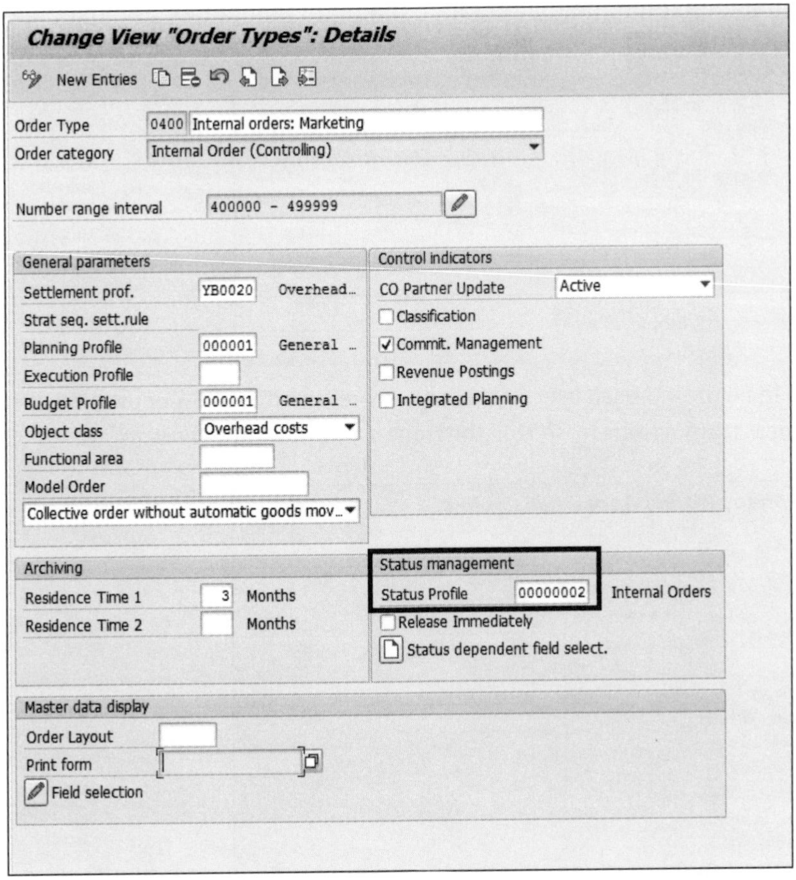

Figure 4.4 Order Type, Status Management Group with Status Profile

As shown in Figure 4.5, the user status profile and its rules allow you to define your own statuses by defining the following:

- User status and short text
- Indicator to set a status as the initial order status
- Lowest/highest status, which controls the subsequent status allowed

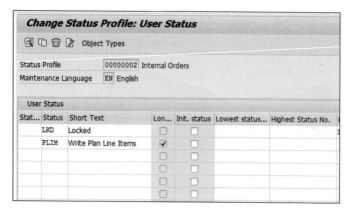

Figure 4.5 User Status Profile

As shown in Figure 4.6, each user status can be configured to allow or prohibit specific business transactions by setting the transaction control indicators.

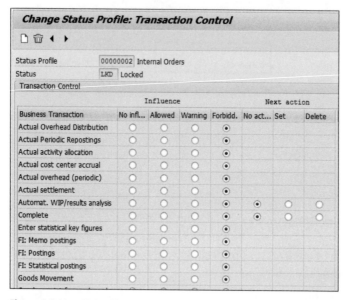

Figure 4.6 User Status Transaction Control

Tip

To prevent a business transaction from posting to an order, use the **Forbidd.** (forbidden) influence indicator in the user status profile.

Internal Order Master Record

Now that we've reviewed the configuration settings for internal orders, let's begin the process of creating an internal order. Internal orders are considered both master data and a cost object and are created on demand, whenever the business requirement exists.

Internal order master records can be created in several ways:

- Using the SAP GUI Transaction KO01
- Using the SAP GUI Transaction KO04
- Using the SAP Fiori app Manage Internal Orders

Using any of these methods, the first step is to enter a controlling area and use the dropdown menu to select an order type, as shown in Figure 4.7. Once selected, you cannot change the order type.

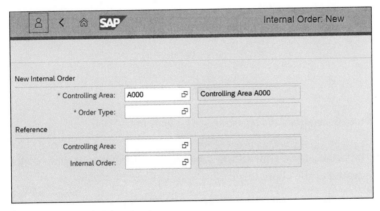

Figure 4.7 Internal Order: Create

In each method of order creation, you can also copy an existing order, which is referred to as "with reference." In this case, under the **Reference** heading, you would enter the **Controlling Area** and the number of the internal order master record from which you want to copy.

> **Note**
> Each internal order can be assigned to only one order type.

Figure 4.8 shows some details from the internal order master record for the **General Data** and **Organizational Assignments** data groups. Required fields are indicated with an asterisk (*).

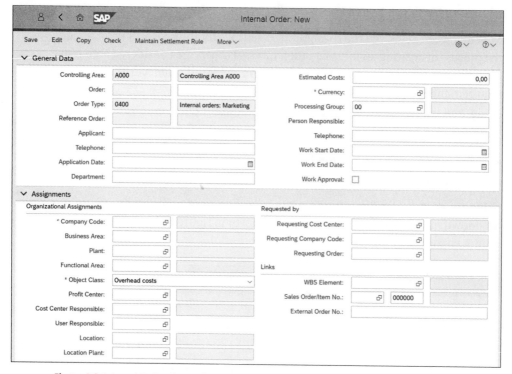

Figure 4.8 Internal Order: General Data and Organizational Assignments

You'll maintain the order at the controlling area level, with reference to an order type, which was created at the client level.

Key fields to fill out in the **General Data** section are as follows:

- **Controlling Area**: Identifies which controlling area the order is valid for.
- **Order**: The system will assign an order number from the number range assignment when the order is saved.
- **Order Type**: The order type was specified at order creation and cannot be changed from this view. If incorrect, exit and begin anew.
- **Currency**: Identifies the currency to be used in regard to the order. This field is required; if left blank, the default company code currency will be used.

For the **Assignments** section, fill out the **Company Code** field. This identifies for which legal entity the order is valid.

> **Warning!**
> A company code must be assigned to the controlling area entered in the **General Data** of the order; you'll won't be able to select a company code here.

The other fields in this group of the master data can be used to make assignments of the order to business area, profit center, and so on. If the order is a real (as opposed to statistical) cost object, the values entered on this order will be defaulted to the line item posted in each business transaction.

Figure 4.9 shows some details of the internal order master record for the **Status**, **Control**, and **Period-End Closing** data groups.

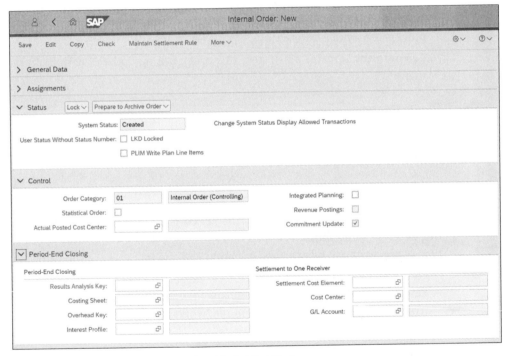

Figure 4.9 Internal Order: Status, Control, and Period-End Closing

Let's take a closer look at each group:

- **Status**
  In this data group, the settings from the **Status Profile** assigned to the **Order Type** are displayed. Once the order is saved, you may maintain the status manually in this group.

- **Control**

  In this data group we can indicate integration with cost centers, planning, and other components. It contains the following:

  - **Order Category**: This value defaulted from the order type and cannot be maintained.

  - **Statistical Order**: If selected, this order will be posted to as a statistical cost object.

  - **Actual Posted Cost Center**: If the **Statistical Order** box is selected, you can maintain the cost center to be posted to as a real cost object.

  - **Integrated Planning**: If selected, this order participates in integrated planning.

  - **Revenue Postings**: If selected, this order can collect revenue via the cost element category of a transaction.

  - **Commitment Update**: If selected, this order will be updated with commitments.

> **Tip**
>
> For commitments to be active, the controlling area must also have the commitment indicator selected as described in Chapter 2. The order type can then provide a default selection to activate commitments.

- **Period-End Closing**

  This data group is divided between the **Period-End Closing** and **Settlement to One Receiver** data groups. The data entered in this data group determines the type of processing to be executed at period end and includes the following key fields:

  - **Results Analysis Key**: This field will control valuation at period end. This is useful if the order contains revenue, or if work in process (WIP) is required for the order.

  - **Costing Sheet and Overhead Key**: This field will control the overhead calculation for the order.

  - **Interest Profile**: This field will control the interest calculation.

  - **Settlement Cost Element**: If there will be one, and only one, receiver of the order value during periodic settlement, then enter the cost element (category 21) in this field (see Chapter 3).

- **Cost Center**: If there will be one, and only one, cost center as receiver of the order value during periodic settlement, enter the cost center in this field.
- **G/L Account**: If there will be one, and only one, general ledger (G/L) account posted to during periodic settlement, enter the G/L account in this field.

> **Note**
> Settlement to one receiver is often referred to as "basic settlement." We'll review more detailed options for settlement, or "extended settlement," in the "Period-End Close" section.

Finally, as shown in Figure 4.10, additional data groups on the order master record include the following:

- **Investment Management**: If the order is integrated with inventory management (IM), those parameters can be entered in this data group.
- **Translation and Long Text**: Language translations, if applicable, will be located in this data group.
- **Change Documents**: This data group is an order-level change log.

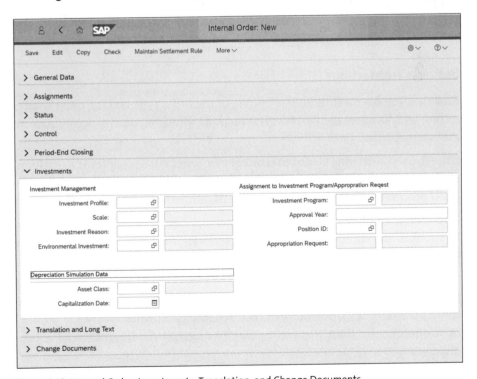

Figure 4.10 Internal Order: Investments, Translation, and Change Documents

Tip

Remember that the order layout of an order type determines what data groups and field statuses default from the order master record.

An internal order master record can be managed by creating order groups. Since the order number depends on the number range assigned in configuration, grouping similar orders together for reporting purposes can be helpful. Groups can be created using two methods:

- Manually using Transaction KOH1: If only a few orders need to be grouped together, you can enter each order number manually.
- Automatic collective processing using Transaction KOK4: If many orders should be grouped together, you can create a rule to automatically include orders in a group if the orders share the same profit center, for example.

In addition to collectively creating groups, Transaction KOK4 contains these additional features:

- Change order status
- Apply substitution rule

Business Transactions

Now that you have a firm understanding of the order type and the order master record, let's focus on the business transactions whose values will accumulate on the internal order.

If the G/L account being posted to is integrated with CO (see Chapter 3), a real (non-statistical) internal order can be entered on the line item of the posting to meet the FI-CO process integration (or CO account assignment) requirement.

Before reviewing the basics of posting financial transactions to internal orders, let's look at the status of an order once again. Figure 4.11 shows the status data group of an order master record. In this data group, the order status can be manually maintained.

Remember that the status profile controls this activity. To see how the transaction control works, click **Display Allowed Transactions**. As shown in Figure 4.12, a listing of business transactions that can be executed against the internal order is then displayed.

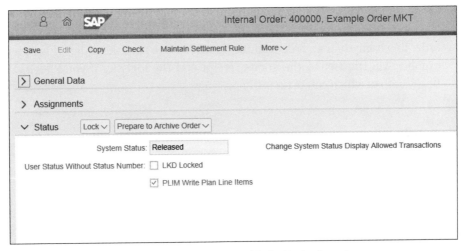

Figure 4.11 Order Status Group as Seen on the Internal Order Master Record

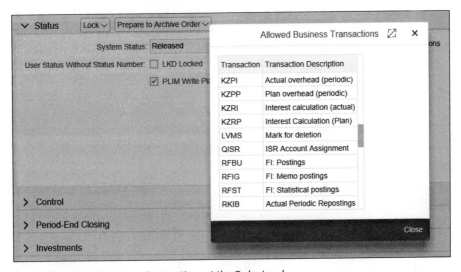

Figure 4.12 Allowed Business Transactions at the Order Level

Posting Integrated Transactions

As financial transactions are being recorded throughout the organization, internal orders are updated in real time—provided the order number was entered in the original FI document. So, exactly where can the internal order number be entered? The following are a few common examples:

- **On a purchase order line item**

  If the buyer enters an account assignment category F (order) on the purchase order line item, then an order number is required to save the order. This order number will transfer to the goods receipt and the logistics invoice verification—both of which create financial postings.

> **Note**
>
> If commitments are active on the internal order, the undelivered purchase order item value will be visible at the order level. This occurs prior to the goods receipt.

- **On a customer invoice**

  If integrated with sales and distribution (SD), the order number can default from the sales order line item. If not integrated, the order number can be manually entered in the FI accounts receivables invoice document.

- **On a vendor invoice**

  If integrated with purchasing, the order number can default from the purchase order (as described in Chapter 2). If not integrated, the order number can be manually entered in the FI accounts payables (AP) invoice document.

- **On a G/L manual posting**

  The order number can be manually entered for any G/L account number that is integrated with CO (see Chapter 3).

Figure 4.13 shows an example of the creation of a vendor invoice (not integrated with purchasing). Notice the internal order number is entered in the **Order** field for the G/L account **Purchased Services**.

> **Warning!**
>
> The internal order number used here must be assigned to the same company code entered in the line item of the FI document. If not, the user will receive an error message.

When the FI document is posted, all relevant data from the internal order master record is transferred to the posting. As shown in Figure 4.14, in our example, the profit center and business area were defaulted from the order for the expense line of **Purchased Services**.

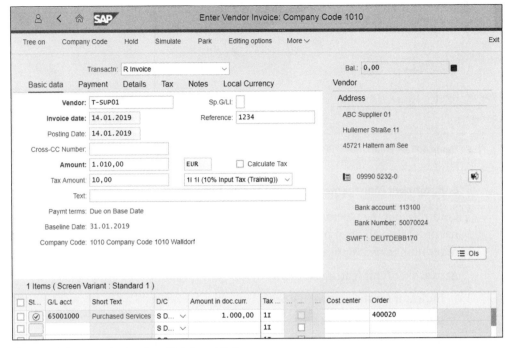

Figure 4.13 Enter Vendor Invoice with Internal Order

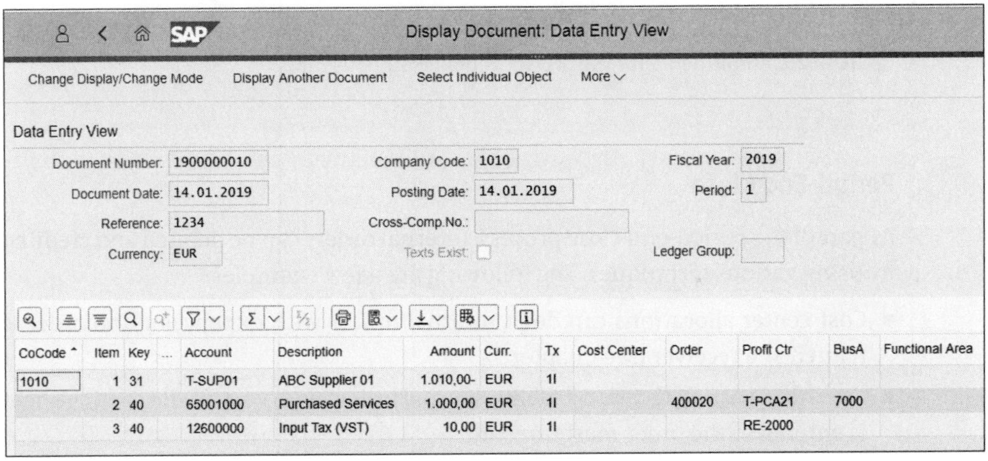

Figure 4.14 Vendor Invoice Posted with Internal Order

When the document is posted, the order information is updated in real time, as shown in Figure 4.15.

Order ▼▲	Order ▼▲	G/L Account ▲	G/L Account ▼▲	Actual Amount ▼▲	Plan Amount ▼▲	Difference ▼▲	%-Difference ▼▲
400020	New Product Brochure	Purchased Services	65001000	1.000,00 EUR		1.000,00 EUR	
Overall Result				**1.000,00 EUR**		**1.000,00 EUR**	

Figure 4.15 Internal Orders: Plan/Actual Report

Commitment Management

Commitment management is an optional feature that allows visibility on an internal order into all open purchase requisitions and purchase orders—provided the order number was entered in the purchasing document.

Activation of this feature is created by:

1. Indicator for the controlling area
2. Indicator for the order type
3. Indicator for the order master data

> **Tip**
> If you are managing a high-value capital project using an internal order, visibility of open purchase commitments for the project could be quite useful.

Period-End Close

As part of the period-end close process, internal orders can be debited and credited by using various techniques. The following are a few examples:

- Cost center allocations can debit internal orders with expenses if the order is named as a receiver (see Chapter 3).
- Overhead costing sheets can debit internal orders with costs if the costing sheet is entered in the order master record.
- Internal orders can be the sender of costs via periodic repostings (see Chapter 3).
- Internal orders can be the sender of costs through the settlement process.

> **Tip**
> As we look at overhead costing, keeping in mind the different "senders" and "receivers" of overhead could be useful. Any real cost object can be a sender/receiver. Think of this scenario as a realignment of responsibility: An internal order was used as a temporary cost object, but at period end, we could determine who is next responsible and transfer the cost to that receiver.

In this section, we'll walk through two key processes for period-end close.

Overhead Costing Sheet

This technique is commonly used to allocate costs in several CO components: cost center accounting, product costing, and internal orders.

Three main elements, or steps, determine the calculation for overhead costing:

1. The *calculation base* is used to identify the amount to which overhead is applied. This amount is expressed by cost elements.
2. The *overhead amount* indicates how much overhead to apply. This value can be expressed as a percentage or using a quantity-based method, and you can also distinguish between actual, plan, and even commitment amounts.
3. The *credit key* indicates the sender (either a cost center or an internal order) of the overhead. With the credit key, you can also identify the secondary cost element (category 41) for the posting to take place on when executed.

Let's look at an example. As shown in Figure 4.16, a simple overhead costing sheet consists of two rows:

- Row 10 defines the calculation base as **X00**.
- Row 20 defines the overhead amount as **Y00**, which is to be applied to the result of row 10. This row also defines the credit key as **Z00**.

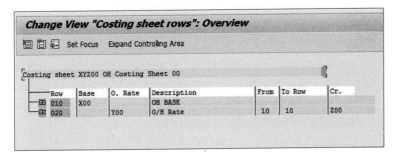

Figure 4.16 Overhead Costing Sheet

To better understand the calculation, let's look at the details found on the costing sheet, as shown in Figure 4.17.

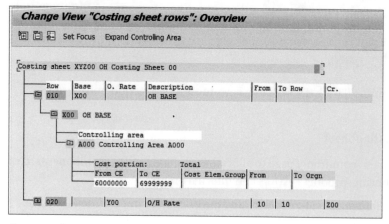

Figure 4.17 Overhead Base X00

By expanding row 10, as shown in Figure 4.17, you'll see the range of cost elements (from **60000000** to **69999999**) defines the calculation base of **X00**. If the internal order has any posted values to cost elements in this range, the total value will be the basis for the overhead calculation.

By expanding row 20, as shown in Figure 4.18, you'll see that the rate of 10% defines the overhead amount of **Y00** and that the credit key of **Z00** determines the cost element as **94111000** and the sender cost object as cost center **10101601**.

Tip
When creating an overhead amount key, you may use a dependency. In this example, the overhead type is the dependency. We could assign a different percentage for plan, actual, and commitments, and other dependencies are available.

How does SAP S/4HANA bring together these various components of a costing sheet? Let's look at a simple example:

1. If overhead costing sheet XYZ00 is assigned to the internal order master record
2. And the internal order has an actual posted value of $1,000 to cost element 60001000
3. Then the overhead amount will be $100 ($1,000 × 10%)
4. And the internal order will be debited $100, and cost center 10101601 will be credited all on cost element 94111000

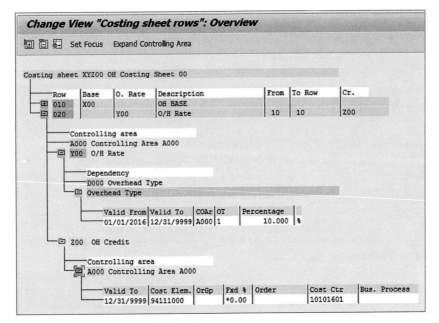

Figure 4.18 Overhead Rate Y00 and Credit Key Z00

Settlement

The last step in the period-end close process for internal orders is referred to as *settlement*. During the accounting period, the temporary cost collector has accumulated costs through actual postings. At period end, our task is to properly pass on to other cost objects their share of these costs.

> **Note**
>
> The settlement of internal orders is not mandatory.

Two settlement procedures are available in SAP:

- Simple settlement: Receiver information is entered on the **Prd-end closing** tab of the order, as shown in Figure 4.19.

- Extended settlement: Receiver information is entered in a *settlement rule*, where you can enter *distribution rules*, as shown in Figure 4.20. These distribution rules can be used to allocate costs to more than one receiver and are controlled by a *settlement profile* assigned to the order type.

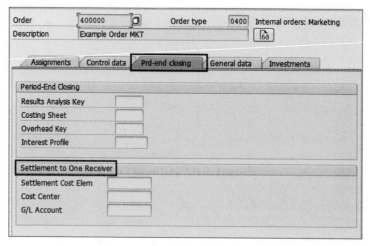

Figure 4.19 Simple Settlement

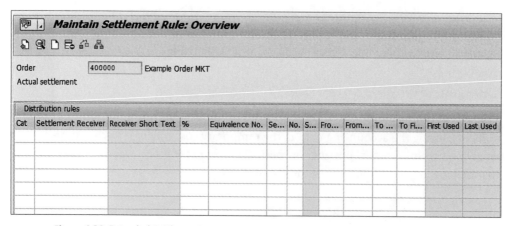

Figure 4.20 Extended Settlement

The settlement profile contains all control parameters for extended settlement and is entered in the **General parameters** section of the order type in configuration, as shown in Figure 4.21.

Tip

A single settlement profile could be assigned to many order types.

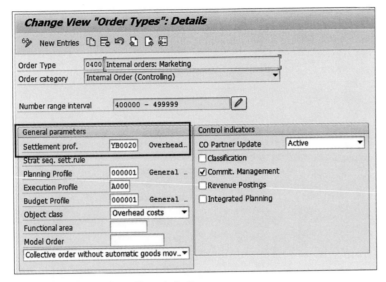

Figure 4.21 Settlement Profile in Order Type

The settlement profile, shown in Figure 4.22, controls the following:

- Determines if an order can be settled
- Indicates the appropriate receivers
- Assigns additional structures, if required
- Controls indicators that determine cost apportionment methods:
  - Percentages
  - Amounts
  - Equivalence numbers
- Determines the document type used in settlement posting
- Controls the number of distribution rules allowed

Warning!

Even if you're using simple settlement, you must have a settlement profile assigned to order types. If no settlement profile exists, the order will not be included in the period-end close settlement.

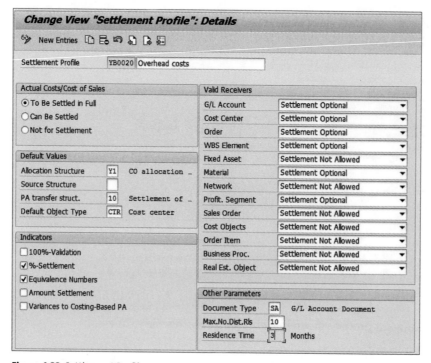

Figure 4.22 Settlement Profile

There are also the following three different structure types, which are assigned to the settlement profile:

- **Allocation structure**

  An *allocation structure* determines which cost elements will be posted to at settlement and is entered in the settlement profile. An allocation structure allows you to choose, by receiver type, either a secondary cost element or the original primary cost element, as follows:

  - For settlement internal to CO: The secondary cost element used for order settlement must have cost element type (category) 21 in its definition.

  - For settlement external to CO: The secondary cost element used for order settlement must have cost element type (category) 22 in its definition. This approach is usually seen when settling an asset for a G/L account.

  Figure 4.23 shows an example of an allocation structure that allows the use of a secondary cost element if the receiver is a fixed asset or a cost center. However, if the receiver is another order, you'll want to use the original cost element of the posted cost.

Allocation Structure	Y1	CO allocation structure
Assignment	040	Secondary costs
Controlling Area	A000	Controlling Area A000

Settlement cost elements

Receiver cat.	By cost element	Settlement Cost Elem	Name
FXA	☐	71115000	
CTR	☐	92112000	Order SettlCost
ORD	☑		

Figure 4.23 Allocation Structure

- **PA transfer structure**
  If you are settling to a costing-based profitability analysis (CO-PA) profitability segment, a CO-PA transfer structure (PA transfer structure) is required to map cost elements used to post settlement to value fields in CO-PA. You'll enter this value into the settlement profile.

- **Source structure**
  This structure allows you to group certain cost elements together for assignment to different receivers in the settlement rules. This structure can be assigned to the settlement profile or entered in the order master record.

> **Tip**
> Let's consider an example. Your order supports a training event. You have a requirement to settle internal personnel costs from the order to the human resources cost center, but any outside service costs should be settled to the training cost center. Use a source structure to group these different cost elements, then enter the distribution by receiver in the settlement rule.

Planning and Budgeting

Planning and *budgeting* are optional features that can be used with internal orders to monitor and control spending against an order. These features can be implemented alone or together.

Planning provides values to compare to actual cost. Often, planning is referred to as "funds requested." Budgeting provides a tighter control by preventing overspending. Often, budgeting is referred to as "funds approved."

Tip

To analyze plan/actual/variance for an order, you may want to plan spending by cost element. Then, using the information system plan versus actual can be analyzed.

To control spending for an order, you may want to create an overall budget and availability control with actions that determine how far over budget the values may go.

Planning

Planning can be performed for costs, activities, and business processes that will be incurred over the life of the order.

The levels of planning include:

- **Overall planning**
  This option is the simplest way to plan for an order. Values are planned at the order header level as overall and/or by year.

- **Primary/secondary cost planning**
  This option is the most commonly used scope. When you have detail about expected spending by cost element, the analysis of plan versus actual is the most meaningful.

  Within this scope, two methods are available:

  - Manual planning: Plan costs are entered manually into a planning layout by cost element, activity input, and revenue.

  - Automatic planning: Plan costs are calculated by use of an overhead rate, distribution, assessment, indirect activity allocation, process costs, and settlement.

- **Unit costing**
  This feature allows for a lower level of planning detail than overall planning.

- **Statistical key figures**
  Key figures such as headcount or square footage can be planned for use in reporting and periodic reposting.

A *planning profile* contains all planning parameters, as shown in Figure 4.24. Planning profiles are assigned to internal order types.

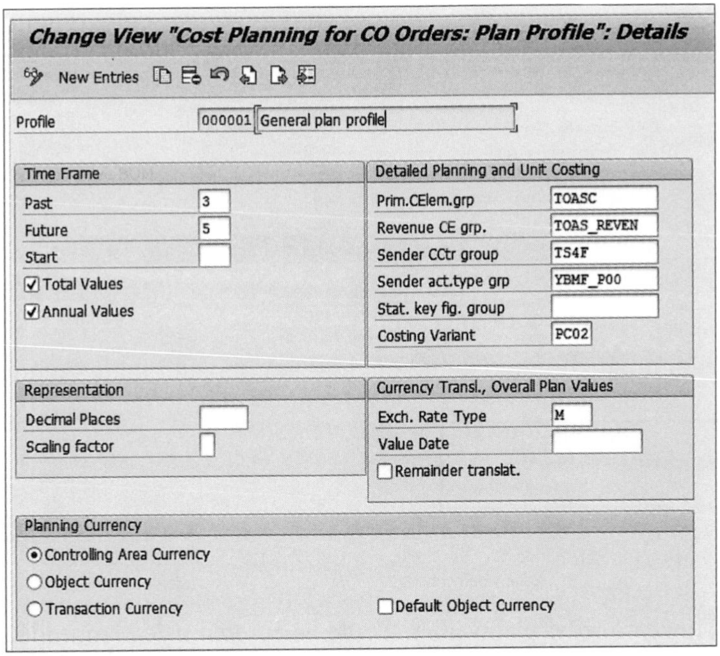

Figure 4.24 Planning Profile

Since planning is often an iterative process, you can use multiple *planning versions* to manage various plan assumptions. This method is the same version control referenced in Chapter 2, with version 0 always indicating actual values.

For planning purposes, two indicators in the version are important, as shown in Figure 4.25:

- The **Integrated Planning** checkbox allows plan values to be passed on to profit center accounting and special purpose ledgers.
- The **Integrated planning with cost centers/bus. processes** checkbox allows order planning to integrate with these components.

> **Tip**
> Order planning is only used for longer-term orders or large values. In other cases, order planning for each internal order would be impractical.

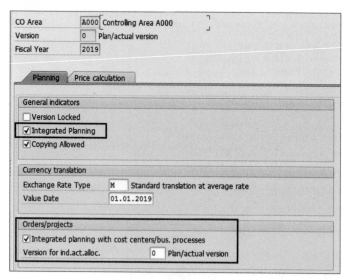

Figure 4.25 Planning Version Indicators

In SAP S/4HANA, internal order plan values should be entered using embedded SAP Business Warehouse (SAP BW) and SAP Analysis for Microsoft Office. This planned data can then be retracted.

Budgeting

Budgeting and availability control are features used to control the actual spending of an internal order. These features are popular when using orders to track capital expenditures and any other large-dollar events with a finite amount of funds available.

A *budget profile* must be created and assigned to the order type. All control parameters are found on this profile, including the activation type for **Availability Control**, as shown in Figure 4.26.

Availability control provides a system response when posting to an order based on three actions:

- Action 1: Warning to user
- Action 2: Warning to user and email to budget manager
- Action 3: Error to user

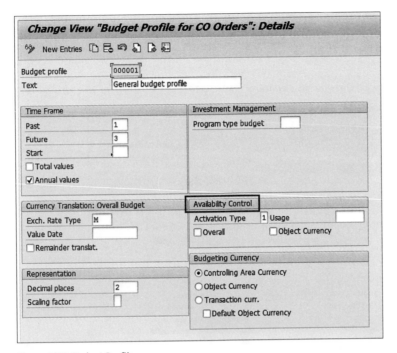

Figure 4.26 Budget Profile

Each of these actions can have a budget tolerance expressed as a percentage or an absolute variance, as shown in Figure 4.27.

COAr	Prof.	Text	Tr.Grp	Act.	Usage i...	Abs.variance	
A000	000001	General budget profile	++	1	95.00		
A000	000001	General budget profile	++	2	105.00		
A000	000001	General budget profile	++	3	115.00		

Figure 4.27 Availability Control Tolerance Limits

Note

Notice that the tolerance is assigned to a budget profile at the controlling area level.

For example, if an order has a budget of $1,000 and a posting is attempted in the amount of $951, the system will trigger a warning message to the user upon posting, as shown in Figure 4.28.

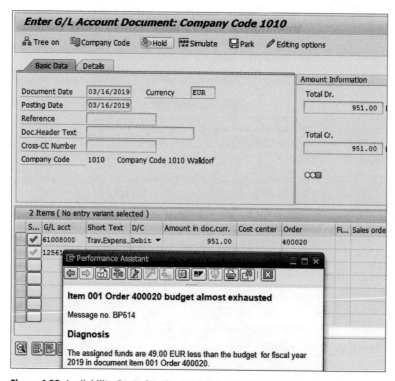

Figure 4.28 Availability Control Action 1 User Warning Message

If an order has a budget of $1,000 and a posting is attempted in the amount of $1,151, the system will trigger an error message to the user upon posting, as shown in Figure 4.29.

If action 2 is in use, you must also configure a budget manager in Customizing.

Tip

During configuration, you can exempt specific business transactions and cost elements from the availability control feature.

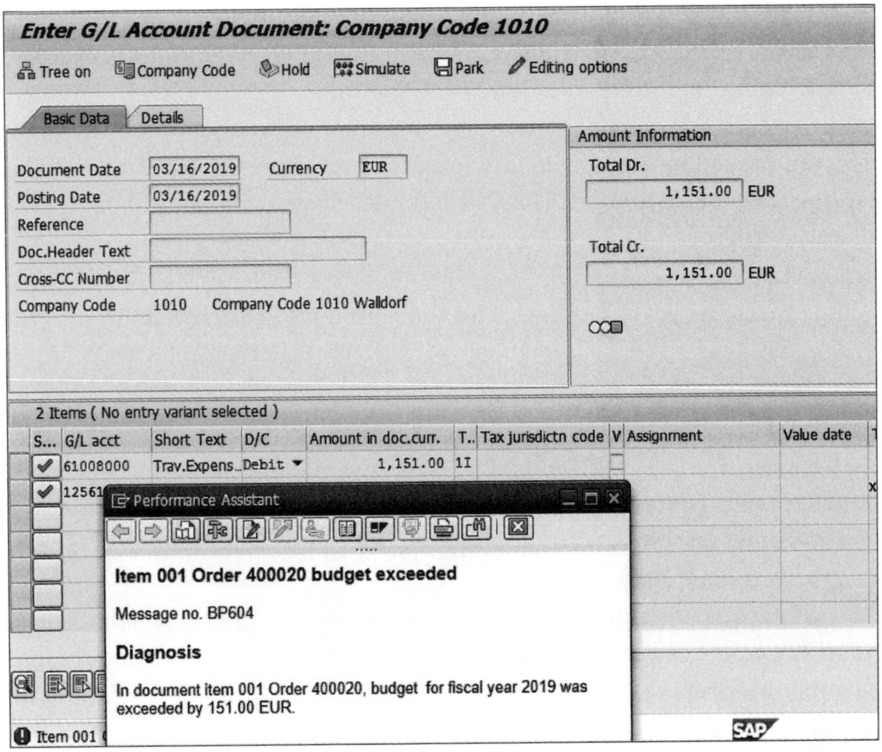

Figure 4.29 Availability Control Action 3 User Error Message

Important Terminology

In this chapter, the following terminology was used:

- **Allocation structure**
  An allocation structure controls how original cost elements are assigned to set-tlement cost elements.

- **Automatic collective processing**
  This kind of processing allows the grouping of multiple orders so that changes can be made at one time using substitution rules.

- **Availability control**
  This feature controls order spending based on tolerance to budget.

- **Budget profile**

  A budget profile controls a budget's settings such as timeframe, exchange rate, currency, and the activation of availability control.

- **Commitment management**

  This process can be used to identify future costs from existing purchase requisitions and purchase orders. This capability is activated at the controlling area level and by order type.

- **Internal order**

  An internal order is a cost collector for short-lived projects or events.

- **Order grouping**

  This flexible tool can manage orders, whether created manually or via automatic collective processing.

- **Order type**

  An order type contains all control parameters, including number range, for internal order master records.

- **Overhead costing sheet**

  The overhead costing sheet holds rules for applying overhead. Its three central elements are its calculation base, the overhead amount, and the percentage/quantity-based approach.

- **Planning level**

  The planning level determines how much detail is used to plan order cost. The three levels are overall, primary/secondary costs, and unit costing.

- **Planning profile**

  A planning profile contains all control parameters for overall planning and is assigned to the order type.

- **Settlement**

  This process is a periodic pass through of order costs to other receivers.

- **Settlement profile**

  A settlement profile contains all control parameters that govern the settlement process.

- **Source structure**

  A source structure controls the settlement to different receivers based on original cost.

- **Status profile**

  A status profile controls which business transactions are valid during the order lifecycle.

Practice Questions

These practice questions will help you evaluate your understanding of the topics covered in this chapter. The questions shown are similar in nature to those found on the certification examination. Although none of these questions will be found on the exam itself, they will allow you to review your knowledge of the subject. Select the correct answers and then check the completeness of your answers in the "Practice Question Answers and Explanations" section. Remember that on the exam you must select all correct answers and only correct answers to receive credit for the question.

1. At what organizational level are internal orders created?

□   **A.** SAP client

□   **B.** Company code

□   **C.** Controlling area

□   **D.** Operating concern

2. True or False: Internal orders can be used to collect revenue.

□   **A.** True

□   **B.** False

3. If activated, availability control offers which benefit?

□   **A.** Used to notify the budget manager that budget is depleted

□   **B.** Uses plan values to create a budget

□   **C.** Used with postings to update commitments

4. Where do you activate commitment management for internal orders? (There are two correct answers.)

□   **A.** Controlling area

□   **B.** Company code

□   **C.** Order type

□   **D.** Budget profile

5.   Which of the following are features of SAP system status? (There are two correct answers.)

☐   **A.** Controls the lifecycle of an order

☐   **B.** Can be configured

☐   **C.** Requires a status profile

☐   **D.** Determines which business transactions can post to an order

6.   Which of the following does the budget profile control?

☐   **A.** Planning level

☐   **B.** Availability control

☐   **C.** Allocation structure

7.   Which of the following are assigned to an order type? (There are three correct
     answers.)

☐   **A.** The number range for orders

☐   **B.** The description of the order

☐   **C.** General parameters for settlement, planning, and budgeting

☐   **D.** The profit center of the order

☐   **E.** The status profile

8.   Tolerance limits are assigned to which organization level?

☐   **A.** Order type

☐   **B.** SAP client

☐   **C.** Controlling area

9.   Which of the following are organizational assignments contained in the order
     master? (There are three correct answers.)

☐   **A.** Company code

☐   **B.** Order type

☐   **C.** Controlling area

☐   **D.** Business area

☐   **E.** Cost center

10. Which of the following can be a receiver for an internal order settlement? (There are three correct answers.)

   ☐ **A.** A fixed asset
   ☐ **B.** A settlement profile
   ☐ **C.** A general ledger (G/L) account
   ☐ **D.** A cost object
   ☐ **E.** A statistical key figure

11. True or False: Planning for internal orders is required in SAP S/4HANA.

   ☐ **A.** True
   ☐ **B.** False

12. When using budgeting and availability control for internal orders, at which action is an email sent to the budget manager?

   ☐ **A.** When the original budget is entered on the order
   ☐ **B.** When spending on the order will exceed the third tolerance limit
   ☐ **C.** When spending on the order will exceed the second tolerance limit

13. Which feature can be used to settle certain costs to different receivers?

   ☐ **A.** Settlement profile
   ☐ **B.** Source structure
   ☐ **C.** PA transfer structure

14. Which element of an overhead costing sheet identifies the sender of the overhead?

   ☐ **A.** Calculation base
   ☐ **B.** Credit key
   ☐ **C.** Overhead amount

15. Which setting controls where fields are positioned on the internal order master record?

☐ **A.** Status profile

☐ **B.** Field selection

☐ **C.** Order layout

Practice Question Answers and Explanations

1. Correct answer: **C**
   Orders are created within a controlling area. In the header of the order, you can then assign a company code and other organizational structures, but the initial creation is by controlling area.

2. Correct answer: **A**
   True. If the order type has the revenue checkbox selected, the orders that are created with this order type can then be used to collect revenue. Remember a checkbox for revenue on the order master record is also available.

3. Correct answer: **A**
   The purpose of availability control is to define the usage limits of a budget based on three actions. The second action triggers a notice to whomever is identified as the budget manager.

4. Correct answers: **A, C**
   First, the controlling area must have commitment management activated. Next, the order type can indicate which commitments are in scope.

5. Correct answers: **A, D**
   These activities are features of SAP-controlled system statuses. The remaining choices refer to a user status, which can be configured to meet specific requirements.

6. Correct answer: **B**
   The budget profile determines the activation type for availability control.

7. Correct answers: **A, C, E**
   Each order type contains all control parameters for creation of the internal order master data. The controls include a number range; profiles for settlement, planning, and budgeting; and a profile to control the status of the internal order. Order description and profit center are fields on the internal order master data.

8. Correct answer: **C**

   Each budget profile can have its own tolerance limits, but they are assigned at the controlling area organization level.

9. Correct answers: **A, C, D**

   An internal order is created by entering a controlling area and an order type. Of these two objects, only the controlling area is considered an organizational assignment. In the **General Data** section of the internal order, you can make the additional organizational assignments of company code and business area. You can also enter a responsible cost center, but this information would be considered master data, not an organizational assignment.

10. Correct answers: **A, C, D**

    The settlement profile assigned to the order type can allow an order to settle to other cost objects or to master data in FI. Of the possible answers, only fixed assets, G/L accounts, and cost objects could act as receivers.

11. Correct answer: **B**

    False. Planning is an optional feature for internal orders. Typically, we plan for orders that require significant spending or need to be managed over a long period of time.

12. Correct answer: **C**

    Three actions are triggered by spending compared to budget: action 1 sends a warning message to the user when the first budget tolerance limit has been reached; action 2 sends a warning message to the user and an email to the budget manager when the second budget tolerance limit has been reached; action 3 sends an error message to the user when the third budget tolerance limit has been reached.

13. Correct answer: **B**

    The source structure allows for the grouping of cost elements to be assigned to different receivers at settlement. The PA transfer structure is used when settling to costing-based CO-PA. Both of these structures are assigned to the settlement profile.

14. Correct answer: **B**

    The components of the overhead costing sheet are the calculation base, which determines the amount to calculate the overhead on; the overhead amount, which determines how much overhead to apply; and the credit key, which determines which cost object is the sender of the overhead as well as the secondary cost element for posting.

15. Correct answer: **C**

    The order layout can be used to position the tabs and fields of orders in a specific way. You can create different order layouts for each customer requirement and for each order type.

Takeaway

In this chapter, we focused on using internal orders as cost objects. We began with a review of how to activate internal orders at the controlling area level and discussed the four categories of internal orders: overhead, investment, accrual, and with revenue.

Next, we looked at the most important configuration object—the order type. Order types are aligned to specific business processes by the controls assigned. Each order type can use different rules, or profiles, to determine how to manage the business processes of settling, planning, and budgeting internal orders. Each profile has its own indicators relevant to the specific business process.

You should now understand how to create an order master record and the basics of the value flow from financial transactions to internal orders, including optional features to measure commitments. The period-end close process, which the optional use of an overhead costing sheet, was also reviewed, and we covered the periodic settlement of orders.

Armed with this information, you should be well equipped to meet the objectives of this portion of the test.

Summary

Internal orders offer a flexible cost collector for short-term projects and events, and a solid understanding of internal orders is necessary to meet your customers' requirements. You should now understand the most common configuration settings, as well as how to manage the order lifecycle.

This chapter completes our review of the components of CO-OM. Now, we can move on to the next component: product cost planning. In the next chapter, you'll learn what objects are needed in configuration to create material cost estimates for product cost planning.

Chapter 5
Product Cost Planning

Techniques You'll Master

- Explain product cost planning tools
- Explain overhead application
- Describe material cost estimates
- Integrate key master data with cost estimates
- Explain master data selection criteria
- Create a material cost estimate
- Update standard prices
- Execute a costing run
- Explain costing variant components
- Explain cost component structure
- Describe overhead tools
- Explain transfer control

Now that you've learned the key components of overhead cost controlling, in this chapter, those concepts will now be applied to product cost planning. You'll gain an understanding of the key costing tools and their application. We'll describe how costing works through costing variants. You'll gain the ability to define master data inputs and prices and thus provide costing information to your business. Once you understand how the costing is performed, you can determine which material prices to change.

Real-World Scenario

To successfully execute cost planning, you must become skilled at understanding and decoding logistics master data. You should comprehend how changes in logistics data will impact costing, since rarely do owners of this master data know how their data influences costing. You'll need an intricate understanding of their data to help translate data requirements. Master data may work appropriately for the logistics team but can cause issues for the costing team.

You may also find that, on occasion, logistics configuration will affect product costing results. For this reason, you'll need to work closely with the logistics team to provide the vital technical settings to achieve the expected costing results. A minor change in a logistics area can cause exceptional changes to costing results. On many occasions, you may find difficulties meeting the technical requirements of all your team members. The challenge is that technical settings that meet the needs of logistics teams could negatively impact costing. Again, translating your requirements to other teams will be your responsibility. You'll need to learn how to be diplomatic to balance the competing needs of various data owners against your need to control impacts on costing.

The results of product cost planning can impact values in the financial balance sheet during standard settings. You'll need to communicate with the finance team and possibly liaison between logistics and finance to ensure accurate costing results.

Objectives of This Portion of the Test

This portion of the certification exam covers the cost planning and material pricing process. The certification exam expects you to have a good understanding of the following topics:

- Define the technical settings for cost planning
- Define the master data structure
- Explain price strategies
- Explain overhead application options
- Define and set up costing variants
- Apply various costing tools

> **Note**
> This product cost planning topic makes up more than 12% of the exam and is also critical to understanding topics later in this book.

Key Concepts Refresher

Product costing planning is the initial process for cost object controlling and is the initial step in setting standard prices for materials. Product cost planning creates cost estimates. A cost estimate is composed of a group of costing items, mainly materials, labor, and overhead. Cost estimates can be used for many purposes beyond standard price setting. An individual material could have many different cost estimates depending on the cost analysis being performed. These estimates can be used for pricing, productivity, seeking alternative methods, determining cost of goods sold (COGS) and cost of goods manufactured (COGM), inventory valuation, and determining cost origins.

Depending on the planning methods you're using, cost estimates can be created manually or automatically. A key element of cost estimating is what's called a *quantity structure*, which refers to the master data that contains the data structures and the items' quantities used for the cost estimate. Once you have a quantity structure, prices can be applied. In this chapter, we'll incorporate the cost center and activity type from cost center accounting to apply labor and overhead costs. We'll review numerous types of logistics master data that provide the quantity structure for costing and provide an overview of key master data fields and how they impact the costing process. Once you've grasped the foundation of master data, we'll walk through key configuration steps while executing a cost estimate for single items or multiple items through the costing run.

Product Cost Planning Methods

Product cost planning has methods designed for all phases of product development. Which planning method you select will depend on where you are in terms of master data creation, available product details, engineering details, prototype information, or product simulation. These tools are designed to develop cost estimates early in the product cycle and continue to be used throughout the product's life. You can also compare cost details throughout each phase. The different planning methods begin with little or no data where the cost estimates are created manually, through development of complete master data that can be used to automatically create cost estimates. The following costing methods can be used:

- **SAP Product Lifecycle Costing**
  SAP Product Lifecycle Costing is an SAP HANA-based solution to incorporate data from an SAP ERP system or many other data sources. SAP Product Lifecycle Costing allows costing data to be developed early in the product development cycle. This solution uses a Microsoft Excel-like tool to determine costs when quantity structure details have not been defined. You can use SAP Product Lifecycle Costing early in the product lifecycle to create cost estimates and perform simulations. If data exists, it can be used to develop a cost estimate. Even without data, you can use this solution to define estimated costs. SAP Product Lifecycle Costing can create costing sheets for overhead and provide cost component views, in addition to item views, and can be used for future comparisons, pricing, quotations, and product collaboration.

Note
As a separate tool that can operate independently of ERP processes, SAP Product Lifecycle Costing is beyond the scope of this book, which focuses on tools within the SAP S/4HANA area.

- **Costing without quantity structure**
  Material cost estimates without quantity structure can be created once a material master record exists. This process uses unit costing to create a cost estimate, and the process is mostly manual. Like SAP Product Lifecycle Costing, existing master data can be used when available. This process is used further along the development process. When a material record exists, standards can be set, or

the data can be used for comparisons with other cost estimates. You can create cost estimates for raw materials or assemblies as well as create both single-level or multilevel cost estimates. We'll discuss costing without quantity structure further in the "Cost Estimate without Quantity Structure" section.

- **Costing with quantity structure**
Costing with quantity structure is used to develop planned cost and can also set prices for materials without reference to orders. You can use the results of material cost estimates with a quantity structure to valuate materials at standard prices. Before a cost estimate can be created, logistics quantity structure data must exist. The cost estimate is created automatically. We'll discuss costing with quantity structure further in the "Cost Estimate with Quantity Structure" section.

Product Cost Planning Basics

Product cost planning is part of product cost controlling and can be used without reference to other cost objects. You can use product cost planning to analyze your product costs for tangible items or intangible items like services. Key questions answered by product cost planning include the following:

- What is the value of specific materials?
- What is the cost of production process steps?
- What does the value add from at different organizational units?
- What are additional overhead costs?
- What are the most cost effective procurement methods?
- How can processes be improved?

These questions can be answered through individual cost estimates. A cost estimate contains all relevant costing details. Each cost estimate is based on a costing variant and a list of costing items. A cost estimate can be built with minimal master data, which requires significant manual effort, or created automatically with extensive master data. Cost estimates have three main views:

- **Cost component split**
You can define the cost component split, which summarizes costs into categories you design. A component may include one or more cost elements. A cost element can be further broken down into different categories. These components can be defined as either COGM, which is used for valuing inventory for manufactured components, or COGS. The COGS view can be transferred to profitability analysis (CO-PA) for use in determining product profitability (see Chapter 7).

- **Itemization**
  The itemization view is created automatically from the categorization of costing items. The itemization view also contains cost elements. The master data included in each item is determined by the item category. Items may contain a material, plant, cost element, quantity, unit of measure, price, fixed value, description, activity type, and currency information. At a minimum, an item will contain a description, a quantity, a cost element, and a price.

- **Costing structure**
  The costing structure, or the indented view, shows the relationship between lower-level items and upper-level assemblies. A costing structure can be built manually with a multilevel unit cost estimate or through a bill of material (BOM) in material costing with quantity structure. The structure represents a "parent" material with lower-level "child" materials, labor, and overhead.

The foundation of cost estimates are costing items. Each costing item type represents a different type of costing information. Costing items can be entered manually, such as adding a labor value directly, or derived automatically through a routing and work center.

Costing Items

Each cost estimate contains a group of costing items. A costing item has a category that will determine specific costing details. The data needed to complete a costing item is defined by the item's category. Item category is a term used throughout CO and is useful for defining and classifying details. Costing items can be divided into three groups:

- **Modifiable**
  Modifiable items allow user input to direct the cost details. An example is "M" for material. The user determines the plant, material, and quantity. The system then values the material and extends the value by the item quantity.

- **Special**
  Special items will be controlled automatically by SAP. If relevant conditions are met, a value is updated. For example, let's say item type G needs a costing sheet. If the conditions of the costing sheet are met, the system adds overhead.

- **Formulas**
  Formula are mathematical calculations. If a cost estimate is created manually, formulas can be entered by your users. SAP uses Boolean logic to build formulas.

At this point, you should understand that, to use product cost planning, you must have a costing variant. At a minimum, the costing variant must contain a costing type and a valuation variant, as shown in Figure 5.1. The costing type identifies the technical attributes for the costing process. The valuation variant identifies the logic to choose a price for the costing items. We'll discuss costing variants in more detail in the "Product Cost Planning Configuration" section.

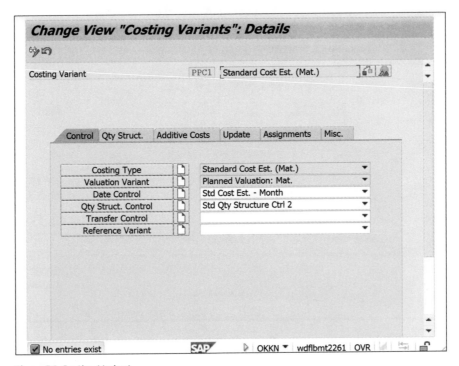

Figure 5.1 Costing Variant

Costing Sheet

The most basic type of overhead application is a costing sheet, which can be used to add costs to materials as well as to cost objects. Think of a costing sheet as a simplified spreadsheet that can add value to materials. A costing sheet is simple to apply but only contains basic logic. As shown in Figure 5.2, a costing sheet contains a set of codes that represents values for three basic elements:

- **Base**: The base identifies cost element values that exist in the cost estimate. If they are present, then the costing sheet will add overhead.

- **Overhead**: The overhead is a percentage of additional value added to the cost estimate. Overhead is also dependency relevant. Think of dependency as a rule about how to dispense overhead. The broadest application of overhead is using an overhead type, which is applied every time the costing sheet is accessed. The most specific application of overhead is using an overhead key; in this case, overhead is only added when the key is assigned to a material.

- **Credit**: The credit represents the sender of overhead (the provider).

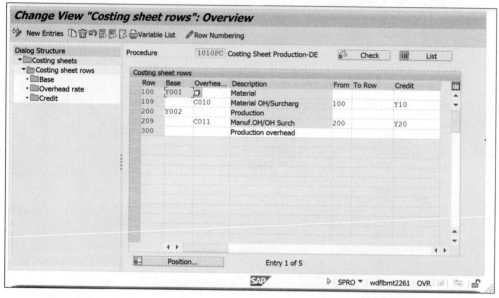

Figure 5.2 Costing Sheet

Let's consider an example of a material-handling cost center providing production with material support. Assume our costing sheet features the following lines:

- **Base Y001**: Material cost elements in the cost estimate = $10
- **Overhead C010**: 10%
- **Credit Y10**: Cost center ML101 (sender/overhead provider)

The calculation would be as follows:

- Overhead calculation: $10 × 10% = $1 overhead
- Credit to sender cost center ML1010: $1
- Debit to material cost estimate: $1

Product Cost Planning Configuration

The configuration for costing is intricate. As you'll see in this section, a costing variant is designed in layers, with each layer addressing a different tier of data. To ensure that a costing variant is complete and accurate, the most practical way to create costing variants is to copy and change a variant provided by SAP. Whenever a costing variant is changed, you should test it extensively before releasing it to production.

Costing Variant

Costing variants contain the control parameters for executing a costing process to create cost estimates. Cost estimates can be used for different purposes. Each use will require different costing parameters and, therefore, different variants.

A costing variant consists of client-level information and can be valid for all plants in all company codes. The first level of the costing variant, shown in Figure 5.3, describes various components that control costing functions, such as costing uses, prices, valid dates, and data transfer control.

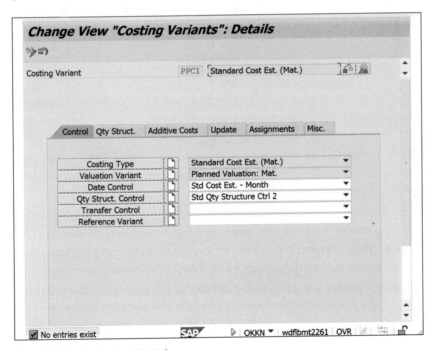

Figure 5.3 Costing Variant Control

Let's first walk through the main tabs:

- **Control**

  The **Control** tab shows the different components in the costing variant. Each selection box has a subset of criteria to control how costing will work.

- **Qty Struct.**

  These settings control whether the costing lot size of the parent part will be used to cost lower-level parts or whether lower-level materials should use their own costing lot sizes. These settings also contains a designation that allows users to override transfer control. You can also control how cost estimates without quantity structure or cost estimates with errors are treated.

- **Additive Cost**

  Additive costs is a feature using unit cost estimates. Additive cost estimates are created manually but provide the flexibility to use specific costs in an automatic cost estimate. This setting determines whether existing additive cost estimates will be included during costing execution.

- **Update**

  In this area, you can define whether the estimate can be saved, whether the dates of an estimate can be changed by a user, whether an itemization is created, and whether the error log is saved. Notice that the cost component view is not an option. The cost component view is required for CO-PA, so it is always saved.

- **Assignments**

  In this area, you'll connect a cost component structure to your costing variant, activate costing versions, and activate cross-company code costing. This area contains the following fields:

  - **Cost Component Structure**: A cost component structure is assigned to each company code. The details of the cost component structure will be discussed later in this section.

  - **Costing Version**: A total of 99 costing versions can be defined daily to cost estimates. During the marking allowance process, one version is defined for standards. Only cost estimates with this version can be used for standards, other versions are used for cost analysis.

  - **Cost Comp. Split in Controlling Area Currency**: In this field, you can activate an alternate currency.

  - **Cross-Company Costing**: Cost estimates can be created and pass values across plants and company codes, but only in the controlling area. This option must first be activated to allow transfers across legal entities.

- **Misc.**

  In this area, you'll indicate how error logs should be handled. Options include online only, log/save/mail, log/save, and log message only.

Under the **Control** tab are key segments in a costing variant. As mentioned earlier, not all components are required. In this tab, you'll configure the components required for your costing needs:

- **Costing Type**

  The costing type is a key setting that restricts how a costing variant can be used by identifying the type of costing being performed. A costing type is not restricted to a single variant but will dictate the type of cost estimates that can be created from the costing variant. A costing type contains the following fields:

  - **Price Update**: Price field in the material master to update and to calculate valuation to post.
  - **Save Parameter**: Start date for cost estimate and additive cost estimate.
  - **Misc.**: Value in the cost estimate to use for costing sheet overhead and partner cost component to activate.

- **Valuation Variant**

  In general, the valuation variant contains all the prices to use with the costing items. A valuation variant can be defined at the costing variant level or the plant level. Each item type has a strategy to determine the price to value the elements of the quantity structure. The system will evaluate each level until it finds a valid price. If a price can't be determined, an error message will be issued. The following details in the cost estimate will define the source of the price for each item:

  - **Material Value**: These settings define the strategy to value M costing item types. In the purchasing event, information is selected then a substructure must also be defined. The system will read the primary strategy, unless it encounters a purchasing price, in which case the system will move to the substructure.
  - **Activity Type/Processes**: The activity price and CO version can be defined in these settings.
  - **Subcontracting**: The price for external assembly is derived from purchasing price data. Once a price category has been selected, a substructure must be defined.
  - **Ext. Processing**: External labor can be valued from data entered in the routing operations or through purchasing prices.

- **Overhead**: There are two settings available for the costing sheet (defined earlier in the chapter). You have the option of choosing a separate calculation base for assemblies and procured items.

- **Misc.**: In this selection, you can set an overall factor to apply, which can be useful for inventory costing.

- **Date Control**

  In this area, you'll determine the dates to begin and end a cost estimate. You'll also define a date for a valid quantity structure and a date for valuation prices.

- **Qty Struct. Control**

  The quantity structure process will be discussed in more detail in the "Cost Estimate with Quantity Structure" section. The setting in this area dictates what master data to use when multiple options exist. A cost estimate must find appropriate master data that falls on a valid date:

  - BOM: Sequence to arrive at a BOM. The strategy defines a set of rules and whether the production planning data strategy will be used or overridden.

  - Routing: The sequence to determine a valid task list or routing.

- **Transfer Control**

  Transfer control dictates how existing costing data will be used, if at all. In this section, you can assign a transfer control. The specific settings will be defined in the "Transfer Control" section. The transfer control logic influences whether the system will re-create costing data or transfer current values into the cost estimate. If a valid transfer control is not defined, then the system recosts the structure by exploding the quantity structure and revaluing the costing items.

- **Reference Variant**

  A reference variant is a special form of transfer control. You can define the elements of a cost estimate to transfer. Like transfer control, the system must first determine if transfer details are valid.

Main Cost Component

The main cost component structure has multiple cost components, as shown in Figure 5.4, which make up the cost component structure identified in the costing variant. Each cost component is assigned to one or more cost elements. Cost components should include all the cost elements that occur in a cost estimate. If you don't include all cost elements, then the different costing views will not be equal.

Each cost component has a setting identifying it as either a variable or both fixed and variable, as shown in Figure 5.5. The components are also assigned to a view.

COGM are components included in FI stock valuation, or the value is included in COGS. You can also include items in commercial or tax inventory price valuation.

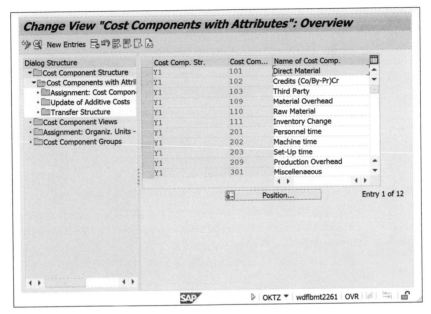

Figure 5.4 Cost Components

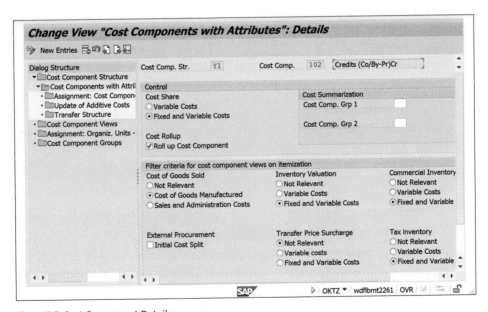

Figure 5.5 Cost Component Details

As shown in Figure 5.6, you can see the flow from costing items to cost components. This flow is followed for all costing items.

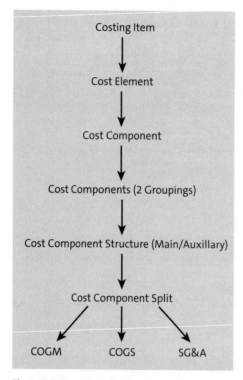

Figure 5.6 Cost Component Flow

> **Note**
>
> During cost element determination for costing items, the system uses automatic account determination. In many areas, the SAP system contains a set of logical steps to determine an account number automatically, referred to as automatic account determination. The logic defined in the materials management (MM) area provides cost elements for the costing process.

Cost elements are derived based on the category of the costing items. The system determines cost elements for costing item by following this logic:

- Each costing item contains an item category. The item category dictates the type of master data required for the line item and is used, in conjunction with master data, to determine a cost element.

- The cost element for each costing item will be entered manually or automatically by the system. The source of cost elements for different item categories is as follows:
  - **M – Stock Material/Plant**: Material master record → valuation class → automatic account determination in configuration
  - **M – Non-Stock Material (BOM)/Plant**: Material master record → valuation class → automatic account determination configuration
  - **M – Non-Stock Material**: No material master → manually entered in the BOM or purchase order (PO)
  - **E – Internal Activity**: Activity type → activity type master data
  - **G – Overhead Costing Sheet**: Credit code → cost element
  - **X – Business Process Template**: Business process master data
  - **V – Variable Items**: Entered manually
- Cost elements are defined and applied for each component of the cost component structure.
- Each component can be assigned to a group for summary reporting.
- Each component has a group of settings that will dictate whether it is valid for inventory, sales, and administration, or excluded.
- The system uses the flags set in the component configuration to place the components into the cost component view.

Primary Cost Component

A primary cost component structure is an alternative view of cost components based on primary cost elements from materials and cost center accounting. Examples are payroll and benefits, rather than overhead and activity labor. The structure illustrates cost center planning details instead of a cost estimate view. To keep the two structures synchronized, you'll need to perform automatic price calculation for activities in the cost center.

In the costing variant, company codes can have unique cost component structures. With this option, the primary cost components will require mapping settings to translate the primary cost components to the main cost component structure. The process for the defining a primary or auxiliary cost component structure is similar to defining the main cost component structure.

To define an auxiliary cost component structure, follow these steps:

1. In the cost component definition, select the **Active** and **Prim. Cost Comp. Split** checkboxes. The main cost component structure **Y1** is set to active, as shown in Figure 5.7. Notice that structure **Y2** is also active, but the primary indicator has been selected, making it the auxiliary component structure.

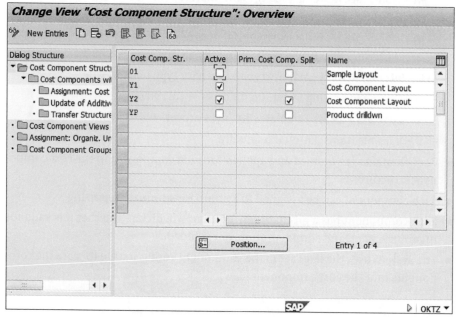

Figure 5.7 Cost Component Initial Setting

2. Once the structure is defined, you must assign a set of component "buckets," as shown earlier in Figure 5.4. The name of the buckets can be different from the set for **Y1**.

3. Each component should be mapped to all relevant cost elements, as shown in Figure 5.8. These cost elements must include any accounts seen in a cost center or in material account determination.

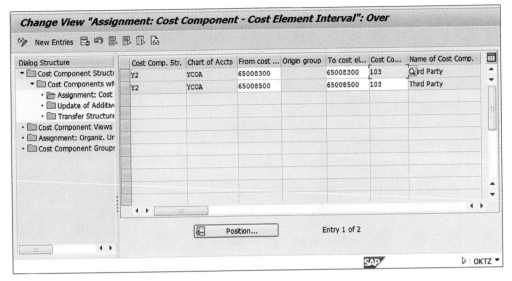

Figure 5.8 Cost Component Account Assignment

4. SAP provides the ability for different plants to use unique cost component structures. In this situation, you must define a third cost component structure to use as a mapping structure and then assign it to a controlling area.

5. Map the third cost component structure to the primary cost component structure and the main cost components using the transfer structure shown in Figure 5.7.

6. If all plants in the controlling area use the same main cost component structure, the previous two steps are not necessary. The newly defined auxiliary structure can be used. The mapping component structure only needs to have the **Active** checkbox selected, as shown in Figure 5.7. You'll still need to perform the component definition and cost element assignment steps discussed earlier.

7. Maintain price calculation details in a planning version under **Settings for Each Fiscal Year** for the controlling area, as shown in Figure 5.9. Assign the primary cost component structure.

8. Perform an automatic price calculation to ensure consistency between the main and primary component views.

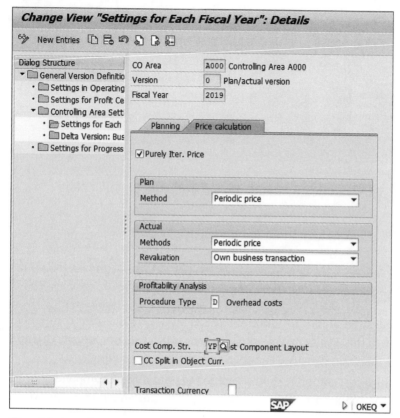

Figure 5.9 Controlling Area Price Details

Business Process Template

Product costing offers the option of calculating overhead costs using a template. A template is like a complex spreadsheet, and this feature is part of the activity-based costing functionality. A cost object providing services to materials is called a *business process*. A business process is like a cost center; however, activity information is defined within the process master data. Again, similar to a cost center, a secondary cost element is assigned to the business process.

The value for business process items is determined by the planned rate of the business process. The rate is assigned to individual business processes.

The business process rate dictates the value of the business process, while the template determines the quantities used for overhead allocation. To calculate business process quantities, the template uses an *environment*, which contains all the data elements that can be used in formulas to calculate quantities. Formulas can be defined for plan, actual, and activation of the line items. Figure 5.10 shows an example of template rows and a formula.

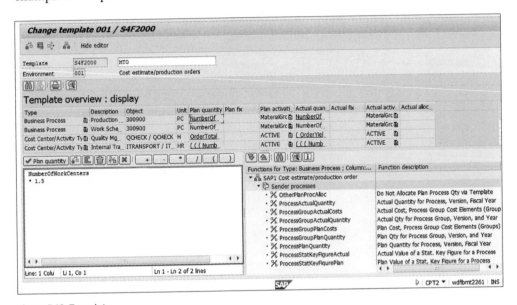

Figure 5.10 Template

These formulas can be complex, using different mathematical operands and different master data elements within the environment. This flexibility offers clear-cut advantages over the costing sheet process.

Once defined, the business process template needs to be linked to the costing process. This link is defined through the costing sheet, which is assigned in the costing variant. The template is then linked to costing sheet, as shown in Figure 5.11.

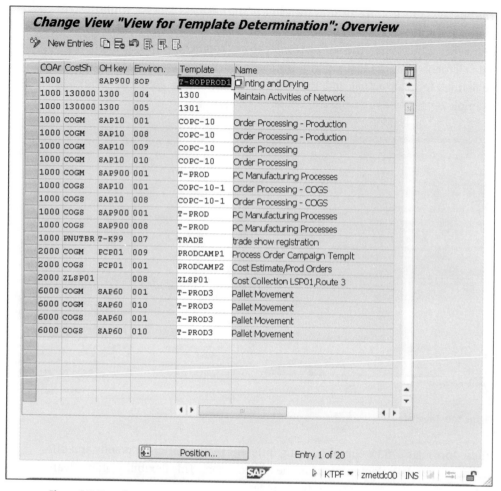

Figure 5.11 Template Assignment

Cost Estimate without Quantity Structure

Cost estimates without quantity structures can be used for many purposes, even to release a standard cost estimate. Cost estimates allow the costing team to build different cost details without reference to production planning data. To begin a cost estimate without quantity structure, a material and plant are required. A plant is the organizational structure for MM. A material number could represent a tangible item or an intangible item, such as a service.

Costing without quantity structure follows this flow:

1. Enter a plant and a material.
2. Select a costing variant.
3. Create costing items.
4. Save items.
5. Save the cost estimate.

These costing items are used to construct a unit cost estimate. Costing items will represent the costing value for this material, including labor and overhead. The cost estimate has a two-step save process. The first step just locks in your current settings, with the ability to review results. The second save commits the record to the database.

Costing without quantity structure doesn't require extensive master data but does require a material master record. The material master record is complex and should be reviewed systematically, which we'll do next.

Material Master

A material master record has different tabs that control how a material is used. These tabs are used to categorize the data, describe the materials, and dictate the applicable uses of the material.

> **Note**
> The discussion of the material master focuses on fields that are relevant to costing. Many other views and fields in the master material that are not relevant to costing.

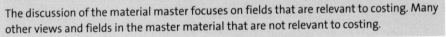

Numerous fields found in each tab on the material master will impact how costing will work:

- **Basic data 1**
  This tab, shown in Figure 5.12, contains the following key fields for costing:
  - **Base Unit of Measure**: Unit of measure for managing materials; other units are converted to the base unit of measure.
  - **X-Plant Matl Status**: Status must be relevant for all plants to cost.
  - **Valid from**: Date record is available.

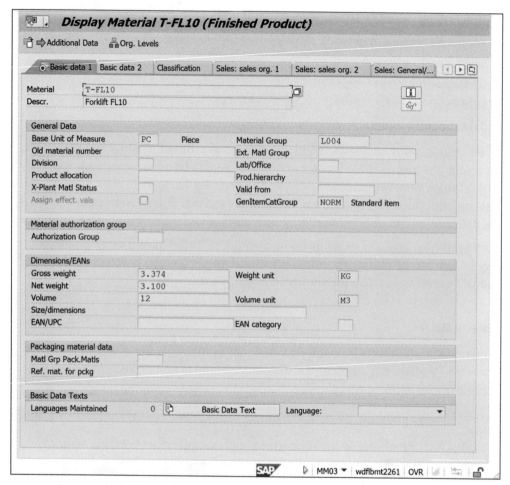

Figure 5.12 Material Master Basic Data 1

- MRP 1

  The **MRP** tabs in the material master record the details about how material requirements planning (MRP) will be processed and also include fields that impact costing. Product costing can observe settings made in these tabs, as shown in Figure 5.13, or can override the settings found under the **Costing** tabs, shown later in Figure 5.17. The **MRP 1** tab contains the following key fields:

  - **Base Unit of Measure**: Same as **Basic data 1** tab.

  - **Plant-sp.matl status**: Status for only materials maintained in the plant. Must be relevant for costing and can't override **X-Plant Matl Status**, as shown in Figure 5.12.

- **Assembly scrap (%)**: The assembly scrap is used in planning in order to increase the quantity to be produced to include the expected scrap quantity.

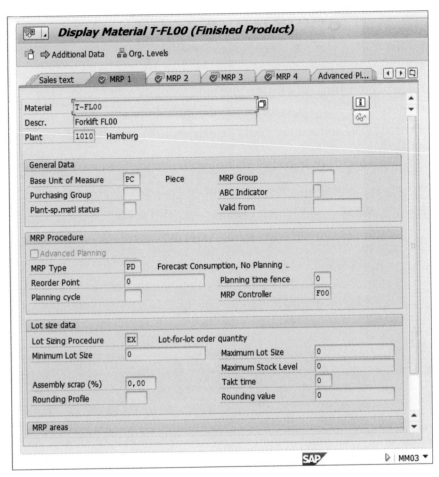

Figure 5.13 Material Master MRP 1

- **MRP 2**

  A key setting in the **MRP 2** tab, shown in Figure 5.14, is the special procurement key. The special procurement key comprises the **Procurement type** and the **Special procurement** type. These two fields formulate a procurement alternative. Product costing uses the procurement alternative to dictate the master data used for costing. The following list describes some example procurement alternatives:

  - Make it internally: Looks for BOM and routing

- Buy it externally: Looks for purchasing data
- Stock from fellow plant (in controlling area): Looks for BOM and routing in alternate plant
- Trigger production in another plant: Reads BOM and routing in alternate plant
- Subcontracting: Looks for BOM and purchasing data for vendor
- External processing (labor): Looks for purchasing data for vendor labor
- Production version: Looks for specified BOM and routing
- Alternate BOM and routing: Looks for existence of alternate BOM or routing

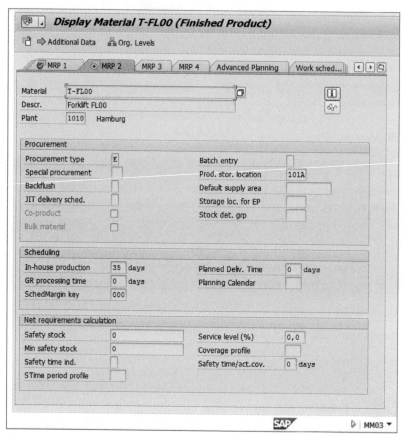

Figure 5.14 Material Master MRP 2

The **MRP 2** tab contains the following key fields:

- **Procurement type**: Identifies make, buy, or either.

- **Special procurement**: Method of internal or external procurement.
- **Co-product**: Materials used in joint production. This setting can also be identified in the master recipe.
- **Bulk material**: High-volume, low-value items. No value in the cost estimate, but visible in the BOM. Value applied through overhead tools. Can be identified in the BOM.

- **MRP 4**

  The **MRP 4** tab, shown in Figure 5.15, contains the following key fields:

  - **ProdVersions** (production version): Designated BOM, routing, lot size, and validity period.
  - **Component Scrap**: Amount of scrap added during the costing process.

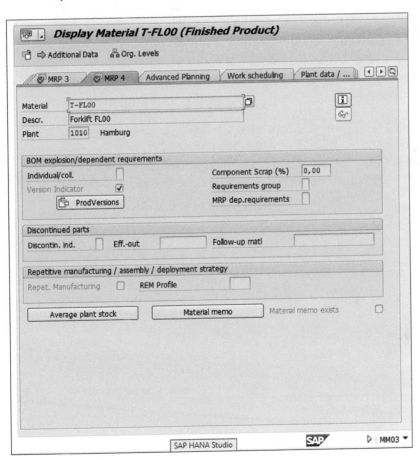

Figure 5.15 Material Master MRP 4

- **Accounting 1, 2**

  The **Accounting** tabs are required to value materials. The **Accounting 1** tab changes significantly with SAP S/4HANA. Since the material ledger is required in SAP S/4HANA, you'll see the material ledger indicator, material price analysis, and the price determination field, as shown in Figure 5.16. The default setting for price determination is **2**, meaning that actual costing is not activated. Multiple currencies and transfer prices can be activated.

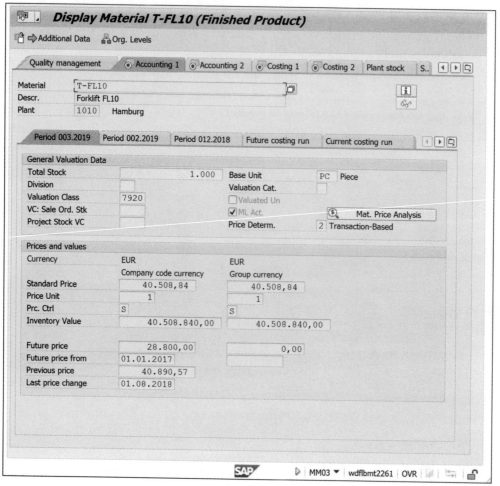

Figure 5.16 Accounting 1 Tab

Note

Prior to SAP S/4HANA, SAP maintained material valuation data in both material tables and financial tables, which resulted in discrepancies in valuation. As the SAP S/4HANA system was designed, SAP made valuation only available in the material ledger function, but since then, confusion about the mandatory material ledger in SAP S/4HANA has persisted.

The material ledger does three things: record materials in multiple currencies, perform parallel valuations for transfer pricing between business entities, and conduct actual costing with price determination 2 in the material master. Additional configuration is required to activate transfer pricing for parallel valuation.

The second price determination option is 3, single-level/multilevel costing, which activates actual costing. Actual costing is still an optional process and requires configuration to activate. This process also requires your diligence in monitoring and tracking price variances. Actual costing stores materials at standard price and collects price variances throughout the month. At period end, the material ledger calculates an actual price.

The material valuation will be maintained in the material ledger. The relevant settings for costing in the **Accounting 1** tab are as follows:

- **Price Determ.**: 2 (transactional) or 3 (single/multilevel [actual]).
- **Standard Price**: Frozen value used for FI inventory, price determination = S.
- **Moving Average Price (MAP)**: Calculated average value used for FI inventory, price determination = V. In an SAP ERP 6 system, you always see a **V** price even if using standard. In an SAP S/4HANA system, you won't see a MAP price without price control V.
- **Prc. Ctrl**: Dictates whether FI will use the S or V field for inventory.
- **Inventory Value**: FI balance sheet value (on-hand quantity × price).
- **Future price**: Manually entered price that can be used for future standards or reporting.
- **Future price from**: Date that the future price can be seen by costing.
- **Previous price**: Previous standard value.
- **Price Unit**: Quantity relevant for the price.

Note

SAP product costing only maintains two decimal places. For materials with very small value but large volume, two decimal places limits pricing precision. The price unit is used to provide pricing precision.

Let's consider an example purchase price of $.6249 for 1,000 pieces:

- Actual purchase value: $.6249 × 1,000 = $624.90
- Costing value:
  - Price unit of 1: $.63 × 1,000 = $630.00
  - Price unit of 10: $6.25 × 1,000 = $625.00
  - Price unit of 100: $62.49 × 1,000 = $624.90

The relevant settings in the **Accounting 2** tab are as follows:

- **Tax 1, 2, 3**: Price fields available to store the results of costing or a price used to create a standard.
- **Inventory 1, 2, 3**: Price fields available to store the results of costing or a price used to create a standard.

- Costing 1

  The costing views are required if you will use product cost planning. You can set a manual price in the **Accounting 1** tab for balance sheet valuation, but product cost planning adds layers of detail and information for analysis in order to provide different views of costing details. The **Costing 1** tab, shown in Figure 5.17, contains the following details about how costing will derive information:

  - **Do Not Cost**: Controls whether a cost estimate is possible.
  - **Material origin**: Records the relevant material ID in a transaction.
  - **Origin group**: Used for assigning overhead.
  - **Overhead Group**: Groups materials to apply overhead.
  - **With Qty Structure**: Controls whether "without quantity structure" can be released for standard.
  - **Variance Key**: Key used for cost object controlling.
  - **Profit Center**: Profit center used for material transactions.
  - **Plant-sp.matl status**: Status for the material at a plant level. Blank will read the MRP tab.
  - **Quantity structure data**: Allows costing to dictate a BOM and routing for costing purposes.
  - **Costing Lot Size**: Quantity used for calculating fixed cost.

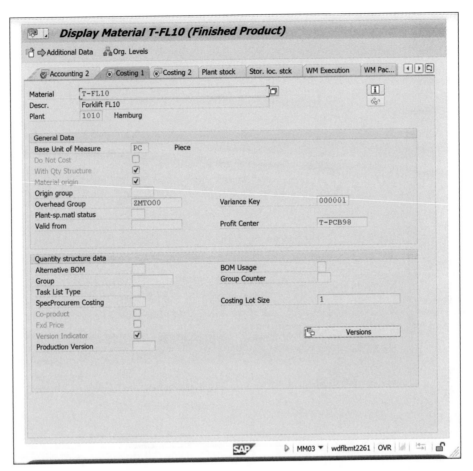

Figure 5.17 Product Costing 1 Tab

- **Costing 2**

    The **Costing 2** tab, shown in Figure 5.18, mainly stores prices. Prices can be designated in the costing variant pricing strategy for a new material, or they can be used to store the results of a cost estimate. This tab contains the following key fields:

    - **Future**: From a marked cost estimate.
    - **Current**: The current released standard cost estimate.
    - **Previous**: The previous released standard cost estimate.
    - **Planned price 1, 2, 3**: Can be used as input for new cost estimates or for cost comparisons.

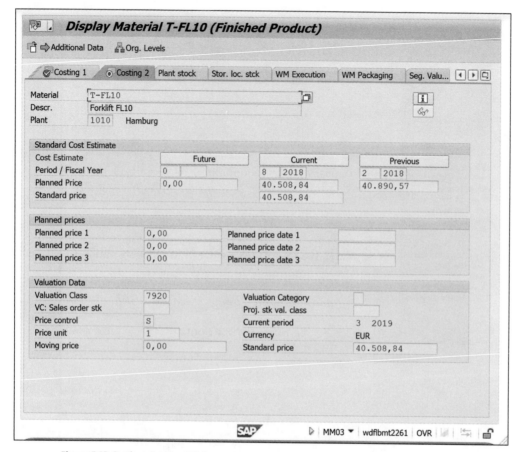

Figure 5.18 Product Costing 2 Tab

Note

Fields in the material master dictate what processes are available for the individual items. The **Accounting** tabs in the material master are the minimum required to maintain an inventory valuation. Material records without this information can be used by material management for other purposes but cannot maintain an inventory value on the FI balance sheet. Materials can be valued without maintaining the **Costing** tabs, but the **Costing** tabs are required to use product cost planning.

Unit Costing

Throughout CO, unit cost estimates can be used, and many different options are available for unit costing. Unit costing can involve a type of spreadsheet that can use existing master data and prices, or you can create items to use as building blocks in a cost estimate. Unit cost estimates can be created without a material record or other master data. The results of the cost estimate can be valid for the entire life of a product or only for a fiscal year.

The following types of unit costing are available:

- **Single-level cost estimate**

  A single-level cost estimate uses the unit costing feature. Single-level costing refers to a data structure that only references one level. This cost estimate requires material, plant, costing variant, version, lot size, costing date from, costing date to, and valuation date.

> **Tip**
>
> At a minimum, you can build a cost estimate with only the V item category. Other item categories are optional and indicate additional data items are available for costing.

- **Multilevel cost estimate**

  A multilevel cost estimate, shown in Figure 5.19, can be accessed via Transaction CKUC and uses the same inputs to build a cost estimate as a single-level cost estimate.

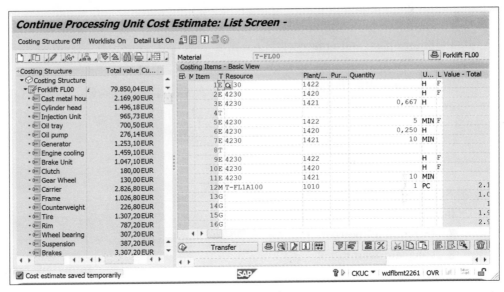

Figure 5.19 Multilevel Unit Cost Estimate (Transaction CKUC)

Building off the basic structure, a multilevel cost element adds the ability to create an indented structure. Tools to assist the creation of the structure by using worklist are available, which gives you a toolset with predefined items to easily add to a cost estimate. You can also view different several cost estimate structures simultaneously. As shown in Figure 5.19, on the right side of the screen, you can construct a single-level cost estimate while creating a multilevel cost element on the left.

Cost Estimate with Quantity Structure

Cost estimates with quantity structures require a material, plant, and quantity structure master data. The material master must contain a **Costing** tab and an **Accounting** tab. You can value a material with only the **Accounting** tab, but product costing requires the **Costing** tabs. When you create a cost estimate, the quantity structure is determined and used to create the estimate, thus enabling cost estimates to be created automatically. To successfully complete an estimate, the master data must be valid, a quantity structure must be determined, and prices must be valid. Cost estimates can be used for the valuation of inventory; the pricing of products; and the exploration production alternatives, engineering options, or origin alternatives.

The following flow is used for costing without quantity structure:

1. Enter a plant and a material.
2. Select a costing variant.
3. Select a costing version.
4. Select standard values:
   - Lot size
   - Quantity structure
   - Dates
5. Create a quantity structure.
6. Valuate the quantity structure.
7. Include additive costs.
8. Calculate overhead.
9. Review results.
10. Save the cost estimate.

> **Tip**
> Quantity structures apply to production and logistics master data. Production processing can be performed in many different ways, and these different methods will require different master data structures. Costing is flexible enough to allow you to select different structures to create cost estimates.

A cost estimate with quantity structure accesses data across production, MM, and CO. Costing has the option of selecting a specific production method or creating a quantity structure specifically for costing. Table 5.1 illustrates the source of quantity structure details.

Costing Data	Source
Component quantity	BOM
Standard times	Routing
Externally procured material	Material master, purchase order (PO), or purchase info record
External operation	PO, purchase info record, or routing
Internal labor	Activity type price
Overhead	Costing sheet
Process costs	Business process template
Stock material	Valuation class—automatic account determination
Non-stock items	Material master, BOM, or PO

Table 5.1 Quantity Structure Elements

Logistics Master Data

The key to understanding costing with quantity structure is to gain a complete understanding of logistics master data. As with the material master settings discussed in the "Cost Estimate without Quantity Structure" section, numerous settings exist under each master data tab and not all are relevant to product costing.

> **Tip**
> The master data discussed in this section is integral to product costing, but often, the cost accounts don't own the master data. Master data settings are directly linked to strategies defined in the relevant costing variant. Different costing variants may look at different settings in the master data depending on the intended use of the costing variant.

Bill of Material

A bill of material (BOM) provides a material list with quantities. A costing variant provides details about valuing those materials.

The BOM contains the following details that will impact costing:

- Header

  The BOM header includes details applicable to all items listed in the BOM, identifying the following:

  - **Base Quantity**: All quantities in the BOM items are extended by to this quantity.

  - **Usage**: BOMs that can be defined for many different uses. The system will first look for a BOM specifically, as shown in Figure 5.20. If a costing BOM is not available a production BOM could be used. Costing usage with plus sign (+) indicates this is the default BOM for costing; in the absence of a plus sign (+), then any BOM with a period sign (.) can be used for costing, and a minus sign (−) indicates the BOM is invalid for costing.

  - **Status**: Identifies if the BOM status currently valid for costing.

  - **Validity Period**: When can the data be read.

  - **Lot Size**: Relevant quantity for costing. Fixed costs are applied to the total lot size.

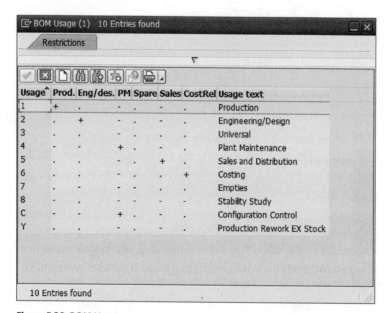

Figure 5.20 BOM Usage

- **Items**

  BOMs in SAP are built one level at a time and then connected to complete a structure. Each level of the BOM is assigned a costing level. Levels are used to build a sequence to determine costs starting from lower-level items to the top final item. The item details shown in Figure 5.21 are the first level below the material in the header. An item with the **Asm** indicator set is a lower-level BOM item.

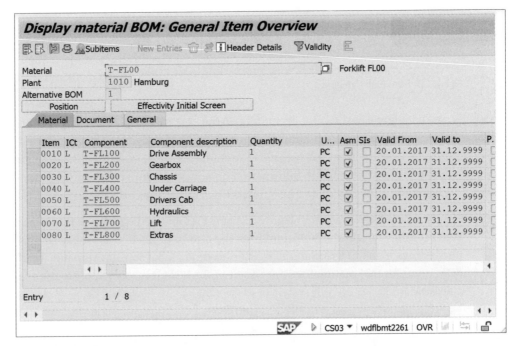

Figure 5.21 BOM Items

- **Item category**

  BOM items are assigned to an item category, as shown in Figure 5.22. The category dictates whether the item is a material managed as stock or other details for manufacturing. **L** items are stock materials and available for costing. **N** items are non-stock items procured at the time of manufacturing and available for costing.

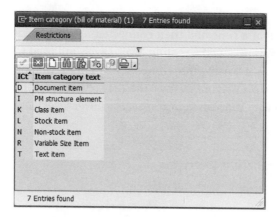

Figure 5.22 BOM Item Categories

The details will be different depending on the item category. The **L** category contains the most prevalent items used in a BOM. This category contains information on how the item will be used in manufacturing. **N** or non-stock items are less prevalent and contain information on how to procure the item. Categories not relevant for costing will be ignored when creating a cost estimate.

The item detail view shown in Figure 5.23 specifies all the data for one BOM item. Some settings seen at the BOM item level can also be defined in the material master. Settings made in the material master become global settings relevant for all BOM items for that material. Settings made at the BOM level only apply to the specific BOM item.

The key item detail fields that impact costing include the following:

- **Quantity**: Quantity of item required to make the base quantity in the header.
- **Item category**: Defines the type of item and dictates how it impacts manufacturing.
- **Assembly indicator**: Low-level items.
- **CostingRelevncy**: Determines if an item will be available for costing.
- **Validity**: Date that item will be valid for usage.
- **Scrap**: Planned scrap amount. Scrap will only be applied to this item.
- **Bulk**: Items of small value, visible to manufacturing but ignored by costing. Bulk can also be defined in the material master.
- **Phantom**: Items needed by manufacturing but ignored by costing. Can be set in the material master through the special procurement key.

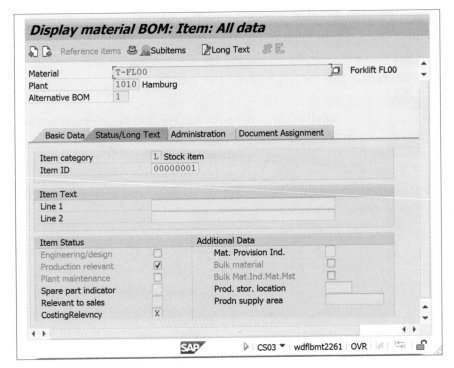

Figure 5.23 BOM Item Details

Routing

The routing is a sequence of steps required to convert a material. These steps, called *operations*, detail the quantity of time, type of work, and the work center where the processing will be executed. The sequence of steps identifies the order the system should be executed.

The routing header has similar settings to the BOM header. An operation contains individual labor steps to convert the material. These labor steps could be defined as internally executed by manufacturing or externally executed by a vendor. You can also include operation items that are not relevant for costing. Let's take a closer look at the structure of a routing, as follows:

- **Header**
  The routing header has similar information to the BOM header. The routing header identifies the material and plant for processing and provides information verifying the availability of the routing. The routing header details the following:

- **Usage**: Business processes that can access the routing.
- **Status**: Release of the routing for process use.
- **Lot Size Range**: Production lot size valid for the routing.
- **Validity Period**: Date the routing can be accessed.

- **Operations**

  Operations represent individual packets of work. The number of operations in a routing depends on the extent of processing required. The operations shown in Figure 5.24 provide the time quantity for costing structure.

Display Routing: Operation Overview

◀ ▶ 🖨 📋 🗒 📝 Work center   Allocation   Sequences 🔧PRT   ✏ 🔍Inspection Characteristics

Material T-FL00   Forklift FL00   Grp.Count1
Sequence   0

Operation Overview

Op...	SOp	Work ce...	Plant	Co...	Standard...	Description	L...	PRT	Cl...	O...	P...	C...	S...	Base Quantity	U...
0010		T-E00	1010	PP01		Alloc. components/Bereitstellung Kompon.	☐	☐	☐	☐	☐		☐	1	PC
0020		T-F00	1010	PP01		Drive Assy-> chassis/Antrieb->Chassis	☐	☑	☐	☐	☐		☐	1	PC
0030		T-G00	1010	PP01		Under Carriage->chassis/Fahrwerk-Chassis	☐	☑	☐	☐	☐		☐	1	PC
0040		T-H00	1010	PP01		Driver's Carb assy/ Fahrkabine montieren	☐	☐	☐	☐	☐		☐	1	PC
0050		T-K00	1010	PP01		Hydraulics with/mit Lift/Hubgerüst assy	☐	☐	☐	☐	☐		☐	1	PC
0060		T-M00	1010	PP01		Lift/Hubgerüst with/mit chassis assy	☐	☐	☐	☐	☐		☐	1	PC
0065		T-L00	1010	PP01		Varnishing /Lackieren	☐	☐	☐	☐	☐		☐	1	PC
0070		T-P00	1010	PP01		Extras assembly/anbringen	☐	☐	☐	☐	☐		☐	1	PC
0080		T-Z00	1010	PP99		Final Inspec/Endkontrolle+Road/Fahr Test	☐	☑	☐	☐	☐		☐	1	PC

◀ ▶

Entry   1   of 9

◀ ▶

SAP   ▷ | CA03 ▼ | wdflbmt2261 | OVR |

Figure 5.24 Operations

Each operation contains a control key. The control key identifies the processes available for each operation. Details in an operation as well as the control key, as shown in Figure 5.25, could be relevant to costing. The system will ignore any operations not relevant for costing, but these operations could still be valid for manufacturing processes. Operations detail the following:

- **Base Quantity**: Quantity output per processing time.
- **Standard Time Value**: Time fields represent the time value for the base quantity. Six time fields are available in the operation.

- **Work Center Assignment**: Location or resource where the work occurs.
- **Material Assignment**: Step where materials in the BOM will be consumed.
- **Control Key**: Identify that controls how the operation will be processed.
- **Scrap**: Scrap % for output to the next step.
- **Relevancy for Costing**: Operation is valid for costing.
- **Assignment of Activity Type**: Activity time linked to the cost center in the operation work center.

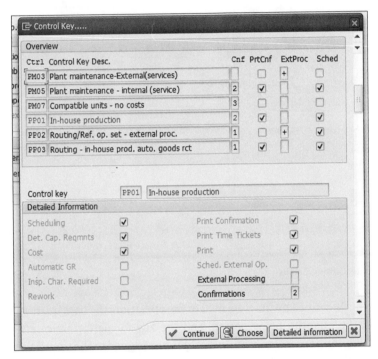

Figure 5.25 Control Key

Work Center

The work center is the location, the machine, the line, or the labor group that performs the processing defined in an operation. The **Basic Data** tab in the work center identifies which time fields will be available for the operation. This tab also contains the key for performance efficiency, which specifies an efficiency factor applied to time calculations. This factor will have the effect of increasing the value of time in the cost estimate. Default values, capacities, and scheduling tabs are used by manufacturing to plan and schedule work in the work center.

The **Costing** tab, shown in Figure 5.26, identifies the remaining setting critical for costing. Each work center is linked to a single cost center. This assignment represents the cost center providing the labor and services to the operation.

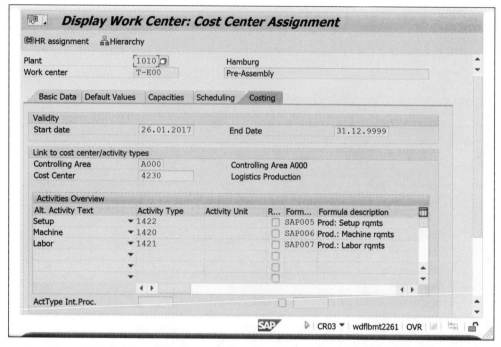

Figure 5.26 Work Center Costing Details

The quantity of time is defined by the time field in the operation, the base quantity of the operation, the quantity being costed, and the key for performance efficiency. The combination of cost center and activity type assigned to the time fields will govern the rate used to value labor. Each time field is assigned a formula, shown in Figure 5.27, to define the time calculation. The formula contains the following parameters:

- **Machine:** Time in the operation machine field.
- **Operation quantity:** Quantity being costed.
- **Base quantity:** Quantity in the operation.

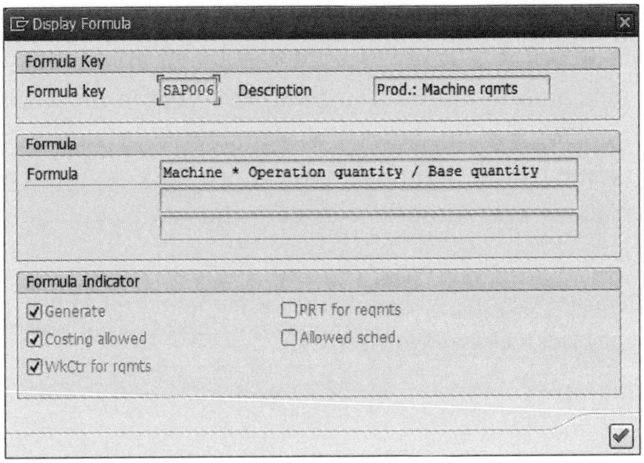

Figure 5.27 Costing Formula

Master Recipe

Up to this point, we've focused on the master data used in discrete manufacturing. Some industries, such as the food and chemical industries, use process manufacturing where materials are processed, not assembled. SAP provides a different manufacturing process to meet the needs of these industries. The master data used for costing is similar between the two manufacturing options. Process manufacturing uses a master recipe, shown in Figure 5.28. A master recipe combines the features of a BOM, routing, and work center.

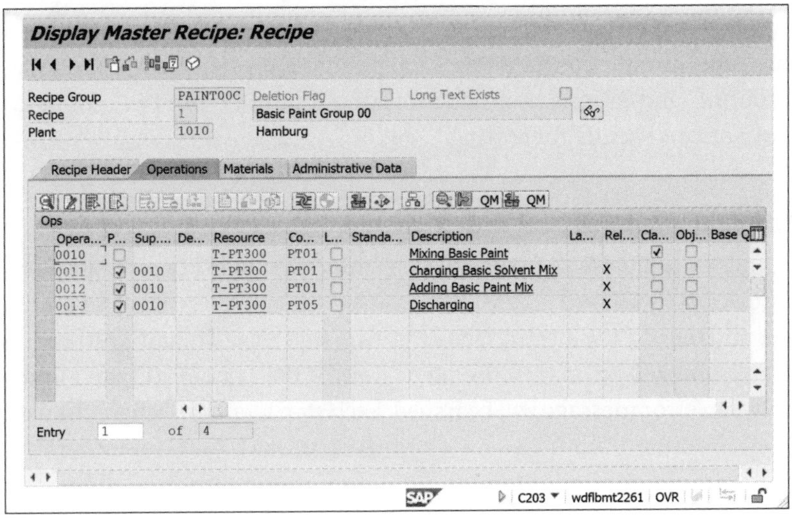

Figure 5.28 Process Recipe

Labor Valuation

The value of labor (the operation price) is determined by the activity type designated in the operation time field and the relevant cost center visible in the work center (shown earlier in Figure 5.26). Activity types and planned prices were discussed in Chapter 3 in the context of cost center accounting. Once defined, a planned price can be applied to an operation. To calculate the labor operation value, use the following formula:

(Costing lot size ÷ Operation base quantity) ÷ Work center performance efficiency x Operation time x Activity type price = Operation price

Let's consider the following example:

- Operation time: 10 minutes
- Operation base quantity: 1 pc/10 minutes
- Costing lot size: 10 pc
- Activity type price: $30/hour
- Work center performance efficiency: 95%

Your formula would look like the following: *(10 pc ÷ 1 pc) ÷ .95 × 10 min × ($30 ÷ 60 min)*, resulting in $52.63 as your operation price.

Production Version

Manufacturing can produce products with different procurement alternatives. To control material planning, manufacturing can dictate a specific BOM, routing, and lot size to apply to individual production processes. These individual production processes are called production versions. Each production version contains a specific BOM, routing, and lot size. A production version can be used in costing to specify the quantity structure for costing.

Determine Quantity Structure

The system follows a precise sequence to determine the quantity structure. The system may discover a valid structure, but the structure must also be valid for the costing dates and the costing lot size. If costing can't find a valid quantity structure in a step, the system will go on to subsequent steps. If the system still can't find a valid structure, an error message will be issued. Each step identifies where the data is specified.

The BOM selection process is as follows:

1. Manually create a single cost estimate by entering the BOM or production version in the cost estimate parameters.

2. Identify the special procurement key in the **MRP 2** tab of the material master. Determine appropriate alternatives and follows the relevant master data.

3. Maintain the production version in the **MRP 4** tab of the material master. This setting reads the production version for manufacturing with valid dates and lot sizes.

4. Follow the menu path **Material Costing with Quantity Structure · Costing Variant Components: Define Quantity Structure Control** and select a **BOM Application** to override the current section and send the system back to master data settings for further analysis. Maintain the following fields, as shown in Figure 5.29:

   - **Selection ID**: This setting will be defined in the next step. It points to a table that has a priority to define the BOM selection.

   - **Alt.det. mult. BOM**: This setting is determined via the following methods:
     - This selection first sends the system back to the material master to evaluate the **Individual/coll.** field in the **MRP 4** tab. If it's set to **1**, the material is make-to-order and it uses the order BOM (as shown earlier in Figure 5.15).
     - If the setting is not **1**, then the system goes to production configuration: **BOMs · Alternative Determination · Define Alternative Determination for Multiple BOMs** and uses the selection.

   - **Production versions**: This selection points to the **Selection Method** field in the **MRP 4** tab of the material master. The settings can be as follows:
     - **2**: Production version is optional. If no valid production version is available, this goes on with selection choices.
     - **3**: Production version is mandatory. If there is no valid production version, an error is issued.

   - **Minimum BOM status requirements**: This setting identifies a minimum BOM status in the master data that is available for costing.

5. Follow the menu path **Material Costing with Quantity Structures · Settings for Quantity Structure Control · BOM Selection · Check BOM Selection** (Transaction OPJI). Select the **Quantity Structure Control** defined in the **Quantity Structure** tab of the costing variant. This table allows you to define a priority for selecting different BOM usages to determine a costing BOM. The settings are as follows:

- **SelID**: The system looks for the **Selection ID** identified in the previous step.
- **SelPr**: Once an ID is found, it follows the priority to determine the appropriate usage.
- **BOMUsg**: The system follows the priority to find a valid BOM usage to use for costing.

6. If a valid BOM with valid dates, status, and quantity has not been found, then the system issues an error message.

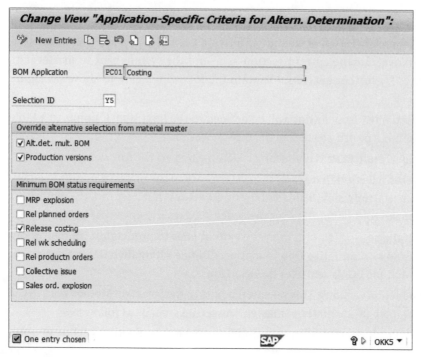

Figure 5.29 BOM Selection Override Settings

The routing process is less complicated than the BOM, but it's still necessary to find a routing for a valid status, valid costing lot size, and valid costing dates. The routing selection process is as follows:

1. Manually create a single cost estimate by manually entering the routing or production version in the cost estimate parameters.

2. Identify the special procurement key in the **MRP 2** tab of the material master (as shown previously in Figure 5.14). Determine appropriate alternatives and follow the relevant master data.

3. Determine a production version from the **MRP 4** tab in the material master. The system first reads the **Selection Method** field in the **MRP 4** tab of the material master. The settings can be as follows:
   - **2**: Production version is optional. If no valid production version is available, goes on with selection choices.
   - **3**: Production version is mandatory. If there is no valid production version, an error is issued.
4. Set the costing routing or production version in the **Costing 1** tab in the material master, using the costing quantity structure.
5. Set the priority of routing types to determine a routing from existing manufacturing data by following the menu path **Material Costing with Quantity Structures • Settings for Quantity Structure Control • Routing Selection • Check Automatic Routing Selection**. The settings are as follow:
   - **ID**: Select the **ID** defined in the **Quantity Structure** tab of the costing variant.
   - **SP**: Selection priority defines the order for selecting a routing.
   - **Task List Type**: Key that classifies task lists or routing according to their functionality.
   - **Usage**: Identifies a usage setting in a valid BOM.
6. Set alternative sequences in manufacturing routing master data.
7. If no routing is found with a valid status, a valid costing lot size, or a valid costing date, the system will issue an error message.

Cost Estimate

A cost estimate with quantity structure has several different views. These screens can be a little intimidating until you develop some experience navigating the screens. These screens contain all the relevant information for the results of costing as well as all details about the creation of cost estimates. These views are relevant to the material selected at the top of the screen, as shown in Figure 5.30:

- Costing details
  Costing details are contained in the tabs shown in the center of Figure 5.30. The material and plant relevant to costing are contained in these details. The costing details view provides on overview of the details used in creating a cost estimate: the quantity structure, the costing configuration settings, the validity dates for master data, and the current use of the estimate. This view also displays the **Cost of Goods Manufactured**, used for balance sheet material valuation, and the **Cost**

of Goods Sold, used for product profitability. These values are determined by the cost component split. The cost component split allows five separate values to be defined from cost components.

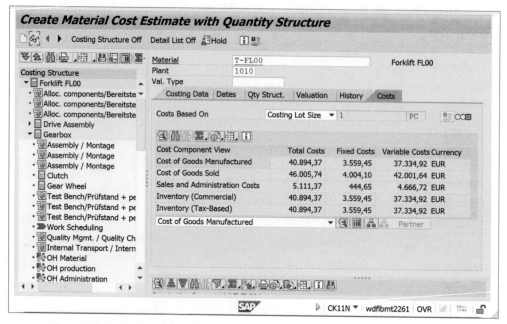

Figure 5.30 Costing Details

- **Indented view**

  The indented view shows all the lower-level materials in a cost estimate, as shown in Figure 5.31. The default view contains only the materials list. In this view, you can activate routing and overhead details. This view includes the extended value of costing items as well as master data details. This view is the only one that shows the lower-level details rolled into the costed materials. By creating screen variants, you can change the details shown in this view.

- **Itemization view**

  The itemization view, shown in Figure 5.32, displays individual costing items, including item category, resource, cost element, total value, quantity, and material. Like the indented view, you can change this view using screen variants. The item category determines the type of costing details displayed. The costing item category was explained in the "Product Cost Planning Basics" section.

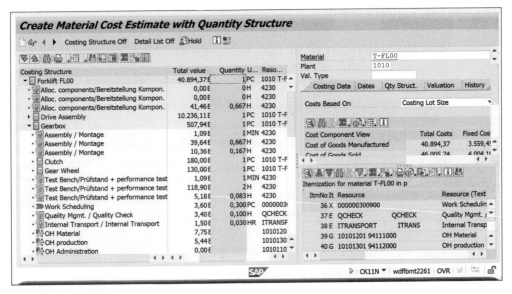

Figure 5.31 Indented View

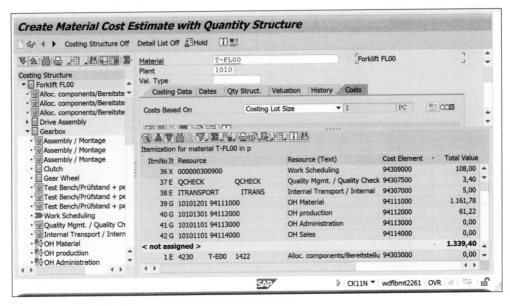

Figure 5.32 Itemization View

- **Cost component view**

  Two cost component views exist. The main view, shown in Figure 5.33, is the only one required by costing. An alternate view, called primary or actual, is available for additional costing detail. The cost component view is required for sending COGM or COGS details to CO-PA. This view is also the only one that keeps material, labor, and overhead separate throughout the costing structure.

  The views discussed earlier are created automatically based on the quantity structure and master data. In contrast, cost component views are defined by the organization. SAP provides a table with 40 different fields. Each variable and fixed value utilizes one field. Values are mapped to the component fields in configuration, as previously shown in Figure 5.6 and described in the "Product Cost Planning Configuration" section. If a primary or auxiliary view is defined, you can toggle between the two views.

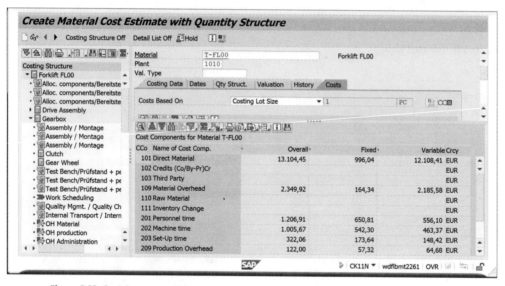

Figure 5.33 Cost Component View

Update Prices

After a cost estimated is reviewed, you can save it for future reference or use it to set prices. As mentioned earlier in the "Cost Estimate without Quantity Structure" section, almost a dozen fields in the material master are available for material prices. To update a price field, the costing variant must identify the valid material master fields to update, as shown previously in Figure 5.3. The cost estimate must use the variant that identifies the desired material master fields designated for price update. At least one cost variant must be designated to update the standard price field. This field will be used for FI inventory valuation. The other price fields are optional and are available for alternate cost analyses.

Prior to setting standard prices for a material, the marking allowance must be activated, as shown in Figure 5.34. The marking allowance can be set in the individual price screen or in the costing run cockpit, as we'll discuss in the "Costing Run" section. This allowance must be set for every period, for each company code. The marking allowance setting can be changed until a standard material price has been released. The marking allowance identifies the costing variant and version that must be used to create cost estimates for standards. These cost estimates must still be activated for standards by performing a mark step and a release step, which we'll discuss in the next section.

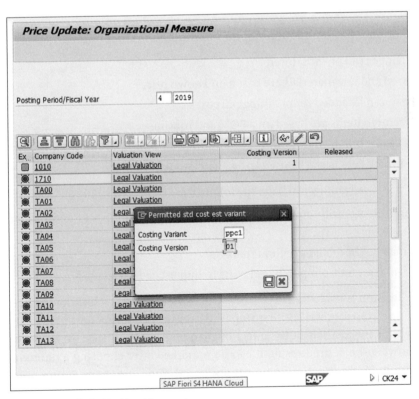

Figure 5.34 Activate Marking Allowance

> **Note**
>
> In an MM environment, you may handle many different types of materials. Costing is only relevant for valuated materials. For valuated materials, you can use two different price controls: price control S and price control V. Remember from the material master discussion earlier in this chapter that in an SAP S/4HANA system, the material ledger indicator can be set to 2 or 3. Either price control S or V can be used only with material ledger indicator 2. Material ledger indicator 3 always require price control S.
>
> S materials will use a frozen price to value inventory. This price can only be changed once per period. V items will be valued using an average price calculated by the system. Both material settings can generate a cost estimate, but V items will not value inventory from the cost estimate.

Before you decide whether to use a standard cost estimate, you'll need to consider both its benefits and disadvantages. The advantages to using a standard cost estimate include the following:

- Inventory valued at consistent price
- Variances captured in price difference account
- Variances are visible at material level
- Price changes can be monitored
- Purchased and raw materials are based on known prices
- Overhead can be added for planning purposes
- Manufactured items are based on a BOM and routing
- Details can be provided to CO-PA
- Cost estimate details can be used to evaluate product changes

However, key disadvantages include the following:

- Standard settings will require significant effort to validate prices and master data.
- Prices may not be realistic in fluid markets.
- Lack of integration from purchased parts to upper-level parent.

Once the decision is made to use price control S, the function to set standards or prices is a two-step process. The first step is to mark a relevant cost estimate. This step allows for the analysis of the effect of changing a price. If the cost estimate doesn't provide the desired result, it can be remarked after choosing a different costing result. Marked cost estimate details can be reviewed in the **Future** price field on the **Costing 2** tab of the material master. Once the costing results are validated, the price can be released.

Released cost estimates are used to set new standards. During the release process, the system moves the cost estimate from the **Future** field to the **Standard** field in the material master. The existing standard is moved to the **Previous** field. Cost estimates can be reviewed from within the material master. Any materials with price control S and on-hand quantities will be revalued in the FI balance sheet.

> **Warning!**
> The process of releasing a standard cost estimate can occur only once per period. The system provides the ability to update a price, but doing so comes with risks. Before discussing updating a standard, we need to evaluate two price fields in the materials master. Under the **Current** heading in **Costing 2** tab, shown in Figure 5.18, you'll see two fields showing the same amount, but these fields do not contain identical data.
>
> The **Standard price** field is the value used for inventory valuation. This value can be set manually through MM processes or through product costing. The second field (**Planned Price**) contains details from the cost estimate including the cost component split used by CO-PA.

The first option is to manually change the FI price for inventory through an MM price change. While FI is correct, a mismatch often occurs between FI and CO-PA, the latter of which receives data through the cost estimate component detail. The second alternative is to delete the current cost estimate and release a new cost estimate. However, during the resetting process, you run the risk of CO-PA not receiving any details.

Cost estimates can also be used to set prices in other price fields. These alternative prices can be used for comparison or reporting procurement alternatives. This feature is controlled by settings in the costing variant configuration, which we discussed in the "Product Cost Planning Configuration" section.

Costing Run

An alternative to setting individual cost estimates and manually marking and releasing is to execute a costing run. Costing run parameters can be set to cost numerous materials simultaneously.

The following list offers suggestions for setting the standards or the data that must be reviewed while preparing for a costing run:

1. Verify the material master information is complete and up to date.
2. Ensure that BOM and routing is correct.
3. Choose the validity periods for prices and master data.
4. Run the costing for raw materials, level 1, to find lower-level errors.
5. Correct level 1 errors, so they don't transfer to upper-level materials.
6. Repeat for subsequent costing levels.
7. Use transfer control to find items that need updated costs.
8. Use error control to find items that need data updates.
9. Designate a data SWAT team (of master data owners) to quickly review and resolve costing issues.
10. Review standard reports to find valid cost estimates with unusual values.

In the following sections, we'll walk you through the steps to executing a costing run.

Selection List

The first step to creating a costing run is to select materials for costing, for which there are two methods. A selection list transaction in the costing menu can be used to build a list of materials, or within the costing run selection step, individual criteria can be entered to determine the materials for costing.

In both options, you can use numerous criteria to select the desired materials. The selection list is created ahead of time and entered during the select step of the costing run. If no selection list exists, material selection parameters must be defined in the costing run. A key advantage of using a selection list is the ability to reuse the same list for multiple costing runs. Once a selection list has been created, it can be edited repeatedly.

Warning!

Selecting the option of having the costing run select materials comes with limits. SAP automatically uses the selection criteria to build an SQL statement for the costing run program. If too many selection parameters are entered, the costing run will encounter a technical error because of character limits in SQL. Using the selection list will alleviate this restriction.

Create a Costing Run

A costing run is executed from a costing run cockpit, which allows you to perform all the required steps from one convenient location. General data must be entered and saved prior to executing any subsequent steps.

The key setting in the general data, shown in Figure 5.35, are **Costing Variant, Costing Version, Controlling Area, Company Code**, and **Transfer Control** (optional).

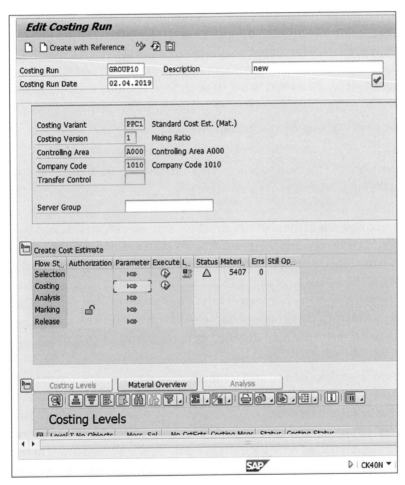

Figure 5.35 Costing Run Cockpit

You must also select the costing, quantity structure, and valuation dates. You can choose a costing variant that will post results to the standard price field or a variant that updates price fields other than standard. You can also set a frequency for regular costing runs. You cannot manually select quantity structure; it is determined automatically.

Once you save the general data, you can begin the costing process. The steps in the costing run are executed in sequence; however, you can go back and reexecute previous steps if needed.

Processing

Each step in the costing run process requires the entry of parameters. The individual parameters are relevant for the specified step. Once a parameter is entered and saved, the execute icon will be available. These steps also create individual logs and error messages. Each step can also be set to execute in the foreground or in the background.

The following steps make up the costing run process:

1. **Selection**
   Determines materials that will be processed in the costing run. In this step, you can manually enter criteria or use a selection list.

2. **Costing**
   Explode and cost levels of the quantity structure. You can execute this step by a specific costing level or select all levels. When a BOM is exploded, the lowest item in the structure is assigned to level 1. The number of levels depends on the complexity of the BOM. Only costing individual levels assists with error management by reducing lower-level errors from transferring to upper levels. This step can be set to cost all selections or only previous estimates with errors. Logging by costing level is beneficial when trying to trace errors.

3. **Analysis**
   Choose from several options to analyze the costing results. Some reports will give you an overview of all the materials and allow you to compare the new cost estimate to the current standard. Once a selection is saved, other options cannot be accessed during this step but can always be executed for the reporting area. The most often used report, shown in Figure 5.36, is a comparison of the current standard price and the future price. This step will also validate the informational revaluation in FI.

Analyze/Compare Material Cost Estimates

Plant   1010

Material	Material description	Plant	Sta.	Costing Result	Unit	Var. costing/...	Value Mat.Mst.Price	Total Value	Total Stock	Lot Size
T-F109	Extreme Group 09	1010	FR	5.291,25	PC	9.228,75-	14.520,00	0,00	0	100
T-F110	Extreme Group 10	1010	FR	12.607,29	PC	1.912,71-	14.520,00	166.980,00	1.150	100
	Extreme Group 10	1010	FR	14.519,65	PC	0,35-	14.520,00	166.980,00	1.150	100
	Extreme Group 10	1010	FR	16.309,71	PC	1.789,71	14.520,00	166.980,00	1.150	100
	Extreme Group 10	1010	FR	5.066,25	PC	9.453,75-	14.520,00	166.980,00	1.150	100
	Extreme Group 10	1010	KA	5.291,25	PC	9.228,75-	14.520,00	166.980,00	1.150	100
	Extreme Group 10	1010	FR	5.291,25	PC	9.228,75-	14.520,00	166.980,00	1.150	100
T-F111	Extreme Group 11	1010	FR	12.607,29	PC	1.912,71-	14.520,00	0,00	0	100
	Extreme Group 11	1010	FR	14.519,65	PC	0,35-	14.520,00	0,00	0	100
	Extreme Group 11	1010	FR	16.309,71	PC	1.789,71	14.520,00	0,00	0	100
	Extreme Group 11	1010	FR	5.066,25	PC	9.453,75-	14.520,00	0,00	0	100
	Extreme Group 11	1010	KA	5.291,25	PC	9.228,75-	14.520,00	0,00	0	100
	Extreme Group 11	1010	FR	5.291,25	PC	9.228,75-	14.520,00	0,00	0	100
T-F112	Extreme Group 12	1010	FR	12.607,29	PC	1.912,71-	14.520,00	1.306,80	9	100
	Extreme Group 12	1010	FR	14.519,65	PC	0,35-	14.520,00	1.306,80	9	100
	Extreme Group 12	1010	FR	16.309,71	PC	1.789,71	14.520,00	1.306,80	9	100
	Extreme Group 12	1010	FR	5.066,25	PC	9.453,75-	14.520,00	1.306,80	9	100
	Extreme Group 12	1010	KA	5.291,25	PC	9.228,75-	14.520,00	1.306,80	9	100
	Extreme Group 12	1010	FR	5.291,25	PC	9.228,75-	14.520,00	1.306,80	9	100
T-F113	Extreme Group 13	1010	FR	12.607,29	PC	1.912,71-	14.520,00	0,00	0	100
	Extreme Group 13	1010	FR	14.519,65	PC	0,35-	14.520,00	0,00	0	100
	Extreme Group 13	1010	FR	16.309,71	PC	1.789,71	14.520,00	0,00	0	100
	Extreme Group 13	1010	FR	5.066,25	PC	9.453,75-	14.520,00	0,00	0	100

SAP   ▷   S_P99_41000111 ▼   wdflbmt2261

Figure 5.36 Costing Value Report

4. **Marking**

   Marks all valid cost estimates. If the marking allowance is not set for the period, it can be saved in this setup. The mark setting can be done for cost estimates with a future date.

5. **Release**

   Releases all valid cost estimates or post results to price fields based on the costing variant. Only cost estimates for the current period can be released.

Each step of the costing run contains details about costing level, material overview, and analysis. The costing run cockpit executes programs that need to update details in the cockpit, so be sure to refresh often. Individual steps have a status indicator and a processing log. As the programs progress, you can verify their status by refreshing the screen.

Error Handling

Handling errors can be difficult since one problem can trigger multiple errors, especially when you are costing several levels simultaneously. As mentioned in the costing step, you can cost by level. This flexibility allows each level to be processed and corrected separately, prior to moving to the next level. At a minimum, logging errors by level identifies the level where the error occurred.

You can configure your own error messages to facilitate the correction process. Setting the user error message **CK318** flag, shown in Figure 5.37, to red flags all cost estimates with errors so you can recost these cost estimates.

Once the message **CK318** is set to error, in the costing step of the costing run, set the indicator **Cost with Errors Only**. During the costing run, the system only reads the cost materials that have an error. It will not recost everything, using less system resources.

User-defined messagesMaterial Cost Estimate

Lig.	Message Process	Msg Type	Area	Message	Message Text
△		W	C2	223	A valid bill of material could not be found for materi
△		W	CK	229	No routing could be determined for material &
△		W	CK	230	Costing item has no material or price
▣		I	CK	240	Cost component split costed with value of zero
▣		I	CK	254	Costing view created for material &1 in plant &2
△		W	CK	256	No cost field for fixed costs has been defined
▣		I	CK	264	There is no costing view for material & in plant &
△		W	CK	299	No alternative to multi-level BOM found for material
△		W	CK	305	BOM for material & in plant & is flagged for deletion
△		W	CK	306	No routing could be determined for material & plant
△		W	CK	310	Material & is marked for deletion
△		W	C2	315	Routing & is flagged for deletion
▣		I	CK	318	Cost estimate for material & contains errors -> Plan
△		W	CK	319	Material & in plant & has no costing status
▣			CKBA	320	Mixing ratio imported from production plan - only di:
▣		I	CK	321	Overhead key & is not suitable for costing sheet &
▣		I	CK	324	Material & in plant & will not be costed because the
▣			CO	328	Routing & & quantity & not within lot size range
▣			CK	340	Costing lot size changed from & & to & &
▣			CO	342	No business area determined for sector & plant &

Figure 5.37 Costing Run Error Management

> **Warning!**
> No easy guide exists for troubleshooting costing errors. The process requires experience. One error could cause several subsequent errors. Since many cost accountants do not own the master data, correcting the sources of errors could be problematic. Having key master data owners available can simplify the process.

Transfer Control

Transfer control allows to you determine if a cost estimate will reexplode the quantity structure and allows you to revalue the costing items with new prices or transfer existing cost values to upper level costing items. Instructing the system to use existing data is more efficient and keeps current costing items frozen at the desired detail. The transfer control can be defined to only transfer within a plant or to transfer existing data across plants, as shown in Figure 5.38.

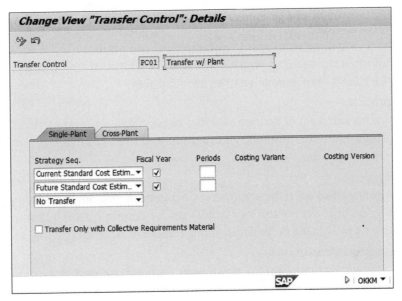

Figure 5.38 Transfer Control

The transfer control details contain a strategy to define valid costs estimates that can be transferred. For materials to receive costing details across plants, a special procurement key should be defined in the **MRP 2** tab, shown earlier in Figure 5.14. This key indicates which plant is sending costing data. The special procurement key instructs the cost estimate to read data from supplying plants within the controlling area and allows the cost estimate to build a quantity structure across plants.

Once defined, a transfer control can be assigned to the costing variant. You can make a transfer control mandatory or allow users to remove it. The costing variant must also be updated with cross-company code costing, if you want to transfer costs from plants in different company codes. You cannot transfer costs across controlling areas.

Important Terminology

In this chapter, the following terminology was used:

- **Automatic account determination**
  This capability is a standard functionality to determine account posting details automatically by the SAP system.

- **Bill of material (BOM)**
  A BOM is a list of materials and quantities converting in manufacturing. A BOM provides information about quantities of materials to the costing quantity structure. Each BOM item is assigned to an item category.

- **Business process**
  A business process is a set of defined activities to support a business scenario. Business processes are cost objects used when applying overhead from support areas to the product cost.

- **Control key**
  A control key identifies which business activities can be carried out in a routing operation. In costing, the control key is relevant for determining internal or external activity processing or for determining relevancy for costing.

- **Cost component structure**
  A cost component structure breaks down costs into defined cost categories. Common components include material, labor, overhead, sales, and administration. This structure allows you to analyze the sources of costs and provides detailed COGS values to CO-PA.

- **Cost estimate**
  A cost estimate is a group of costing items used to value materials and services. Each costing item must contain a quantity, a price, and a cost element. This capability is used for analysis or for setting prices.

- **Cost estimate without quantity structure**
  This kind of cost estimate is built manually from selected costing items. Cost elements are the only master data required to build a cost estimate.

- **Cost estimate with quantity structure**
  This kind of cost estimate is built automatically using relevant master data structures from production planning or process industries.

- **Costing items**
  Costing items are individual values and quantities required to build a cost estimate. Each item has an item category, which contains logic directing the data required for the item and how the item will be valued.

- **Costing level**
  A costing quantity structure is exploded and assigned a level. The lowest level of the structure is level 1, indicating a procured part. Each subsequent level receives a higher number in sequence.

- **Costing sheet**
  A costing sheet defines the control data to calculate and apply overhead to costing items. Costing sheets contain three main components: a calculation base, an overhead rate, and credit.

- **Costing variant**
  A costing variant contains all the essential parameters for creating cost estimates. Each costing variant must contain a costing type and valuation variant.

- **Date control**
  This feature specifies the effective dates for a cost estimate, the applicable validity dates for valuation prices, and the validity dates for a quantity structure data.

- **Intangible items**
  This kind of item represents services or materials without a physical structure (for example, freight, design, or installation services).

- **Key for performance efficiency**
  This key allows an operational efficiency rate to be applied to the time fields of the routing operations. If no rate is defined, the key is assumed to be 100%.

- **Main cost component split**
  This is a set of cost elements that summarizes costs into categories to be analyzed in the cost estimate. A group of components is defined and then assigned to a costing variant.

- **Operation**
  An operation is a processing activity required to process material. Operations

are a sequence of processing steps. Each operation has control parameters and is assigned to a work center.

- **Primary cost component split**
  This split creates an alternate group of cost components based on primary spending in manufacturing cost centers. This structure is optional and linked to the main cost component structure.

- **Production version**
  A production version serves as a link between a BOM, a routing, and a processing lot size and represents a specific processing alternative for manufacturing.

- **Quantity structure control**
  This control is a set of structured master data from logistics used to create cost estimates. This set contains the quantities used by the costing variant to value costing items.

- **Routing**
  A routing is a list of operations detailing the activities required to process materials. A routing identifies a valid processing quantity to determine if the process is valid for a costing lot size.

- **Special procurement key**
  This key is a combination of the procurement type and the special procurement types. It influences the determination of a procurement alternative. In product costing, this key guides the determination of the quantity structure.

- **Tangible items**
  This kind of item represents physical materials that can be used in the costing process.

- **Template**
  A template provides a flexible method for assigning overhead costs using an environment structure.

- **Transfer structure**
  A transfer structure is a selection of data elements mapped to other fields.

- **Unit cost estimate**
  A unit cost estimate is a flexible tool for planning costs manually using various master data elements.

- **Valuation variant**
  A valuation variant is a structure containing logic for selecting and assigning values to items in a cost estimate.

- **Work center**

  A work center represents a resource where manufacturing activities are performed. A work center could indicate a machine, a group of operators, an assembly line, or equipment.

 Practice Questions

These practice questions will help you evaluate your understanding of the topics covered in this chapter. The questions shown are similar in nature to those found on the certification examination. Although none of these questions will be found on the exam itself, they will allow you to review your knowledge of the subject. Select the correct answers and then check the completeness of your answers in the "Practice Question Answers and Explanations" section. Remember that on the exam you must select all correct answers and only correct answers to receive credit for the question.

1. What can you use to differentiate two or more cost estimates for the same material? (There are two correct answers.)

   ☐ **A.** Costing variant

   ☐ **B.** Transfer control

   ☐ **C.** Costing version

   ☐ **D.** Valuation variant

2. What do you do to create a primary cost component split? (There are two correct answers.)

   ☐ **A.** Assign the same cost element main components

   ☐ **B.** Assign a cost component structure to the CO version

   ☐ **C.** Run an activity price calculation

   ☐ **D.** Enter split activity prices manually

3. True or False: A cost component split can have as many categories as you wish.

   ☐ **A.** True

   ☐ **B.** False

4. What do you get if you mark a standard price cost estimate? (There are two correct answers.)

☐ **A.** A new status in the cost estimate

☐ **B.** A future standard price

☐ **C.** A costing-based CO-PA document for material revaluation

☐ **D.** An accounting document for the material ledger

5. What do you use to map the primary cost component split to the product cost component structure?

☐ **A.** Assignment scheme

☐ **B.** Cost component groups

☐ **C.** Allocation structure

☐ **D.** Transfer structure

6. What is required before you can create a multilevel material cost estimate without quantity structure?

☐ **A.** Material master with accounting view and with MRP views

☐ **B.** Specific valuation variants for material costings without quantity structure

☐ **C.** Material master with costing view

☐ **D.** Specific costing variants for material costings without quantity structure

7. Which cost estimates must you reuse with the transfer control functionality?

☐ **A.** Cost estimates with same cost component structure

☐ **B.** Cost estimates with quantity structure

☐ **C.** Cost estimates within the same plant

☐ **D.** Cost estimates across company codes

8. Which object do you configure to reuse material cost estimate for the costing process?

☐ **A.** Group costing

☐ **B.** Quantity structure control

☐ **C.** Valuation variant

☐ **D.** Transfer control

9. True or False: A BOM and routing can be created specifically for costing.

☐   **A.** True
☐   **B.** False

10. Which object do you have to assign the cost component structure to?

☐   **A.** Valuation variant
☐   **B.** Costing type
☐   **C.** Costing variant
☐   **D.** Material master record

11. Which parameters can you enter when you create a costing run? (There are three correct answers.)

☐   **A.** Transfer control
☐   **B.** Costing variant
☐   **C.** Production version
☐   **D.** Costing version
☐   **E.** Valuation variant

12. Which views can you use to analyze the costing results within the costing run tool? (There are three correct answers.)

☐   **A.** Variance report
☐   **B.** Costing levels report
☐   **C.** Work in process (WIP) report
☐   **D.** Material list report
☐   **E.** Analysis report

13. You want to use a template for activity and process assignment to your material cost estimate. What do you need to do?

☐   **A.** Use the costing sheet of the **Costing 1** tab
☐   **B.** Use the template allocation function in a material cost estimate
☐   **C.** Assign a template to an operation in the routing of the material
☐   **D.** Assign a template directly to **Costing 1** tab of the material master record

14. True or False: Materials can be marked and released every week.

☐   **A.** True

☐   **B.** False

15. What are features of a cost estimate created with unit costing? (There are three correct answers.)

☐   **A.** Allows costing early in product lifecycle

☐   **B.** Material number is required

☐   **C.** BOMs and routings can be used

☐   **D.** Estimate is created automatically

☐   **E.** Requires cost element

16. True or False: The costing variant is client-level data.

☐   **A.** True

☐   **B.** False

17. A cost estimate is made up of several costing items. What data is maintained in a costing item? (There are three correct answers.)

☐   **A.** Item category

☐   **B.** BOM item

☐   **C.** Cost element .

☐   **D.** Price

☐   **E.** Validity date

18. What are uses of a cost estimate? (There are three correct answers.)

☐   **A.** Cost origin

☐   **B.** Continuous improvement

☐   **C.** Activity prices

☐   **D.** Productivity

☐   **E.** Cost center valuation

19. What is a feature of the valuation variant?

☐   **A.** Strategies are defined by costing item

☐   **B.** Strategies are defined at the BOM level

☐   **C.** Strategies must have at least two options

20. In the costing variant date control, which date will trigger different prices?

☐   **A.** Costing to and from dates

☐   **B.** Quantity structure date

☐   **C.** Valuation date

☐   **D.** BOM validity date

21. Material cost estimates with quantity structure try to find a valid BOM and routing. What are some data elements that trigger a BOM or routing? (There are three correct answers.)

☐   **A.** Valid status

☐   **B.** Valid lot size

☐   **C.** Valid dates

☐   **D.** Valid material items

☐   **E.** Valid control keys

22. What is the benefit of the primary cost component structure?

☐   **A.** Divide the COGS into more detail

☐   **B.** Show COGM

☐   **C.** Provides an alternate primary cost view

Practice Question Answers and Explanations

1. Correct answers: **A, C**
    The costing date, material, plant, costing variant, or version will create a new costing record in the database (in other words, a different cost estimate). Transfer control and valuation variants will only update the current record (in other words, giving an existing cost estimate new values).

2. Correct answers: **B, C**

   The primary cost component structure is an alternative to the main structure. The primary or auxiliary structure is optional and can use different components because it will assign primary cost elements from the cost center. To do this, you must use the activity price calculation to ensure no cost center variance exist. The automatic price calculation must have a component structure assigned in the CO version.

3. Correct answer: **B**

   False. Each cost component split can have only 40 fields. If the component is variable, then only 1 of the 40 fields will be assigned. If the field is fixed and a variable is used, then 2 of the 40 fields are assigned.

4. Correct answers: **A, B**

   Marking a cost estimate updates the status and places the value in the **Future** field of the material master. At this point, you can analyze the price and possible valuation changes. It cannot be used for postings at this point, so no documents are created.

5. Correct answer: **D**

   You must map the components in the main and primary cost component structures. This mapping is created in the transfer structure. Cost component groups are an optional setting to group similar components together to provide alternative views for reporting.

6. Correct answer: **C**

   The definition of material cost estimate specifies its structure and whether it requires a material master record. For any cost estimate to be created, the material must contain costing views. A quantity structure means master data with quantity information exists, for instance, a material BOM with material quantity or a routing with time quantities.

7. Correct answer: **A**

   Transfer control is activated during the creation of a cost estimate. Since data can be transferred across plants and across company codes, the same main cost component structure must be used for data consistency. You could use a different cost component for individual plants, but then data couldn't be transferred.

8. Correct answer: **D**

   Transfer control brings existing lower-level costing details into the current costing structure. This process doesn't explode and recalculate lower-level items but only brings in existing value. Without transfer control, full structures are exploded, and new prices are read. If any master data changes have occurred in the quantity structure, that information is used to build the cost estimate.

9. Correct answer: **A**

   True. Costing can use manufacturing master data or create a structure specifically for product costing. The BOM and routing specified in the header record controls which data will be used. If costing doesn't specify data, costing will use the manufacturing data.

10. Correct answer: **C**

    A costing variant contains all the parameters for creating a cost estimate. In its details, a cost component structure is assigned. It contains different costing variants that can use different cost component structures. In the material master, it contains many costing-relevant settings but not logic for selecting quantity data or prices. A valuation variant contains prices relevant for costing.

11. Correct answers: **A, B, D**

    Unlike individual cost estimates, you can only enter a transfer control, a costing variant, and a costing version. Other parameters are determined automatically or from selection criteria. A valuation variant is defined inside the costing variant.

12. Correct answers: **B, D, E**

    The costing run has three standard views for analyzing the costing run process. There are additional reports available to review the costing run output. The variance and WIP reports are reports used to analyze production orders.

13. Correct answer: **B**

    You need to set up the template allocation function. To activate the template, you'll link the template to costing sheet in configuration. You can't assign a template, a costing sheet, or operations in the material master; it must come through the costing variant assignments in configuration. The costing sheet and template can be assigned directly in a cost object, allowing updates in master data and not configuration.

14. Correct answer: **B**

    False. You can mark a material repeatedly, as often as you like. Marking a cost estimate sets a status flag so that reporting and comparisons can occur. Releasing a cost estimate creates valuation postings and can happen only once in each fiscal period.

15. Correct answers: **A, C, E**

    Unit cost estimates can be created prior to master data creation. Since you are creating a cost estimate, cost elements aren't required. If other master data exists, you can enter this information, which is not required. Materials, BOMs, and routings are required when creating material costing with quantity structure, since they are created automatically.

16. Correct answer: **A**

    True. The costing variant is a client-level setting that allows any controlling area, any plant, and any material in the client to access the costing variant. However, the valuation variant can be defined at the plant level but only provides a separate strategy for determining prices. If a different set of costing rules is needed, then you must configure additional costing variants.

17. Correct answers: **A, C, D**

    The details contained in all costing items are item category, cost element, and price. Other details will vary based on the specific to the item category type. For example, M requires plant and material data, E requires a cost center and activity price, and G would require a costing sheet.

18. Correct answers: **A, B, D**

    At first glance, a cost estimate is used to set standards but, in some cases, can have many other purposes. A few common uses for cost estimates is to identify cost origin, to indicate productivity levels, and to identify continuous improvement.

19. Correct answer: **A**

    Strategies in a valuation variant are defined per costing item category. Strategies do not specify a required number of options. Not all valuation settings are required, but in most cases, a strategy will be included if material planning uses the process in their BOMs or routings.

20. Correct answer: **C**

    The valuation date will activate prices valid on that date. The costing to and from dates define the relevant data of the costing record. The quantity structure date determines the validity date for the availability of quantity structure master data. The valuation date determines the availability of prices.

21. Correct answers: **A, B, C**

    Master data for costing must have a valid status, a valid lot size for the costing lot size, and valid dates. The items must also be flagged as relevant for costing.

Valid material items are not determined directly but through a combination of other settings.

22. Correct answer: **C**

The auxiliary or primary cost component structure provides addition component views based on primary cost center values. This view, along with the main cost component structure, can be used for comparison and can be sent to CO-PA for additional COGS analysis.

Takeaway

The previous chapters in this book have focused on overhead management. Product cost planning is an introduction into product cost controlling functionality and is a prerequisite to cost object controlling, which we'll discuss in the next chapter.

The planning process creates cost estimates that can be used for many purposes, not just setting material standards. The product costing solution contains functionalities for creating estimates at various stages of product development and at various stages of master data creation.

The product costing process is controlled by the costing variant. A costing variant is an intricate set of parameters that control how costing will operate. You can create costing variants for exploring many different costing scenarios.

Product costing is highly integrated with the master data throughout the system. Logistics master data can be used for cost planning, as well as manufacturing and logistics processes. Understanding all the master data options for cost estimates is a daunting but necessary part of the costing processes. This master data also gives product costing the flexibility to evaluate alternatives and provide detailed costing information for analyzing logistic functions.

Summary

Product costing is a complicated subject, using features from CO, FI, and logistics to determine product valuations. While master data integration allows the costing process to be automated, trying to follow the flow or determine the source of errors can be complicated. Cost planning provides the tools you need to meet all your costing requirements but requires a high level of knowledge to understand the interaction of all the data elements.

The second phase of product cost controlling is cost object controlling, which you'll master in the next chapter. You'll also see additional uses for costing variants. Note that the costing variant used in cost object controlling is different than the ones used for standard price setting. The parameters will be different, but the foundation is the same as you've seen in this chapter.

Chapter 6
Cost Object Controlling

Techniques You'll Master

- Configure cost object controlling by period and by order
- Manage orders from preliminary costing through simultaneous costing
- Understand work in process (WIP) calculations
- Understand variance calculations
- Understand the settlement of cost objects
- Manage sales order-related production scenarios
- Explain simultaneous costing and stock valuation
- Understand results analysis calculations
- Understand the settlement of sales orders

In this chapter, we'll explain the purpose and design of cost object controlling by discussing the different cost objects available, the basic configuration of each, and the costing phases from preliminary costing through final costing.

Real-World Scenario

Cost object controlling is one of the most complex components in controlling (CO). As a CO consultant, you may be asked to decide which of the three cost objects to implement. You'll need a solid understanding of how these three cost objects differ from both a business process view and from a technical view.

The calculation of plan and actual (or simultaneous) values are a few of the tasks performed in the scope of cost object controlling, and you'll need to be able to configure these calculations and explain them to your customers.

You may also need to explain how SAP S/4HANA calculates values such as WIP and the different variance categories, as well as handle more complex results analysis steps for sales order controlling.

This component of CO builds on the knowledge you've gained regarding product cost planning in Chapter 5, as these two processes are tightly integrated in valuating the cost objects used for cost object controlling. In addition to integration with CO, as a CO consultant, you'll also need a foundation in the integration with logistics in the areas of production planning (PP), material requirements planning (MRP), and sales and distribution (SD).

Objectives of This Portion of the Test

The objective of this portion of the certification exam is to test your understanding of configuring core objects as well as test your understanding the main business processes of cost object controlling.

The certification exam expects you to have a good understanding of the following topics:

- Cost object controlling by period
- Cost object controlling by order
- Sales order-related controlling

- Work in process (WIP)
- Variance categories
- Settlement

> **Note**
> The cost object controlling accounting topic makes up 12% of the total exam.

Key Concepts Refresher

Cost object controlling is a subset of product costing, which includes product cost planning as a prerequisite. In Chapter 5, we reviewed the requirements of creating material cost estimates: the quantity structure and the resource prices needed to plan a cost at a point in time.

In cost object controlling, our task is to measure the cost of producing goods and services against material cost estimates (usually the standard cost estimate) created during product cost planning. You'll accomplish this task by using a cost object. Depending on the CO requirements, you can use any of the following objects as the cost object:

- Sales orders
- Production orders
- Process orders
- Project systems
- Product cost collectors

Functions supported by cost object controlling include the following:

- Valuation of material movements
- Allocation of overhead cost from cost centers and business processes
- Calculating WIP
- Calculating variances
- Settlement to FI-CO, with details for valuation if results analysis is in scope

In the following sections, we'll review three cost object controlling scenarios and walk through examples of the configuration steps involved in deploying each scenario.

Methods and Valuation Phases

In SAP S/4HANA, three scenarios are available for use in cost object controlling:

- Controlling by period
- Controlling by order
- Controlling by sales order item (SDI)

Let's begin with a high-level comparison of these three scenarios, or controlling methods, as listed in Table 6.1.

SAP Scenario	By period	By order	By sales order
Cost Object	Product cost collector	Production order	SDI
Manufacturing Scenario	Repetitive	Make-to-stock (MTS)	Make-to-order (MTO)
Periodic WIP	WIP and variance	WIP or variance	No
Periodic Variance	WIP and variance	WIP or variance	No
Periodic Results Analysis	No	No	Yes
WIP Method	At target	At actual	N/A

Table 6.1 Comparison of Scenarios

> **Tip**
> As you can see, many factors are involved in the decision of which scenario to deploy. All shop floor processes and accounting requirements require a thorough review during the project blueprinting phase to determine the best choice.

Regardless of the scenario you choose, each cost object used will require similar valuation phases, each with its own calculation method and each tightly integrated with logistics processes:

- **Preliminary costing**
  This phase calculates the preliminary (or planned) costs by applying the strategy of a preliminary costing variant to the quantity structure of the cost object. An example of this method could be valuating the quantity of the raw material required on a production order according to the standard price of the raw material. In the information system, you can measure actual costs against these values.

- **Simultaneous costing**
  During this phase, goods are being issued and received in the warehouse, and labor times are being confirmed by the shop floor, each with reference to the cost object. These actual quantities are reported by logistics workers and are valuated on the cost object by the actual costing variant in real time.

- **Periodic costing**
  During this phase, additional costs not already included can be calculated, and activity prices can be revaluated from a plan price to an actual price.

- **Final costing**
  This phase calculates the value of any unfinished inventory (WIP) and variances between the actual cost and a standard cost estimate as well as, in the case of cost objects with revenue, *results analysis* (often referred to as RA). The last step of final costing is to post these calculations to FI-CO through *settlement*.

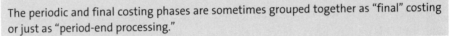

Note
The periodic and final costing phases are sometimes grouped together as "final" costing or just as "period-end processing."

You can align these CO valuation phases to the lifecycle of a production order or process order in logistics as follows:

1. An order is created, scheduled, and released (in logistics), and preliminary costing occurs (in CO).

2. Materials are withdrawn, confirmations posted, and goods receipts posted (in logistics); simultaneous costing occurs (in CO).

3. The order status is maintained, ultimately to **TECO** (technically complete) (in logistics): final costing takes place (in CO).

Product Cost Controlling by Period

This scenario is most often deployed in a *repetitive manufacturing* environment. Repetitive manufacturing involves the rapid manufacturing of goods, often in an automated factory, for example, automobiles and electronic goods. An assembly line is run until all available raw materials are consumed, and then the line switches to another product.

In many cases, a planned production order is used on the factory floor. A planned order is not considered to be a "real" order and cannot collect costs. A planned order presents an opportunity for costing, famously called a *decoupling scenario* in SAP S/4HANA. This decoupling is quite simple: The PP order type has an indicator to "decouple" the order from costing.

To accommodate this PP requirement, SAP S/4HANA offers standard order types for CO: order type RM01 and order type YBMR. These order types create a *product cost collector* that will be linked to the PP orders. All quantities are reported on the PP order, but all valuation occurs on the CO product cost collector.

In this section, we'll walk through the key components to configure for cost object controlling by period.

Order Type for Controlling by Period

The product cost collector master record is created by selecting an appropriate order type. All the control functions of the order type are then transferred to the product cost collector being created.

The order type is created and maintained in the configuration menu. The order type for CO is a client level object, created as category **05-Product Cost Collector**.

As shown in Figure 6.1, all control parameters are contained in the order type including:

- **Number range interval**: Controls the number assigned to the product cost collector at creation.
- **Settlement prof.**: Controls settlement routine of the product cost collector.
- **Planning Profile**: Controls how overall values are planned on the product cost collector.
- **Commit. Management**: If selected, the product cost collector will be updated with commitments.

> **Note**
> Commitments are first activated at the controlling area level, as discussed earlier in Chapter 2. Once active, you'll be able to see the open purchase documents for the cost object.

The profiles mentioned earlier are created independent of the order type and can be assigned to many order types. We'll review various profiles in later sections of this chapter.

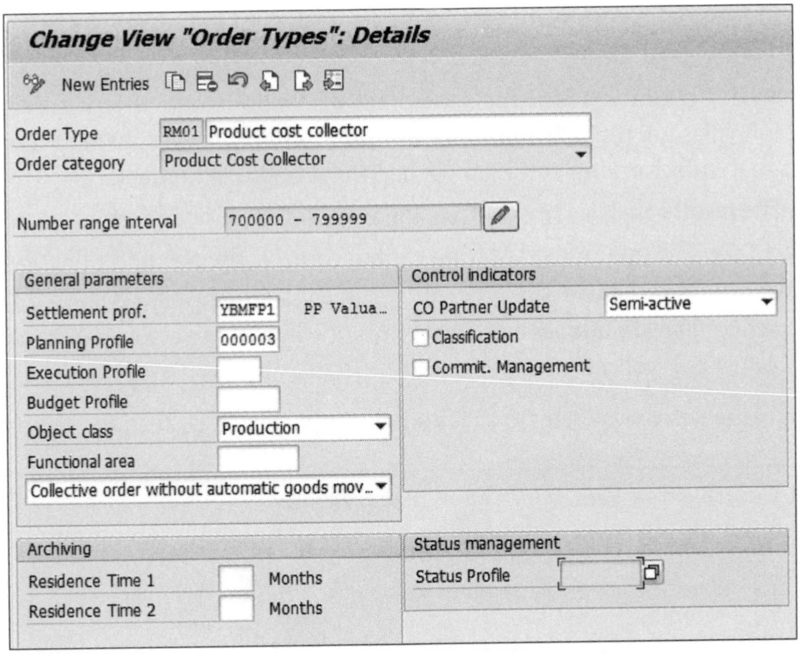

Change View "Order Types": Details

New Entries

| Order Type | RM01 | Product cost collector |
| Order category | Product Cost Collector | |

Number range interval 700000 – 799999

General parameters

Settlement prof.	YBMFP1	PP Valua...
Planning Profile	000003	
Execution Profile		
Budget Profile		
Object class	Production	
Functional area		
Collective order without automatic goods mov...		

Control indicators

CO Partner Update	Semi-active
☐ Classification	
☐ Commit. Management	

Archiving

| Residence Time 1 | | Months |
| Residence Time 2 | | Months |

Status management

| Status Profile | | |

Figure 6.1 Order Type RM01 for Product Cost Collector

Cost Accounting-Relevant Defaults

As order types are defined at the SAP S/4HANA client level, SAP S/4HANA provides an additional level of detail for cost accounting default values to the order. As shown in Figure 6.2, these defaults are assigned at the plant level.

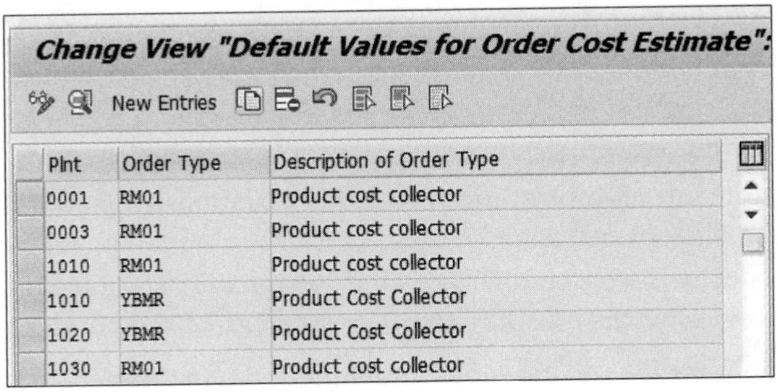

Change View "Default Values for Order Cost Estimate":

New Entries

Plnt	Order Type	Description of Order Type
0001	RM01	Product cost collector
0003	RM01	Product cost collector
1010	RM01	Product cost collector
1010	YBMR	Product Cost Collector
1020	YBMR	Product Cost Collector
1030	RM01	Product cost collector

Figure 6.2 Default Values by Plant (Transaction OKZ3)

As shown in Figure 6.3, each plant can define its own rules for costing by order type, including:

- **Default Rule**: Determines how the settlement distribution rule is structured. The default rules are predefined by SAP S/4HANA and cannot be changed. For product cost collectors, this setting must be **STR** (periodic settlement).
- **RA Key**: The results analysis key controls the WIP process at period end.
- **Prel./Vers.Cstg**: The preliminary costing variant controls the planned valuation of the product cost collector.
- **Simul. Costing**: The simultaneous costing variant controls the actual valuation of the product cost collector.

All the default values will transfer to the product cost collector at creation.

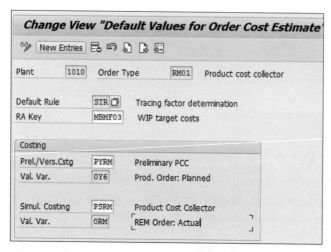

Figure 6.3 Plant-Level Default Values for Order Cost (Transaction OKZ3)

Costing Variant for Controlling by Period

The costing variant contains all control parameters for valuation. As shown in Figure 6.4, various tabs and control features of a preliminary costing variant can be maintained for a product cost collector. This costing variant will determine the cost estimate calculation when the product cost collector is created and saved.

This process looks similar to the costing variants we introduced in Chapter 5, but with one major difference—the costing type. As shown in Figure 6.5, **No Update** is selected for **Price Update ❶**, and the indicator for **Prelim Costg For Prod. Cost Collectors** must be selected ❷ on the costing type.

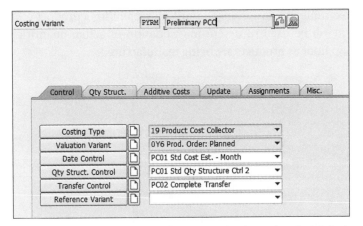

Figure 6.4 Costing Variant Preliminary Costing for the Product Cost Collector

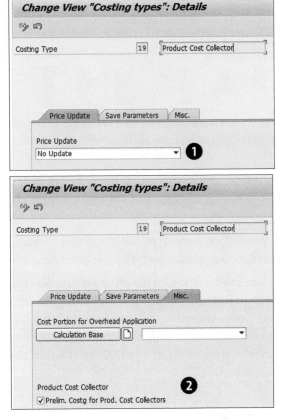

Figure 6.5 Costing Type for the Product Cost Collector

Figure 6.6 shows an example of a simultaneous costing variant for a product cost collector. This variant will be used to determine valuation of actual quantities reported from the shop floor as products are being manufactured.

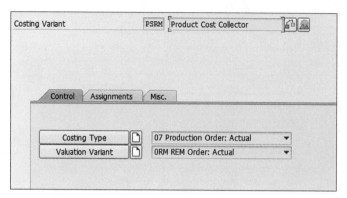

Figure 6.6 Costing Variant Simultaneous Costing for the Product Cost Collector

In the "Product Cost Controlling by Order" section, we'll review more details about each costing variant.

Order Type for Logistics

The logistics production order master record is created by first selecting an appropriate order type. All control functions of the order type are then transferred to the order being created.

The order type is created and maintained in the configuration menu. For an understanding of the process integration between logistics and CO, you'll need basic knowledge about this order type.

Figure 6.7 shows an example of a production order type for use in this scenario. Any cost-related settings are assigned to the product cost collector order type.

To trigger the decoupling scenario, one more setting for the production order type is important. In shop floor control configuration, as shown in Figure 6.8, the **Cost Collector** checkbox must be selected. Once selected, at creation, production orders will first search for a valid product cost collector to assign itself to for controlling valuation. If found, the production order status will indicate **PCC**. If not found, the production order defaults as the cost object.

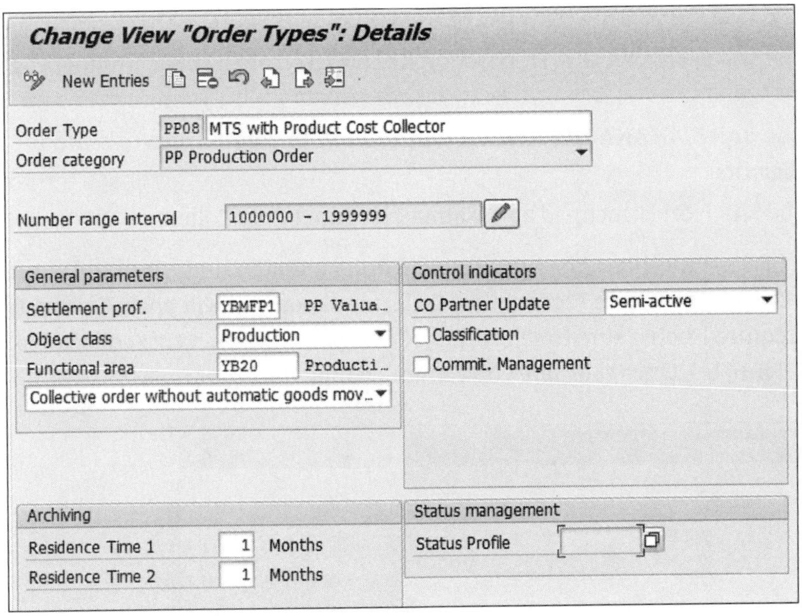

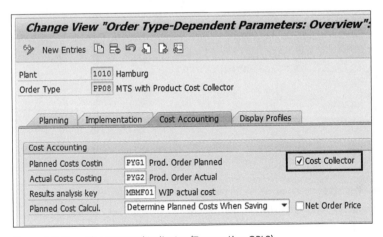

Figure 6.7 Order Type PP08 Production Order Example

Figure 6.8 Shop Floor Control Indicator (Transaction OPL8)

Preliminary Costing for Controlling by Period

Preliminary costing is the planned value of the product cost collector and is calculated when the product cost collector is created and saved.

Product cost collector master records can be created in several ways:

- Using the SAP S/4HANA GUI Transaction KKF6N to create a single product cost collector
- Using the SAP S/4HANA GUI Transaction KKF6M to create collective product cost collectors
- Using the SAP Fiori launchpad app Maintain Product Cost Collectors

Using any of these methods, the first step is to enter a material number and plant, then click **Create**. The **Create Product Cost Collector** dialog box will open. Complete the fields required, being sure to select the order type for product cost collector, as shown in Figure 6.9. Once selected, you cannot change the order type.

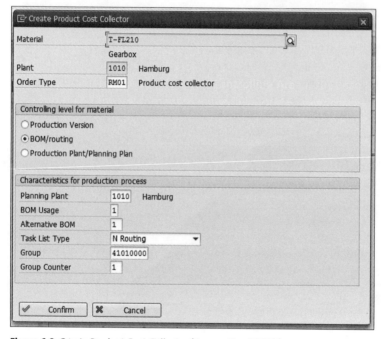

Figure 6.9 Create Product Cost Collector (Transaction KKF6N)

After selecting the **Controlling level for material**, the fields required in the **Characteristics for production process** section will differ. For example, if the controlling level is **Production Version**, you must enter a production version number. If the controlling level is **BOM/routing**, you must maintain the **BOM Usage** field, and so on.

Click **Confirm** to continue, and the system will display the tabs for maintaining the product cost collector, as shown in Figure 6.10.

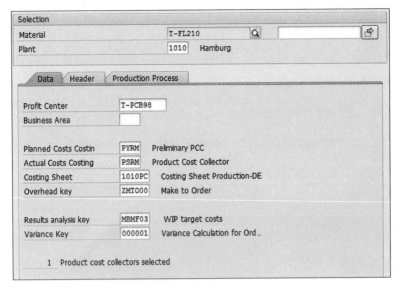

Figure 6.10 Product Cost Collector Data Tab

On the product cost collector **Data** tab, the defaults shown in Table 6.2 will be populated.

Field	Value	Defaulted From	Purpose
Profit Center	T-PCB98	Material master	Profit center accounting
Planned Cost Costin	PYRM	Order type RM01	Plan valuation
Actual Costs Costing	PSRM	Order type RM01	Simultaneous valuation
Costing Sheet	1010PC	Order type RM01	Overhead calculation
Overhead key	ZMT000	Material master	Overhead calculation
Results analysis key	MBMF03	Order type RM01	WIP calculation
Variance Key	000001	Material master	Variance category calculation

Table 6.2 Product Cost Collector Data Tab Defaults with Source and Purpose

Next, let's review the **Header** tab, shown in Figure 6.11.

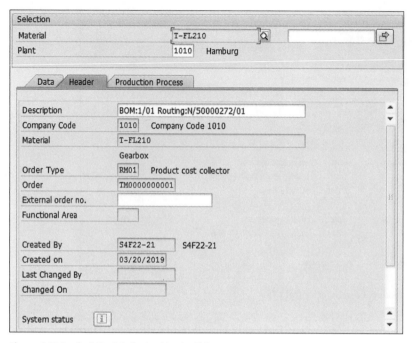

Figure 6.11 Product Cost Collector Header Tab

The defaults values shown in Table 6.3 are displayed.

Field	Value	Defaulted From	Purpose
Description	Routing:N/50000272/01	Routing: N/50000272/01	Indicates the routing and bill of material (BOM)
Company Code	1010	Plant	FI
Order	TM0000000001	Temporary until saving	Temporary until saving

Table 6.3 Product Cost Collector Header Tab Defaults with Source and Purpose

Finally, let's review the **Production Process** tab, shown in Figure 6.12.

On this final tab, you'll see values we previously entered and explained—with one exception: the **Production Process No** field. This new field is very important for integration with logistics production orders. As we entered details into the **Characteristics for production process** section, shown earlier in Figure 6.9, the system was assigning this unique production process number to identify this unique combination of controlling level characteristics. We'll see in a moment how this unique identifier integrates with logistics.

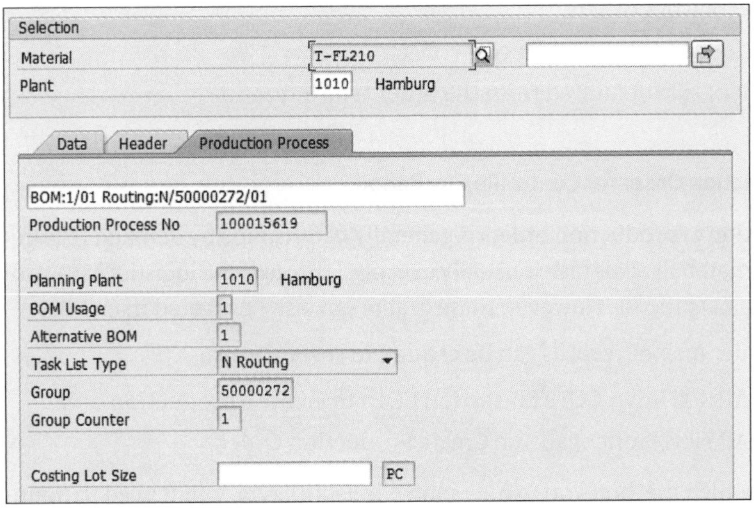

Figure 6.12 Product Cost Collector Production Process Tab

Upon saving the product cost collector, a preliminary cost estimate will be created for this cost object, and its itemization will be displayed immediately, as shown in Figure 6.13. You can verify the itemization immediately by comparing this information to the preliminary costing variant.

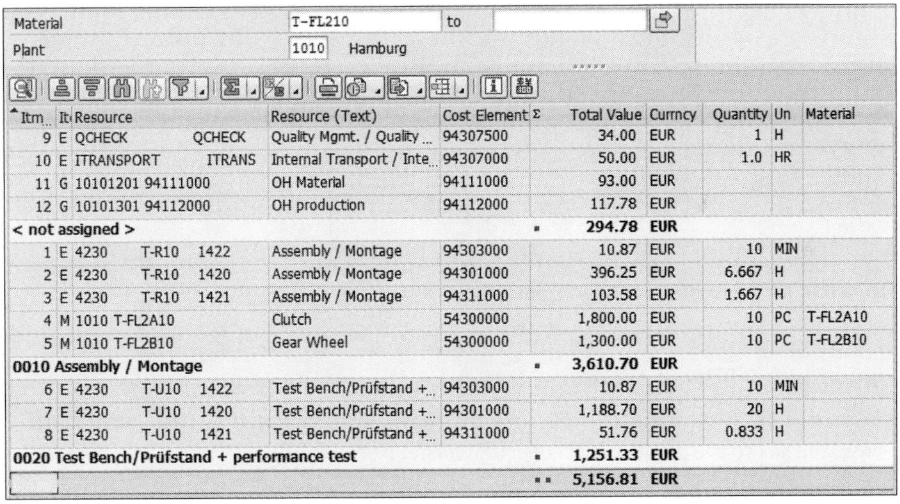

Material T-FL210 to

Plant 1010 Hamburg

Itm..	It	Resource	Resource (Text)	Cost Element	Σ	Total Value	Currncy	Quantity	Un	Material
9	E	QCHECK QCHECK	Quality Mgmt. / Quality...	94307500		34.00	EUR	1	H	
10	E	ITRANSPORT ITRANS	Internal Transport / Inte...	94307000		50.00	EUR	1.0	HR	
11	G	10101201 94111000	OH Material	94111000		93.00	EUR			
12	G	10101301 94112000	OH production	94112000		117.78	EUR			
< not assigned >					▪	**294.78**	**EUR**			
1	E	4230 T-R10 1422	Assembly / Montage	94303000		10.87	EUR	10	MIN	
2	E	4230 T-R10 1420	Assembly / Montage	94301000		396.25	EUR	6.667	H	
3	E	4230 T-R10 1421	Assembly / Montage	94311000		103.58	EUR	1.667	H	
4	M	1010 T-FL2A10	Clutch	54300000		1,800.00	EUR	10	PC	T-FL2A10
5	M	1010 T-FL2B10	Gear Wheel	54300000		1,300.00	EUR	10	PC	T-FL2B10
0010 Assembly / Montage					▪	**3,610.70**	**EUR**			
6	E	4230 T-U10 1422	Test Bench/Prüfstand +...	94303000		10.87	EUR	10	MIN	
7	E	4230 T-U10 1420	Test Bench/Prüfstand +...	94301000		1,188.70	EUR	20	H	
8	E	4230 T-U10 1421	Test Bench/Prüfstand +...	94311000		51.76	EUR	0.833	H	
0020 Test Bench/Prüfstand + performance test					▪	**1,251.33**	**EUR**			
					▪▪	**5,156.81**	**EUR**			

Figure 6.13 Product Cost Collector Itemization

After saving, the **Header** tab will be updated with the following information:

- The product cost collector order number
- Links to any logistics orders
- The cost estimate of the product cost collector
- The settlement rule defaulted from the order type RM01

Logistics Production Order for Controlling by Period

The mass creation of production orders is generally determined by demand requirements for the materials. This task is usually executed through the logistics MRP processes, not by a CO process. However, these orders can also be created manually.

Production order master records can be created in several ways:

- Using the SAP S/4HANA GUI Transaction CO01 to create a production order
- Using the SAP Fiori launchpad app Create Production Order

Regardless of which method you use, as shown in Figure 6.14, you'll need to maintain the following fields:

- **Material** (material number)
- **Production Plant**
- **Order Type**

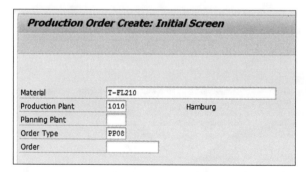

Figure 6.14 Create Production Order (Transaction CO01)

Warning!

Be sure to enter the logistics order type that has been configured as decoupled! Otherwise, the link to the product cost collector will not be found.

After any logistics-required fields have been entered, the system will indicate that a product cost collector has been found for this controlling level by displaying the status **PCC** in the order, as shown in Figure 6.15.

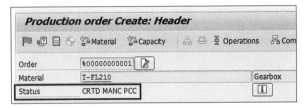

Figure 6.15 Production Order Status Indicator PCC

To see additional details related to the product cost collector, navigate to the **Control** tab of the production order, as shown in Figure 6.16.

Production order Create: Header

Order	$00000000001
Material	T-FL210	Gearbox
Status	CRTD MANC PCC

General   Assignment   Goods Receipt   Control   Dates/Qties   Master Data   Long Tex

Order

Reference Order		Deletion Flag	☐
Reserv./PReq	2 From release		

Costing

PlnCstgVar	PYG1	ActCstgVar	PSRM	Product Cost Collector
Costing Sheet	1010PC	Overhead key	ZMT000	
RA Key		Variance Key		
PlannedCostCalc	2 Determine Planned Costs When Savi... ▾			
Prod. Process	100015619	BOM:1/01 Routing:N/50000272/01		

Figure 6.16 Production Order Control Tab

In the costing group of the **Control** tab, costing variants and other costing-related defaults may exist. However, these variants are not valid because this production order is not a cost object. Double-click the **Product Cost Collector** button to transfer to the cost object, the product cost collector, as shown in Figure 6.17. Note that the production process number is the same on both objects, in this case, **100015619**.

Figure 6.17 Transfer to the Product Cost Collector

Return to the production order and complete the process by releasing and saving the order. An order number will be assigned based on the number range assigned to order type PPO8.

> **Note**
>
> The product cost collector and the production order will *not* have the same number assignment. Each order type has its own unique number range.

Simultaneous Costing for Controlling by Period

As logistics shop floor reporting progresses, the quantities of materials and labor are reported to the production order. Valuations of these quantities are posted to the product cost collector based on the simultaneous costing variant. The design and purpose of this variant is the same as found in CO by order, and we'll review its settings in the "Product Cost Controlling by Order" section.

> **Note**
>
> As the product is being made, logistics reports to the production order, not to the product cost collector.

You can analyze both orders using the following transactions:

- Production order: Transaction CO03 and Transaction COOIS
- Product cost collector: Transaction KKBC_PKO

On the product cost collector, all values flow through the profit and loss (P&L) statement according to the account determination of the materials and the activity types. More details on simultaneous costing will be covered in the "Product Cost Controlling by Order" section of this chapter.

Final Costing for Controlling by Period

At period-end close, the steps for final costing are executed, which may include all or some of the following steps:

- Template allocation: If cost objects are senders of overhead via templates.
- Revaluation at actual prices: Cost center activity prices are recalculated at actual, and their consumption is revalued.
- Overhead: If cost objects are senders of overhead via costing sheets.
- WIP: If a legal requirement exists to capitalize unfinished inventory.
- Variances: If reporting requirements exist for analysis by category.
- Settlement: To post the result of WIP and variance to FI.

More details on final costing will be covered in the "Product Cost Controlling by Order" section. However, an important topic to discuss is how WIP is calculated for a product cost collector.

WIP is calculated using a target cost method for the product cost collector. Let's take a closer look at what this means.

Product cost collectors can calculate both variances and WIP in the same accounting period. This feature of the product cost collector cost object is unique, and several settings make this capability possible:

- The default rule of the product cost collector order type—we reviewed this setting in Figure 6.2. For a product cost collector, this rule must be set as **STR** (periodic settlement).
- In configuration, you must complete the Define Valuation Method (Target Costs) transaction (Transaction OKGD).
- In configuration, you must complete the Define Valuation Variant for WIP and Scrap (Target Costs) transaction.

An example of the defined valuation variant is shown in Figure 6.18. In these settings, you'll indicate which cost estimates will be used and assign a priority to each. In our example, the first priority is to use the product cost collector plan cost; if this value is not available, the second priority is to use the current standard cost estimate.

Tip

The priority you assign in this step may depend on your accounting policy. You may require the standard cost estimate to be the basis for WIP, depending on your country.

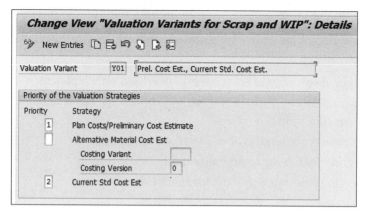

Figure 6.18 Define Valuation Variant for WIP and Scrap (Target Costs)

When WIP is calculated for a product cost collector, the system determines the unfinished quantities at each operation based on the quantity reported as complete, then valuates those quantities based on the incremental (by operation) cost estimate defined in the valuation variant.

❷ Target cost estimate per piece:

Operation#	Material	Labor	Overhead
10	$ 100	$ 20	$ 10
20	$ -	$ 30	$ 15
Total =	$ 100	$ 50	$ 25

❶ Shop floor reporting:

Op#	Description	Quantity reported	Quantity remaining
10	Withdraw raw material from warehouse	100	25
20	Grind housing	75	50

Quantity received as finished =	25

❸ Incremental cost by operation:

Quantity remaining		Material	Labor	Overhead
25	10	$ 2,500	$ 500	$ 250
50	20	$ -	$ 1,500	$ 750
WIP =		$ 2,500	$ 2,000	$ 1,000

Figure 6.19 WIP at Target

Figure 6.19 shows a simple example of the calculation:

❶ Quantities have been reported for two operations and as finished goods. The system can calculate how much material is left unfinished at each operation. For example, if 100 pcs of raw material were issued and 75 pcs were complete through grinding, 25 pcs must remain at the end of the first operation.

❷ The target cost estimate exists with incremental costs by operation. In this example, these costs are broken down by material, labor, and overhead costs.

❸ The system can calculate WIP as the value of the unfinished quantity left at each operation:

- Operation 10 = 25 pcs × target cost at operation 10 = $2,500 material, $500 labor, $250 overhead
- Operation 20 = 50 pcs × target cost at operation 20 = $0 material, $1,500 labor, $750 overhead

SAP S/4HANA calculates the WIP and variance of a product cost collector using the following steps:

1. Calculate WIP at target, as shown in Figure 6.19.
2. Calculate the variance according to following formula:

   Variance = Product cost collector order debits – Goods receipts – WIP at target.

In the "Product Cost Controlling by Order" section, you'll see how order WIP is calculated and get an overview of the configuration settings.

In closing, let's review the costing phases and value flow for period controlling, as shown in Figure 6.20.

Preliminary Costing	FI-CO Posting	Simultaneous Costing			FI-CO Posting	Periodic Costs		FI-CO Posting
Order Type Preliminary Costing Variant x Product Cost Contoller Quantity Structure		Debit	Quantity Goods Issue x Price Control		Yes	Debit	Template Allocation	Yes
		Debit	Labor Confirmation x Simultaneous Costing Variant		Yes	Debit	Revaluation at Actual Prices	Yes
		Credit	Quantity Goods Receipt x Price Control		Yes	Debit	Overhead Costs	Yes
Plan Value of Product Cost Controller	No		Actual Order Balance				Actual Order Balance	

		Final Costing	FI-CO Posting
		Calculate WIP at Target and Calculate Variance	No
			No
		Settlement	Yes

Figure 6.20 Period Controlling Value Flow

Product Cost Controlling by Order

This scenario is most often deployed in a *discrete manufacturing* environment. In discrete manufacturing, each product is manufactured in individually defined lots. Examples include any lot-based production.

> **Note**
> You may be familiar with the phrase "process manufacturing." For our purposes, this kind of manufacturing falls under controlling by order.

Production (or process) orders are created and released to the shop floor to produce specific quantities of semifinished and finished goods. These logistics orders are the CO cost objects—all quantities are valuated on the logistics order. SAP S/4HANA offers several standard order types for this scenario, including order type PIO1 and order type YBM2 (category 05) for process orders and order type PPO1 and order type YBM1 (category 10) for production orders.

Each order type is created within a specific category that determines what master data is required. If you create an order with order type PIO1, the system will search for a master recipe. If you create an order with order type PPO1, the system will search for a BOM and a routing.

In this section, we'll walk through the key components you'll need to configure for cost object controlling by order.

Order Type for Controlling by Order

A production order is created by first selecting an appropriate order type. All the control functions of the order type are then transferred to the production order being created.

The order type is created and maintained in the configuration menu. The order type for CO is a client-level object, created as category **10-PP Production Order**. As shown in Figure 6.21, all control parameters are contained in the order type, including:

- **Number range interval**: Controls the number assigned to the order master record at creation. This range can be an internal or an external number range.
- **Settlement prof.**: Controls the settlement routine of the order.
- **Commit. Management**: If selected, this order will be updated with commitments.

The profiles mentioned earlier are created independent of the order type and can be assigned to many order types. We'll review various profiles later in this chapter.

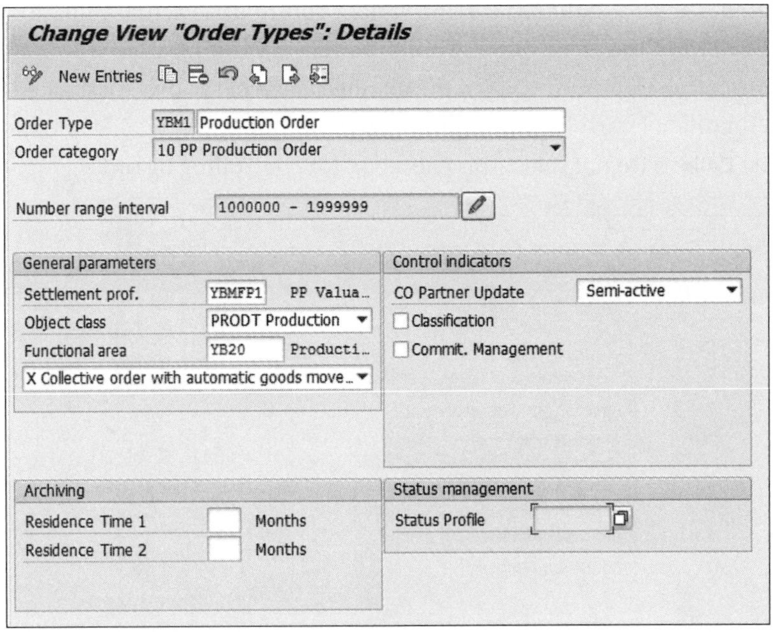

Figure 6.21 Order Type YBM1 for Production Order

Cost Accounting-Relevant Defaults for Controlling by Order

As order types are defined at the SAP S/4HANA client level, SAP S/4HANA provides an additional level of detail for cost accounting default values to the order. As shown in Figure 6.22, these defaults are assigned at the plant level. Notice that, compared to the same setting for controlling by period shown in Figure 6.3, only a few additional indicators are required.

As shown in Figure 6.22, each plant can define its own rules for costing by order type, including the following:

- **Default Rule**: Determines how the settlement distribution rule is structured. The default rules are predefined by SAP S/4HANA and cannot be changed. For orders, this rule must be **PP1** (full settlement).
- **RA Key**: The results analysis key controls the WIP process at period end.
- **Prel./Vers.Cstg**: The preliminary costing variant controls the planned valuation of the production order.

- **Simul. Costing**: The simultaneous costing variant controls the actual valuation of the production order.
- **Planned Cost Calcul**: Determines when the planned value of the order is created. This indicator did not exist for controlling by period.
- **Product Cost Collect**: Do *not* select this checkbox for controlling by order.

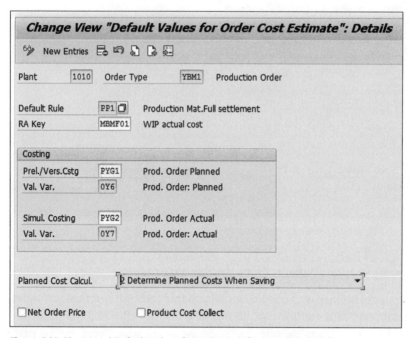

Figure 6.22 Plant-Level Default Values for Order Cost (Transaction OKZ3)

All default values will transfer to the order at creation.

Costing Variant for Controlling by Order

The costing variant contains all control parameters for valuation. Figure 6.23 shows the various tabs and control features of a preliminary costing variant for an order. This variant will determine the plan cost estimate when the production order is created and saved, much like the costing variants introduced in Chapter 5.

> **Note**
> This costing variant does not have quantity structure control parameters like the product cost collector variant did because the quantity structure will be taken from the BOM and routing assigned to the production order.

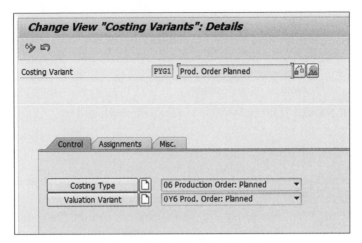

Figure 6.23 Costing Variant Preliminary Costing for Order

Figure 6.24 shows the various tabs and control features of an actual costing variant for an order. This variant will be used to determine the valuation of quantities reported from the shop floor to the production order.

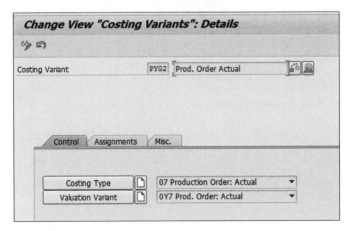

Figure 6.24 Costing Variant Simultaneous Costing for Order

Order Type for Logistics

Unlike product cost controlling by period, CO and logistics use the same production order. No separate order type is required for this method unlike controlling by period, where the CO and logistics orders were distinct or decoupled.

Preliminary Costing for Controlling by Order

Preliminary costing is the planned value of the order and is calculated when the order is created.

Order master records can be created in several ways:

- Using the SAP S/4HANA GUI Transaction CO01 to create a single order
- Executing MRP
- Using the SAP Fiori launchpad app Create Production Order

Using any of these methods, the first step is to enter a material number, plant, and order type and then press Enter. Figure 6.25 shows the transaction for creating orders (Transaction CO01). Once you press Enter, you cannot change the order type.

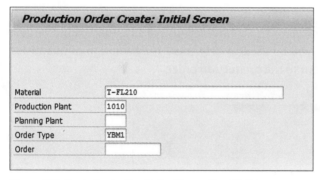

Production Order Create: Initial Screen

Material	T-FL210
Production Plant	1010
Planning Plant	
Order Type	YBM1
Order	

Figure 6.25 Create Production Order (Transaction CO01)

Once an order quantity and other logistical requirements have been entered, navigate to the **Control** tab to verify default values from the order type, as shown in Figure 6.26.

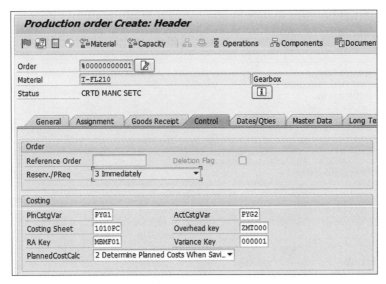

Figure 6.26 Production Order Control Tab

Under the order **Control** tab, as shown in Figure 6.26, the default values listed in Table 6.4 are displayed.

Field	Value	Defaulted From	Purpose
PlnCstgVar	PYG1	Order type YBM1	Plan valuation
ActCstgVar	PYG2	Order type YBM1	Simultaneous valuation
Costing Sheet	1010PC	Order type YBM1	Overhead calculation
Overhead key	ZMT0000	Material master	Overhead calculation
RA Key	MBMF03	Order type YBM1	WIP calculation
Variance Key	000001	Material master	Variance category calculation

Table 6.4 Order Control Tab Defaults with Source and Purpose

Tip

The profit center defaults to the order from the material master and can be found on the **Assignment** tab of the order.

Upon saving the order, a preliminary cost estimate will be created for this cost object. You can display its itemization immediately, as shown in Figure 6.27. You can verify the itemization immediately by comparing this information to the preliminary costing variant.

Order	1000124 T-FL210
Order Type	YBM1 Production Order
Plant	1010 Hamburg
Material	T-FL210 Gearbox

Planned Quantity 100 PC Piece

Cumulative Data
Legal Valuation
Company Code Currency/Object Currency

Transaction	Origin ▲	Origin (Text)	Σ	Total Plan Costs	Total plan quantity
Goods Issues	1010/T-FL2A...	Clutch		18,000.00	100
	1010/T-FL2B...	Gear Wheel		13,000.00	100
Goods Issues			▪	**31,000.00**	
Confirmations	4230/1420	Logistics Production ...		15,849.30	266.667
	4230/1422	Logistics Production ...		21.74	0.334
	4230/1421	Logistics Production ...		1,553.41	25
Confirmations			▪	**17,424.45**	
Overhead	10101201	Purch & Store 1 (DE)		930.00	
	10101301	Manufacturing 1 (DE)		1,144.67	
Overhead			▪	**2,074.67**	
Miscellaneous	300900	Work Scheduling		36.00	3
Miscellaneous			▪	**36.00**	
Goods Receipt	1010/T-FL210	Gearbox		51,524.00-	100-
Goods Receipt			▪	**51,524.00-**	
			▪ ▪	**988.88-**	

Figure 6.27 Order Preliminary Cost

Simultaneous Costing for Controlling by Order

During this phase, logistics is reporting material quantities consumed and delivered as well as labor quantities against the logistics production order. The logistics process is the same as for controlling by period.

Valuation of these quantities is posted to the production order based on the simultaneous (or actual) costing variant, which we reviewed in Figure 6.24.

You can analyze these orders using the following transactions:

- Production order: Transaction CO03 and Transaction COOIS
- Process order: Transaction CO03 and Transaction COOISPI
- Production and process order, costed: Transaction KKBC_ORD

The value flow for this phase of the order is unique to SAP S/4HANA. Cost elements for the transactions are derived from MM account determination, specifically in the P&L accounts of the general ledger (G/L).

> **Note**
> Many legacy systems post this kind of transaction on the balance sheet. For example, often raw materials issued to a production order are credited to the raw material inventory account and debited to the WIP inventory account.

Let's look at a simple example of issuing raw materials and confirming a labor operation for a production order. As listed in Table 6.5, the order as a cost object is debited from these transactions. In the G/L, the P&L section of the income statement is affected.

Transaction	Account Determination	FI—General Ledger			Cost Object	
		Inventory (Balance Sheet)	Material Consumption (P&L)	Labor Activity Allocation (P&L)	Cost Center	Order
Issue raw material to order	MM account determination	Credit	Debit	–	–	Debit
Labor confirmation to order	Secondary cost element of activity type	–	–	Debit/credit	Credit	Debit

Table 6.5 Simultaneous Cost Flow to Order for Consumption

> **Tip**
> In SAP S/4HANA, all value flows are through the P&L accounts in the G/L. A P&L account number exists for each secondary cost element.

Another common transaction during simultaneous costing is a goods receipt for finished materials. As shown in Table 6.6, the order as a cost object is credited for the value of the finished quantity. Again, an offsetting entry is posted to the P&L account in the G/L.

| Transaction | Account Determina-tion | FI—General Ledger | | | Cost Object | |
		Inventory (Balance Sheet)	Material Consump-tion (P&L)	Labor Activ-ity Alloca-tion (P&L)	Cost Center	Order
Goods receipt of fin-ished materi-als	MM account determination	Debit	Credit	–	–	Credit

Table 6.6 Simultaneous Cost Flow to Order for Goods Receipt

Let's also look at an example of values that accumulate on an order during the simultaneous costing phase. Figure 6.28 shows an example of debits to an order from shop floor reporting and a credit to the order from finished goods received. These debits and credits, all from simultaneous costing, ❶, result in the $40 order balance.

Figure 6.28 Order Balance through Simultaneous Costing

Final Costing for Controlling by Order

Within the order lifecycle, postings occurring during period-end close are referred to as *final costing*.

At period end, additional costs not already represented in a BOM and routing can be debited to an order. In SAP S/4HANA, the following features support these peri-odic cost requirements:

- Template allocation: A technique often used to allocate business process cost to orders.

- Revaluation at actual prices: A technique to apply the actual activity price calcu-lated as part of cost center period-end close to orders that consumed those activities (see Chapter 3).

- Overhead costs: A technique using overhead costing sheets to allocate cost to orders (see Chapter 4). A common use of overhead costing sheets is to allocate incoming freight and duties/tariffs to material costs.

Note

Each of these periodic cost features creates a financial posting.

As shown in Figure 6.29, the periodic costs ❷ have debited the order, thereby increasing the order balance.

Transaction	Production Order
❶ Issue Raw Materal to Order	$100
Labor Confirmation to Order	$20
❶ Goods Receipt	($80)
Actual Order Balance	$40
❷ Template Allocation	$5
Reval. at Actual Prices	$5
Overhead	$10
Actual Order Balance	$60

Figure 6.29 Order Balance through Periodic Costing

Local accounting requirements usually involve valuation of the unfinished inventory still in process at period end as well as a full reporting of variances incurred from the actual cost compared to the standard price. In SAP S/4HANA, the following features support these final costing requirements:

- WIP calculation: Executes a calculation defined by the results analysis key for valuation of unfinished products
- Variance calculation: Executes a calculation defined by the variance key for valuation of eight variance categories

Production orders can calculate variances *or* WIP in the same accounting period. A few settings make this possible:

- The default rule of the order type—we reviewed this setting earlier in Figure 6.22—must be set as **PP1** (full settlement).
- In configuration, you must use Transaction OKG3 (Define Valuation Method (Actual Costs)).

> **Note**
> Each of these final costing features calculates a value. No financial posting occurs until settlement.

Work in Process for Controlling by Order

We've learned that when posting to an order during simultaneous costing, all value flows were through the profit and loss section of the financial statements. Statutory reporting requires that any unfinished inventory (or asset) be capitalized at period end. The WIP calculation applies the rules we've created in configuration to each order balance, and determines the value for capitalization.

> **Note**
> Mastering the WIP configuration requires time and patience because this process is one of the most complex in CO. In this book, our focus is on a solid understanding of the steps involved.

Figure 6.30 shows the configuration menu for calculating order WIP.

▼ Cost Object Controlling	
▶ Product Cost by Period	
▼ Product Cost by Order	
▶ Basic Settings for Product Cost by Order	
▶ Manufacturing Orders	
• Define Goods Received Valuation for Order Delivery	SIMG_CFMENUORKKOPK9
▼ Period-End Closing	
▼ Work in Process	
• Define Results Analysis Keys	SIMG_KKSORKKOKG1
• Define Cost Elements for WIP Calculation	SIMG_ORKK_WERK_KA02
• Define Results Analysis Versions	SIMG_CFMENUORKKOKG9
• Define Valuation Method (Actual Costs)	SIMG_KKSORKKOKG3
• Define Line IDs	SIMG_ORKK_WERK_ZID
• Define Assignment	SIMG_KKSORKKOKG5
• Define Update	SIMG_KKSORKKOKG4
• Define Posting Rules for Settling Work in Process	SIMG_KKSORKKOKG8
• Define Number Ranges	SIMG_KKSORKKOKG6
▶ User-Defined Error Management	

Figure 6.30 WIP Configuration Menu for Order Controlling

Let's take a closer look at each:

- **Define Results Analysis Keys**: A 6-character alphanumeric key that will be further assigned in each remaining menu option.

- **Define Cost Elements for WIP Calculation**: This link creates G/L account numbers for results analysis calculations. These cost elements must be of cost element category 31 for CO integration.
- **Define Results Analysis Versions**: You may use this version to calculate WIP using different methods (we'll describe each of these methods later). Only one version can settle to FI, version 0.
- **Define Valuation Method (Actual Costs)**: By using results analysis key, you can indicate if target or actual WIP is to be calculated and specify what effect order status has on the calculation, as shown for example in Figure 6.31.

Change View "Valuation Method for Work in Process": Overview

CO Area	RA Vers...	RA Key	Status	Status Nu...	RA Type
A000	0	MBMF01	REL	2	WIP Calculation on Basis of Actual Costs
A000	0	MBMF01	DLV	3	Cancel Data of WIP Calculation and Results Ana
A000	0	MBMF01	PREL	1	WIP Calculation on Basis of Actual Costs
A000	0	MBMF01	TECO	4	Cancel Data of WIP Calculation and Results Ana

Figure 6.31 Define Valuation Method

- **Define Line IDs**: Line IDs are used in a later step to separate different types of costs for capitalization. In this setting, you'll define a 3-character alphanumeric key to serve as a line ID. Examples of line IDs include material cost, labor cost, and packaging cost.
- **Define Assignment**: In this setting, you'll bring together several pieces of this puzzle. The results analysis version and results analysis key are assigned to cost elements and line IDs. An example of the assignment table is shown in Figure 6.32.

Change View "Assignment of Cost Elements for WIP and Results Analysis"

CO Area	RA ...	RA Key	Masked Cost Ele...	Origin	Masked Co...	Mask...	Business Proc.	D	V	Appo...	Acco...	Valid-Fr...	ReqToCap	OptToCap	CannotBeCap
A000	0	MBMF01	0051100000	++++				+	+	++	++	001.2007 MAT			
A000	0	MBMF01	0051500000	++++				+	+	++	++	001.2007 MAT			
A000	0	MBMF01	0051600000	++++				+	+	++	++	001.2007 MAT			
A000	0	MBMF01	0051700000	++++				+	+	++	++	001.2007 MAT			

Figure 6.32 Define Assignment

Using this example, you can state the following:

1. If an order is created within controlling area A000
2. And the results analysis version entered in the calculate WIP transaction is 0

3. And the RA key on the production order is MBMF01

4. And order costs have posted to cost element 51100000

5. Then the amount will be determined as line ID MAT and will be capitalized.

> **Warning!**
> Enter the line ID in the correct column to the far right to indicate the capitalization rule of the costs.

- **Define Update**: Each line ID must be assigned to a results analysis cost element in this setting, which supports reporting in CO.

- **Define Posting Rules for Work in Process**: The G/L account numbers posted to at settlement are defined in this setting.

- **Define Number Ranges**: Number range control of the CO settlement documents.

Examples of the definitions for each setting are listed in Table 6.7.

Step	Description	Transaction	Definition
1	Define results analysis key	Transaction OKG1	■ Results analysis key: MBMF01 ■ Text: WIP actual cost
2	Define results analysis version	Transaction OKG9	■ Controlling area: A000 ■ Results analysis version: 0 ■ Post to FI: Yes
3	Define valuation method	Transaction OKG3	■ Controlling area: A000 ■ Results analysis version: 0 ■ Results analysis key: MBMF01 ■ Status: – REL: WIP calculation on basis of actual costs – DLV: Cancel data of WIP calculation and results analysis – PREL: WIP calculation on basis of actual costs – TECO: Cancel data of WIP calculation and results analysis
4	Define line ID	Transaction WERK_ZID	■ Controlling area: A000 ■ Line ID: MAT ■ Text: Material Costs

Table 6.7 Examples of WIP Configuration Settings

Step	Description	Transaction	Definition

5	Define assignment	Transaction OKG5	■ Controlling area: A000
			■ Results analysis version: 0
			■ Results analysis key: MBMF01
			■ Cost element:
			  – 51100000
			  – 51500000
			■ Line ID: MAT

6	Define update	Transaction OKG4	■ Controlling area: A000 ■ Results analysis version: 0 ■ Results analysis key: MBMF01 ■ Line ID: MAT ■ Category: K ■ Cost element: 93118000
7	Define posting rule	Transaction OKG8	■ Controlling area: A000 ■ Company code: 1010 ■ Results analysis version: 0 ■ Results analysis category: WIPR ■ P&L: 54200000 ■ Balance sheet: 13200000

Table 6.7 Examples of WIP Configuration Settings (Cont.)

Using this chart, you can state the following simple example of the calculation process:

1. If the results analysis key found on the order is MBMF01

2. And the results analysis version 0 is used to calculate WIP (which is entered in the execution transaction)

3. And the order status is REL, then the actual order balance will be the basis for WIP

4. If line ID MAT represents material costs

5. And there are material consumption costs debited to the order on cost element 5110000 and/or 5150000 they will be classified as line ID MAT

6. Then material cost in WIP will post to results analysis cost element 93118000 in the WIP layout of KKBC_ORD

7. And the G/L accounts 54200000 and 13200000 will be posted to at WIP settlement

Variance for Controlling by Order

The variance calculation measures *control cost* against *target costs*. During configuration, you can determine the meaning of the control cost and the target cost by assigning actual or plan as the control and a specific cost estimate as the target.

For controlling by order, variances are calculated by category. SAP S/4HANA provides eight categories of variance. Table 6.8 lists and explains these eight categories. Input variances result from the cost assigned to the order. Output variances result from the valuation of the material being produced on the order.

Input Variance	
Category	**Example**
Input price	Difference between target and actual price of resources
Input quantity	Difference between target and actual quantity of resources
Resource usage	Use of an unplanned resource
Remaining	All others, including rounding
Output Variance	
Category	**Example**
Lot size	Difference between target and actual lot size of material produced
Mixed price	Difference due to mixing ratio
Output price	Difference between the planned and actual price of material produced
Remaining	All others, including rounding

Table 6.8 Variance Categories

As shown in Figure 6.33, the variance key is assigned to the material master. If assigned, variance categories will be calculated.

The variance key is created in configuration. Select the optional **Scrap** indicator, shown in Figure 6.34, if you need to calculate scrap variance.

Figure 6.35 shows the configuration menu for order variance.

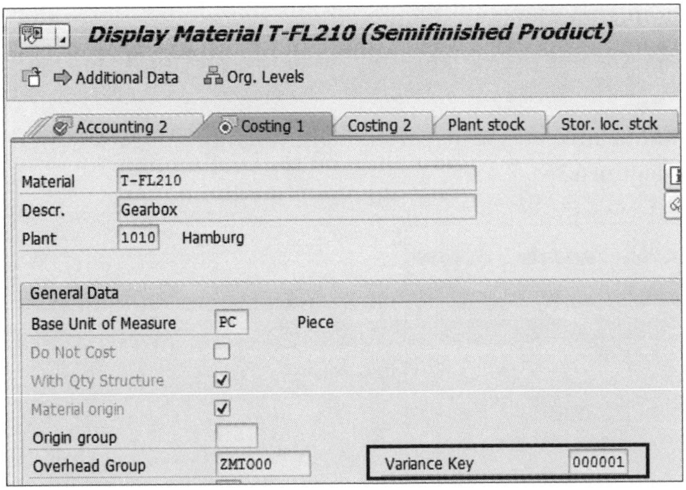

Figure 6.33 Material Master Variance Key

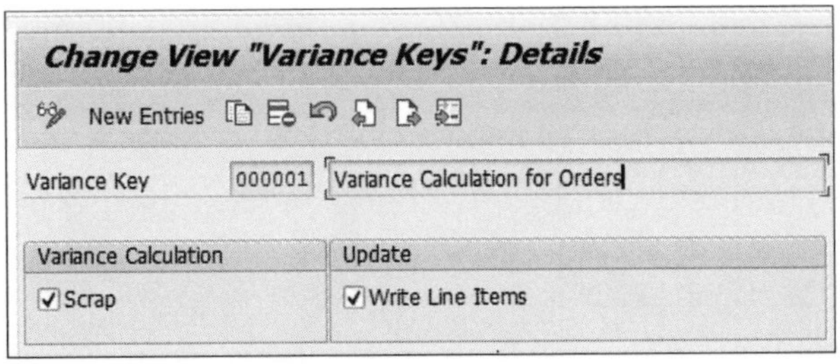

Figure 6.34 Variance Key (Transaction OKV1)

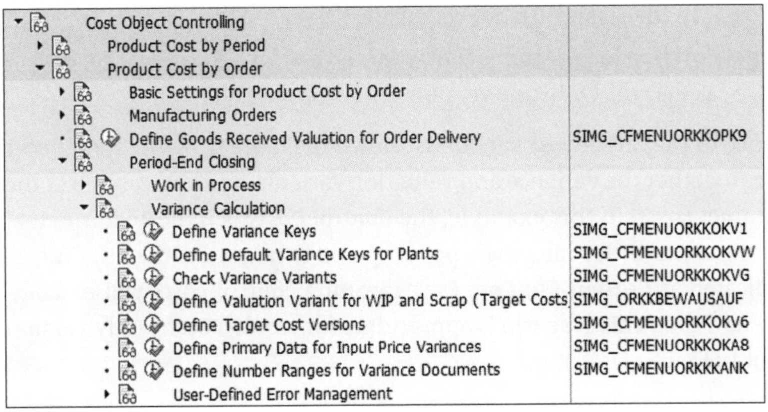

Figure 6.35 Variance Configuration Menu for Order Controlling

The following settings are important:

- **Define Variance Keys**: Creates the variance key, as shown previously in Figure 6.34.
- **Check Variance Variants**: Indicates which of the eight variance categories to calculate, as shown in Figure 6.36.

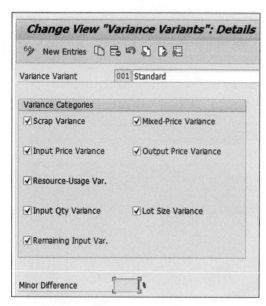

Figure 6.36 Variance Variant (Transaction OKVG)

- **Define Valuation Variant for WIP and Scrap**: Indicates, by priority, which cost estimate to use in the scrap variance calculation.
- **Define Target Cost Versions**: Defines the variants, control cost, and target cost of the variance calculation. Only one version can settle to FI, version 0.

The importance of the target cost version is shown in Figure 6.37. The target cost version brings together the variance and valuation variants, and you can select the control and target costs. In this example, the **Control Costs** is indicated as **Actual Costs**—meaning actual order values will be compared to target. Further, the **Target Costs** are indicated as **Current Std Cost Est**—meaning control costs will be compared to standard cost. This scenario is appropriate for version 0, the only version for settlement to FI.

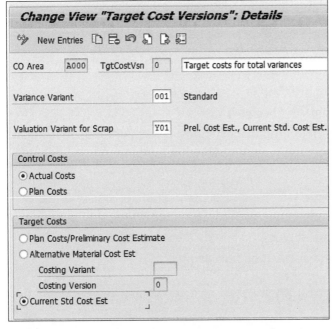

Figure 6.37 Define Target Cost Versions (Transaction OKV6)

> **Tip**
>
> What if we also needed measure the difference between the order plan values and the current standard? This information could explain differences in the costing variants used for each calculation. In this case, you would set **Control Costs** as **Plan Costs** and **Target Costs** as **Current Std Cost Est**.

Settlement

The periodic calculated values for WIP and variance are posted to FI-CO by executing the settlement process.

As shown back in Figure 6.21, the order type contains a settlement profile. This profile controls the overall settlement process.

In Chapter 4, we reviewed settlement profiles for internal orders. Settlement profiles for production orders are similar, but in this section, we'll review some additional fields for integration with CO-PA.

The settlement profile, shown in Figure 6.38, controls the following:

- Whether the order can be settled
- Indicates the receivers
- Assigns the following additional structures, if required:
  - Allocation structure (see Chapter 4)
  - PA transfer structure (see Chapter 7)
- Controls the following indicators that determine cost apportionment methods:
  - Percentage
  - Amount
  - Equivalence numbers
- Control indicator to settle variances to costing-based CO-PA
- Determines the document type used in settlement posting
- Controls the number of distribution rules allowed

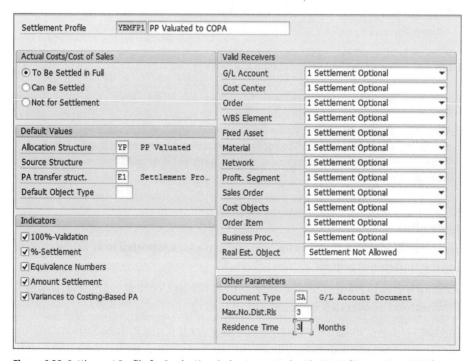

Figure 6.38 Settlement Profile for Production Order, Integrated with CO-PA (Transaction OKO7)

The FI account determination for the posting of variance settlement is taken from the MM account determination settings. The debit and credit account numbers are assigned to Transaction PRD for price difference, modifier PRF for price differences from orders. An example by valuation class is shown in Figure 6.39.

Configuration Accounting Maintain : Automatic Posts

◀ ▶ ☐ ☐ ☐ Posting Key ⚏Procedures Rules

| Chart of Accounts | YCOA | Standard Chart of Accounts (Training) |
| Transaction | PRD | Cost (price) differences |

Account assignment

General m...	Valuation ...	Debit	Credit
PRF	3040	52070000	52570000
PRF	3050	52041000	52541000
PRF	3100	52041000	52541000
PRF	7900	52070000	52570000
PRF	7920	52070000	52570000

Figure 6.39 MM Account Determination (Transaction OMWB)

In SAP S/4HANA, you can create an optional *splitting profile* to assign a G/L account by variance category. To find this well-hidden setting in the configuration menu, follow the menu path **Financial Accounting · General Ledger Accounting · Periodic Processing-Integration · Materials Management · Define Accounts for Splitting Price Differences**.

As shown in Figure 6.40, a price splitting profile can be used to assign each of the eight variance categories, plus scrap, to separate G/L account numbers. The system will execute this process in two steps:

1. The total variance is posted to the G/L account determined by Transaction OMWB.

2. A second posting offsets the amount posted via Transaction OMWB to the G/L accounts specified by the price splitting profile.

Change View "Detailed Price Difference Accounts": Overview

New Entries

Splitting of Price Differences	Price Diff. Splitting Profile	ZYA000	CC Variances
▼ ☐ Price Differences Splitting Prof	Controlling Area	A000	Controlling Area A000
· ☐ Detailed Price Difference A	Chart of Accounts	YCOA	Standard Chart of Accounts (Training)
· ☐ Company Code Settings			

Detailed Price Difference Accounts

Line	Description	Cost Elem. From	Cost Elem. To	CElem Group	VCat	Target Account	Default
0010	Scrap			TCOST	SCRP	52701000	☐
0020	Input Price Variance			TCOST	PRIV	52702000	☐
0030	Mixes Price Variance			TCOST	MXPV	52703000	☐
0040	Quantity Variance Material			CONSUME	QTYV	52704000	☐
0050	Quantity Variance Production			COGS	QTYV	52705000	☐
0060	Recource Usage Variance			TCOST	RSUV	52706000	☐
0070	Remaining Input Variance			TCOST	INPV	52707000	☐
0080	Lot Size Variance			TCOST	LSFV	52708000	☐
0090	Output Price Variance			TCOST	OPPV	52709000	☐
0100	Remaining Output Variance			TCOST	REMV	52710000	☑

Figure 6.40 Price Splitting Profile

To post these same variances to value fields in costing-based CO-PA, a PA transfer structure is also required (refer to Chapter 7).

The FI account determination for posting WIP is taken from the Define Posting Rules for Work in Process transaction (Transaction OKG8) mentioned earlier in this section. Figure 6.41 shows an example of this assignment.

Change View "Posting Rules in WIP Calculation and Results Analysis":

New Entries

CO A...	Com...	RA Version	RA categ...	Bal./Cr...	Cost Elem...	Recor...	P&L Acct	BalSheetAcct	A
A000	1010	0	WIPR			0	54200000	13200000	
A000	1010	0	RUCR			0	54040000	21700000	
A000	1010	0	POCI			0	43401400	13711400	

Figure 6.41 Define Posting Rules for Work in Process (Transaction OKG8)

Let's return to our actual order balance diagram, shown in Figure 6.42, to understand what occurs during settlement. After periodic costing, the actual order balance is $60. If the production order status is REL (released) or PDLV (partially delivered), the $60 will be calculated as WIP ❸. If the order status is DLV (delivered) or TECO (technically complete), the $60 will be calculated as variance ❹ and can be passed to costing-based CO-PA by the variance category and to table ACDOCA by the price splitting profile.

	Transaction	Production Order
❶	Issue Raw Materal to Order	$100
	Labor Confirmation to Order	$20
❶	Goods Receipt	($80)
	Actual Order Balance	$40
❷	Template Allocation	$5
	Reval. at Actual Prices	$5
	Overhead	$10
	Actual Order Balance	$60
❸	If REL, PDLV = WIP	$60
❹	If DLV, TECO = VAR	
	Material Price	$10
	Lot Size	$20
	Scrap	$15
	Resource	$15

Figure 6.42 Actual Order Balance at Settlement

In closing, let's review the costing phases and value flow for order controlling, as shown in Figure 6.43.

Preliminary Costing	FI-CO Posting	Simultaneous Costing		FI-CO Posting	Periodic Costs		FI-CO Posting
Order Type Preliminary Costing Variant x Product Cost Controller Quantity Structure		Debit Quantity Goods Issue x Price Control		Yes	Debit Template Allocation		Yes
		Debit Labor Confirmation x Simultaneous Costing Variant		Yes	Debit Reval. at Actual Prices		Yes
		Credit Quantity Goods Receipt x Price Control		Yes	Credit Overhead Costs		Yes
- - - - - - - - - - - - -		- - - - - - - - - - - - -			- - - - - - - - - - - - -		
Plan Value of Order	No	Actual Order Balance			Actual Order Balance		

	Final Costing		
	If Order Status = REL, PDLV or If Order Status = DLV, TECO	Calculate WIP at Target	No
		Calculate Variance	No
		Settlement	Yes

Figure 6.43 Order Controlling Value Flow

Sales Order-Related Scenarios

Sales order-related costing is a more focused costing method and requires detailed integration among the logistics components of SD, PP, and of course with CO.

For example, if your company manufactures a product for a specific customer using a particular process, you may need to control the plan and actual values for production costs at the SDI level.

Often, the "assemble-to-order" and "engineer-to-order" production processes are used to support this type of requirement. From a cost object controlling perspective, these processes present some unique opportunities.

Before reviewing how SAP S/4HANA features support this scenario, let's begin with some basic terms and features related to controlling by order.

Make-to-Order Controlling

The following are features of MTO controlling:

- Manufacturing is for a specific customer.
- Quantities are produced for a specific SDI. Quantities cannot be reassigned to another SDI.

- Components can be procured for a specific SDI.
- MRP can create an independent requirement for SDIs.
- Stock can be managed by the SDI.

Two key MTO controlling scenarios exist:

- **Without product cost by sales order**
  - Cost and revenue postings occur in real time.
  - Sales order stock can be valuated by the SDI cost estimate or the manufacturing preliminary cost.
  - A production order is the cost object.
  - WIP is based on the production order.
- **With product cost by sales order**
  - Cost and revenue postings can occur in real time; adjustments are made at period end based on the results analysis method.
  - Stock can be either unvaluated or valuated.
  - The SDI is the cost object.
  - Results analysis by method is calculated for the SDI.

Table 6.9 compares these two controlling scenarios.

	MTO Controlling Scenarios	
	Without Costing by Sales Order	**With Costing by Sales Order**
Cost Object	Production order	Sales order line item
Use Case	High-volume production, controlling on the product level	Complex MTO, controlling focus on the sales order
MRP	Independent requirement	Independent requirement
Plan Cost	SDI to production order	Sales order line item
Simultaneous Cost	Production order	Sales order line item
Final Cost	Production order	Sales order line item

Table 6.9 MTO Controlling Scenarios

Note
With controlling by sales order, the SDI is a cost object.

Our focus is on the most common MTO scenario with product cost by SDI. With controlling by sales order comes the option to valuate stock in several ways:

- Valuated: The quantity and the valuation of materials post at the same time:
  - Goods movements post in real time because inventory is "valuated."
  - Period-end settlement will post to costing-based CO-PA.
- Unvaluated: The quantity and valuation are decoupled, with valuation occurring separate from quantity:
  - No accounting posting with goods movements occur.
  - Period-end settlement will transfer CO-relevant production costs to the SDI.
  - Results analysis method will determine settlement postings based on revenue-based percentage of completion, cost-based percentage of completion, and other system-delivered methods.

Table 6.10 compares these options.

	With Costing by Sales Order	
	Valuated Stock	**Unvaluated Stock**
Production variances	Calculate and settle to CO-PA.	N/A, as SDI has actual cost.
COGS	Quantity sold with cost component split.	At settlement of the SDI.
Flow	Quantity reported is valuated with each goods receipt/goods issue.	Quantity reported with each goods receipt/goods issue. Value reported with each invoice for goods and/or at settlement of the SDI.

Table 6.10 Valuated versus Unvaluated Stock

Note
Unvaluated stock is only possible with costing by sales order.

Like our earlier overview of the costing phases in the "Methods and Valuation Phases" section, valuation can occur at certain points in the overall CO process:

- Preliminary costing
- Simultaneous costing
- Periodic costing
- Final costing

Sales order management is a bit more complex than our earlier management of other cost objects. You can still align the costing phases to the SD sales order life-cycle as follows:

1. Presales: Customer inquiries are made, and quotes are produced (in SD).

2. Order processing: An order is placed, a customer and material are entered, pricing and conditions calculate values (in SD); preliminary costing occurs (in CO).

3. Procurement: A determination is made about whether the material is in stock, needs to be procured, or is an MTO material (in SD); simultaneous costing occurs (in CO).

4. Delivery: The material is delivered to the customer, and goods issues are posted (in SD); simultaneous costing occurs (in CO).

5. Billing: Billing documents/invoices are created for the delivered goods (in SD); simultaneous costing occurs, and final costing can occur (in CO).

6. Payment: The customer remits payment for the invoice (accounts receivable [AR]).

Requirements Type

Each sales order item contains a requirements type, which defines the planning strategy for production. This setting is also an important indicator for CO as it will determine the requirements class, which we'll discuss in the next section.

To view the requirements type, navigate to the **Procurement** tab of a sales order line item, as shown in Figure 6.44.

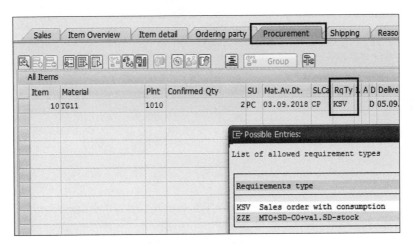

Figure 6.44 Requirements Type in Sales Order Item

When a sales order is created, various parameters from the SDI are used to assign the requirements type. Once the requirements type has been determined, SAP S/4HANA will then assign a requirements class to the SDI. An overview of the determination of a requirements class from the requirements type is shown in Figure 6.45, including the configuration transaction codes where each setting is determined: Transaction OPPS, Transaction OVZ1, and Transaction OVZH.

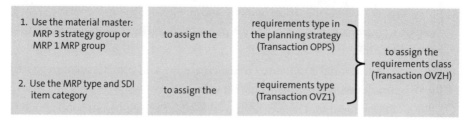

Figure 6.45 Requirements Type Assigns Requirements Class

The requirements type is assigned to the requirements class, as shown in Figure 6.46.

RqTy	Requirements type	ReqCl	Description
VSEM	Plng assemblies w/o final ass.	107	Plng assy w/o fn.ass
VSEV	Planning the planning material	104	Planning plng mat.
VSF	Planning with final assembly	101	Plnng with assembly
VSFB	Planning for assemblies	105	Assembly planning
YB1	3rd Party with SN	CB1	3rd Party with SN
YB2	3rd Party	CB2	3rd Party MV
YB4	Bought-In	CB4	Bought-In
YME	MTO w/o Prod. and CO	YME	MTO w/o Prod and CO
YSE	MTO w/o Prod. and CO	YSE	MTO w/o Prod and CO
ZPS1	PS: Project single stock (Q)	ZP1	PS: Proj.account Q
ZPS2	PS: assbly netwrk /acct proj.Q	ZP2	PS: Assem./ProjAcc Q
ZZE	MTO+SD-CO+val.SD-stock	ZZE	MTO+SD-CO+valSDstock

Change View "Requirements Types": Overview — New Entries

Figure 6.46 Requirements Type Assigned to Requirements Class (Transaction OVZH)

Requirements Class

With this method of CO, the requirements class contains all SDI control parameters, similar to the order types used in the two methods previously discussed. Figure 6.47 shows an example of requirements class **ZZE**.

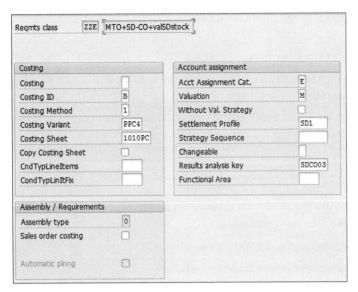

Figure 6.47 Requirements Class (Transaction OKVG)

The most important fields in the **Costing** group are:

- **Costing**: This field indicates if a sales order cost estimate is permitted, required, or prohibited.

- **Costing ID**: This field determines if the sales order cost estimate is created when saving the sales order, is created and marked when saving the sales order, or is created manually.

- **Costing Method**: This field determines if unit costing or product costing is used.

- **Costing Variant**: This field contains all control parameters for the cost estimate.

- **Costing Sheet**: This field determines the overhead calculation.

The most important fields in the **Account assignment** group are:

- **Account Assignment Cat.**: This field determines if costs are collected on the sales order. The categories are as follows:
  - **E** = Sales order controlling is active, with settlement at period end.
  - **M** = Sales order controlling is not active; no costs are collected, and no settlement occurs at period end.

- **Valuation**: This field determines if the sales order stock is valuated or non-valuated. The options are as follows:
  - **M** = Sales order stock is valuated based on the SDI or manufacturing order cost estimate. Valuated stock can be displayed using Transaction MMBE.

- **A** = Sales order stock is valuated based on the standard cost estimate of the material.
- Blank = Sales order stock is non-valuated.

- **Settlement Profile**: This field controls the settlement routine and is needed only if settlement is required.
- **Results analysis key**: This field controls the valuation method of results analysis calculation at period end.

Preliminary Costing for Controlling by Sales Order

The costing method of the requirements class determines the method of calculating plan cost for the SDI. The methods are:

- Product costing by reference to a BOM and routing
- Unit costing with no reference to a BOM and routing

> **Warning!**
> Unit costing output does not produce a cost component split; therefore, analysis by cost component isn't possible.

The valuation variant of the requirements class determines the plan costs for all resources, including materials with individual requirements. This plan value is then transferred to the production order used to manufacture the material.

Revenue is also planned for the SDI, based on the pricing conditions and procedures of the sales order.

Simultaneous Costing for Controlling by Sales Order

To understand the costing flow for this method, you'll need a foundation in how MRP indicators affect costing. This integration point is important, but you don't need comprehensive expertise; some basic knowledge should suffice.

Let's expand on the design of individual material requirements in the sales order controlling scenario. On the material master, **MRP 4** tab, locate the **Individual/coll.**, as shown in Figure 6.48.

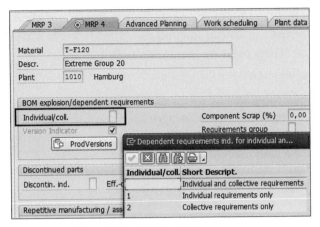

Figure 6.48 MRP4 Individual/Coll. Indicator

The **Individual/coll.** indicator plays a role in MRP. In sales order controlling, this indicator also signifies whether the material is treated as *sales order stock*.

Sales order stock is indicated as individual requirements and is strictly assigned to the SDI that created the requirement. This stock is valuated separately from other stock quantity for the same material. During simultaneous costing, goods movements for sales order stock are not valuated by the requirements class valuation variant; rather, the actual procurement cost is assigned.

For example, if a raw material consumed in a sales BOM is treated as an individual requirement, this material will be valuated as sales order stock. If the purchase order for this material is created at $100 per piece, the purchase order value will be the actual cost of the goods receipt and will be posted to the SDI.

Non-sales order stock is valuated based on the requirements class costing variant and costing method.

As goods issues and goods receipts are reported, the SDI is debited and credited for the values resulting in a balance on the cost object.

Final Costing for Controlling by Sales Order

At period-end close, the steps for final costing are executed. These steps may include all or only some of the following:

- Template allocation: If cost objects are senders of overhead via templates.
- Revaluation at actual prices: The cost center activity prices are recalculated at actual.

- Overhead: If cost objects are senders of overhead via costing sheets.
- Results analysis: To apply the calculation for unfinished inventory/reserves and to reconcile CO-PA and FI data based on the results analysis method.
- Settlement: To post the result analysis to CO-PA and FI.

We've already discussed these closing steps, with the exception of results analysis. Results analysis configuration is unique to SDI costing. Its purpose is similar to the result analysis key configuration for orders, but more complex. Figure 6.49 shows an example of a definition for results analysis.

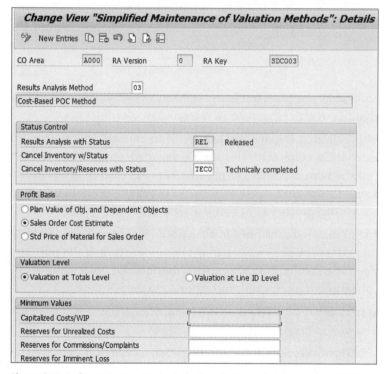

Figure 6.49 Define Valuation Methods for Results Analysis (Transaction OKG3)

In this view, you'll define the following control parameters:

- **Results Analysis Method**: Determines revenue in excess of billing, capitalized cost, and reserves.
- **Status Control**: Determines at which SDI status to calculate/reverse the result analysis method by selecting from the following:
  - **REL (Released)**

- – FNBL (Final Billing)
- – TECO (Technically Complete)
- **Profit Basis**: Determines which cost to use when calculating profitability.
- **Valuation Level**: Determines if calculations are performed on the SDI total amount or by line ID as defined in configuration (if using line ID, amounts can be separated by material, labor, etc.).
- **Minimum Values** (for the calculations): Determines if immaterial amounts are capitalized.

> **Note**
> This assignment is by controlling area and result analysis version. Only result analysis version 0 can post to FI.

In SAP S/4HANA, results analysis can calculate the following for each sales order item:

- Inventory values
- Reserves
  - – For unrealized costs
  - – For imminent losses
  - – For complaints/provisions
- Cost of sales

These calculated values can update FI and CO-PA at settlement. Why is this necessary? Hasn't FI recognized revenue and costs as billing and goods issue occurred? Of course, FI has these postings, but the values were determined by the SD pricing condition and the price control of the inventory. The profit calculation is a simple equation:

Revenue – Cost of sales = Profit

FI lacks the tools to calculate reserves, nor can FI provide complicated revenue recognition calculations. CO offers 17 predefined results analysis methods, shown in Figure 6.50. Each method contains the rules for the specific calculation.

For a better understanding of the purpose of results analysis, let's look at a basic calculation used in method **01 Revenue Based Method**.

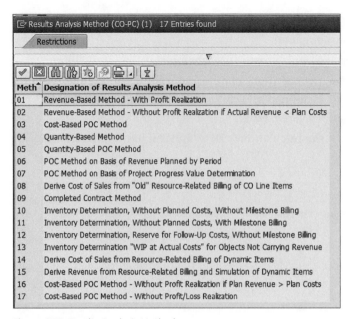

Figure 6.50 Results Analysis Methods

Before we begin, understanding the acronyms used to identify the values will be helpful:

- *a*: Actual
- *p*: Plan
- *pa*: Profitability analysis
- *R(pa)*: Revenue profitability analysis
- *C(pa)*: Cost of sales profitability analysis
- *R(a)*: Revenue actual
- *R(p)*: Revenue planned
- *C(a)*: Cost actual
- *C(p)*: Cost planned
- *POC*: Percentage of completion

To calculate results analysis, the first step is to determine the percentage of completion (POC). This value is based on SDI plan versus actual values for revenue, cost, and quantities, in other words, on any of the 17 methods shown in Figure 6.50.

Let's consider an example calculation for method **01 (Revenue Based Method)**. In this example, profit is determined by revenue POC × planned costs. The calculation steps are as follows:

1. **POC = R(a) ÷ R(p)**
   Calculate the POC by dividing actual revenue by plan revenue.

2. **R(pa) = R(a) ÷ R(p) × R(p)**
   Calculate the CO-PA revenue.

3. **C(pa) = R(a) ÷ R(p) × C(p)**
   Calculate the CO-PA cost.

4. **If C(a) > C(p), then WIP = C(a) – C(pa), else Reserve = C(pa) – C(a)**
   If actual costs are greater than plan cost then WIP will equal the actual cost minus the calculated cost; otherwise, the reserve will equal the calculated cost minus the actual cost.

Next, let's assume the SDI contains the revenue and cost shown in Table 6.11.

	Plan	Actual
Revenue	$3,000	$0
Cost	$2,000	$1,000

Table 6.11 SDI Revenue and Cost

Keep in mind that FI has already recognized this cost of $1,000 when the goods issue was posted.

Now, let's apply the calculation to the SDI values. The results analysis calculation will involve the following steps:

1. POC will equal the actual revenue divided by the planned revenue. In this example, this value is 0.00% ($0 ÷ $3,000).

2. Revenue for pa will equal *POC × Planned revenue*. In this example, this value is $0 ($0 ÷ $3,000 × $3,000).

3. Cost for pa will equal *POC × Planned cost*. In this example, this value is $0 ($0 × $2,000).

4. Actual costs are greater than pa cost, so WIP is calculated as the difference. In this example, this value would be $1,000 ($1,000 – $0).

When this SDI is then settled, the values previously posted in FI will be brought into alignment with this calculation:

1. The balance sheet will be adjusted for WIP with a debit for $1,000.

2. The P&L offsetting account will be credited for $1,000. This credit will counter the $1,000 debit previously posted to cost of sales, bringing the P&L impact to $0.

> **Tip**
>
> Simply stated, result analysis is a calculation to adjust FI postings to align them with revenue recognition rules.

In closing, let's review the costing phases and value flow for sales order controlling, as shown in Figure 6.51.

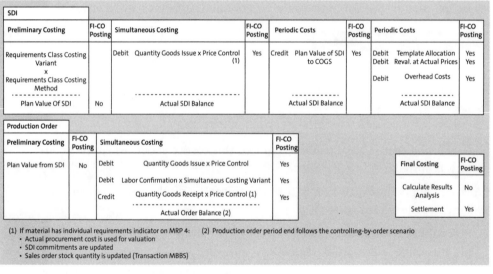

Figure 6.51 Sales Order Controlling Value Flow

Important Terminology

In this chapter, the following terminology was used:

- **Commitment**
  A commitment represents the value of a purchase requisition or a purchase order for sales order controlling to fulfill individual requirements.

- **Condition type**
  This key is used with sales order controlling and identifies a condition used to calculate a price, a surcharge, or a discount.

- **Final costing**
  Final costing calculates WIP, variances, and results analysis. Postings are made to FI-CO at settlement.

- **Independent requirements**
  These requirements are used with sales order controlling to indicate when material can only be used for a specific SDI.

- **Input side variances**
  This kind of variance is based on cost object spending (i.e., goods issue, activity allocations, overhead allocations). The four input variance categories are input price, resource usage, input quantity, and remaining input.

- **Order type**
  An order type is an object containing all the parameters necessary for managing orders. Every order is created with reference to an order type, which passes parameters to the order.

- **Output side variances**
  These variances are based on the cost object output resulting from making more or less than planned or due to a valuation difference in the material manufactured. The four output variance categories are mixed price, output price, lot size, and remaining variance.

- **PA transfer structure**
  This structure is used when settlement involves costing-based CO-PA to assign cost and revenue to value and quantity fields.

- **Preliminary costing**
  This calculation is performed when creating cost estimates for production orders, product cost collector, and sales orders.

- **Product cost collector**
  A product cost collector is a cost object that collects target and actual cost at the controlling level of a material. These objects are required for repetitive manufacturing but optional in other contexts.

- **Production order**
  A production order is a cost object that collects plan and actual cost at the order level of a material. These orders include manufacturing and process orders.

- **Requirements class**
  In sales order controlling, a requirements class is an object containing all the parameters necessary for managing the SDI.

- **Requirements type**
  In sales order controlling, the requirements type is an object that assigns a requirements class to an SDI.

- **Results analysis**
  In sales order controlling, results analysis calculates costs to be capitalized and reserves and reconciles FI and CO-PA for SDIs.

- **Results analysis key**
  This key is assigned to the cost object to indicate that WIP must be calculated.

- **Results analysis version**
  A results analysis version defines different methods of results analysis; only version 0 can post to FI.

- **Sales order stock**
  This stock can be allocated directly to an SDI and delivered only to that customer.

- **Settlement profile**
  This profile controls the parameters for settlement processing and is assigned to an order type.

- **Settlement rule**
  A settlement rule determines the cost allocation to receivers and is found in the header of the cost object.

- **Settlement type**
  This type determines whether settlement is made in each period (**PER**, periodic) or after the last delivery (**FUL**, full). The default rule of the order type controls this setting as either **STR** (**PER**, periodic) for the product cost collector or **PP1** (**FUL**, full) for production orders.

- **Simultaneous costing**
  This kind of costing records actual cost for cost objects (i.e., goods issues, labor confirmations, good receipts). Simultaneous costing can determine the valuation of actual quantities as these values are reported from the warehouse and shop floor.

- **Target cost**
  A target cost is a plan cost adjusted for delivered quantity. With product cost collectors, a goods receipt is required for this calculation.

- **Target cost version**
  The target cost version is used in variance calculations to determine the basis for target costs (what to measure actual against). Only version 0 can post to FI.

- **Variance category**
  The cost object balance is divided into variance categories during variance calculation. four categories exist on the input side, and another four categories on the output side.

- **Variance key**
  This key defaults from the material master to the order or product cost collector and determines whether variance and scrap will be calculated.

- **Variance variant**
  A variance variant specifies which of the eight variance categories are calculated and is assigned to the target cost version.

- **Work in process (WIP)**
  This calculation capitalizes the value of unfinished inventory at period end. A product cost collector uses the WIP at target method, while production orders use the WIP at actual method.

Practice Questions

These practice questions will help you evaluate your understanding of the topics covered in this chapter. The questions shown are similar in nature to those found on the certification examination. Although none of these questions will be found on the exam itself, they will allow you to review your knowledge of the subject. Select the correct answers and then check the completeness of your answers in the "Practice Question Answers and Explanations" section. Remember that on the exam you must select all correct answers and only correct answers to receive credit for the question.

1. Which of the following configuration settings are used for calculating work in process (WIP)? (There are three correct answers.)

☐   **A.** Create settlement profile

☐   **B.** Define assignment of cost elements

☐   **C.** Define update

☐   **D.** Create allocation structure

☐   **E.** Define posting rules

2. Which order status is relevant for creating WIP calculations when using controlling by order?

☐ **A.** Created

☐ **B.** Delivered

☐ **C.** Partially delivered

☐ **D.** Technically completed

3. Product cost collectors calculate WIP and variances each period. What is the calculation for variance?

☐ **A.** Actual Debits + Scrap – Goods Receipt

☐ **B.** Actual Debits – Goods Receipt – WIP

☐ **C.** Actual Credits – Goods Receipt – WIP – Scrap

☐ **D.** Actual Credits – WIP – Scrap

4. The setting that controls settlement by PER (periodic) or FUL (full) is determined by which of the following?

☐ **A.** Settlement profile

☐ **B.** Allocation structure

☐ **C.** Settlement type

5. In controlling by sales order, when using a sales order with an assigned production order and valuated sales order stock. Which process is used to post costs to the sales order in SAP S/4HANA? (There are two correct answers.)

☐ **A.** Production order confirmation

☐ **B.** Delivery from production order to sales order stock

☐ **C.** Production order settlement

☐ **D.** Externally procured sales order stock

6. When using controlling by sales order, to which object do you settle values of results analysis?

☐ **A.** Profit center

☐ **B.** Cost center

☐   **C.** Segment

☐   **D.** Profitability segment

7.   Which tasks can be performed on a production order in a controlling by sales order scenario with valuated stock? (There are two correct answers.)

☐   **A.** Perform results analysis

☐   **B.** Transfer reserves for realized costs

☐   **C.** Settle the production variances to CO-PA

☐   **D.** Calculate production variances

8.   In controlling by sales order, the planned value can come from which of the following? (There are two correct answers.)

☐   **A.** Pricing conditions on the sales order

☐   **B.** Unit costing

☐   **C.** Product costing

☐   **D.** Cost estimate of the planned production order

9.   In controlling by order, if the order has neither status delivered nor status technically completed, WIP is calculated based on which of the following?

☐   **A.** Actual cost

☐   **B.** Target cost

☐   **C.** Plan cost

10.   What needs to be specified to calculate WIP for a product cost collector?

☐   **A.** Default rule

☐   **B.** Order type

☐   **C.** Results analysis key

☐   **D.** Settlement type

11. Using a production order, which of the following could cause a difference between the standard cost estimate and the planned cost for the order?

☐ **A.** Different order types

☐ **B.** Different results analysis keys

☐ **C.** Different costing variants

12. For cost objects with the settlement type PER, how is WIP calculated?

☐ **A.** Based on the standard cost estimate

☐ **B.** Based on target costs

☐ **C.** Based on actual costs for the orders

13. What can cause production order variances? (There are two correct answers.)

☐ **A.** Using the wrong order type

☐ **B.** Debits to the order in excess of the credits

☐ **C.** Consuming unplanned materials

☐ **D.** The splitting profile

14. When using controlling by sales order, which of the following applies to results analysis?

☐ **A.** Individual/collective indicator

☐ **B.** Non-valuated stock

☐ **C.** Determining the percentage of completion

15. What is the purpose of a splitting profile? (There are two correct answers.)

☐ **A.** To post variance categories to CO-PA value fields

☐ **B.** To provide more variance information in the G/L

☐ **C.** To post variance categories to separate G/L accounts

☐ **D.** To determine which variance categories to calculate

16. When using controlling by period, how is decoupling the cost object from the production order accomplished?

☐ **A.** Create a new order type

☐ **B.** Select the **Cost Collector** indicator on the logistics order type

☐ **C.** Assign the settlement type PER

17. Product cost collectors and logistics production orders are linked through which of the following?

☐ **A.** The results analysis key

☐ **B.** The production process

☐ **C.** The order numbers

18. True or False: Simultaneous costing refers to the valuation phase when WIP is calculated.

☐ **A.** True

☐ **B.** False

19. True or False: Product cost collectors can calculate WIP and variance in each accounting period.

☐ **A.** True

☐ **B.** False

20. True or False: Unvaluated stock can be used with the costing by period scenario.

☐ **A.** True

☐ **B.** False

21. True or False: Unit costing can produce a cost component split.

☐ **A.** True

☐ **B.** False

22. True or False: All order values flow through the profit and loss section of the income statement.

☐   **A.** True

☐   **B.** False

Practice Question Answers and Explanations

1. Correct answers: **B, C, E**

   These three settings apply to the WIP calculation: define assignment links the result analysis version and result analysis key to cost elements by line ID; define update assigns each line ID to a cost element used only in CO reporting; and define posting rules determines the G/L account number for WIP postings. The settlement profile and allocation structure apply only to settlement, not to WIP calculations.

2. Correct answer: **C**

   Controlling by order relies on the order status at period end to determine if WIP or variance are going to be calculated. The status of released or partially delivered results in WIP; the status of delivered or technically complete results in variance.

3. Correct answer: **B**

   The actual cost debited to the product cost collector are reduced by the value of goods receipts and the WIP at target calculation; the remaining balance of the product cost collector is the basis for variance.

4. Correct answer: **C**

   The settlement type is defined by the default rule, found on the order type. The settlement type triggers full settlement (controlling by order) or periodic settlement (controlling by period).

5. Correct answers: **B, D**

   Because sales order stock is an individual requirement, the "actual" costs of goods receipt and external procurement flow to the SDI.

6. Correct answer: **D**

   Results analysis calculations are compared to what has previously been posted in FI. At settlement, a profitability segment in CO-PA is updated. (An adjustment posting to FI may occur, but G/L account was not a choice here.)

7. Correct answers: **C, D**

   In a valuated stock scenario, variances are assigned to the production order.

8. Correct answers: **B, C**

   For SDI planned costs, both unit costing and product costing can be used. However, unit costing cannot provide a cost component split; product costing will provide a cost component split. The requirements class costing method indicates if unit or product costing will be used. Pricing conditions calculate values on the sales order like sales price and discount but have no effect on SDI planned costs.

9. Correct answer: **A**

   In this scenario, the actual cost reflected in the order balance becomes the basis for WIP.

10. Correct answer: **C**

    If no results analysis key is found, no WIP will be calculated.

11. Correct answer: **C**

    Each costing variant can have unique controls, such as the valuation variant for materials and internal operations.

12. Correct answer: **B**

    The settlement type PER is used in the controlling by period scenario, meaning a product cost collector is the cost object. WIP is always calculated using a target cost estimate for this method. The standard cost estimate may be defined in configuration as the target cost estimate for WIP, but so could any other cost estimate—therefore, you must be careful in this type of question, using the word "target" not the word "standard." WIP based on actual costs for the order applies in settlement type FUL, not PER.

13. Correct answers: **B, C**

    Overspending could be categorized as price variance, while consuming unplanned resources could be categorized as resource usage variance.

14. Correct answer: **C**

    Determining the percentage of completion is always the first step of results analysis. The exact calculation is dependent on which result analysis method is being applied.

15. Correct answers: **B, C**

    The splitting profiles provide more granularity about variance categories (and also cost of goods sold) in the G/L by assigning each category to a distinct G/L account number. Prior to SAP S/4HANA, you could only get that level of detail in costing-based CO-PA. To post variance categories to value fields in CO-PA, a PA transfer structure is required, not a splitting profile. The variance variant determines which variance categories will be calculated.

16. Correct answer: **B**

   By selecting the **Cost Collector** indicator on the logistics order type, we have decoupled it from CO. This indicator causes the system to search for a product cost collector with the same production process as the logistics order being created. When found, both orders are linked, and cost flows will be reported on the product cost collector.

17. Correct answer: **B**

   The production process is taken from the controlling level of the material/plant and is found on the product cost collector and on the production order.

18. Correct answer: **B**

   False. Simultaneous costing refers to the phase of goods movements and labor confirmations as products are being manufactured.

19. Correct answer: **A**

   True. This decoupling feature is unique to product cost collector used in costing by period.

20. Correct answer: **B**

   False. Unvaluated stock can only be using in costing by sales order.

21. Correct answer: **B**

   False. Unit costing cannot produce the cost component split. There is no cost component structure assignment in configuration.

22. Correct answer: **A**

   True. In each scenario, the orders are cost objects. Posted values for cost objects are always made in the profit and loss section of the income statement. At period-end close, WIP settlement, any valuation for unfinished inventory is moved back to the balance sheet for statutory reporting purposes.

Takeaway

In this chapter, our focus has been on three scenarios, or controlling methods, for cost object controlling: by period, by order, and by sales order. We compared similarities and differences among these methods as they relate to each cost object: a product cost collector, a production order, and an SDI.

You should now have a good understanding of the configuration settings required for the main objects: the order type and the requirements class. These settings contain the control parameters for each valuation phase of the order lifecycle, from creation to final costing.

We also revisited the purpose and design of costing variants, building on your first introduction to these concepts in Chapter 5. Rather than controlling a material cost estimate, in cost object controlling, costing variants control the plan and simultaneous costing.

From our review of WIP process and variance calculations, you should be able to answer questions related to periodic and final costing and describe the postings that occur at settlement.

From a business process perspective, we've reviewed the valuation phases and related flow of values for preliminary costing, simultaneous costing, and periodic/final costing.

Summary

At this point, you should be able to explain the basic concepts and benefits of each cost object controlling scenario: controlling by period, controlling by order, and controlling by sales order item. You can explain these options to your customers and propose deployment options. You can also help end users with basic knowledge.

Now that we've covered how values flow through the cost object controlling scenarios, we're ready for our next chapter on CO-PA. In the next chapter, we'll once again review how values flow from one cost object to another, but this time to the profitability segment.

Chapter 7
Profitability Analysis

Techniques You'll Master

- Identify differences between account-based and costing-based profitability analysis (CO-PA)

- Define organizational and data structures in CO-PA

- Understand characteristic derivation

- Understand the purpose of valuation

- Understand the dynamic creation of profitability segment master data

- Define actual data flows

- Explain the planning process

- Explain the reporting options

- Explain predictive accounting

In this chapter, we'll discuss the purpose and design of account- and costing-based CO-PA. We'll begin with a review of how an operating concern is generated, and then explain how actual data flows to CO-PA. Finally, we'll take on the most commonly used planning and reporting features.

Real-World Scenario

As a controlling (CO) consultant, you'll need tools for analyzing contribution margin. Depending on the industry of your customers, this requirement could be high level—with perhaps material cost and total overhead cost being the focus. If your customer produces goods or services, requirements could be far more detailed—with perhaps more cost buckets and a need for splitting fixed costs and variable costs. CO-PA is the SAP solution that meets these reporting requirements.

CO-PA is fundamentally a reporting tool. As the recipient of data flowing from all other financial accounting (FI) and CO components, in many ways, all roads lead to CO-PA. As CO design decisions are made, you must consider the end reporting requirements of your clients and determine where CO-PA integration should occur.

A good example is integration with cost object controlling. In Chapter 6, we discussed the settings required for production order variances to flow to CO-PA as well as the complex sales order results analysis methods that can be used to align FI postings with revenue recognition calculations.

Objectives of This Portion of the Test

The objective of this portion of the certification exam is to test your understanding of customizing the core CO-PA master data objects as well as your understanding the main business processes in CO-PA.

The certification exam expects you to have a good understanding of the following topics:

- Account-based versus costing-based CO-PA
- Configuration of the operating concern

- Data structures
- Characteristic derivation
- Configuration of the valuation strategy
- Planning
- Reporting

> **Note**
> The CO-PA accounting topic makes up 12% of the total exam.

Key Concepts Refresher

In this section, we'll discuss operating concerns as organizational structures, the data structures required, and how data flows from FI-CO to CO-PA. We'll also review some basic planning and reporting features.

Overview of Profitability Analysis

CO-PA is a quite different component of CO as compared to others in this text. CO-PA, the acronym for profitability analysis, is purely a reporting feature in SAP S/4HANA. CO-PA receives postings as business transactions are occurring and stores this data in various tables to be used in *contribution margin* reporting.

Each company may have its own specific definition and calculation method for contribution margin. A good place to start is with a simple formula:

Revenue – Variable cost – Fixed cost = Contribution margin

Right away, you can see this formula is a bit different from the usual external reporting requirement, which looks something like this formula:

Revenue – Cost of goods sold (COGS) – Taxes = Net profit

To further complicate the design of a contribution margin formula, likely, you'll need information at the material/quantity level to effectively determine where your company is making and losing profit. The usual reporting methods just can't support that level of detail. CO-PA is the only component that can handle these challenges.

Account-Based CO-PA

With account-based CO-PA, you can analyze data at the general ledger (G/L) account level. Within the posted values for the G/L revenue account, you can slice and dice data by, for example, customer, product, and region. Values posted in this account are quite easy to reconcile to FI by G/L account. Until SAP S/4HANA, this type of CO-PA was not widely used. One shortcoming is easy to understand by looking at the G/L COGS account. While you could still slice and dice data by, for example, customer, product, and region, you could not distinguish between the variable and fixed portions of that value. CO does not pass that level of detail to FI.

With SAP S/4HANA, many improvements have been made to "account-based" CO-PA—so many that you may now be hearing the phrase "profitability analysis from the Universal Journal" rather than "account-based CO-PA." We'll look at those improvements throughout this chapter.

Costing-Based CO-PA

Costing-based CO-PA can analyze data at the *value field* level. A value field is created to contain the amounts and quantities you want to analyze. Various techniques are used in configuration to map objects, such as pricing conditions, G/L accounts, and cost components to value fields. Within the posted values for the value field **Revenue**, you can slice and dice data by, for example, customer, product, and region. Within the posted values for the value fields **Material Cost** and **Labor Cost**, you can slice and dice data by, for example, customer, product, and region and by variable and fixed content. This ability to separate variable and fixed cost is why costing-based CO-PA has long been a requirement for manufacturers.

Figure 7.1 shows a comparison between these two types of CO-PA before SAP S/4HANA. Notice the revenues and the result/contribution margin 3 are the same values. Also, notice the level of detail in the costing-based report—variable and fixed cost are split, and selling, general, and administrative (SG&A) costs are below contribution margin 2.

Account-Based			Costing-Based	
Cost and Revenue Elements			**Value Fields**	
800 000	Revenues	1,000,000	Revenues	1,000,000
808 000	Sales deductions	100,000	Sales deductions	100,000
Net revenues		**900,000**	**Net revenues**	**900,000**
893 000	Cost of sales	690,000	Variable material costs	400,000
231 000	Price differences	10,000	Variable production costs	190,000
651 000	R&D	10,000	Production variances	10,000
671 000	Marketing	50,000	**Contribution margin 1**	**300,000**
655 00	Sales and admin.	40,000	Material overhead	50,000
Result		**100,000**	Production overhead	50,000
			Contribution margin 2	**200,000**
			R&D	10,000
			Marketing	50,000
			Sales costs	40,000
			Contribution margin 3	**100,000**

Figure 7.1 Account-Based versus Costing-Based CO-PA Prior to SAP S/4HANA

CO-PA in the Universal Journal

In SAP S/4HANA, data that was historically stored in several tables is now found in the *Universal Journal*. The Universal Journal is technically named table ACDOCA for actual data and table ACDOCP for plan data, which together contain all the details from all applications (see Chapter 3).

Regarding CO-PA, account-based CO-PA data is now stored in table ACDOCA. Additionally, SAP S/4HANA includes features to provide most of the contribution margin data (previously only available in costing-based CO-PA) in table ACDOCA. Now, far more detail can be contained in a single reporting table than was possible prior to SAP S/4HANA. As we continue in this chapter, we'll look at these features in more detail.

Organizational Structures

As we've seen since Chapter 2, organizational structure is always the first definition you'll make in configuration. CO-PA has a unique organizational structure: the operating concern. Before we review its definition, let's first understand the all-important SAP client-level object.

> **Tip**
> The following settings are quite technical as they deal with ABAP objects and table structures, two topics you should have basic knowledge of, both as a CO consultant and for the purposes of the certification exam.

Within an SAP client, you must create *characteristics* and *value fields* in the field catalog, which are defined as follows:

- Characteristics: These elements define items or objects for the user to analyze; they are the "by" words (i.e., what do you want to analyze data by in a report: by customer, by product, by region, etc.).
- Value fields: These elements contain the amounts and quantities you want to analyze in a report (i.e., revenue, material cost, labor cost, etc.).

> **Note**
> Characteristics are used by both account-based and costing-based CO-PA. Value fields are used by costing-based CO-PA only.

In this section, we'll take a closer look at both characteristics and value fields, as well as the operating concern itself.

Characteristics

When creating characteristics, you can choose between the following four categories:

- Fixed: These characteristics are mandatory objects required by the SAP system. Generally, these objects reference the organizational structure and master data from the posted line item. Examples include company code, controlling area, profit center, material number, plant, etc.
- Predefined: These characteristics are sample/example objects found in the system. These objects may have been created from a sample operating concern.
- Referenced to SAP tables: These objects already exist in other applications such as materials management (MM), production planning (PP), and sales and distribution (SD). Examples include material group, customer group, etc.
- Custom created: These objects do not exist in other applications and are created for use only in CO-PA reporting. An example is a strategic business unit. The names of these objects must begin with "WW."

When using referenced or custom created characteristics, you will have the option of using check tables to validate characteristic values entered at the time of posting.

Let's look at a few characteristics. When transferring a posting to CO-PA, you'll need an analysis by the material group. As shown in Figure 7.2, the CO-PA characteristic material group **KMMAKL** will be copied from the origin table **MARA** and origin field **MATKL**. The status of this characteristic is **A** (**active**).

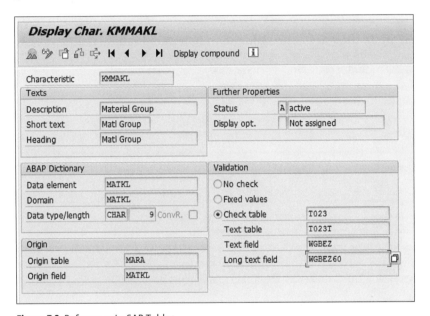

Figure 7.2 References to SAP Tables

> **Warning!**
> A characteristic must be marked as active for it to be assigned to an operating concern.

You'll also need to analyze by an internal designation called the *strategic business unit*. This object does not exist in any table used by another SAP application. As shown in Figure 7.3, the CO-PA characteristic **WWSBU** (**Strat. Business Unit**) has been created with no origin table. The status of this characteristic is **A** (**active**).

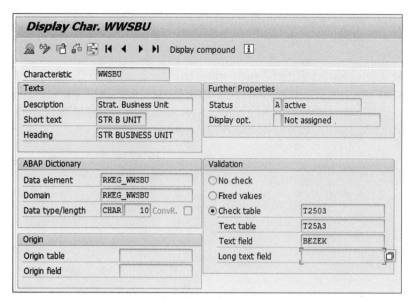

Figure 7.3 Custom Characteristic Created

> **Note**
> If you create a referenced characteristic, since that data exists in SAP, the system will cre-
> ate a check table to be used to validate the field content at posting. If you create a custom
> characteristic and select a check table, you must create your own list of possible entries
> for that field using Transaction KES1 (Maintain Characteristic Values).

Value Fields

The next objects to create are the value fields. Two categories of value fields exist:

- Predefined: These value fields are sample/example objects found in the system.
  These objects may have been created from a sample operating concern.
- Custom: These value fields are created to meet your customer's requirements.
  Custom value fields must begin with "VV."

There are no fixed value fields like fixed characteristics.

Value fields have an indicator for amount or quantity as well an aggregation rule
(because these fields can collect amount and quantities). Three aggregation rules
are available:

- **SUM**

  All amounts will be "summed" (i.e., the value field will be increased/decreased with each posting). For example, if the first posted amount to the value field for revenue is $100, and the second posted amount to the value field for revenue is $50, the sum of the value field is $150 ($100 + $50).

- **AVG**

  All amounts will be averaged. For example, if the first posted quantity to the quantity field number of orders is 10, and the second posted quantity is 50, the average of the quantity field is 30 ((10 + 50) ÷ 2).

- **LAS**

  Only the last posted amount/quantity will appear. For example, if the first posted quantity to the quantity field number of employees is 25, and the second posted quantity is 30, the last posting of 30 is displayed in the value field.

Let's look at a few value fields. As shown in Figure 7.4, the value field **Revenue** uses the **SUM** aggregation rule and is of the **Amount** value field type. The status of this value field is **A** (**active**).

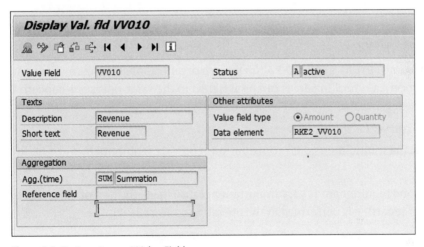

Figure 7.4 Custom Amount Value Field

As shown in Figure 7.5, the value field **Invoiced Quantity** uses the **SUM** aggregation rule and is of the **Quantity** value field type. The status of this value field is **A** (**active**).

Warning!

If a value field is not marked as active, it cannot be assigned to an operating concern.

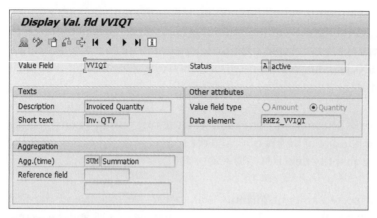

Figure 7.5 Custom Quantity Value Field

Warning!

As of the time of writing (summer 2019), the system limits the number of value fields you can assign to an operating concern. The current limit is between 120 and 200 value fields.

Operating Concern

As you learned in Chapter 2, CO-PA has its own organizational structure: the operating concern. Controlling areas can be assigned to the same operating concern if the following are true:

- The fiscal year is the same.
- The same multidimensional contribution reporting requirement must be fulfilled.

This second requirement is very important because the definition of objects used in CO-PA reporting is performed at the operating concern level.

Three tabs are maintained to define an operating concern:

- **Data Structure**: Under this tab, characteristics and values fields are added to the operating concern from the client-level field catalog.
- **Attributes**: Under this tab, the currency and fiscal year variant are defined.
- **Environment**: Under this tab, indicators govern the generation of objects.

As shown in Figure 7.6, the **Data Structure** tab has indicators for both types of CO-PA—account-based and costing-based—and is where characteristics and value fields are assigned.

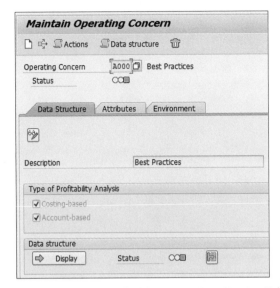

Figure 7.6 Maintain Operating Concern: Data Structure Tab

Click the **Display/Change** button to navigate to **Edit Data Structure** screen, as shown in Figure 7.7. Select characteristics from the **Transfer from** list on the right to add them to your operating concern.

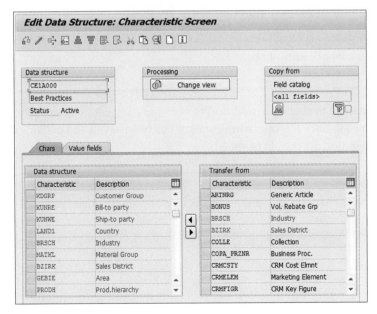

Figure 7.7 Edit Data Structure

Under the **Value fields** tab, you can add value fields using the same method.

As shown in Figure 7.8, the operating concern currency and fiscal year variant are defined on the **Attributes** tab.

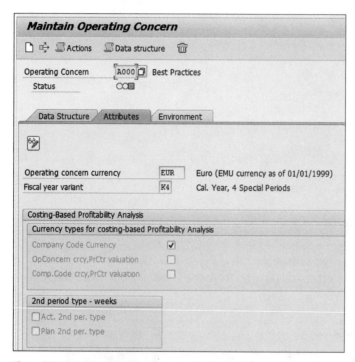

Figure 7.8 Maintain Operating Concern: Attributes Tab

For costing-based CO-PA, you may also select company code types and profit center currency types to be evaluated in addition to the operating concern currency. As shown in Figure 7.9, once the operating concern has been saved and activated (generated), these indicators should be green.

Warning!

If you make changes to characteristics or value fields of the operating concern, you must reactivate (regenerate) these structures; otherwise, the operating concern status remains inactive and changes to these structures are not effective.

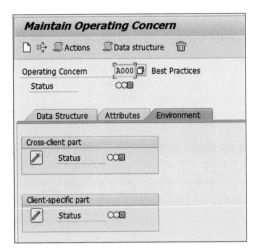

Figure 7.9 Maintain Operating Concern: Environment Tab

Let's now summarize the tasks required to define CO-PA data structures:

1. Create characteristics and values.

2. Create the operating concern (define attributes and save).

3. Define data structures by copying characteristics and value fields and activating/ generating the operating concern.

When the operating concern is generated, many tables are created for the data to be stored in. The following list shows some of the main tables, with "xxxx" indicating the 4-character key for the operating concern:

- **Account-based CO-PA**
  Uses the following tables, which exist also for other cost objects:
  - Table COEP: Actual line items for value types other than value types 4 and 11
  - Table COEJ: Plan line items
  - Table ACDOCA: Universal Journal

> **Note**
> In SAP S/4HANA, CO-PA characteristics are not captured in the FI line item table BSEG; rather, characteristics are captured in table ACDOCA. As the operating concern is generated, table ACDOCA is extended.

- **Costing-based CO-PA**

  Uses the following set of tables, which are unique:

  - Table CE1xxxx: Actual line items
  - Table CE2xxxx: Plan line items
  - Table CE3xxxx: Summary records (profitability segment)
  - Table CE4xxxx: Profitability segment definitions

Account- and costing-based CO-PA share a single table: table CE4xxxx. This table controls the creation of the profitability segment, which is technically the cost object for CO-PA. In other components of CO, you must create a master record/cost object before any postings can occur. CO-PA creates the profitability segment dynamically as postings are occurring. The table CE4xxxx manages the creation and numbering of profitability segments.

Master Data

As we've established, CO-PA is a bit different in its design and configuration than other CO components. This theme will continue as we discuss master data configuration.

Two important settings are required for CO-PA master data:

- Characteristic derivation: A series of steps (called a *strategy*) to populate characteristic values, for example, using a table lookup to get a customer group from the customer master.
- Valuation: A strategy to determine which material cost estimate to use to populate material and labor value fields, for example, using the material standard cost component split to get the fixed and variable COGS. Valuation can also be used with a CO-PA costing sheet to calculate values not present on the posting or with a user exit.

We'll take a look at both settings in the following sections.

Characteristic Derivation

A characteristic derivation strategy may contain several steps to derive the needed characteristics. When the operating concern is generated, the system will create as many derivation steps as possible. You may make changes to some system generated steps. You'll need to create your own steps for any user created (WW) characteristics.

Each step is built on one of four customizable techniques:

- Derivation of organizational units: This technique consists of fixed steps automatically generated by the system. Examples of fixed steps include the derivation company code and controlling area.

- Table lookup: Accessing an existing SAP table for the characteristic value. An example is looking up the material group from the material master table.

- Rule: These can be used to incorporate user-defined logic. Example: If SAP characteristic division = 21, use A as the strategic business unit.

- Move and clear: These can be used to transfer one characteristic value to another, or to remove a value under specified conditions. Example: If ship-to party is blank, move sold-to party to the ship-to characteristic.

Let's look at a few characteristic derivation steps. Figure 7.10 shows an example of a table lookup derivation step. In this case, we need to derive a material group from the CO-PA product number. Under the **Definition** tab, in the **Source Fields for Table Lookup** section, the **MARA** table is specified as the source for the CO-PA product number characteristic. In the **Assignment of Table Fields to Target Fields** section, the field **MATKL** from the **MARA** table will be used as the characteristic value for the CO-PA characteristic MATKL.

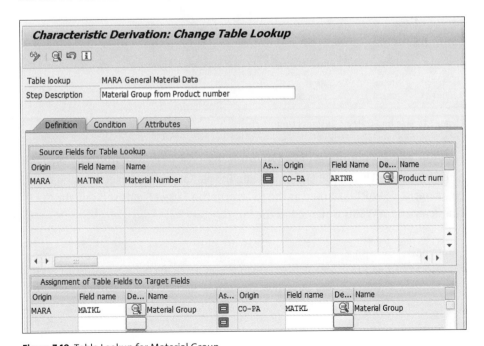

Figure 7.10 Table Lookup for Material Group

> **Tip**
> Use the **Condition** tab to indicate under what conditions this step should be applied. Use the **Attributes** tab to indicate if the system should return an error if this step fails.

Figure 7.11 shows an example of a rule derivation step. First, remember that our **WWSBU Strat. Business Unit** characteristic is a user-created characteristic (as shown earlier in Figure 7.3)—this object does not exist in standard SAP.

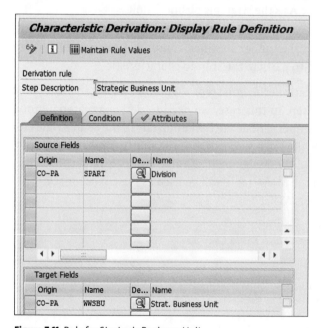

Figure 7.11 Rule for Strategic Business Unit

Let's say we want to use the CO-PA division characteristic to assign a custom characteristic value. Under the **Definition** tab, in the **Source Fields** section, the CO-PA characteristic **SPART** is named as the source. In the **Target Fields** section, the CO-PA characteristic **WWSBU** is named as the target.

> **Warning!**
> The system cannot create derivation steps for custom characteristics; you must create these steps. If you do not, the system cannot capture the characteristic's values for reporting.

As shown in Figure 7.12, the CO-PA **Division** values have been assigned to the CO-PA **Strat. Business Unit** values. In a CO-PA document, if the division number is **21**, then the system will derive **A** to fill out the **Strat. Business Unit** field, for example.

Characteristic Derivation: Display Rule Values

Optimize Column Widths

Derivation rule   Strategic Business Unit

No value filter active

Division	Division Name	to Division	to Division Name	Assigned	Strat. Business U...	Strat. Business Unit Name
21	Forklift 21				A	Fork Lift
00	Cross Division	17	Furniture 17		C	Cross
19	IT Services 19				C	Cross
18	Consulting Sces 1.				B	Consulting

Figure 7.12 Rule Value for WWSBU

As each posting occurs, the derivation strategy is executed. The system assigns as many characteristic values as possible and determines a profitability segment number based on each unique combination of these characteristic values. Unlike other master data we've seen in this book, your users don't need to keep track of this profitability segment master data number. Profitability segments are technical objects only. Instead of a specific master record number, users can analyze all the data by the characteristic values themselves; for example, by customer, by region, or by product.

Valuation

Due to its special design, valuation is used with costing-based CO-PA only. Remember that account-based CO-PA reports by cost element and ties off to FI G/L account values. Valuation can provide calculated amounts that were not posted to FI as well as more granular details than FI about product cost.

A valuation strategy may contain several user-defined steps to supplement details about costs. When the operating concern is generated, the system does not create a valuation strategy.

A user-defined valuation strategy may contain the following:

- CO-PA costing sheet: Used to calculate imputed/accrued values in costing-based CO-PA only
- SD pricing procedures (available for planning only): Used to plan revenue and cost of sales
- Product costing details: Used to transfer the material cost component split to costing-based CO-PA only
- User exit: Used to create custom ABAP coding not supplied by the three preceding points

A user-defined valuation strategy must be assigned to a point of valuation and a record type. Optionally, a valuation strategy may be assigned to a plan version.

The *point of valuation* indicates when the strategy is going to be executed. The selections supplied by SAP are:

- **01: Realtime valuation of actual data**
- **02: Periodic revaluation of actual data**
- **03: Manual planning**
- **04: Automatic planning**

A *record type* is used to identify the source of a posting in costing-based CO-PA. Record types are supplied by SAP, but you can change their descriptions. The available selections are:

- **A: Incoming sales order**
- **B: Dir. Posting from FI**
- **C: Order/proj.settlemnt**
- **D: Overhead costs**
- **E: Single trans costing**
- **F: Billing data**
- **G: Customer agreements**
- **H: Stat. key figures**
- **I: Order-rel. project**
- **L: Goods Issue**

An example of assignments is shown in Figure 7.13. In this example, if a posting to costing-based CO-PA is being made in real time (**PV 01**) from an SD billing document (**Rec. F**), then valuation strategy **001** will be called/executed.

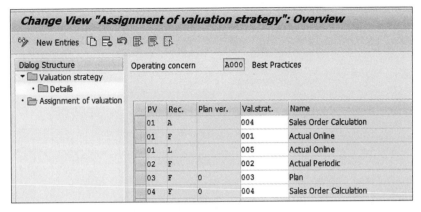

Figure 7.13 Assignment of Valuation Strategy

The most common use of valuation is the ability to capture and assign a material cost component split to costing-based CO-PA value fields. By use of a *costing key*, you can assign a specific material cost estimate as follows:

1. Select the **Mat. cstg** checkbox and maintain the CO-PA **Qty field**, as shown in Figure 7.14.

| Operating concern | A000 | Best Practices |
| Val. strategy | 001 | Actual Online |

Sequence	Appl.	Costg s...	Description	Mat. cstg	Qty field
10				✓	VVIQI

Figure 7.14 Material Costing Checkbox

2. Create a **Costing Key** to indicate which material cost estimate to use, as shown in Figure 7.15.
3. Assign the costing key to any characteristic. For example, should a different cost estimate be used for finished goods instead of semifinished goods? If so, then assign the costing key to a material type.
4. By cost component structure (see Chapter 5), assign each cost component to a costing-based CO-PA value field, as shown in Figure 7.16.

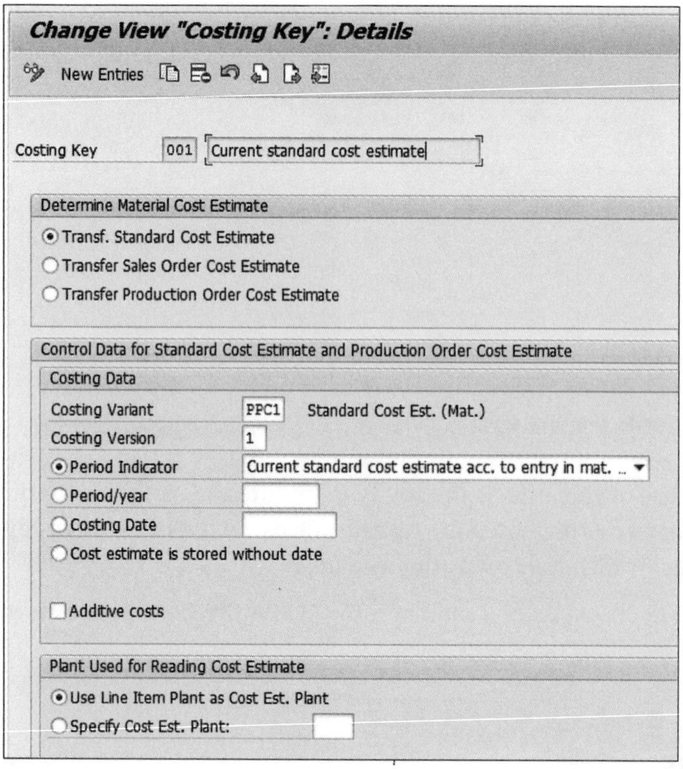

Figure 7.15 Costing Key

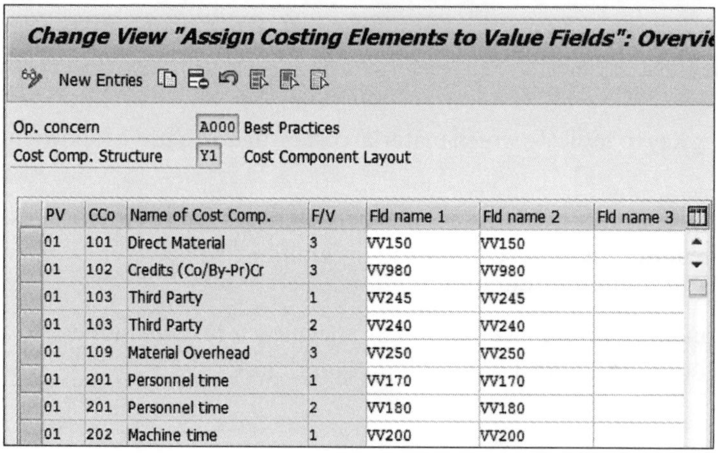

Figure 7.16 Assign Cost Component Structure to Value Field

Enhancements with the Universal Journal

Now that you have a basic understanding of the design of CO-PA prior to SAP S/4HANA, let's return to the features available in SAP S/4HANA that enhance the legacy account-based and costing-based CO-PA features.

Splitting Structures/Profiles

To bring the required level of detail about COGS and production variances (see Chapter 6), SAP S/4HANA introduced two splitting structures (often referred to as profiles) to assign cost components to G/L account numbers. These profiles, in effect, replace costing-based mappings created by the PA transfer structures.

The next few figures show examples of each splitting structure/profile.

As shown in Figure 7.17, cost components are assigned to G/L account numbers by controlling area and chart of accounts. In SAP S/4HANA, CO-PA from the Universal Journal replaces the costing-based valuation/costing key design by splitting these costs directly in the G/L.

Cost Splitting Profile	0YA000
Source Account	54083000
Valuation View	
Basis	SAP
Cost Component Structure	Y1
CO Area	A000
Chart of Accounts	YCOA

Target Accounts

Cost Component	Name of Cost Component	Target Account	Target account text	Default
101	Direct Material	50301000	COGS Direct Material	☑
102	Credits (Co/By-Pr)Cr	50308000	COGS Credit Co/By-Pr	☐
103	Third Party	50302000	COGS Third Party	☐
109	Material Overhead	50303000	COGS Material Overhd	☐
201	Personnel time	50304000	COGS Personnel Time	☐
202	Machine time	50305000	COGS Machine Time	☐

Figure 7.17 COGS Splitting Profile

As shown in Figure 7.18, production variance categories are also assigned to G/L account numbers by controlling area and chart of accounts. In SAP S/4HANA, CO-PA from the Universal Journal also replaces the costing-based PA transfer structure design by splitting these costs directly in the G/L.

Price Diff. Splitting Profile	ZYA000	CC Variances
Controlling Area	A000	Controlling Area A000
Chart of Accounts	YCOA	Standard Chart of Accounts (Training)

Detailed Price Difference Accounts

Line	Description	Cost Elem. From	Cost Elem. To	CElem Group	VCat	Target Account	Default
0010	Scrap			TCOST	SCRP	52701000	☐
0020	Input Price Variance			TCOST	PRIV	52702000	☐
0030	Mixes Price Variance			TCOST	MXPV	52703000	☐
0040	Quantity Variance Material			CONSUME	QTYV	52704000	☐
0050	Quantity Variance Production			COGS	QTYV	52705000	☐
0060	Recource Usage Variance			TCOST	RSUV	52706000	☐
0070	Remaining Input Variance			TCOST	INPV	52707000	☐
0080	Lot Size Variance			TCOST	LSFV	52708000	☐
0090	Output Price Variance			TCOST	OPPV	52709000	☐
0100	Remaining Output Variance		🔍	TCOST	REMV	52710000	☑

Figure 7.18 Price Difference Splitting Profile

Tip

These splitting profiles are found in the **General Ledger-Periodic Processing · Integration-Materials Management** section of the configuration menu.

Activate Derivation for Items without Profitability Segment

With this feature, you can activate the derivation of profitability characteristics for line items in the Universal Journal that do not carry an account assignment to a profitability segment. This process is possible for cost or revenue line items with the following account assignments:

- Cost center
- Production order
- Internal order
- Project
- Sales order

One benefit is the ability to report these costs with detailed characteristic values prior to the periodic settlement of each cost object. You may hear this SAP S/4HANA feature referred to as the "attributed profitability segment."

Flow of Actual Data

For account-based CO-PA in the Universal Journal, the flow of actual data is achieved simply by posting to a G/L account and including the relevant characteristic values. These will populate table ACDOCA. There are a few actual postings that require automatic account assignment to a profitability segment in Transaction OKB9 to pass characteristics to account-based CO-PA. These postings originate in materials management (MM) and include the following:

- Purchasing price differences on material purchases
- Changes from inventory revaluations
- Changes from the transfer of inventories

For costing-based CO-PA, you must determine which value fields to use for posting all business transactions. In the configuration menu, a separate folder exists for each type of value flow from FI to costing-based CO-PA. Table 7.1 summarizes this process.

Component	Source of Business Transaction	Example of Value Fields to Update	Method
Sales and distribution (SD)	Billing document	Revenue, COGS	Pricing condition to value field
Product cost controlling	Material cost estimate	Variable material cost, fixed labor cost	Valuation strategy and costing key
Financial accounting (FI)	G/L posting	Commission, bad debt	PA transfer structure
Overhead management (CO-OM)	Cost center and internal order settlement	SG&A cost	PA transfer structure
Project systems (PS)	Work breakdown structure (WBS) settlement	R&D cost	PA transfer structure
Cost object controlling	Production order settlement	Variances by category	PA transfer structure

Table 7.1 Source of Value Fields

Each SD pricing condition that flows to costing-based CO-PA must be assigned to a value field, as shown in Figure 7.19.

Change View "CO-PA: Assignment of SD Conditions to Value Fields

   New Entries 　　　　　

Op. concern   A000   Best Practices

CTyp	Name	Val. fld	Description	Transfer +/-
PR00	Price	VV010	Revenue	☐
PR02	Graduated Price	VV010	Revenue	☐
R100	100% discount	VV030	Customer Discount	☐
RA00	% Discount from Net	VV030	Customer Discount	☐
RB00	Discount (Value)	VV030	Customer Discount	☐
RC00	Quantity Discount	VV030	Customer Discount	☐

Figure 7.19 SD Conditions to Value Fields

A *PA transfer structure* is used to assign cost by cost element to a value field. Let's look in detail at the example shown in Figure 7.20:

- The PA transfer structure **FI** contains two assignment lines: **010 Costs** and **020 Revenue**.
- For assignment line **010 Costs**, in **Controlling Area A000**, use the cost element group **TCOST** for assignment to value field **VV366 Other cost**.
- For assignment line **020 Revenue**, in **Controlling Area A000**, use the cost element group **REVENUE** for assignment to value field **VV010 Revenue**.

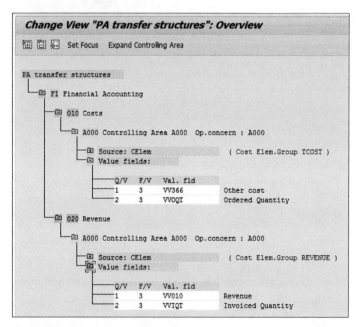

Figure 7.20 PA Transfer Structure "FI"

For example, if a posting is made in the FI G/L to a CO-PA-relevant cost element in the group **TCOST**, costing-based CO-PA will update the value field **Other cost**.

For actual postings that are transferred from FI, PA transfer structure FI is required. To transfer production order variances at settlement, you must create a separate PA transfer structure. This structure is similar to the structure **FI** reviewed earlier, but it has one additional level of detail in the definition of **Source**.

As shown in Figure 7.21, you assign a cost element by range or by group to the assignment row of the transfer structure along with the category of variance that was calculated during the period-end close of cost object controlling (see Chapter 6).

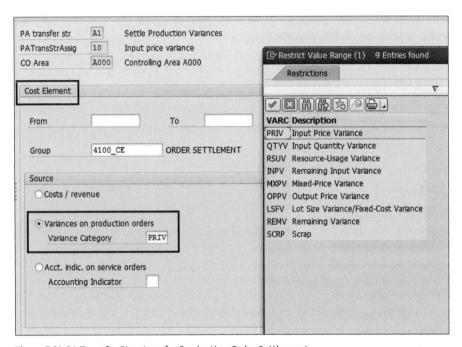

Figure 7.21 PA Transfer Structure for Production Order Settlement

You must then assign the PA transfer structure for production order settlement to the production order settlement profile, as discussed in Chapter 6.

Planning

Planning is an optional feature that you can use for revenue and cost planning with CO-PA characteristics, which provides more detail than planning by G/L account, by leveraging our "by" words, for example, revenue by customer and product rather than only by the revenue G/L account.

For account-based CO-PA in the Universal Journal, planning would be entered via embedded SAP Business Planning and Consolidation (SAP BPC). For costing-based CO-PA, the two most commonly used planning methods for costing-based CO-PA are as follows:

- *Manual planning*, where planning data is entered in the system manually.
- *Automatic planning*, where planning data is calculated by the system, specifically using the feature *top-down distribution*. Top-down distribution can use reference data against high-level planning to provide more granularity.

Before we look at some examples of each planning method, we need to review the purpose and design of the *planning layout*.

Planning Layout

For the entry of plan data, you can customize a layout of columns, rows, and characteristics you want to plan for. These attributes can be assigned to each value column in the layout, as follows:

- A currency or a unit field for the value field
- A long text
- Characteristics
- A distribution key, for example, to divide an annual value evenly over the period being planned
- A formula

Let's review the example shown in Figure 7.22. In this example, we want to plan the value fields **Invoiced Quantity** and **Revenue** by the characteristics **Customer** and **Product**.

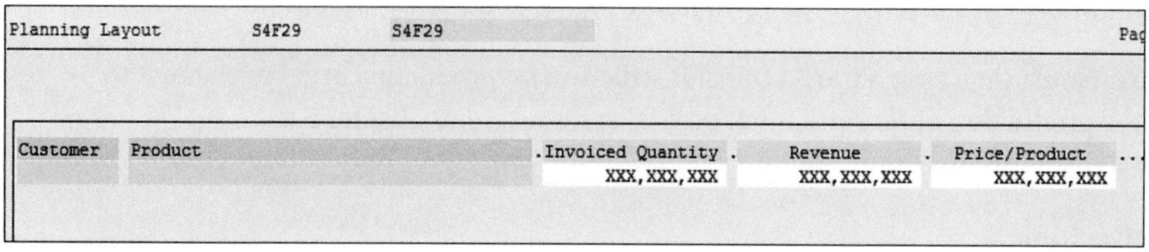

Figure 7.22 Planning Layout

> **Tip**
> The **Price/Product** column is not a value field; rather this field represents a formula.

Manual Planning

To enter plan data manually, you would first navigate to Transaction KEPM in the application menu, as shown in Figure 7.23. Within Transaction KEPM, you would make the following selections:

- The *planning level* (**S4F29**) indicates what objects are to be planned, in this example, customer, record type, and the year 2018.
- The *planning package* (**S4F290**) indicates which version to plan, in this example, version 0.
- The *planning method* indicates whether you enter, display, or change the planning data, in this case **Enter planning data**.
- The *parameter set* indicates the planning layout, as shown in Figure 7.24—in this case, **S4F29**.

Figure 7.23 Transaction KEPM Enter Manual Planning

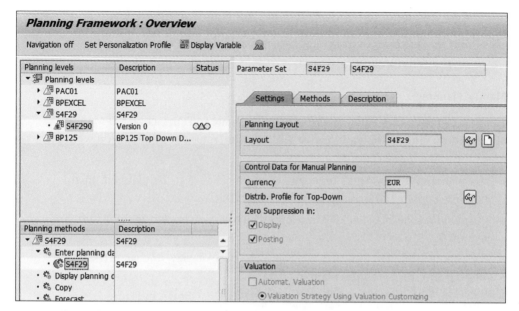

Figure 7.24 Parameter Set S4F29 with Planning Layout S4F29 Assigned

Top-Down Distribution

Top-down distribution can use reference data against high-level planning to provide more granularity. The following capabilities are enabled by top-down distribution:

- Planning can be input by product group and revenue.
- Reference data by product group for the past year can be assigned.
- The system can distribute the planned revenue by the individual products sold from the reference data.

Figure 7.25 shows a simple example of the top-down distribution process:

❶ This table represents plan entries in Transaction KEPM. We've planned revenue dollars by the characteristic product group A at a fairly high level.

❷ This table represents the reference data we want to use to deconstruct product group A, in this case, the billing documents (record type F) from the year 2018.

❸ In this table, we've executed the top-down distribution calculation using Transaction KEPM. The system found three products with sales quantities for product group A:

- Product A1 had a quantity of 100.
- Product A2 had a quantity of 200.
- Product A3 had a quantity of 100.

❹ This table represents the output of the top-down distribution calculation. The $10,000 revenue planned for product group A in table ❶ has now been distributed to the product level.

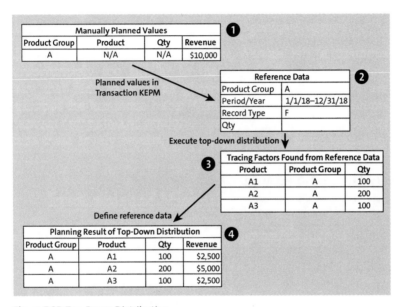

Figure 7.25 Top-Down Distribution

Reporting

Let's start with account-based CO-PA. Since all data resides in the Universal Journal (table ACDOCA), standard reports are available for contribution margin analysis. Figure 7.26 shows an example of the Market Segment SAP Fiori app. In this example, you'll see G/L account balances in company code currency, with the characteristic **Product Sold Group** in the lead column. Now, you can analyze cost and revenue by the "market segment" of product group in a standard report.

Alternatively, you must create your own drilldown reports for costing-based CO-PA using the Report Painter tool (see Chapter 9). These reports use a matrix of data that allows you to select one or more characteristics for a "slice and dice" analysis. User access can be restricted to various levels of the drilldown information. An example of a user-created contribution margin report is shown in Figure 7.27.

Product Sold Group ≜	Product Sold Group ⤙≜	G/L Account ≜	G/L Account ⤙≜	Actual Amount in Company Code Crcy ⤙≜	
		63004000	Insurance	6.000,00 EUR	
		63006000	Telephone and other	6.000,00 EUR	
		63007000	Fax and Internet	6.000,00 EUR	
P001	Services	65100000	Office Supplies	6.000,00 EUR	
		65150000	Computer Supplies	6.000,00 EUR	
		65301000	Marketing Expenses	5.800,00 EUR	
		Result		**35.800,00 EUR**	
Result				**35.800,00 EUR**	
		41000000	Rev Domestic Prod	-59.900,00 EUR	
		50301000	COGS Direct Material	507,00 EUR	
		50303000	COGS Material Overhd	4,15 EUR	
		50304000	COGS Personnel Time	4.958,15 EUR	
L004	Finished Goods	50305000	COGS Machine Time	3.749,90 EUR	
		50306000	COGS Setup Time	25,05 EUR	
		50307000	COGS Productn Overhd	212,80 EUR	

Figure 7.26 Universal Journal Market Segment App

Execute Drilldown Report Cross Margin Detail: Detail List

Cross Margin Detail

Global Profit Analysis
Year:2018   From Period: 1   To Period: 12

Navigation
Country
Customer
Industry
Sales Group

Lead column	Plan Version: 0	Actual	Abs. Var.	Var. %
Invoiced Quantity	2,320.000	115.000	2,205.000-	95.04310-
Revenue	1,390,840.00	157,864.04	1,232,975.96-	88.64973-
Sales Deduction	0.00	0.00	0.00	✗
Net Revenue	1,390,840.00	157,864.04	1,232,975.96-	88.64973-
Material input	33,573.00	1,614.29	31,958.71-	95.19170-
Production labor var	57,516.56	5,517.38	51,999.18-	90.40732-
Product. machine var	14,499.88	1,387.98	13,111.90-	90.42764-

Figure 7.27 Costing-Based User Created Report (Transaction KE30)

Predictive Accounting

Account-based CO-PA can benefit from the use of the optional *prediction ledger*. The prediction ledger supports the analysis of activities which haven't yet occurred, and therefore aren't yet financial postings.

This feature is activated in several steps:

1. First, the prediction ledger must be created by company code. In FI configuration for **Ledger** settings, a new ledger can be created as ledger type **Prediction and Commitments**.

2. Once active, you can use Transaction SE11 to maintain table `FINSV_PRED_RLDNR` with the new ledger.

3. Then, you can activate predictive accounting for incoming sales orders. This will create postings in the prediction ledger for the equivalent of costing-based record type A.

An additional option for using the prediction ledger is to include statistical pricing conditions from the SD sales order.

These new options enable forecasting of future revenue, COGS, and the contribution margin of sales orders that have yet to be delivered and billed by reporting from the predictive ledger.

Important Terminology

In this chapter, the following terminology was used:

- **Account-based CO-PA**
  Account-based CO-PA can analyze data at the G/L account level by characteristic.

- **Characteristic**
  Characteristics define items or objects for your users to analyze. In a report analyzing data by customer, the customer is the relevant characteristic. Other common uses for characteristics include reporting by product or by region.

- **Characteristic derivation**
  This technique determines a characteristic's value based on steps in a strategy. When an operating concern is generated, the system will create as many steps as possible, but you can also create your own steps.

- **Costing-based CO-PA**
  Costing-based CO-PA analyzes fixed and variable data at the value field level by characteristic.

- **Costing key**
  A costing key indicates which material cost estimate to use during valuation for costing-based CO-PA.

- **Operating concern**
  An operating concern is an organizational structure for CO-PA that has its own fiscal year variant and currency. Controlling areas are assigned to operating concerns.

- **PA transfer structure**
  This structure can be used to assign costs by cost element to a value field in costing-based CO-PA.

- **Point of valuation**
  The point of valuation indicates when the valuation strategy will be executed in costing-based CO-PA. Four options are available depending on the kind of data. For actual data, you can choose between real-time and periodic valuation strategies; for plan data, you can choose between manual and automatic valuation strategies.

- **Prediction ledger**
  An FI extension ledger that can be used for posting incoming sales orders and statistical SD condition types. This optional feature supports predictive accounting.

- **Record type**
  The record type identifies the source of a posting in costing-based CO-PA. Record types are supplied by SAP, but you can change their descriptions.

- **Splitting profile**
  A splitting profile can be used to assign cost components to G/L account numbers for account-based CO-PA/Universal Journal.

- **Top-down distribution**
  This distribution is the use of reference data against high-level planning data to provide more granularity.

- **Universal Journal**
  Data that was historically stored in numerous tables is now found in the Universal Journal in SAP S/4HANA. The Universal Journal is technically named table ACDOCA for actual data and table ACDOCP for plan data and contains all details from all applications.

- **Valuation**
  This process is used in costing-based CO-PA to supplement details about cost.
- **Value field**
  This field is used in costing-based CO-PA to contain the amounts and quantities you want to analyze in a report.

Practice Questions

These practice questions will help you evaluate your understanding of the topics covered in this chapter. The questions shown are similar in nature to those found on the certification examination. Although none of these questions will be found on the exam itself, they will allow you to review your knowledge of the subject. Select the correct answers and then check the completeness of your answers in the "Practice Question Answers and Explanations" section. Remember that on the exam you must select all correct answers and only correct answers to receive credit for the question.

1. What tables are used to store CO-PA data? (There are two correct answers.)

  ☐ **A.** Tables CE1xxxx and CE2xxxx are used by costing-based CO-PA

  ☐ **B.** Table BSEG is used by account-based CO-PA

  ☐ **C.** Table ACDOCA is used by account-based CO-PA

  ☐ **D.** Table COSS is used by account-based CO-PA

2. Which of the following apply to costing-based CO-PA? (There are two correct answers.)

  ☐ **A.** Characteristics

  ☐ **B.** Splitting structures

  ☐ **C.** Value fields

  ☐ **D.** Cost elements

3. For which characteristics does the system automatically create a derivation step?

  ☐ **A.** Derivation rules

  ☐ **B.** Fixed characteristics

  ☐ **C.** Custom characteristics

4. To which of the following can a valuation strategy be assigned? (There are two correct answers.)

☐   **A.** Point of valuation

☐   **B.** A value field

☐   **C.** Record type

☐   **D.** Costing key

5. Which of the following is needed to transfer data from FI directly to costing-based CO-PA?

☐   **A.** Valuation strategy

☐   **B.** PA transfer structure

☐   **C.** Splitting structure

6. When you create a planning layout, which objects can you use to define the data columns? (There are two correct answers.)

☐   **A.** Formulas

☐   **B.** Characteristics

☐   **C.** Planning level

☐   **D.** Planning package

7. Which objects are fixed characteristics for CO-PA in SAP S/4HANA? (There are three correct answers.)

☐   **A.** Controlling area

☐   **B.** Company code

☐   **C.** Product category

☐   **D.** Plant

☐   **E.** Region

8. Which object do you use when you assign costs and revenue to the value fields in costing-based CO-PA?

☐   **A.** Overhead group

☐   **B.** PA transfer structure

☐   **C.** Allocation template

☐   **D.** Allocation structure

9.   Which of the following define an operating concern when it is created? (There are three correct answers.)

☐   **A.** Valuation strategy

☐   **B.** Type of profitability analysis

☐   **C.** Derivation strategy

☐   **D.** Data structure

☐   **E.** Operating concern currency

10.   True or False: Companies can choose which type of CO-PA to activate.

☐   **A.** True

☐   **B.** False

11.   Which of the following apply to both account-based and costing-based CO-PA? (There are three correct answers.)

☐   **A.** Valuation strategy

☐   **B.** Characteristics

☐   **C.** PA transfer structure

☐   **D.** Table CE4xxxx

☐   **E.** Derivation strategy

12.   True or False: Fixed characteristics usually represent organizational structure and master data derived on a posting.

☐   **A.** True

☐   **B.** False

13.   True or False: Once an operating concern has been generated, you cannot make any changes to its settings.

☐   **A.** True

☐   **B.** False

14. Which of the following applies to cost splitting profiles?

☐ **A.** They are used in costing-based CO-PA.

☐ **B.** They are used to supply more costing detail to the G/L.

☐ **C.** They are assigned to an operating concern.

15. True or False: Top-down distribution can be used to provide more granular planning details.

☐ **A.** True

☐ **B.** False

16. True or False: Planning for costing-based CO-PA is created in SAP BPC.

☐ **A.** True

☐ **B.** False

17. For costing-based CO-PA, SAP S/4HANA provides standard reports that can be used by all customers.

☐ **A.** True

☐ **B.** False

Practice Question Answers and Explanations

1. Correct answers: **A, C**
    Remember that in SAP S/4HANA, account-based CO-PA data is stored directly in table ACDOCA, the Universal Journal. Costing-based CO-PA has its own unique tables for data storage. Each table carries the characters of the operating concern key as its last four characters.

2. Correct answers: **A, C**
    While characteristics are utilized in both types of CO-PA, only costing-based CO-PA uses value fields. Cost elements are now G/L accounts in SAP S/4HANA and are used in account-based CO-PA. Splitting structures are not used in costing-based CO-PA; they provide more details, by G/L account, for account-based CO-PA.

3. Correct answer: **B**

    Of these choices, only fixed characteristics is correct. However, the system will also attempt to create a derivation step for any table lookup characteristic.

4. Correct answers: **A, C**

    Valuation strategies are assigned to point of valuation, for example, real time or periodic, and to record types, for example, billing or settlement documents. You can also assign the valuation strategy to a plan version. Costing keys are used within a valuation strategy to determine which material cost estimate to use in a valuation, but they are not used for assignment of the strategy.

5. Correct answer: **B**

    The PA transfer structure is used to assign the G/L accounts from an FI posting directly to a value field in costing-based CO-PA. Splitting structures apply only to account-based CO-PA.

6. Correct answers: **A, B**

    Formulas can be used in planning layout columns to calculate ratios or totals. Characteristics can be used in planning layouts to plan specific amounts; for example, a material group may be a lead column with a material number as the second column.

7. Correct answers: **A, B, D**

    Remember that fixed characteristics generally represent the organizational structure and master data from the posting. In this question, three characteristics are qualifying: Controlling area, company code, and plant are each organizational structures in SAP S/4HANA.

8. Correct answer: **B**

    The PA transfer structure is used to make the assignment of cost and revenue to a specific value field for use in reporting.

9. Correct answers: **B, D, E**

    When creating a new operating concern, you must indicate if account-based and/or costing-based CO-PA will be in scope. Each operating concern has its own currency settings, separate from other currencies you've defined for FI-CO. You must also add characteristics and value fields to the new operating concern; these elements define the data structure.

10. Correct answer: **A**

    True. This decision is first made in the definition of the operating concern. While both types of CO-PA are optional, in SAP S/4HANA, a best practice is to

390 Chapter 7 Profitability Analysis

activate account-based CO-PA. Costing-based CO-PA remains an optional feature.

11. Correct answers: **B, D, E**

    Both types of CO-PA use characteristics, the "by" words for reporting, and both use the derivation strategy to determine the characteristic values. Table CE4xxxx is shared by both types of CO-PA as a control of the profitability segment. Costing-based CO-PA only uses a PA transfer structure and the valuation strategy.

12. Correct answer: **A**

    True. Remember that fixed characteristics are mandatory and are controlled by SAP. They are derived from each posting's organizational structure and master data.

13. Correct answer: **B**

    False. If changes are made to characteristics or value fields after generating the operating concern, the operating concern must be regenerated to expand the various table structures to accommodate the new characteristics or value fields.

14. Correct answer: **B**

    Cost splitting profiles proved more granular details by assigning cost components to G/L account number and therefore are used only in account-based CO-PA. They are assigned initially to a controlling area.

15. Correct answer: **A**

    True. Top-down distribution is a technique to use historical reference data to deconstruct data. Our planning example was to reference product numbers and their sales quantities from a prior year to revenue planned only at the product group level.

16. Correct answer: **B**

    False. In SAP S/4HANA, SAP BPC is embedded and is where you'll plan for account-based CO-PA. To plan in costing-based CO-PA, you can use Transaction KEPM.

17. Correct answer: **B**

    False. All reports for costing-based CO-PA must be created using the Report Painter tool. No standard reports come predelivered. In SAP S/4HANA, reporting apps have been standardized following SAP Fiori design principles.

Takeaway

In this chapter, you gained a good understanding of all basic CO-PA objects and configuration settings. We reviewed the two types of CO-PA, and you should now be familiar with both account-based CO-PA and costing-based CO-PA. Basic integration with other modules has been introduced as actual value flows. We reviewed improvements in CO-PA, which now benefits from the use of SAP S/4HANA's Universal Journal.

We covered the unique organizational structure of the operating concern and the role of characteristics and value fields to the data structures created during generation. You've also been introduced to the characteristic derivation strategy and its importance in defining the profitability segment master record as well as its role in supplying the "by" words used in reporting.

Specifically for costing-based CO-PA, we discussed the valuation strategy as a tool to supplement product costing details and reviewed integration with other modules as actual value flows using features like PA transfer structures.

Finally, we introduced you to planning and reporting options in SAP S/4HANA.

Summary

CO-PA is a powerful tool for contribution margin reporting. Being able to explain its structures and participate in the design phase is crucial for a CO consultant. You should now understand the most common configuration settings as well as understand how to distinguish between account-based and costing-based CO-PA.

Now that we've covered CO-PA as a profitability reporting tool, let's move on to another component used to measure profitability from another perspective—profit center accounting.

Chapter 8
Profit Center Accounting

Techniques You'll Master

- Define profit center organizational units
- Explain profit center master data structure
- Define the features of document splitting
- Introduce the concept of new general ledger (G/L) segment reporting
- Define profit center update process
- Outline integration with financial accounting (FI)
- Outline integration with materials management (MM)
- Outline integration with cost object controlling
- Outline integration with sales and distribution (SD)
- Describe the period-end allocation in profit centers

In this chapter, we'll outline the use of profit centers. We'll define the process of creating profit centers, as well as their integration with other business processes. We'll also outline the similarity and differences between profit center accounting (PCA) and FI. We'll finish our discussion of controlling (CO) with period-end closing for profit centers.

Real-World Scenario

As a CO consultant, several common questions will arise when explaining profit centers. One of your first tasks will be to convey the concept of statistical value tracking versus actual values. Profit center posting are always initiated in conjunction with other objects, either in CO or FI. You'll also need to understand the differences between business areas, functional areas, profit centers, and segments and be tasked with advising which options to implement.

You might encounter customers that do not use profit centers but could benefit from their use. You should also be clear that a new G/L version of profit centers is different from a classic version of profit centers. While using the classic version of profit centers is still possible, customers should be discouraged from their use. If your customer is currently using classic profit centers, you should advise them to migrate to using new G/L profit centers. Once you understand the capabilities of PCA, you'll be able to advise your customers about how it fits with their business functions.

Objectives of This Portion of the Test

This portion of the certification exam will test your knowledge of process integration between FI, CO, and PCA as well as test your knowledge of the design and purpose of standard profitability tools provided in SAP. An essential understanding of profit centers will require knowledge of real versus statistical objects.

The certification exam expects you to have a good understanding of the following topics:

- Utilize SAP profit analysis tools
- Explain PCA changes with FI and the new G/L
- Explain uses and derivation of segments
- Describe relationships between FI, CO, and PCA

- Explain profit center standard hierarchy definition
- Explain profit center derivation options within business processes
- Define profit center transaction data
- Explain period-end allocation for PCA

> **Note**
> The PCA topic makes up less than 8% of the exam.

Key Concepts Refresher

When SAP uses the term "profitability analysis," both profitability analysis (CO-PA) and PCA are included. As discussed in the previous chapter, CO-PA covers product, market, and service profitability. PCA is defined as organizational-level profitability analysis. The two tools provide different information. CO-PA is margin reporting for product and market analysis, while PCA uses account-level detail including an income statement and balance sheets.

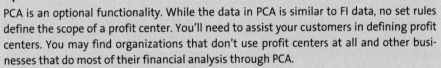

> **Tip**
> PCA is an optional functionality. While the data in PCA is similar to FI data, no set rules define the scope of a profit center. You'll need to assist your customers in defining profit centers. You may find organizations that don't use profit centers at all and other businesses that do most of their financial analysis through PCA.

Profit centers are a reporting dimension and a statistical assignment object. Profit centers cannot receive standalone postings; they must always have a companion of a real assignment object, such as a company code or controlling cost object. Profit centers are posted in conjunction with company codes or controlling cost objects. You can, however, move postings from one profit center to another, which can be done with manual entries or period-end allocations.

Two versions of PCA currently exist. The initial version, classic PCA, was a subarea of CO. Data was stored in separate technical structures and had limitations when balance sheet postings were available. During the design of the new G/L accounting, PCA was integrated into the FI technical structure. The new structure of PCA, referred to as EC-PCA, is integrated into the enterprise controlling function of the new G/L

In SAP S/4HANA, the new G/L is mandatory, but both options of PCA are still possible. The recommended best practice is to use EC-PCA in SAP S/4HANA. Since SAP S/4HANA is built on a foundation of the new G/L, EC-PCA data is stored in the Universal Journal. To simplify our discussion here we will just use the term PCA.

The first step to grasping the functionality of PCA is understanding the organizational structure of profit centers, which we'll discuss first. We'll then discuss transfer pricing, and the integration with enterprise controlling for account-level details like finance. We'll close with a look at period-end close for PCA.

Master Data

Profit centers are defined at the controlling area level, which gives them features similar to other CO elements discussed previously. Profit centers are also assigned to other master data objects like cost centers, orders, fixed assets, and materials. In the following sections, we'll discuss how these assignments are used to derive profit centers during business processes.

Standard Hierarchy

The initial step for activating PCA is designating a standard hierarchy. Figure 8.1 shows how a standard hierarchy is defined at the controlling area in configuration. The guidelines for determining the profit center hierarchy are similar to the cost center hierarchy. Every profit center in the controlling area must be assigned to the standard hierarchy. You can also assign the profit center to multiple alternate hierarchies.

Once the hierarchy is defined, you can define up to 99 levels. You can organize groups at your discretion. The structure of the hierarchy should correspond to the desired organizational control.

Warning!
The assignment to a group occurs immediately. Any changes to the group structure occur immediately; no previews are available before changes are committed.

A standard hierarchy, shown in Figure 8.2, shows the structure of the hierarchy including the assignment to group levels and an activation status.

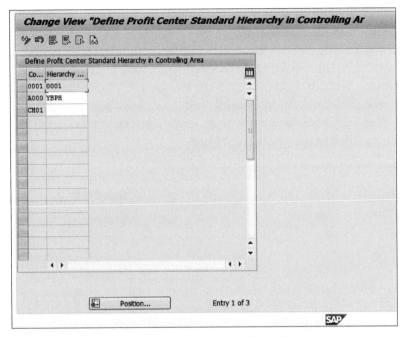

Figure 8.1 Define Profit Center Standard Hierarchy in Controlling Area

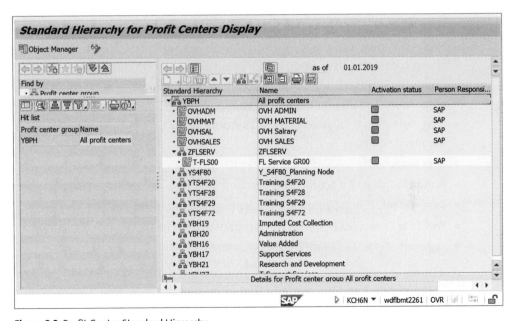

Figure 8.2 Profit Center Standard Hierarchy

Many organizations make frequent changes to their hierarchies, which thus require significant effort spent maintaining the hierarchy structure. SAP S/4HANA's enhanced functionality with flexible hierarchies can generate hierarchies based on master data attributes. This capability can be used for reporting based on profit center master data attributes. With the SAP Fiori app Manage Flexible Hierarchies, you can set up a new flexible hierarchy by defining a sequence of selected attributes. This app also provides a fast and efficient way to set up different hierarchies in parallel just by specifying different sequences of attributes.

> **Note**
> The Manage Flexible Hierarchies app supports mass changes to master data attributes as well.

Profit Center

The initial settings for profit center master data include an ID, an assignment to a controlling area, and validity dates. Other relevant master data fields are shown in Figure 8.3. Notice the similarities between cost center master data and profit center master data. Some additional settings for profit centers include the following:

- **Status**: Profit center must be activated. To receive postings, a profit center must have valid dates and be activated.
- **Analysis Period**: Valid dates for the current master data settings. This setting allows before and after reporting for profit center information.
- **Name**: This field contains a short text to define the profit center. Think of this name as a nickname for the profit center.
- **Long Text**: This field gives you the ability to assign an extended description to the profit center.
- **User Responsible**: An SAP system user ID.
- **Person Respons.**: An actual person's name or title.
- **Department**: Free assignment field for business organization.
- **Profit Ctr Group**: Level within the standard hierarchy.
- **Segment**: ID for a relevant business segment.

A segment is a subarea of a company. This concept was introduced with the new G/L to provide a dimension for reporting to meet legal requirements for market or geographical reporting. This requirement was directed in International Financial Reporting Standards (IFRS) 8 and US Generally Accepted Accounting Principles (US GAAP) for reporting, beginning in 2009. These instruments require companies to disclose business segments that are 10% or more of their business operations. A segment can be assigned to multiple profit centers. Generally, a segment is not entered manually but instead derived from the profit center. SAP provides a tool in Customizing to derive segments from a prior document posting.

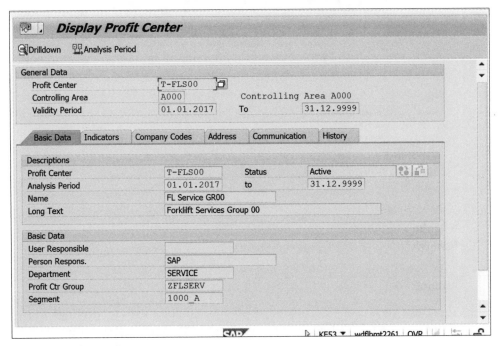

Figure 8.3 Profit Center Master Data

A key indicator in the profit center is the **Company Code** column, shown in Figure 8.4. The profit center to company code relationship is many to many (*n:n*). This indicator allows profit center postings to all selected company codes, assuming that the period is valid and that the profit center status is active and is not locked.

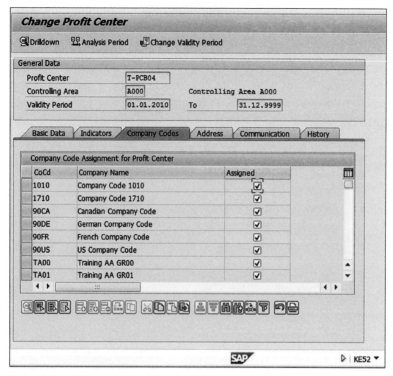

Figure 8.4 Profit Center Company Code Assignment

Accounts

The classic version of PCA had unique account numbers used for postings. In SAP S/4HANA, PCA uses G/L account master records. The technical structure of profit centers allows the utilization of all four G/L account types. These account types were discussed in Chapter 3. The effect is that profit centers can post to all FI accounts as well as to all accounts relevant to CO, essentially seeing all postings.

Statistical Key Figures

CO traits continue with another master data element. Profit centers can use statistical key figures, shown in Figure 8.5, which are the same master data element seen in cost center accounting (refer to Chapter 3) and serve the same purpose. Statistical key figures can be used as tracing factors and for key performance indicator (KPI) reporting.

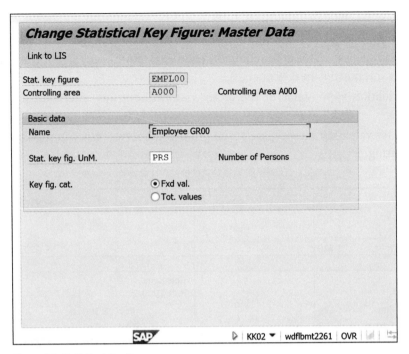

Figure 8.5 Statistical Key Figure

Transfer Pricing

Transfer pricing has become more prevalent with the expansion of multinational companies. Statutory reporting requirements are increasingly complex as companies move goods between business units and across legal boundaries. To facilitate this reporting requirement, companies employ transfer pricing.

Transfer pricing is part of the material ledger functionality, which is compulsory in SAP S/4HANA. There are three technical options in the material ledger: parallel valuation (transfer pricing), parallel currencies, and actual costing. Parallel valuation and parallel currencies are available out-of-the-box but require additional setup. Actual costing is an optional functionality that must be activated and configured.

Transfer pricing is used to accommodate accounting requirements to value products at *cost plus pricing* as goods traverse across business units. Cost plus pricing markup is defined by the applicable accounting principles. This has become more significant as organizations become more multinational.

Parallel valuation can be maintained in three prices simultaneously, as shown in Figure 8.6:

- Legal valuation view: Value at the company code level required for FI reporting. Eliminates internal business upcharges.
- Group valuation view: Value at the group view without any intercompany upcharges.
- Profit center valuation view: Value at the profit center level to accommodate PCA reporting.

Group View	Corporate				PROFIT
	Rev.	$ 300			
	Cost	$ 80			
	Profit	$ 220			$ 220

Legal View	Company Code 1000			Company Code 2000		
	Rev.	$ 170		Rev.	$ 300	
	Cost	$ 70		Cost	$ 180	
	Profit	$ 100		Profit	$ 120	$ 220

Profit Center	Profit Center 1000		Profit Center 1500		Profit Center 2000		
	Rev.	$ 100	Rev.	$ 170	Rev.	$ 300	
	Cost	$ 60	Cost	$ 110	Cost	$ 180	
	Profit	$ 40	Profit	$ 60	Profit	$ 120	$ 220

Figure 8.6 Parallel Valuation Example

The steps to activate transfer pricing are extensive and go beyond the scope of the exam. For the purposes of this book, let's review the steps and associated key decisions at a high level.

The first step in the process is to set up the value-add logic or upcharges. PCA has a key role in transfer pricing, because it maintains the upcharge between business levels. The substance of the upcharge is dependent on accounting principles or business requirements. In conjunction with the transfer price, the material ledger maintains the three values separately for inventory valuation, which are then maintained in the Universal Journal. The menu shown in Figure 8.7 illustrates where transfer pricing logic is defined in the IMG.

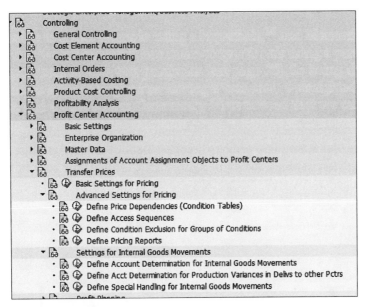

Figure 8.7 Transfer Price Setup

Transfer prices also need to be activated using the IMG menu activities shown in Figure 8.8.

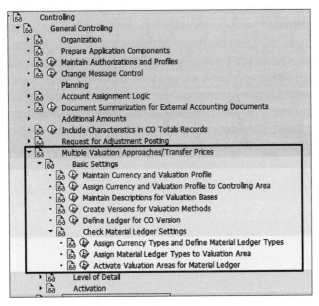

Figure 8.8 Transfer Price Activation

At this point, you need to decide which of the three valuation views to activate. You also need to define a version in the CO area in which to store the different prices. This allows the system to maintain price details for the different valuations. Finally, you need to assign a currency type to each valuation. The material ledger can maintain up to three parallel valuations.

After activating transfer prices, you need to determine how the values will be stored in the Universal Journal. The configuration path is **Financial Accounting · Financial Accounting Global Settings · Ledgers · Ledger · Define Settings for Ledger and Currency Types**. These settings, shown in Figure 8.9, determine how your values will post to a ledger.

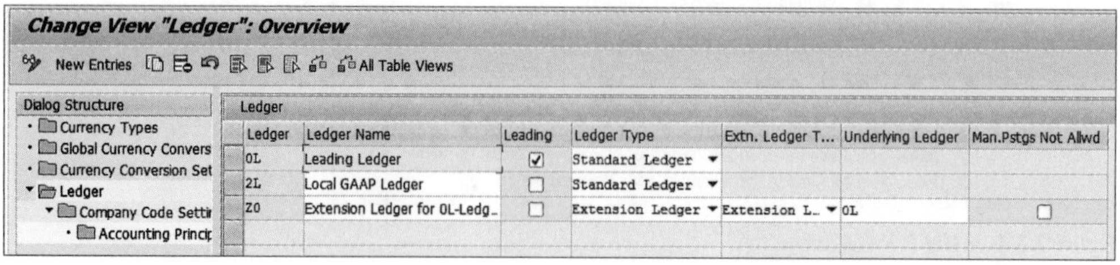

Figure 8.9 Settings for Ledgers and Currency

You have two options: parallel single-valuation ledgers or multi-valuation. Parallel single valuation stores the transfer price values in separate ledgers. This requires you to report the values in separate parallel ledgers.

The second option, multi-valuation, stores the values in one ledger; however, additional currency types need to be defined in order to store the different transfer price valuations. The **Currency Type** settings shown in Figure 8.10 are in the same menu as ledgers.

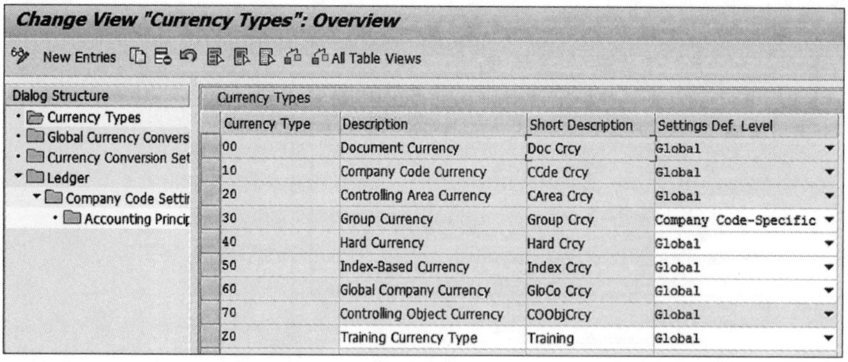

Figure 8.10 Currency Type Settings

Integration with Financial Accounting

To begin processing postings to profit centers, understanding how the profit center is determined is critical. In most cases, profit centers are derived during the data entry process. The system will try to determine a valid profit center and fill in the profit center field in a line item. Figure 8.11 shows the master data connections used to derive a profit center. Wherever possible, the system will also derive a segment from the master data associated to the profit center.

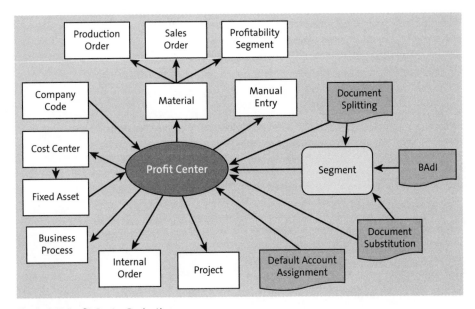

Figure 8.11 Profit Center Derivation

Segments and profit centers can be determined through master data assignment, a program business add-in (BAdI), a substitution (discussed in Chapter 3), or the document splitting process discussed in the next section. The processes shown in Figure 8.11 will be explained in further detail throughout the integration sections of this chapter. We'll begin profit center derivation through FI account assignment means.

FI Posting

During manual FI postings, several sources can impact profit center assignment. The simplest derivation is using primary cost elements. Primary cost elements require the assignment of a cost object. As shown in Figure 8.12, the cost object is entered in the document, and the profit center is derived from the cost object master data.

The example shown in Figure 8.13 illustrates profit center assignment. Cost objects can be entered manually in the posting, assigned through CO automatic account assignment (Transaction OKB9), or determined through substitution rules. Automatic account assignment in CO was discussed in Chapter 3.

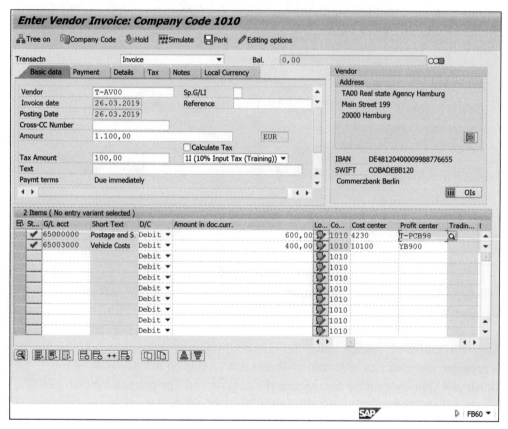

Figure 8.12 FI Account Assignment

> **Warning!**
> Note that, when profit centers are derived from cost objects, the system will validate the assignment from the cost object's master data, shown in Figure 8.13. It will issue an error if a different profit center is entered.

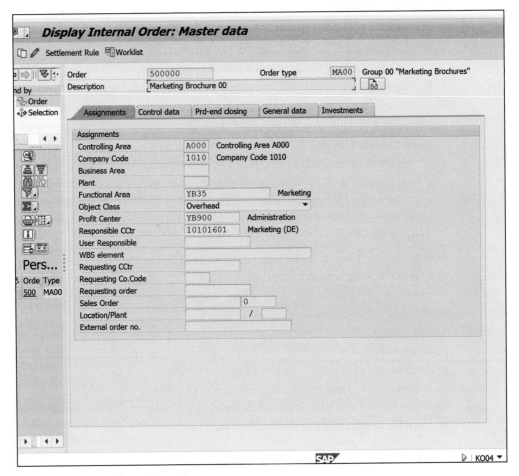

Figure 8.13 Internal Order Assignment

If a cost object is created without reference to a profit center, the profit center must be entered manually or derived by one of the following means:

- **Document splitting**

  Classic PCA had a limitation when receiving balance sheet postings. Most balance sheet accounts were loaded during the close process, drastically limiting the ability to see real-time profit center reports. To resolve this problem, EC-PCA uses a process called document splitting, which comes in three types:

  - *Passive splitting*: Derivation through an automatic process that uses data in existing postings, which doesn't allow user intervention. An example would be clearing a payment in an automatic payment process.

  - *Active splitting*: A set of rules defined in Customizing that trigger derivation logic. An example would be splitting the FI company code balance sheet account to a profit center and segment level.

  - *Zero balance splitting*: This process ensures the profit center and the segment always balance to zero. When an FI document is unable to balance the posting to zero, the system uses a designated account to offset the difference and thus "zero balance" the posting. The system automatically generates a line item for the offsetting account.

Active splitting is the most familiar document splitting method, since this process occurs during accounts payable (AP) invoices. In this section, we'll provide an overview of active document splitting. The other document splitting options are beyond scope of this book.

Active splitting characteristics must to be defined to identify the fields to be populated. Figure 8.14 shows the settings that select characteristics to split. Three possible characteristics to be split are profit center, segment, and business area. These characteristics can also be set to zero balance and mandatory. Once document splitting has been defined, you'll need to activate the process, which will also identify the method to apply.

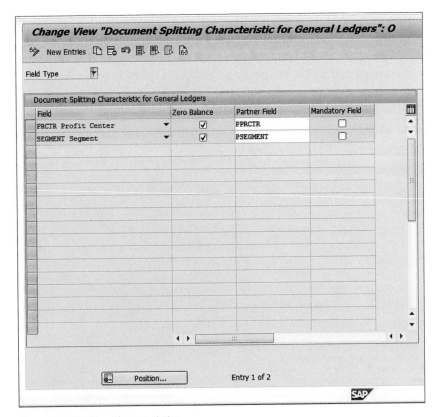

Figure 8.14 Splitting Characteristics

Once a splitting characteristic has been defined, parameters must be entered to facilitate the splitting process. The main components of active document splitting are:

- *Item category*: Categorize G/L accounts together, accounts in the group will be handled with similar logic.
- *Business transactions*: SAP program logic that is executed when you perform a transaction posting.
- *Business transaction variant*: An identifier to represent this combination of item category and business transactions. Validates accounts and business processes can use a splitting rule.
- *Splitting method*: All possible splitting rules for the business transaction.
- *Splitting rule*: Specifies which item categories will be split and used to derive account assignment.

The effect of document splitting can be seen in the G/L view of an FI document, as shown in Figure 8.15. The initial document entry split the expense to two different cost objects. The initial profit centers were derived from the cost object master data used in the expense posting. Document splitting took the ratio for the two expense accounts and applied it to taxes payable and the vendor payable. The document is balanced to 0 for the company code and the profit center. The effect of the document is real-time posting of payables.

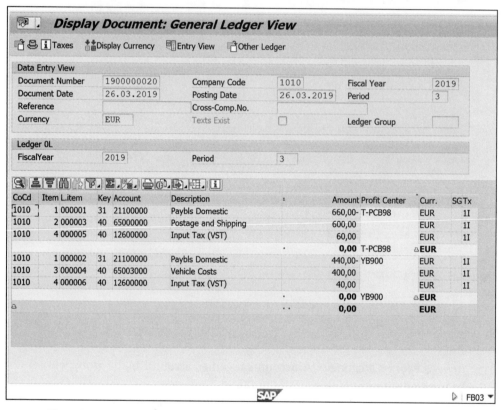

Figure 8.15 Document Splitting

- **Constant profit center and segment**

  In classic PCA, one profit center was designated as the "dummy." The dummy would accept postings if the system could not determine a valid profit center. The effect was FI and PCA were kept in sync. At period end, a process was needed to reallocate these postings.

In SAP S/4HANA, a dummy is no longer required. If the system cannot derive a profit center, then the field is left blank. In the document splitting settings, shown in Figure 8.16, you can define a "constant" profit center, if desired. Doing so will have a similar effect to having the dummy to assist in the reconciling processes. In these same settings, you can also set a constant segment, which can act as a fallback if a segment cannot be derived. In the event a profit center or segment is not desired, then entries without the field populated become reconciling items. At period end, any postings to the constant should be reassigned to valid profit centers.

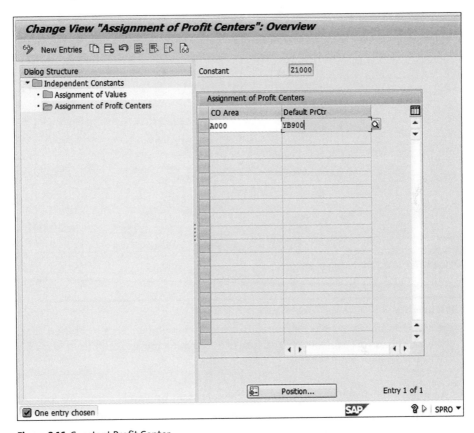

Figure 8.16 Constant Profit Center

- **Default account assignment**
  In the profit center settings, you can assign specific accounts to a default profit center. This assignment is typically used to help the data entry process for non-

operating or balance sheet accounts. The challenge with setting default account assignments, however, is reduced flexibility. Example profit center assignments are shown in Figure 8.17. Since these settings are at the profit center level, these settings are also a CO-level setting. As a result, all postings across the controlling area will go to one profit center.

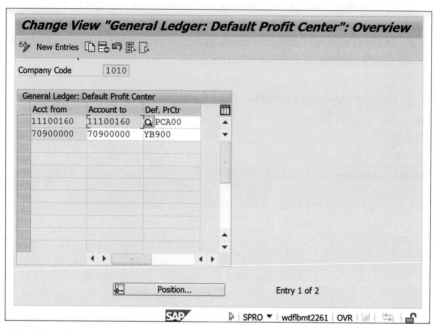

Figure 8.17 PCA Account Assignment

> **Warning!**
> The accounts are assigned in configuration, which is a limitation since most users that don't have access to configuration. This type of information can also be difficult to maintain as master data updates occur.

An additional account assignment process is assigning an FI company code. As shown in Figure 8.18, this process is similar to the previous process but is more specific, since accounts are signed at the company code level. This adds the flexibility of assigning a profit center directly at the company code level.

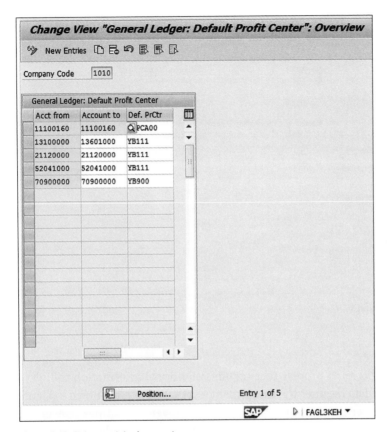

Figure 8.18 FI Account Assignment

- **Document substitution**

  A flexible account assignment tool, the document substitution process is available throughout the system. Each substitution is made up of defined steps, shown in Figure 8.19. Each step can be considered an "if-then" statement. The steps contain a prerequisite and a substitution. The prerequisite is a rule identifying the parameters to consider. If the requirements are met, then the substitution determines the next action. This process offers you the ability to apply more advanced logic to assign a profit center.

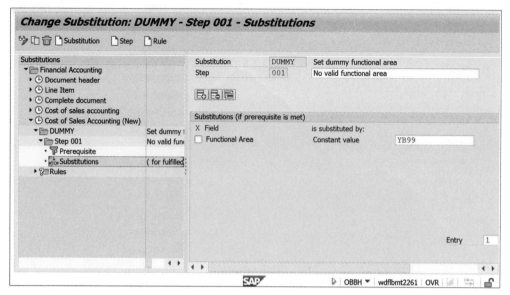

Figure 8.19 Substitution

Asset Accounting

Asset accounting is an FI process that requires additional information to link to CO. Asset master data requires the assignment of a cost center, as shown in Figure 8.20. The cost center is needed to post expense or revenue postings relevant to assets. The link between cost centers and profit centers provides profit center detail, plus the link between profit center and segment assigns all three characteristics to the asset.

> **Note**
>
> Many times, questions arise about the difference between cost centers and profit centers. Even though cost centers can receive revenue posting, they usually only have cost postings. Profit center receive all cost and revenue postings. In addition to expense and revenue postings, profit centers can receive balance sheet postings, which is not possible for cost centers.

The master data assignment for segments is not adequate for asset reporting. Segment reporting must be activated, as shown in Figure 8.21. You simply activate the switch (**Segment Rptng Active**).

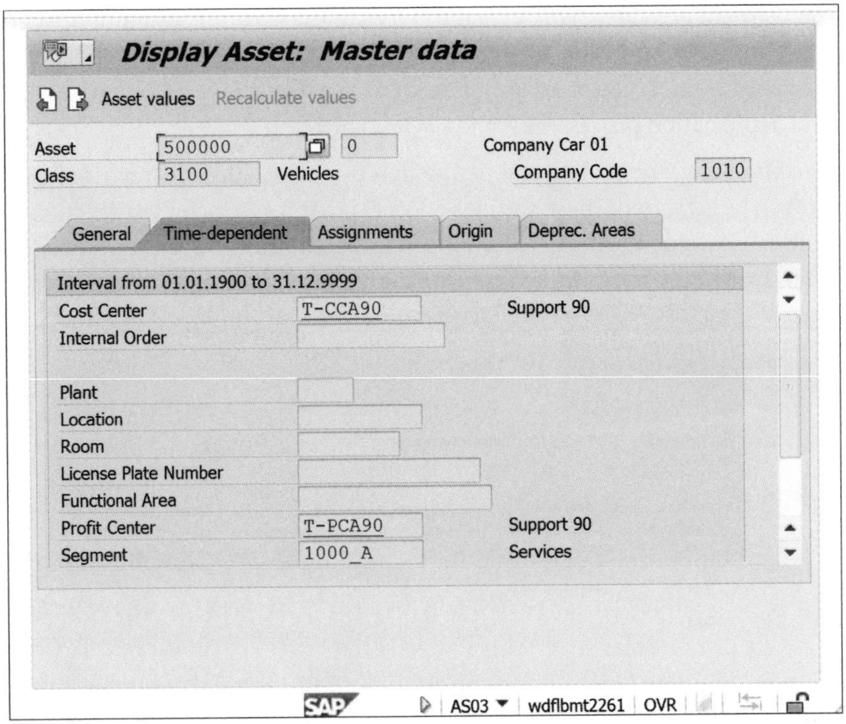

Figure 8.20 Asset Accounting Assignment

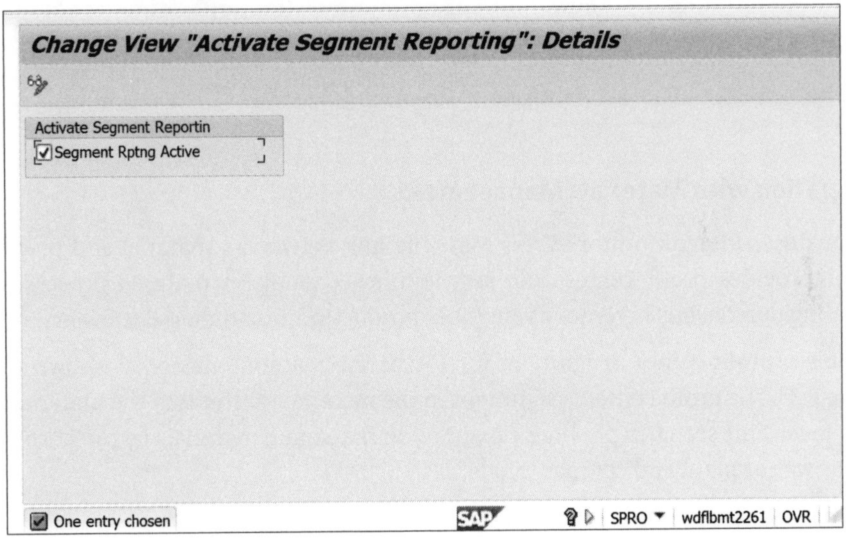

Figure 8.21 Activate Segment Reporting

Once the segment activated, you'll need to activate the account assignment characteristics for asset accounting, as shown in Figure 8.22. This activation directs the system to record the account assignment for acquisition transaction processing (APC) and depreciation processing.

Other account assignments like cost center and work breakdown structure (WBS) elements can be activated. These settings allow FI postings to include segment and profit center assignments. If assets have been initiated prior to activation of additional objects, you can use standard tools to derive account assignment objects.

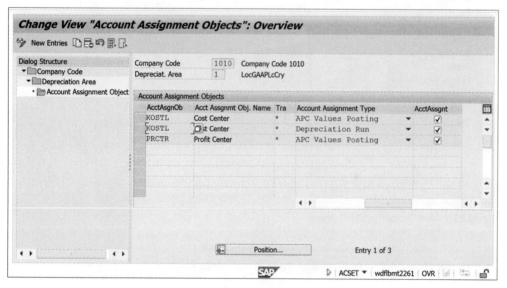

Figure 8.22 Activate Profit Center and Segment Account Assignment

Integration with Materials Management

The business integration for PCA is MM. The link between a material and profit center provides profit center- and segment-level detail for material processes including purchasing, inventory valuation, production, and material transfers.

The initial profit center assignment for MM is the material master, as shown in Figure 8.23. The profit center assignment in the material master is at the material/plant level. This scenario provides flexibility in managing materials by profit centers, as well as plant and company code.

To further understand the implications, remember that plants are assigned to a company code. Materials are not assigned to a company code directly but through the plant/company code assignments. One plant can have different materials assigned to different profit centers.

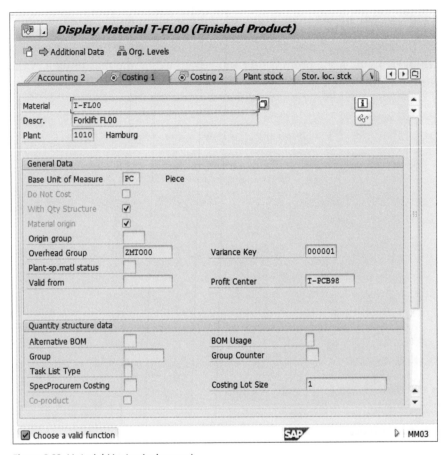

Figure 8.23 Material Master Assignment

Tip
A material in different plants could have the same profit center but different company codes. You could have all the materials in a plant all belong to the same profit center.

Let's now evaluate the link between materials and profit centers for specific logistics processes.

Purchasing

At the line item level of a purchase order is the account assignment indicator. If the indicator is blank, then the item will be posted to the relevant stock account. The assignment for the profit center will be derived from the material master record. If an account assignment is populated in the purchase order line item, as shown in Figure 8.24, the profit center will be defined by the master data of the account assignment object.

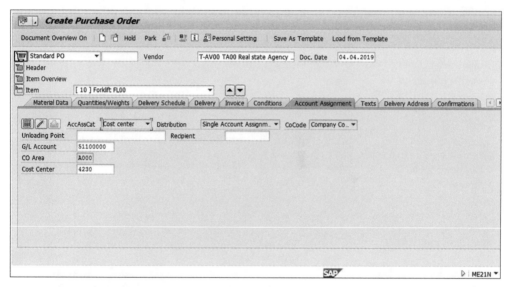

Figure 8.24 Purchase Order Assignment

Procure-to-Pay Process

Purchasing does not require a material, so we'll focus on the account assignment field at the PO line item. If the item will be valued on the FI balance sheet, the field is blank, and a material record is required, which will derive the profit center for balance sheet posting.

A purchasing line item will require an account assignment, as shown earlier in Figure 8.24. The account assignment determines the purchase item is for a purpose other than inventory. The key in the account assignment field indicates the purpose. Material records are not required for account assignment items. The profit center will be derived from the account assignment object.

The procure-to-pay (P2P) process is shown in Figure 8.25. The PCA boxes identify when a profit center value is posted. In classic PCA, these boxes represent individual profit center documents. In SAP S/4HANA, these boxes represent profit center values posted to the Universal Journal (table ACDOCA).

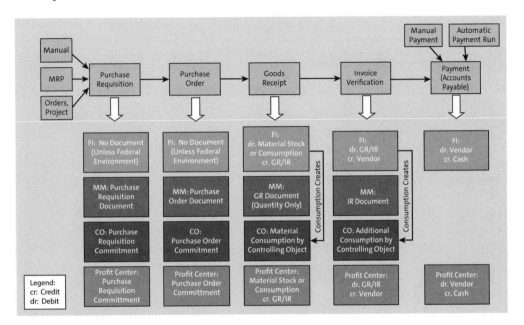

Figure 8.25 P2P Value Flow

Production Planning

Notice, in the production order, that assignments can have several assignments, as shown in Figure 8.26. In make-to-stock (MTS) environments, the profit center is derived from the plant material assigned to the order. In make-to-order (MTO) environments, the profit center is derived from the MTO object, such as a sales order or a project.

Postings to the production order will follow a similar path. Labor postings to the production order will credit the profit center of the sending cost center and debit the profit center on the production order. Overhead assigned to the order will debit the profit center assigned to the order and credit the profit center of the sending object. This process will use the overhead account assigned in the overhead function.

MTS materials issued out of stock will credit the stock account of the plant material profit center and debit the consumption account of the order profit center. MTO stock issues will credit the stock account of the material profit center and debit the consumption account of the order profit center. Goods receipt from the order to stock will credit the production output account of the order profit center and debit the stock account of the plant material profit center.

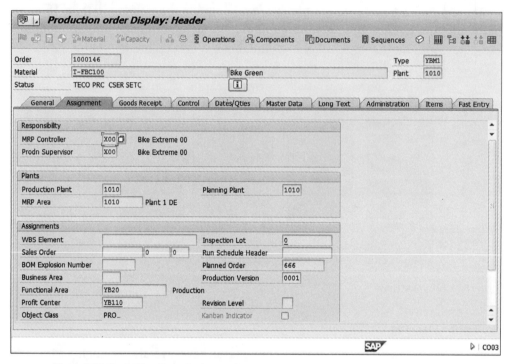

Figure 8.26 Production Order Assignment

Integration with Sales and Distribution

All postings to sales and distribution (SD) require the assignment of a material; however, the sales item does not automatically accept the material-to-profit center assignment. The system provides a derivation process to select a profit center for SD, which gives your business the flexibility to manage revenue and cost of goods sold (COGS) by different profit centers.

A sales order will first check for a substitution rule. A few settings in a substitution rule that can initiate a profit center are:

- Business area
- Customer
- Distribution channel
- Material group
- Order reason, sales district
- Sales group

If the prerequisite in the substitution rule is not met, then the profit center of the line item material will be used. The profit center assignment, shown in Figure 8.27, can be found in the item-level detail under the **Account Assignment** tab.

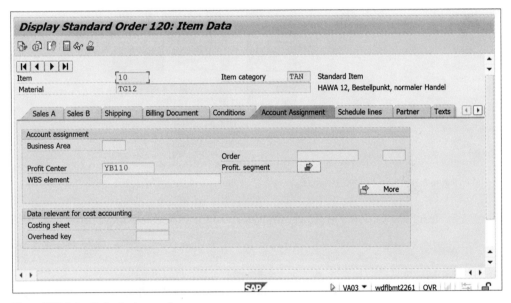

Figure 8.27 Sales Order Assignment

Now, we've come to the order-to-cash process. Goods issues to sales orders will credit the profit center of the plant material and debit the COGS account of the sales order line item profit center. The COGS account will also debit the profit center in CO-PA. Billing the order will debit revenue on the order profit center and the customer's accounts receivable (AR) account. The revenue will also be posted to the profit center in CO-PA.

Figure 8.28 shows the order-to-cash process. Similar to the P2P processes, the boxes represent when the individual lines of business (LoBs) receive postings. The easiest way to understand when a profit center receives value is to keep in mind that FI and CO postings will trigger profit center postings.

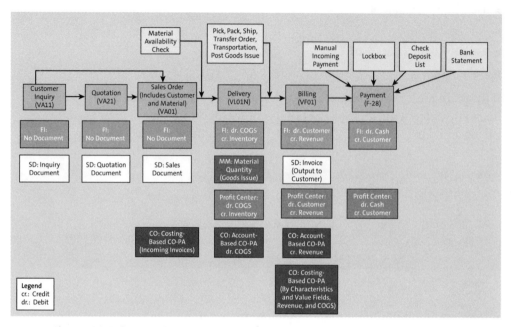

Figure 8.28 Order-to-Cash Value Flow

Table 8.1 shows how a profit center is derived for various business processes.

Posting Detail	Profit Center Derivation
Cost elements	■ CO object master data profit center ■ Automatic account assignment (Transaction OKB9) ■ CO allocations: Credit sending object profit center/debit receiving object profit center
CO labor allocation	Credit sending cost center profit center/debit production order profit center
Non-operating/balance sheet account	■ Constant (IMG) ■ Document splitting (IMG) ■ Substitution (Transaction/table OBBH) ■ EC-PCA account assignment (IMG) ■ FI default account assignment (Transaction FAGL3KEH)

Table 8.1 Profit Center Derivation

Posting Detail	Profit Center Derivation
Assets	Asset master data
Goods receipt stock	Material
Goods receipt non-stock	Account assignment object in PO
Material transfer	Credit sending plant material profit center/debit receiving plant material profit center
MTS production	Material master
MTO production	MTO account assignment profit center
Goods issue stock ·	Credit material profit center/debit account assignment profit center
Sales order	Sales order material or substitution
Post goods issue	Credit material profit center/debit sales order profit center
Billing	Sales order profit center
EC-PCA allocations	Credit sending profit center/debit receiving profit center

Table 8.1 Profit Center Derivation (Cont.)

Period-End Close

In this section, we'll see that the steps for profit center closing are similar to other CO functions. The challenge for period-end close is coordination among all CO and FI functions. One common process for PCA is reconciliation between FI, CO, and PCA.

No standard process exists for period-end closing in CO. The process will be unique to each business depending on the desired data flow and the SAP functions that have been activated. For example, one business may choose to perform cost center allocations, then order settlement, then profit center allocations. Conversely, another business may perform order settlement and then cost center allocations, but no profit center allocations at all.

As demonstrated in business processes, the derivation of a profit center is most likely to happen through master data assignment. SAP has a tool to review the assignment of profit centers and objects. The Assignment Monitor, shown in Figure 8.29, will show you profit center assignments to objects and objects without profit center assignments.

Tip

This process should be executed periodically to verify profit center assignments are correct or if profit center postings are found to be inaccurate. After SAP ERP Enhancement Pack (EHP) 4, changing profit center assignments requires a project be created. The requirement was set up to protect against master data inconsistencies. The same process was implemented for segments in SAP ERP EHP 5.

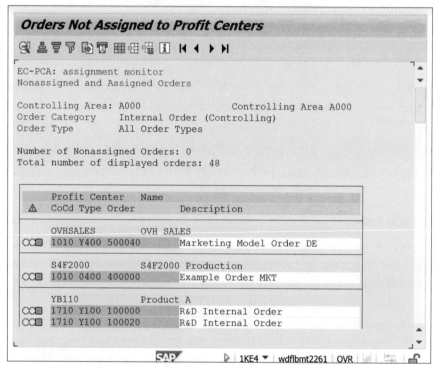

Figure 8.29 Profit Center Assignment Monitor

You have the option of using cost center allocations at period end, which includes the profit center. You can also perform allocations directly in profit centers. In SAP S/4HANA, you can use assessments and distributions for profit centers, segments, and functional areas.

Note

Distributions in profit centers also allow you to allocate between balance sheet accounts, as well as profit and loss (P&L) accounts.

These allocations are built on the structure of allocations in cost center accounting and use the cycle segment method. Using profit centers as an example, you can allocate primary cost elements with a distribution and allocate secondary cost elements with an assessment, as shown in Figure 8.30. A distribution allocation works in a similar fashion to a cost center distribution; it retains the original primary cost element from the sender to the receiver. An assessment summarizes many accounts into a secondary cost element. The difference is that secondary cost elements are statistical postings so the only sending and receiving objects are profit centers.

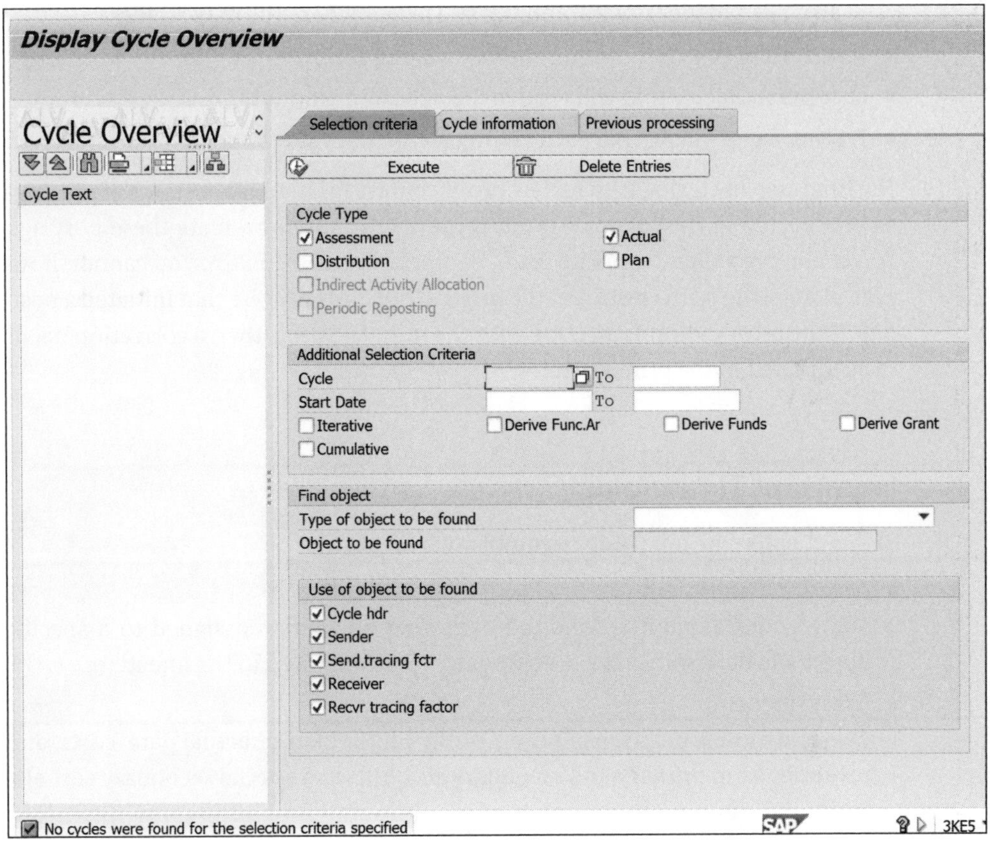

Figure 8.30 Profit Center Assessment

A cycle can contains multiple steps. Each step in the cycle has one allocation rule, which are executed in sequence. These steps are called *segments*. Segments contain the following information:

- Tracing factor: The allocations rule how the values will be transferred from the sender to the receiver. Values can be entered in the following ways:
  - Fixed amount: Manually enter values per receiver.
  - Percentages: Percentage value entered by receiver.
  - Portions: Statistical key figure values. The system totals all the key figures and calculates a proportion. Statistical key figures used in profit center allocation are the same master data values use in cost centers. It is still necessary to enter profit center level quantitates. The values can also be derived from the Logistics Information System (LIS) quantities. In the allocation, you'll also need to identify the appropriate ledger where the data resides.
- Senders: Objects that contain the value being sent.
- Receivers: Objects that will receive the allocated amounts.
- Tracing factor values: For each tracing factor, the value applied to each receiver.

The final step in closing is to review profit centers for manual postings. If postings have occurred in the constant profit center, you should evaluate these postings. You can move values from one profit center to another in PCA. You cannot, however, change the prima nota (i.e., the original business process that initiated a posting). If the error indicates an issue with the initial posting, then a correction needs to be initiated in the prima nota.

Important Terminology

In this chapter, the following terminology was used:

- **Account assignment**
  The account assignment indicates whether an item is assigned to a specific object and determines the specific data will be required in the line item.
- **Assessment**
  The assessment function allocates profit center plan or actual data, costs, and revenues from primary and secondary accounts to a special secondary cost element.
- **Assignment Monitor**
  The capability provides an overview of the assignment of profit centers to other objects. Its basic use is to ensure the assignment of profit centers is correct and complete.

- **Business transactions**
  Business transactions are a basic SAP functionality prompted at specific points in a business process. Transactions generally lead to an update in values.

- **Business transaction variant**
  A business transaction variant is a set of characteristics that identify valid item categories for a business transaction. This kind of variant is assigned to a document type.

- **Derivation**
  A derivation process involves profit center assignment to line items based on information in a posting. A default profit center can be defined to ensure an automatic profit center assignment in the event derivation fails.

- **Distribution**
  A distribution involves the allocation to the distribution balance sheet as well as the distribution of costs and revenues to another profit center. The initial account is retained in the allocation.

- **Document splitting method**
  This method contains the relevant splitting rules for a business transaction.

- **Document splitting rule**
  A document splitting rule defines the instructions for business transactions and item categories to fill the profit center or segment characteristics in a document line item. This rule is assigned to the splitting method and contains three fields: the document splitting method, the business transaction, and the business transaction variant.

- **Fixed assets**
  These assets are long-term, tangible items that have value. Fixed assets are used to support business operations and are generally items owned by a business that are not intended for sale.

- **Flexible hierarchy**
  A flexible hierarchy is a tool for defining hierarchy structures by defining a sequence of various attributes.

- **Functional areas**
  Functional areas are organizational units that classify cost and revenue accounts by operational area. Functional areas enable cost of sales accounting without the addition of separate G/L accounts.

- **Inheritance**
  Document splitting characteristics are posted to subsequent lines that lack

assignments. To be successful, the splitting characteristics must be unique within a document.

- **Item category**

  An item category is a group of G/L accounts that will be treated in a similar manner during document splitting.

- **Multi-valuation ledger**

  This option stores parallel valuations in a single ledger. To facilitate the separate values, additional currency types must be defined.

- **Parallel currency**

  Parallel currency is a feature of the material ledger. It allows inventory to be posted in up to three currencies in real time.

- **Parallel single-valuation ledgers**

  This option stores parallel valuations in separate ledgers using FI currencies.

- **Parallel valuation**

  Parallel valuation is a feature of the material ledger. Parallel valuation allows inventory and COGS to be valued with and without upcharges for different business unit levels.

- **Prerequisite**

  Prerequisites are conditions that must be met for a substitution step to be executed.

- **Profit center**

  A profit center is a defined FI organizational unit for capturing the profitability for an internal operational unit.

- **Segment**

  A segment is an alternate organizational unit for report financial statements by market. Segments are often defined to meet legal requirements for financial reporting.

- **Splitting characteristic**

  This characteristic is an account assignment object used in document splitting to fill the characteristic field in line items for balance sheet postings.

- **Statistical object**

  Account assignment object used to provide additional detailed reporting. Statistical objects must always be assigned to a "real" object that actually carries the posting.

- **Substitution**

  Substitution is rule-based logic used to validate and update information during document posting. The rules are validated against a condition or prerequisite.

Practice Questions

These practice questions will help you evaluate your understanding of the topics covered in this chapter. The questions shown are similar in nature to those found on the certification examination. Although none of these questions will be found on the exam itself, they will allow you to review your knowledge of the subject. Select the correct answers and then check the completeness of your answers in the "Practice Question Answers and Explanations" section. Remember that on the exam you must select all correct answers and only correct answers to receive credit for the question.

1. In the profit center assignment to a cost center, you get an error. What is the cause?

☐ **A.** Profit center validity is within the cost center validity.

☐ **B.** Cost center validity is outside the profit center validity.

☐ **C.** Profit center lock indicator had been set.

2. In an SAP S/4HANA system, you have two profit centers with the same profit center code and the same validity period, but different names. What does this indicate about the configuration of the profit centers?

☐ **A.** They are defined in separate controlling areas.

☐ **B.** They are defined in separate company codes.

☐ **C.** They are assigned to different functional areas.

3. Is it possible to post a value directly to a standalone profit center?

☐ **A.** True

☐ **B.** False

4. In your company, you tend to go through many reorganizations, which often leads to extra master data maintenance work. Which grouping functionality can save you time maintaining profit center groups?

☐ **A.** Creating multidimensional sets

☐ **B.** Configuring derivation rules

☐ **C.** Defining flexible hierarchies

☐ **D.** Copying groups with suffixes

5. On which organizational level do you maintain PCA in SAP S/4HANA?

☐ **A.** Company code

☐ **B.** Financial statement version

☐ **C.** Controlling area

☐ **D.** Operating concern

6. True or False: In SAP S/4HANA, if PCA is active, the profit center field is mandatory.

☐ **A.** True

☐ **B.** False

7. Which document splitting Customizing settings do you maintain to ensure that financial statements can always be produced separately for each profit center?

☐ **A.** Zero-balance

☐ **B.** Dummy profit center

☐ **C.** Standard account assignment

☐ **D.** Inheritance

8. True or False: Parallel valuations' multi-valuation ledger updates multiple ledgers.

☐ **A.** True

☐ **B.** False

9. What is a document splitting method?

☐ **A.** Transaction splitting rule

☐ **B.** Set of business transactions

☐ **C.** Set of item categories

10. True or False: In SAP S/4HANA, EC-PCA accounts post separate profit center documents for transactions.

☐ **A.** True

☐ **B.** False

11. Which characteristics define extension ledgers in SAP S/4HANA? (There are two correct answers.)

☐ **A.** Extension ledgers can be posted from CO.

☐ **B.** Extension ledgers must be assigned to a base ledger.

☐ **C.** Extension ledgers contain all the postings for an accounting principle.

☐ **D.** Extension ledgers should be viewed as standalone ledgers.

12. In an SAP S/4HANA system, let's say two parallel ledgers and one extension ledger exist. Which is true?

☐ **A.** A journal entry will post to all three ledgers automatically.

☐ **B.** A journal entry will post to the two parallel ledgers simultaneously.

☐ **C.** A journal entry to the extension ledger will simultaneously post to the base ledger.

13. In SAP S/4HANA, how is the organizational element segment derived?

☐ **A.** Assignment to a company code

☐ **B.** Assignment to a profit center

☐ **C.** Assignment to a controlling area

14. Indirect profit center assignment is based on which of the following?

☐ **A.** Characteristics in the current document

☐ **B.** Characteristics in a preceding document

☐ **C.** Characteristics in document splitting

15. True or False: Profit centers and cost centers can receive revenue postings.

☐ **A.** True

☐ **B.** False

16. Which of the following are standard characteristics for document splitting? (There are two correct answers.)

☐ **A.** Functional area

☐ **B.** Company code

☐ **C.** Segment

☐   **D.** Business area

☐   **E.** Profit center

17. The derivation of profit center can happen through assignments to which objects? (There are three correct answers.)

☐   **A.** Material assignment

☐   **B.** Cost center assignment

☐   **C.** Document splitting

☐   **C.** Cost estimate assignment

☐   **E.** Fixed asset assignment

18. The first step in profit center derivation process is which of the following?

☐   **A.** Substitution

☐   **B.** Document splitting

☐   **C.** Cost or revenue type

19. The purpose of document splitting is which of the following?

☐   **A.** Assign relevant characteristics to a G/L line item

☐   **B.** Split payables and receivables

☐   **C.** Include a balance sheet in CO

20. To ensure all that profit center master data is accurate and complete, we use which of the following?

☐   **A.** Assignment Monitor

☐   **B.** Profit Center Monitor

☐   **C.** Customizing Monitor

21. What kind of process is document splitting?

☐   **A.** Substitution

☐   **B.** Passive

☐   **C.** BAdI (program)

Practice Question Answers and Explanations

1. Correct answer: **B**

   Cost center is not valid for the profit center dates. The lock indicator stops further postings to the profit center. If the profit center validity is within the cost center dates, but not for the current date, the system will not allow postings. The lock indicator allows an assignment but will issue error at the time of posting.

2. Correct answer: **A**

   The profit center ID is unique, but the name is not unique. You cannot have profit centers with the same master data ID, so profit centers must be in different controlling areas. The system doesn't check for unique names; it only validates that the profit centers exist.

3. Correct answer: **B**

   False. Profit centers are statistical and cannot receive postings directly without the assistance of a real cost object or company code. Once a profit center has a posting, it can be transferred to other profit centers.

4. Correct answer: **C**

   The flexible hierarchy feature allows you to easily build a reporting hierarchy from master data fields. Prior to SAP S/4HANA, the grouping function was a CO feature. The technical function of the SAP HANA database allows hierarchies to be built from any set of indicators. The suffix feature also seen in the cost center unit captures or freezes a current view of a hierarchy.

5. Correct answer: **C**

   Profit centers exist at the controlling level. An operating concern is the organizational level for CO-PA, which is above the controlling area.

6. Correct answer: **B**

   False. A profit center may be a desired element, but the field is not automatically mandatory. You can use features such as document splitting, FI field status groups, or the constant profit center to ensure a profit center assignment.

7. Correct answer: **A**

   Zero balance indicators ensure that each posting for the profit center balances to zero. Dummy profit centers are a classic PCA feature that is activated for derivation issues.

8. Correct answer: **B**

   False. Parallel valuations are updated in multiple currencies on one ledger. The currency types need to be defined and attached to each of the parallel valuations. Parallel single-valuation ledgers store the values in separate ledgers. This does not require additional currency types beyond those defined for FI.

9. Correct answer: **A**

   A document splitting method is a set of rules to split a document. This method combines characteristics for a set of accounts and business process transactions to derive a profit center or segment in a document. A common example is the balance sheet accounts for an AP posting.

10. Correct answer: **B**

    False. EC-PCA posts a document to the Universal Journal (table ACDOCA). In certain migration scenarios, classic PCA can be activated in SAP S/4HANA, but doing so is not recommended. This scenario will create separate profit center documents because the data is not stored in the Universal Journal.

11. Correct answer: **A, B**

    An extension ledger cannot stand alone; it must be posted in combination with a base ledger or leading ledger. An extension ledger will only contain delta postings from designated postings. All parallel ledgers receive a posting unless a ledger group is included in the posting, to exclude ledgers.

12. Correct answer: **B**

    Only the parallel ledger will post automatically, unless it is excluded through the ledger group setting. The extension ledger will receive posting only when triggered through a ledger group assignment at document entry.

13. Correct answer: **B**

    The segment will usually be derived through the profit center assignment. A segment can't be assigned to a company code or controlling area directly.

14. Correct answer: **B**

    Most profit center assignments are direct or through document splitting. Indirect means the system is basing the assignment on a previous document in the process.

15. Correct answer: **A**

    True. While not common, cost centers can receive revenue posting if activated in the cost center master data. Profit centers always receive revenue posting, ensuring reconciliation with FI and CO.

16. Correct answers: **C, D**

    The standard assignment characteristics are segment, business area, profit center, and cost center. A company code is required data for the FI prima nota postings, so it's always entered directly. Document splitting was introduced in the new G/L to reconcile FI and PCA.

17. Correct answers: **A, B, E**

    Profit center assignment is available through master data fields in the material master, cost center and fixed asset. Document splitting is a set of rules and cost estimates are assigned to a material.

18. Correct answer: **C**

    The first step of derivation in the SD process is to determine the cost or revenue type; substitution and document splitting are subsequent steps. If these functions do not initiate a profit center assignment, the system will use the material master assignment.

19. Correct answer: **A**

    Document splitting assigns a characteristic to the G/L line items. While it may be used with payable and receivables, it is not limited to those features. CO does not contain a balance sheet.

20. Correct answer: **A**

    The Assignment Monitor reports the master data assignments to profit centers and identified any missing assignments. It is a master data process not involved with Customizing. The monitor should be evaluated periodically to preclude incorrect profit center postings.

21. Correct answer: **B**

    Document splitting is a passive technical process that reads the current entries and populates a field in the line item. It doesn't change or alter existing information like a substitution or BAdI. This is not to be confused with passive document splitting.

Takeaway

Profit centers are an optional function in CO. Profit centers are an organizational structure that provide for the flexible analysis of internal operational entities, enabling you to report across financial boundaries by providing financial statement views of internal organizations. Profit centers can report P&L as well as balance sheet information in real time.

Profit center reporting can include all your G/L accounts, including secondary cost elements, thus enabling you to perform allocations for profit centers using both primary and secondary cost elements. Profit centers also enable you to build hierarchy groups for reporting and analysis.

Details in the profit centers are filled in during FI and CO postings. In most cases, this information is derived from the parameters entered during a posting. In some cases, data must be entered manually. The derivation of a profit center can trigger a subsequent derivation of the segment. These characteristics can then be used to build additional views of financial information.

Summary

Profit centers are the last topic in our journey through CO. Profit centers are freely definable and can be added at any time depending on the requirements of your organization.

Profit centers are one mechanism in CO to facilitate the internal management of your organization. Each tool in CO has a specific purpose and distinct information provided for analysis. No mandatory requirements exist for activating any areas of CO. Each organization must evaluate the tools individually and determine which are appropriate for their business processes.

In the next chapter, we'll conclude with an overview of relevant reporting functionality.

Chapter 9
Reporting

Techniques You'll Master

- Understand the different tools available for reporting in management accounting (CO)

- Describe the features of each tool

- Position reporting tools in CO functions

Reporting has appeared at various points throughout this book, which goes to show that it's difficult to separate reporting into a standalone topic. In this chapter, we'll set out to provide general knowledge regarding the reporting tools, referring back to where they appear within relevant process-focused chapters.

Real-World Scenario

You've now completed the setup of various controlling functions. As a CO consultant, you must now work with your customer to determine the appropriate reporting tools. Prior to creating customized reports, you need to become familiar with existing standard reports. There are several different tools provided in the standard system, and each tool has specific characteristics to provide the required details. The same information may be presented in different reports. Using your skills in reporting, you'll be able to recommend the appropriate reporting tools to support customers' needs.

Objectives of this Portion of the Test

This portion of the exam tests your knowledge of standard SAP reporting tools. Many standard reporting tools deliver various standard reports and provide the primary tools to create your own reports. This portion of the exam will test your ability to discern the features of each tool and to apply the appropriate tool for each reporting situation.

The certification exam expects you to have a good understanding of the following topics:

1. SAP S/4HANA reporting techniques
2. List displays
3. Using the Report Painter
4. Using drilldown reporting

Note
The reporting topic makes up 8%–12% of the total exam.

Key Concepts Refresher

Reporting accurate results is critical to the function of a company. The go-to solutions for reporting tend to be standard SAP-delivered functions. SAP has also developed new reporting methods built on the features of SAP S/4HANA. These reporting options offer improvements in speed, granularity, and flexibility.

SAP has made the conversion to SAP S/4HANA as nondisruptive as possible. An enormous advantage of core data services (CDS) views, which access data directly from the new SAP S/4HANA data model, is that they use the vast library of existing reports. Traditional reporting tools are still available in SAP S/4HANA. The tables on which these tools rely have been eliminated; however, SAP has provided another solution through CDS views. The system simulates the original table structure on the fly using the new SAP data structure in table ACDOCA. This also allows businesses to capitalize on their current investments in reporting without immediately re-creating custom reports. Note that businesses should be encouraged to transition away from these tools and into the new tool sets that are more efficient and have expanded capabilities.

Most SAP reporting tools are structured to allow moderate technical users to construct their own reports without programing knowledge. To segregate users, SAP groups individuals into three categories:

- **IT users**
  IT users will create customized programs and new CDS views.

- **Key users**
  Key users may not be part of the IT group but have the ability to build ad hoc reports or queries using standard tools.

- **Casual users**
  Casual users consume the data. For the purposes of CO, this is the group we'll discuss options for in this chapter.

In this section, we'll start with a look at the new SAP S/4HANA reporting methods, before reviewing the classic Report Painter tool and your drilldown reporting options.

SAP S/4HANA Reporting

In SAP S/4HANA, the CO submodules update the Universal Journal (table ACDOCA) at the line item level directly. SAP S/4HANA tools are built to read this data directly. The SAP HANA database structure allows users to access online transaction processing (OLTP) and online analytical processing (OLAP) information in real time. Historically, reports in the core system were predominantly OLTP. OLAP reports were mainly achieved through the SAP Business Warehouse (SAP BW) tool, due to the summarization of the data. In SAP S/4HANA, transactional and analytical reports access the same tables. The robust features of the SAP HANA database are used to handle the OLAP functions, allowing the user community to get instant insight into operations.

SAP HANA has also reduced the need for periodically extracting data to a business warehouse. The new database structure eliminates redundant data records, which complicated the reporting process in the past. The SAP HANA in-memory computing feature increases reporting efficiency, reducing the need for background reporting.

The following are the key user reporting tools for casual users:

- **Multidimensional report**
  Flexible data analysis uses rows and columns as well as flexible hierarchy. Multidimensional reports help answer unexpected business questions and provide graphical, filtering, sorting, and pivoting views for data analysis.

- **SAP Smart Business key performance indicators (KPIs)**
  This is a set of SAP Fiori apps that you use to manage KPIs across your business.

- **Query Browser**
  The Query Browser provides on-demand reporting. You can select an analytical query and perform on-demand reporting on that query. The analytical query is specified via a URL parameter, so it's possible to create a tile that directly starts the analytical query.

- **Analytical SAP Fiori apps**
  Analytical apps use the power of SAP HANA and combine with the SAP Fiori user interface to provide real-time operational data. These apps provide a visual overview of complex topics.

- **SAP Analysis for Microsoft Office**
  Microsoft Excel and PowerPoint tools provide multidimensional, real-time reporting directly from the SAP HANA database by using Microsoft Office. Originally a feature of SAP BusinessObjects, SAP has expanded the function to additional applications.

- **SAP Lumira**
  SAP Lumira is an easy-to-use tool that can access data from multiple sources. One of its best features is the ability to present visualizations of complex data sets.

List Display

A highly useful reporting option are list displays, which include traditional list displays and ABAP list viewer (ALV) displays. The ALV list displays are the most user friendly. List displays are just lists, such as a list of documents or a list of master data elements, and are most commonly used to track down issues.

List displays are used throughout all areas of the system. With list display reports, you can sort, filter, and arrange columns; export them to Excel; and select or drill down to the original transactions. See the "Cost Center Reporting" section in Chapter 3 for more details.

Report Painter

The most common ad hoc reporting tool is Report Painter. Report Painter is a what-you-see-is-what-you-get (WYSIWYG) reporting tool. This term characterizes how the reports are created. The developer can view a simulation of the report as it's created. SAP also refers to this as a graphical reporting tool because it uses rows and columns to format and present data.

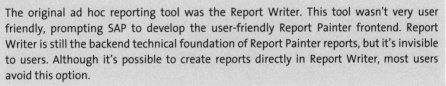

Note
The original ad hoc reporting tool was the Report Writer. This tool wasn't very user friendly, prompting SAP to develop the user-friendly Report Painter frontend. Report Writer is still the backend technical foundation of Report Painter reports, but it's invisible to users. Although it's possible to create reports directly in Report Writer, most users avoid this option.

SAP delivers thousands of Report Painter reports, traversing most SAP modules and functionalities. Report Painter reports are commonly referred to as "sailor" reports because the SAP report transaction codes start with S_ALR. These reports allow users to do the following:

- Access thousands of standard delivered reports.
- Use data from many different applications.
- Use external data loaded in reporting structures.
- Choose from flexible report layout options.
- See end report output during development.
- Access real-time data.
- Calculate and report KPIs.

- Access archive data.
- Use Excel in-place.
- Format reports.
- Access SAP HANA data using CDS views.

More details about Report Painter reporting are discussed in Chapter 3, in the "Cost Center Reporting" section in the context of cost center accounting.

Drilldown Reporting

Drilldown reporting supports a "slice and dice," or matrixed, report style. These types of reports are frequently used in profitability analysis (CO-PA) and profit center reporting. Similar to Report Painter, these reports are often referred to as graphical reporting tools because they use columns and rows for presentation, as shown in Figure 9.1.

Figure 9.1 CO-PA Drilldown Report Design

Some report creation functions are unique to drilldown reporting, such as the following:

- Use of forms to create report structures
- Multiple axes, with or without key figures
- Variables for data selection, including the following:
  - Global variables: Can be used in all reports
  - Local variables: Can be used in one form or report

SAP delivers drilldown reports for profit center accounting (PCA). These report transaction codes start with S_PLO.

SAP requires drilldown reports for costing-based CO-PA but doesn't supply standard reports due to the flexible, company-defined nature of costing-based CO-PA. Each report must be created to meet requirements.

More details about drilldown reporting are discussed in the "Reporting" section of Chapter 7.

Important Terminology

- **CDS view**
  A database tables or view in the ABAP Dictionary. The table view is an entity that isn't persistent in the database; instead, it's a projection of other entities.

- **Drilldown report**
  Drilldown reporting is a dialog-oriented reporting tool that analyzes a data set according to all available characteristics. This interactive tool allows reports to evaluate data according to multiple characteristics.

- **Graphical report structure**
  Related data is structured and formatted into rows and columns to allow for the creation of customized reports.

- **Key performance indicator (KPI)**
  A KPI is a calculation or measurable value that demonstrates the effectiveness of business operations.

- **Online analytical processing (OLAP)**
  OLAP is a technology that allows multidimensional data models to be analyzed in online reports. OLAP allows complex data to be organized into structures that can be accessed through standard SAP reporting tools.

- **Online transaction processing (OLTP)**
  OLTP reports extract and display transactional level data for business operations and master data.

- **Report Painter**
  A user-friendly reporting tool you can use to quickly create specialized reports via the graphical report structure that formats data in rows and columns.

- **SAP Analysis for Microsoft Office**
  This Microsoft Office add-in allows processing both in Excel and PowerPoint. You can easily run ad hoc analyses from OLAP sources or connect directly with SAP HANA and embed live data in PowerPoint presentations.

- **SAP Lumira**
  A SAP HANA visualization reporting for users that grew out of SAP Business Explorer. It can be used to alter data, create correlations, and then resubmit the data back to the system.

- **Structure**
  Data for Report Painter has been prebuilt into a reporting structure that combines pertinent data from different core tables. The data is arranged in columns and rows and represents the data elements used to create a report.

- **WYSIWYG**
  In Report Painter, this term describes the simulation of data output that the report developer can see and that simplifies the report creation process.

Practice Questions

These practice questions will help you evaluate your understanding of the topics covered in this chapter. The questions shown are similar in nature to those found on the certification examination. Although none of these questions will be found on the exam itself, they will allow you to review your knowledge of the subject. Select the correct answers, and then check the completeness of your answers in the "Practice Question Answers and Explanations" section. Remember that on the exam, you must select all correct answers and only correct answers to receive credit for the question.

Additional information and questions are provided in previous chapters where reporting options are detailed for specific controlling functions.

1.   True or False: Controlling data extracted with Report Painter in SAP S/4HANA is read directly from historical tables.

☐   **A.** True

☐   **B.** False

2.   What are the benefits of SAP Analysis for Office? (There are two correct answers.)

☐   **A.** Execute drilldown reports

☐   **B.** Real-time data views

☐   **C.** Excel spreadsheet functions

☐   **D.** Graphical analysis

3.   What are the functions of CDS views? (There are two correct answers.)

☐   **A.** Data is read from SAP HANA tables.

☐   **B.** All historical reports are replaced.

☐   **C.** Traditional reports aren't disrupted.

☐   **D.** Data is written to historical tables.

4.   True or False: Report Painter can be used across SAP business processes.

☐   **A.** True

☐   **B.** False

5.   When is it appropriate to use SAP Lumira? (There are two correct answers.)

☐   **A.** Data visualization is required.

☐   **B.** Real-time transactions are required.

☐   **C.** Day-to-day operations efficiency is needed.

☐   **D.** Data is contained in different sources.

6.   What are characteristics of drilldown reports? (There are two correct answers.)

☐   **A.** You can use drilldown reporting in Report Painter reports.

☐   **B.** You can slice and dice the data in different ways.

☐   **C.** You must re-execute a report to see a new view.

☐   **D.** You can analyze complex data.

7.   What are the benefits of WYSIWYG reporting functions? (There are two correct answers.)

☐   **A.** Report developers can see output prior to execution.

☐   **B.** Reports can use drilldown functions.

☐   **C.** Report developers can see report changes immediately.

☐   **D.** Reports are displayed in a visual format.

8.   What are good applications of drilldown reports? (There are two correct answers.)

☐   **A.** Production order analysis

☐   **B.** Profit center analysis

☐   **C.** CO-PA data analysis

☐   **D.** Cost center analysis

9.   Which reporting tools require IT support? (There are two correct answers.)

☐   **A.** ABAP reports

☐   **B.** CDS views

☐   **C.** Drilldown reports

☐   **D.** SAP HANA queries

10.   True or False: The Query Browser only accesses SAP HANA foundation tables.

☐   **A.** True

☐   **B.** False

Practice Question Answers and Explanations

1.   Correct Answer: **B**
     False. Report Painter reports read data from traditional tables. In SAP S/4HANA, these tables have been deleted, requiring Report Painter to read data from CDS views that are accessing data from table ACDOCA.

2.   Correct Answer: **B, C**
     The benefits of SAP Analysis for Microsoft Office include the ability to use the features of Excel and access data directly from SAP HANA in real time. Originally, the data for SAP Analysis for Microsoft Office was accessed through SAP

BW queries. SAP has expanded the function to additional uses, including SAP BW, SAP S/4HANA planning, and SAP Business Planning and Consolidation (SAP BPC) analysis.

3. Correct Answer: **A, C**

   CDS views read data from core SAP HANA tables. They can be used to query data from a table for reporting. SAP has delivered CDS views that replicate deleted tables, so that historical reports can continue making conversion less disruptive. The original tables don't exist, so you can't write to them.

4. Correct Answer: **A**

   True. Report Painter can be used to report data for many different areas of the system. As long as a reporting structure exists, Report Painter can provide data. It's also possible to bring data into the system from external sources and use Report Painter to output reports.

5. Correct Answer: **A, D**

   SAP Lumira is an ideal tool for presenting complex data in a visual format. It can also be used to acquire data from different sources such as SAP HANA and SAP BW. While you might be able to output many types of data, there are other reporting options that are more efficient for transactional or operational data.

6. Correct Answer: **B, D**

   Drilldown reports allow you to review and examine complex data by different characteristics simultaneously. Users can select different characteristics without exiting and re-executing the report. Report Painter can be used as a form to help format a drilldown report, but you can't use drilldown characteristics in a Report Painter report. You can slice and dice the data in different ways.

7. Correct Answer: **A, C**

   WYSIWYG refers to the ability of the report developer to see a representation of a report and the ability to see the effect of changes immediately. It doesn't refer to output of the data in a visual format. You can create graphs of the data as an output format, but it's a very rudimentary function.

8. Correct Answer; **B, C**

   Drilldown reports are valuable when trying to evaluate data with many different parameters, including financial, CO-PA, and profit center data. Production orders and cost centers are better reviewed with data queries or Report Painter reports. In those two areas, you're more interested in transaction postings.

9. Correct Answer: **A, B**

   ABAP reports and new CDS views require programming code, which means an IT expert with coding expertise must create these objects. Drilldown reports or queries can be created by users with some technical experience. Although they don't require programming experience, they must have data structure knowledge.

10. Correct Answer: **B**

   False. After IT creates a table or data view, the Query Browser can access the data. The new table structure in SAP HANA has been simplified, but it has also created large, complex line item tables. Data views allow report developers to access more simplified data views while excluding data that isn't required for their purposes.

Takeaway

Reporting is a key function in an ERP system as it provides information for decision-making and operational analysis. In any business environment, it's critical to gather and examine data to evaluate the health of operations and set the company's future direction. It's also important to gather information on markets and products to develop strategic goals. The SAP S/4HANA system offers a variety of tools to meet all business needs, including the ability to make customized reports. The selection of reports available allows businesses to select reporting options to meet a variety of needs.

Summary

The end result of most ERP functions is extracting and evaluating data. This chapter has finalized our CO journey by providing reporting options in an SAP S/4HANA environment. The standard toolset offers a variety of options to complete data analysis and provide a basis for decision-making.

We hope this book has given you the skills and knowledge to understand the different components available in CO. You should now be able to design and implement CO for a variety of businesses.

The Authors

Theresa Marquis is the founder of Circle City FICO Experts, LLC, a consulting firm. Previously, she was a principal education consultant for SAP, where she focused on the Controlling and Project System components. In her new role, she still interacts with the SAP community, holding training and participating in events. She has contributed to multiple SAP certification exams and facilitated the corresponding updates to SAP Education training books. As an education consultant, she works with companies to perform learning needs analysis to design tailored training plans for their employees. Terri hosts the SAP Learning Room page for Project System certifications.

Marjorie Wright is the founder of Simply FI-CO, LLC, a boutique SAP training consulting company. She is an accomplished subject matter expert in SAP ERP business process and customizing, and a highly respected education consultant for the financial accounting, management accounting, and financial supply chain management components. With more than 25 years of training and accounting experience across multiple industries including financial services, manufacturing, technology, utilities, telecommunications, and healthcare, she has conducted training for over 3,500 learners in traditional face-to-face classrooms and web-based, or virtual, meeting rooms.

Index